The
Future
of the
Organisation

To Susan Coulson-Thomas

The
Future
of the
Organisation

Achieving Excellence through Business Transformation

Colin Coulson-Thomas

KOGAN
PAGE

YOURS TO HAVE AND TO HOLD
BUT NOT TO COPY

First published in 1997

Kogan Page Limited
120 Pentonville Road
London N1 9JN

© Colin Coulson-Thomas, 1997

British Library Cataloguing in Publication Data
A CIP record for this book is available from the British Library.
ISBN 0 7494 1935 0

Typeset by Saxon Graphics Ltd, Derby
Printed in England by Clays Ltd, St Ives plc

Contents

List of figures

List of tables

Preface

Walk on the beach and expect to get tar on your shoes.

During the working day do you grow and thrive or merely cope and survive? Does your job, or role, excite and stimulate you or just tire and exhaust you? Is it all as much fun as it used to be? Do you 'log off' eager to enjoy your hobbies, friends and families or feeling the worst for wear? For how much longer will it, or can it, go on like this?

Let's turn to organisations – will they continue in their current form, or any other form, for any length of time? Network type organisations composed of knowledge workers are heralded as signposts to the future. Yet they are inherently unstable, and can easily fragment as interests diverge or different factions struggle to take them over. What about innovation and new product developments that require trust and cooperation? Where will the changes, and a lack of continuity, leave customers, suppliers, investors and business partners?

As both employees and consumers we have become less loyal and more ready to switch our allegiances to competitors. Restless, and increasingly rootless, we move on to new groups, or leave to set up our own businesses. Given these changes and the uncertainty they cause, how should we sustain relationships? Can we justify longer-term investments?

As more people come, through choice or *force majeure*, to manage themselves and take personal responsibility for delivering agreed outputs, where does this leave managers? What about our careers? Who will help the independent contractor to adjust to changing technologies or to develop new capabilities?

At the level of society as a whole, will governments be able to continue to meet their commitments to those who are no longer employed? Just as the realisation dawns that states across Europe may not have the ability to support their citizens in old age we are fast losing the protection of traditional and benevolent employers. As organisations become 'virtual' and full-time jobs are replaced by contracts for specific services, where does all this leave the individual and the family?

The 'feel-good' factor eludes us. We are confronted by unintended and undesirable consequences of our own actions and of policies that have been pursued by corporate leaders. Where are the new mechanisms and institutions that could fill the emerging gaps? It's all happening so quickly. How might we buy ourselves the time needed to properly prepare for different lifestyles? Could new life be breathed into existing organisations long enough for some alternative provision to emerge?

Improvements in financial performance have occurred at some companies such as BT that are large enough to be significant in national economic terms. However, these 'turnarounds' have generally been achieved at the expense of job losses and the lower morale of those who remain. A third of those at BT, some 90,000 people, lost their jobs during the first half of the 1990s. Have we got the right balance between the various interests in today's company?

Securing such gains as have occurred has also been tough. Sustaining them will not be easy. According to one weary chief executive officer: 'It seems to get harder all the time. You can't assume any more that others share your commitment. As for the longer-term interests of our various stakeholders, who knows?'

For many people the situation at work is rather like that portrayed in Edvard Munch's 1893 painting 'The Scream' – while others continue in a straight line to strive for 'better ratios' they feel ever more isolated within their individual hells.

Purpose and structure of book

Should organisations rethink what they are about in order to give their people richer lives? Does a new style 'contract' need to be struck to accommodate the changing needs of both people and the organisations that require their services? Whether one looks at it from the perspective of an individual, the organisation or a society as a whole, some elements seem to be missing from current approaches to management and transformation.

There must be a better way. In this book we will examine where organisations, and those who lead them, may be going wrong and whether within our current management approaches there might lie the seeds of alternative courses of action.

Our point of departure in several chapters will be to remind ourselves of what corporate leaders have been attempting to do since the start of the 1990s. We will examine their preoccupations and priorities, and the trends, as identified by surveys of senior management, before moving on to subsequent discussion of how organisations are coping and responding. In so doing we will draw upon the results of extensive programmes of interviews and discussions with managers and directors who have reflected upon their experiences and how we might move forward from 'where we are' as opposed to from 'where we would prefer to be'.

While our focus is upon the achievement of transformation rather than quality, much of the dialogue which occurred with interviewees concerned quality. There are three main reasons for this:

- Firstly, various approaches to 'quality' and 'total quality' are such a prominent and ubiquitous feature of 'where we are'.
- Secondly, they often result in corporate frameworks that tend to absorb other much championed approaches such as 're-engineering' or 'empowerment'.
- Thirdly, a consensus emerged that if only the emphasis could be switched within existing quality programmes they could help to lead us in desired directions.

The purpose of this book is to identify issues and trends, speculate about possible future developments, suggest priorities, and offer practical guidance on how best to proceed. In order to facilitate the collective development of a new philosophy of management, it is intended to encourage reflection and open up internal debates, and not to be overly prescriptive.

Before we can introduce the required changes we need to understand where we are with quality and such phenomena as 're-engineering' and 'restructuring'. In part one:

- We begin the review process in a 'scene setting' chapter by examining what quality is or might be, how it has evolved, and both perceptions of it and reactions to it.
- Having considered how 'quality' is perceived we move on in Chapters 2 and 3 to some issues and concerns and its contemporary relevance and role.
- In Chapters 4 and 5 we will reflect upon the growing gap between vision and reality, and what our priorities and aspirations ought to be.

Understanding of itself will not necessarily lead to action. In part two of this book we are also concerned with implementation:

- In Chapter 6 we will address the question of corporate leadership before turning in Chapters 7 and 8 to what quality does and could mean for customers and the people of organisations.
- Chapter 9 focuses upon the role of management, while Chapter 10 adopts a process perspective and examines the contribution of re-engineering.

- After looking in Chapter 11 at various other approaches, tools and techniques we will set out in Chapter 12 the basis of an agenda for moving ahead.
- Chapter 13 highlights the missing elements most mentioned in the course of interviews and discussions, while Chapter 14 suggests we have little more to lose and 'everything to play for'.

In essence, *this book advocates a further attempt to introduce more holistic and people-centred approaches to management and transformation into the organisations and institutions that surround us before we opt either to abandon them or to let them die.* It adopts this approach in the belief that there is insufficient time for more than a minority of citizens to learn how to establish, properly contribute to and manage whatever replacement structures and systems would be necessary to sustain the various support services and general standards of living to which we have become accustomed.

Acknowledgements

I would like to thank all those whose support has made this book possible, especially colleagues at the Faculty of Management of the University of Luton, Adaptation Ltd, Attitudes Skills and Knowledge Ltd, ASK Multimedia Ltd and Policy Publications Ltd, and Tony Mason and the team at Kogan Page Ltd. I owe special debts of gratitude to Willmott Dixon Ltd, and to Susan Coulson-Thomas to whom the book is dedicated.

A central theme of this book is speculation concerning where quality and BPR might be heading and whether they might yet be used as a basis for achieving beneficial change. It draws in part upon the results of COBRA (Constraints and Opportunities in Business Restructuring – an Analysis), an international and independent investigation of business restructuring which has been led and coordinated by the author. The study has examined experience and practice with contemporary phenomena such as BPR, and the implications for new forms of organisation and new patterns of work.

COBRA's aim has been to encourage the adoption of more vision-led, balanced, holistic and strategic approaches to corporate transformation that will lead to greater benefits for *all* stakeholders. COBRA has led to reports, case studies and detailed methodologies for: (a) ensuring that issues relating to new ways of working are fully taken into account during re-engineering, and (b) using the enabling technologies of electronic commerce to re-engineer supply chains. Further European Commission supported projects are applying the COBRA approach to the re-engineering of industrial companies, and of hospital, healthcare and other public sector processes.

The COBRA project team has consisted of transformation specialists and has been advised by an international panel of acknowledged authorities. While the core funding for COBRA was provided by the Commission of the European Communities, additional support was obtained from sponsoring organisations in the corporate, consultancy, public and academic sectors.

Further information

Those who would like to learn more about the COBRA project are invited to contact the Project Leader (Professor Colin Coulson-Thomas) at the COBRA Project Office (Tel:+44 (0)181-857 5907; Fax:+44 (0)181-857 5947).

The views of several of those involved in the COBRA project are summarised in the book: Colin Coulson-Thomas (ed.), *Business Process Reengineering: Myth and Reality*, London, Kogan Page, 1994 (ISBN 0 7494 1442 1) and 1996 (paperback edition: ISBN 0 7494 2109 6).

The formal outputs of the COBRA project consist of:

- A three-volume cased set of reports: Colin Coulson-Thomas (executive ed.), *The Responsive Organisation: Re-engineering New Patterns of Work*, London, Policy Publications, 1995 (ISBN 1 872980 01 5). The set consists of a methodology manual, 21 case studies and the key lessons arising from them, briefings on 101 tools and techniques, and a guide to relevant resources.

- A further report, *The Competitive Network*, London, Policy Publications, 1996 (ISBN 1 872980 26 0) based upon research by Peter Bartram, Colin Coulson-Thomas and Lee Tate, contains a methodology for re-engineering supply chains, nine case studies, briefings on re-engineering and electronic commerce, and details of organisations offering relevant services.

Management myopia: perceptions and reactions

Neither ashore nor afloat.

Options and choices

Questioning, challenging and confronting a reality of entrenched attitudes and assumptions can be tough, even for those individuals who
instinctively fight against corporate 'groupthink'. It is still harder for
those overworked managers who are already struggling to keep up. An
earlier programme of organisational surveys reported that: 'Too many
managers conceal problems rather than solve them'.[1] As one middle manager confided: 'We are not stupid, ... we just look the other way'.

Yet it is worth examining the options. We have everything to play for.
So much has been invested over generations to bring us to where we are
today. We are the lucky ones. No generation in history has had so much
choice in terms of how, when, where or with whom to work, learn and
consume. The barriers between home and office, and work and play have
never been so easy to overcome. We are the first generation for whom
'activity' rather than 'work' is a realistic choice.

Let's take an example. It has never been so easy to set up in business.
Barriers to entry are tumbling down. Vast numbers of customers world
wide, more than have died in most of human history, can be reached
within seconds by means of electronic communication, telecommunications
and the broadcast media. Stimulated by 'word of keyboard', people in dis-
tant places can beat an electronic path to the door of an internet site.

The case of quality

Managers face acute personal dilemmas, for example to press on, try
alternatives or 'cut and run'. There are difficult choices to be made, but

we often feel 'neither ashore nor afloat'. While many of today's management approaches may not be 'delivering' as expected, or as we had hoped, we remain reluctant to ignore or discard them. So much energy and emotion has been devoted to establishing foundations that might yet support a new Jerusalem.

While acknowledging that we don't feel as well as we would like, should we be seeking the support and solace of new bandwaggons, miracle cures, trends and fads? An alternative would be to step back and consider whether the answer might be to adopt a healthier lifestyle rather than try yet another instant remedy for whatever symptoms bother us the most.

Given a different attitude to life, we might be able to build our new assumptions and priorities into some of today's approaches. Maybe even traditional remedies could have their place. Perhaps the answer is under our noses and the familiar could be used to better purpose. What if we are almost there? Having travelled for so long, and blinkered by disappointment and frustration, we could be unaware of how close we might actually be to our goal.

This brings us to quality in its various forms, but first a qualification. This is not another book on how to 'do quality', 're-engineering' or 'transformation', or about what needs to be done to implement 'tick-list' approaches. The author's book *Transforming the Company* presents an overview of how to successfully bring about major change,[2] while the author's recent books on directors and boards examine the role of corporate leadership in the transformation process.[3]

'Quality' is worthy of our consideration because it has become a universal phenomenon. Its concepts and terminology are used by organisations of many forms and sizes that operate in a great diversity of situations and circumstances. Its adoption is encouraged and, in some contexts, imposed.

The tentacles of quality even reach into the depths of the forests of Indonesia. The country's largest producer of market pulp Indorayon has adopted a 'comprehensive quality assurance system' that, according to an executive director of the company Dr Per Haugen, 'will further enhance our commitment to product quality and meeting the exact needs of our customers'.

Why question quality?

Why has quality had such a widespread appeal? To play 'devil's advocate': why are approaches, tools and techniques that were developed by engineers and statisticians to improve the quality of 'things' now being used by so many people to change the attitudes, perceptions, feelings and behaviours of human beings?

Returning to the roots of quality, which lie in the work, during the 1920s and 1930s, of such pioneers as Walter Shewhart at Western Electric, one might have foreseen the adoption of statistical techniques to improve processes and reduce variation in manufacturing and engineering environments, or that the notion of 'conformance to customer requirements' would be understood by IT suppliers offering 'solutions to customers' problems'. What is surprising is that such a diverse and extensive range of businesses have embraced quality with every emotion from enthusiasm to desperation.

There are few major companies that do not have quality programmes. Most managers one meets have been quality trained, and some form of 'quality system' is usually in place within their organisations. A recent survey of FT 500 companies found 69 per cent to have 'quality improvement programmes' with another 12 per cent in the process of setting them up.[4] Against this background, what is there to add?

Surely quality is by now widely accepted? Yes and no. On the basis of definitions, quality seems reasonable enough. For example, within Unisys it is viewed as: 'A strategy for improving business performance through the commitment of all employees to fully satisfying agreed customer requirements at the lowest overall cost through the continuous improvement of products and services, business processes and the people involved.' Such a broad perspective appears to embrace more recent developments such as Business Process Re-engineering (BPR) and to benefit just about everyone and everything.

Yet there is disquiet even among the faithful. BT and other companies are finding that the rate at which customer satisfaction is increasing is either tailing off or the level has plateaued. The 1990 Institute of Management report *Beyond Quality* concluded that: 'Increasingly customers assume reliability and performance. Quality of itself may no longer differentiate alternative suppliers. In markets in which all suppliers have their quality programmes managers need to consider what lies beyond quality.'[5]

Many quality leaders are finding that competitors are catching up while past improvements are quickly taken for granted by ever more demanding customers. British Airways is responding with a wide-ranging 'Leadership 2000' initiative designed to change how the organisation is managed. As with other companies such as Unilever and Rank Xerox renewed emphasis is being put upon improving the quality of management and the quality of contribution from people throughout the organisation.

Xerox and Rank Xerox have together won major quality awards around the world. And yet the company has singularly failed to exploit the pioneering role played by its Palo Alto Research Centre or Xerox PARC in developing windows, icons, the mouse, pop-up and pull-down menus, and local area networking, all central building blocks of an information technology revolution.

The apparent generality of quality accounts significantly for its appeal. But is it too general and unfocused, in a world of increasing concentration upon core activities, critical processes and 'vital few' actions? Perhaps it is being adopted as a universal panacea, because this is a less demanding option than thinking through what is needed in each context?

Widespread concerns

The use of the rhetoric of quality is widespread, but so to are concerns. Over the last six years, in various consultant–client relationships and survey interviews, many of the early adopters of quality have increasingly confided their misgivings and worries to the author. The following are a small selection of the comments that have been made:

> There comes a point when you have to say – if the benefits haven't come yet, will they ever come? ... I don't buy all this stuff about how long it takes to change attitudes, corporate culture and the rest of it. Who knows what business we will be in next year or the year after? The attitudes we need are changing all the time ... we need the impacts more quickly.

> There is always some fad around the corner ... quality or BPR ... that is going to revolutionise my business. Why hasn't anything really happened yet? ... It sometimes seems all a game. We're now trying thinking it out for ourselves, in effect 'doing our own thing'.

> Quality has been given a fair crack of the whip. How many other things are there out there that might have given us a better return, if we had invested in them only a fraction of the massive commitment we have made to quality?

> I shouldn't be assuming, or hoping, or feeling we have benefited from quality – I should know. We have spent millions on quality training and all the rest of it. People say they feel good ... I would feel better if we really had a stronger, more capable and competitive business.

> Why should I wait and have faith? Life is full of opportunities, things you can do and receive an instant feedback. Society is like that ... things are speeding up ... people don't want to wait around any more.

These, and many other views that could have been quoted, suggest that quality may be 'outliving its welcome'. People in many organisations are just getting bored and tired with 'the same old phrases':

> My overseas people tell me the same thing – quality may have had its day. Quality is now old hat ... The debates are all about what comes next. I'm interested in the next steps, not the past.

> Quality dosen't really interest me any more so far as future competitive advantage is concerned. By now we must have got whatever benefit is to be had ... We have got to keep moving. We must move onto new things in the race to stay ahead.

While some clearly feel they have 'done' quality, others are more positive. For example:

> Quality is a set of shared attitudes, goals and values. It's a sort of spirit that flows through the organisation. It holds us together.

Shared beliefs about a quality of life or the quality of motives and intentions can and do hold some organisations together for hundreds of years.

> Quality should support the establishment and building of mutually beneficial relationships. It could be everything from the attitudes, perspectives, approaches and values of a philosophy or way of life, to a toolkit.

The key to success is selecting what is relevant.

People do exist, beyond the ranks of those whose business is quality, who see 'the benefits'. However, our concern is moving ahead, which requires that we both understand and address the areas of disquiet. Let us look at some further representative comments:

> Quality is perceived as about paperwork, filing the right reports at the right time. It is not about relationships, about talking, feeling, understanding ... We are expected to write it all down, but we are an oral culture. The system does not take account of this.

> It doesn't reach the hearts and minds. It just doesn't get to us. At the end of the day we put up with it, but it is not really wanted. It is forced upon us ... it is an organisational requirement.

> When the quality people shift their ground, you know they are worried. Each time the latest craze comes along our quality people grab it. I'm now told all this process re-engineering stuff is quality ... If all these new things have to be taken on board, does this mean the quality toolkit we had last year was rubbish?

> Each of us has our own view of what the quality system is. To most it's become a bit of a joke. Whatever you suggest we do, don't call it quality.

> Our staff don't jump out of bed each morning looking for new ways to screw up our customers. They actually want to do a good job. Quality should help and not hinder them.

One could go on with more in the same vein, and we will return to some specific areas of concern in the next chapter.

Business process re-engineering

More recently, another phenomenon, BPR, has come into vogue which is complementing quality, and either succeeding it or being embraced and absorbed by it according to the context. A response typical of one particular viewpoint is:

> Quality is too much about incremental change. It's a 'me too' approach for the unimaginative. We need to make bigger, more dramatic steps. 'Greenfield' thinking or re-engineering is the only way to break away from the pack.

What should the relationship be between BPR and quality? We shall return to this question, particularly in Chapter 10. Meanwhile some would argue we are already too late. Another group of interviewees perceive BPR to be 'going the way of quality':

> Where is the drive and excitement about quality? It comes across as something we have done. It's not even last year's priority. People have moved on, tried BPR and are now trying to make a mark with something else.

For a period hardly a day went by without an invitation to yet another BPR event arriving in the in-tray. The initial trickle of books on the subject soon became a flood. In some larger organisations, 'me too' exercises abound, as people have jumped onto the BPR bandwagon in order to keep up with colleagues and rivals.

Can the momentum be maintained? How many companies face such a challenge, if not a crisis, that they actually need to undertake BPR in place of quality or alongside it? Does BPR encourage creativity, or lead to the avoidance of difficult choices? How many BPR exercises have a fundamental impact upon how, where, when and with whom we work? Will it stay the course, or will it be forced out of the limelight by a more alluring and even better marketed alternative?

What will happen to BPR when all the obvious sources of wasted time and non-value added activity have been cut out, and everyone is squeezed to breaking point? Will the BPR bubble burst leaving organisations stranded in mid-stream, locked into half-complete exercises? Will the fickle move on to the next fashionable term? Already conference organisers are having to differentiate their events in order to attract an audience, extending the application of BPR to ever more specialist and obscure fields.

Survey evidence

The comments on quality which have been quoted above are far from atypical. The author's experience is also supported by survey results. For example, considering the situation in Europe:

- An Economist Intelligence Unit report has broadly concluded that many European companies, as a consequence of their quest for quality, are actually damaging the prospects of improving their service and competitive positioning.[6] In particular, involvement with quality can 'inoculate the organisation against real change'.
- An A T Kearney survey has found that 80 per cent of TQM programmes do not produce any tangible benefit.[7] This is most often the result of a failure of management to set realistic goals or to seek measurable achievements at the outset of programmes.
- A London Business School study has found that many quality pro-

grammes are running out of steam and lack management support. Quality drives have been undermined by the economic recession, and the study concludes that: 'Lip service is not enough'.[8]

The situation is similar in the US, the heartland of many of the earliest champions of quality. Arthur D Little found that among 500 manufacturing and service companies in the US only a third of total quality programmes were having a 'significant impact' upon competitiveness.

Overall, a gap appears to have emerged between the rhetoric of quality and the reality of corporate experience (Figure 1.1). Aspiration has run ahead of achievement, and outcomes have not matched initial intentions. More recently, evidence from across Europe suggests that BPR is likewise 'going the way of quality'.[9]

Taking stock of where we are

Are people overreacting? Has it become fashionable to rubbish quality? The PIMS Associates database actually reveals a positive relationship between return on investment and superior relative quality and strong market differentiation. Companies such as Rank Xerox regard profitability as the consequence of quality that is measured in terms of both customer and employee satisfaction.

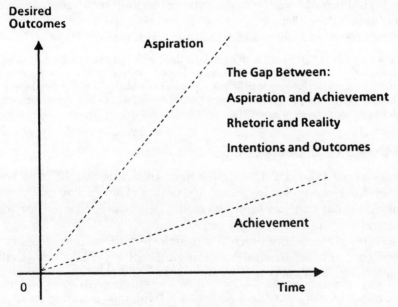

Figure 1.1 The rhetoric/reality gap

PIMS is linking financial performance with achieved quality in the marketplace. The issue is whether what is measured as 'delivered quality' is actually the result of some specific quality programme or initiative, the adoption of quality principles, or the consequence of a great many other things.

Quality is a 'help' or a 'hinder' more often than it is a decisive factor. Very rarely is it seen by itself to be the single cause or solution. Gary Hamel and C K Prahaled consider quality to be but one requirement for market entry.[10] Continuing survival will depend upon more than learning from the best today, namely the creativity and imagination to build new markets and be tomorrow's leader. The quality heritage with its roots in the pioneering work of W Edwards Deming and others to identify and remove faults in 'what is' may provide little guidance about 'what ought to be'.

Is there a problem with the concept of quality, or is the implementation of quality at fault? Professor Harry Roberts of the University of Chicago has concluded that most of the problems with quality management stem from application rather than theory. He also notes that the most effective implementations involve moulding quality to fit a particular.culture and calling it something else.

With so many changes occurring within organisations it is difficult to measure the distinct contribution of one element of a change programme. A team at Surrey University have been able to demonstrate a link between ISO 9000 registration and above average financial performance, but it could well be that companies seeking registration are more likely to be 'above average'.

The Economist Intelligence Unit study concluded:

> Total Quality (TQ) needs rethinking. In the way it has been tackled by most companies, TQ has failed to deliver the hoped for results. It has been internally focused, lacking a clear link to customers or business results. At best, it has led to incremental improvements; at worst, it has made it more difficult for organisations to increase their competitiveness.[6]

All things to all people

According to Donald Petersen, a former chairman and CEO of Ford: 'Everywhere you go lately, people are talking about quality as if it were something that had just been invented.'[11] It has been around for some time and now appears in all manner of forms.

Beyond generalisations such as 'meeting customer requirements at the lowest cost' or 'cost effectively achieving fitness for purpose', views differ greatly as to what quality is or means:

● The enthusiast, stumbling across something that works, gives quality the credit.

- The specialist interested in maintaining a quality registration may be largely concerned with 'internal' matters such as reviewing responsibilities, contract reviews, and process and document control.
- A cynic's description could be along the lines of: 'A variable and shifting selection of generally misunderstood principles and approaches that often confuse and distract, and which rarely have a direct and beneficial impact upon the historical determinants of corporate success or failure.'

Quality is often used as an adjective or attribute, as, for example, when Woo Kwong-Ching, Chairman and CEO of the Hong Kong property company The Wharf (Holdings) Ltd, expresses the view that: 'Wharf's success relies on the quality of its people, its land and infrastructural resources and a vision for the future.'

David Brunnen, Managing Director of Advanced Business Facilities, after limping to a conference podium, explained that he had been involved in an accident. He felt there was some compensation: 'At least it was a quality accident – I was knocked down by a Harley Davidson, in Pall Mall and outside of the Institute of Directors.'

Quality can be a 'sheep dip' into which people are dropped, a package that is imposed, or an area that people can be encouraged to think about and relate to their own circumstances. It can drop like a ton of cement, or evolve and grow naturally. It can constrain or liberate.

What is quality?

There are those who draw a distinction between conformance quality with its emphasis upon 'doing things right', and strategic quality with a focus on 'doing the right things'. Of course 'excellent' companies 'do the right things right', but doing the right things today will not guarantee success in 'competing for the future', the creation of the markets of tomorrow.[10]

Some practitioners draw a distinction between the 'hard' quality of installing and monitoring the quality system, and the 'soft' quality of encouraging cooperation and sharing. At a simplistic level, the 'hard' concentrates on techniques for controlling behaviour, while the focus of the 'soft' is upon influencing attitudes and the 'human factors'. Such a distinction is convenient for those wishing to concentrate upon one area or the other. Quality can mean whatever we wish it to mean. Herein lies its utility for the future.

Quality may be viewed as a goal, as a journey, or as a combination of both. As an objective, it could be regarded as but one step en route to a broader and longer-term goal. In one context, it could be defined so as to make it obtainable, while others might prefer to keep it as an aspiration that is just out of reach. Pursuing the journey analogy, quality could be conceived in route map terms as defined stages to be mechanically followed, or as a pilgrimage, at the end of which the person may never be the same again as a consequence of the experience.

The Institute of Management Services defines total quality management as 'a strategy for improving business performance through the commitment and involvement of all employees to fully satisfying agreed customer requirements at the optimum overall cost through the continuous improvement of the products and services, business processes and the people involved'.

Implementing a strategy, according to the definition just given, could involve the total redesign of an organisation. The 'European Model for Total Quality Management' of the European Foundation for Quality Management (EFQM) appears to be an adaptation of approaches to business excellence pioneered by Xerox and other companies and offers a sufficiently broad framework to embrace almost any contributor to the improvement of performance.

The relationship between quality and other factors

Project managers with responsibilities for delivering certain outputs within agreed parameters of cost and time may have a 'zero sum' approach to quality. Thus to get more of it, something else may have to be given up in terms of time or cost (Figure 1.2). Great importance is attached to establishing to what extent the client or customer is, or is not, prepared to wait or pay more to obtain extra quality.

Others take a 'positive sum' approach, believing the right combination

Figure 1.2   Trade-offs or combinations?

of quality elements can result in gains right across the board. Many advocates of quality regard it as an element of something else, perhaps the 'Q' in QCD or 'Quality, Cost, Delivery', with continuous improvements being sought in all three areas.

Indorayon recognises the importance of the trinity price, service and quality (Figure 1.2). Per Haugen believes the company has sustained its profitability in the face of falling market prices and competitive pricing by being 'one of the lowest cost pulp producers' and by its 'emphasis on product quality and service to customers'.

Quality is often distinguished from price in order to establish the trade-off between them. In the case of commodities, a 'market' level of quality may be perceived as an entrance ticket, purchase decisions being taken on the basis of price. Elsewhere, price needs to be seen for what it is, and not used as a rationalisation for lost orders.

IBM takes the view that quality is quite distinct from price, and a high level or quality of service is remembered by customers long after an original purchase price is forgotten. Continuing service may be a current reality while historic price quickly becomes an item in the records.

Quality as a business philosophy

To some quality is a set of tools, or a quality kitemark, while others talk more broadly of a 'business philosophy', 'paradigm', 'system of attitudes and behaviour' or 'way of doing things'. The 'driver' of 'quality' might be seen by one organisation to be a 'focus upon the customer', while for another it could be 'learning' or 'continuous improvement'.

Charles Handy regards quality as truth. He believes that to survive organisations need to guarantee quality in their goods and services: 'Short-term profit at the expense of quality will lead to short-term lives. In that sense quality is, to my mind, the organisational equivalent of truth. Quality like truth will count in the end.'[12]

The notion of an honest corporation may seem a trifle woolly to some while an inspiration to others. On occasion, the rhetoric of quality values is found wanting, as in the case of British Airway's apparent campaign of 'dirty tricks' against its rival Virgin. However, abstract concepts are given meaning in certain contexts. Thus the concern of Japanese car manufacturers with the 'integrity' of the product results in a holistic approach to design that embraces lifestyle as well as technical considerations.

If reality is truth, then many management teams and advocates of quality are 'living a lie'. Their preoccupation is with the lure of appearance. The inconveniences of reality are avoided by groupthinking clones, hidden in the small print or wordsmithed away by the slick and the smooth.[2]

Perhaps morality is a better analogy than truth. Whereas people tend to view truth in absolutist terms, they are generally more willing to regard morality as relative to the context. As with quality, what is appropriate in one context may not be acceptable in another, and a degree of sensitivity to local requirements and practices can avoid both embarrassment and distress.

Total quality

As a 'business philosophy' quality, and especially its resistant strain TQM, has great staying power to the point of being virulent. It displays imperialist designs and appears able to effortlessly absorb whatever is the current fashion or necessity. Thus one by one 'lean production', 'downsizing', 'flattening the organisation', 'intrapreneurship', 're-engineering' and many other concepts are 'claimed' by 'total quality' and incorporated under its banner.

Some stretch 'total quality management' to embrace almost every aspect of corporate operation. According to one chief executive officer (CEO): 'Total quality is like total war – you throw everything at it, and hope that something, perhaps brute force, works.'

Across companies, what is included under the quality umbrella varies greatly. For example, continuous improvement might appear to many as a key and integral element of the essence of quality, while to others it may be regarded as an attitude or approach in its own right that can be applied outside of their view of what constitutes quality. Thus John Potter, Chief Executive of Bundy within the TI Group distinguishes four key elements of 'Bundy's commitment ... to deliver customer value', namely 'knowledge and service, global leveraging of technology, world-class quality [and a] philosophy of continuous improvement'.

The 'total' in TQM suggests its advocates are adopting a more comprehensive, if not holistic, approach. Include too much and TQM becomes rather like saying 'everything needs to be better', while leave something out and people complain it is incomplete.

The language of quality

In many companies, especially where a wide range of activities are placed under a TQM umbrella, quality appears to have a language of its own. Those used to traditional terms may have taken some time to become accustomed to the new jargon. People also frequently use quality terminology without being certain of precise meanings, or having the same shared understanding as others. Too rarely is understanding tested.

Certain companies use a language that is more familiar. For example, Jurgen Hintz, President and CEO of the French company CMB

Packaging, recognising the competitive nature of the markets within which it operates, refers to the commitment that has been made 'for CMB to achieve world-class operating excellence in three areas':

- *Manufacturing standards:* 'We have many good plants, but we can see ample room for further improvement in the way we operate them. This is the key to raising productivity, and to improving customer service and product quality.'
- *Sales and marketing operations:* 'We must get better at identifying customer needs, and better at answering them. These skills are also necessary for turning our superior technology into higher sales and profits.'
- *Management systems, starting with information handling:* 'Our many decentralised business units need to be 'wired together' more effectively. We need advanced systems to help each unit operate better, and to allow the Group to learn.'[13]

Within CMB, the key elements of corporate objectives are expressed in traditional terms, to help people to understand what needs to be done in each functional area. In many companies, people are familiar with the concepts of quality while at the same time uncertain of how to apply them in a local context.

The evolution of quality

A key issue for quality is how broad a church it is prepared to be. In an age of 'business excellence' models, diversity, restructuring, re-engineering and fragmentation, who or what will be included or excluded?

Understanding what is quality is complicated by its capacity to transform and mutate. For example:

- Quality within IBM has passed through various stages, including an emphasis on the cost of quality, quality circles and process management en route to 'Market Driven Quality'.
- In several major companies, the tools and approaches of quality are now being incorporated in the methodologies and toolkits being assembled to support the simplification or redesign of management and business processes.
- Rank Xerox experienced benchmarking, employee involvement and Leadership Through Quality phases before arriving at a business excellence model that incorporates the main elements needed to achieve corporate transformation.
- Within General Motors, the concept of 'Network Quality' embraces the supply chain and consists of 'a collection of interdependent values, concepts and techniques which represent the best-known manufacturing and business practices in the world' at any moment in time.

With the benefit of hindsight such experiences can be portrayed as a steady evolution based upon learning and adaptation, as one by one vital building blocks needed to succeed are put in place, each building upon previous foundations. At the time, and to those involved, it all seems bitty and jerky as people stumble forward, with some stages seeming to be dead ends, incomplete, half-hearted or periods of treading water. A typical reaction is: 'If we could start again, we would be here in half the time.'

The evolution of BPR

Let us turn our attention for a moment to BPR which in some form is probably here to stay, simply because the need for fundamental change, even if periodic, is likely to be a continuing feature of business life. Also many of the individual elements of BPR are not new, their roots in some cases going back to the 1960s, even though 'packaging' under the BPR label has occurred more recently.[9]

Various combinations of elements or 'principles' of BPR and transformation (fundamental change of the whole organisation) were produced in the form of 'manuals' or 'guidance notes' within individual companies throughout the 1980s. Different compilations of these began to enter the public domain towards the end of the decade as major consultancy firms began to consolidate the experiences of their clients and strove to differentiate their offerings.

Although its main elements had been successfully utilised by internal change teams within certain corporations for several years before being 'packaged' for a wider audience, the impact of the first few articles and books on BPR was dramatic. However, in the course of selection and packaging some of the key 'principles' of transformation developed in leading edge companies in the 1980s seem to have been forgotten. For example:[9]

- *Internally, focus upon harnessing more of the potential of people and applying it to those activities which identify and deliver value to customers.* The first part of this principle has generally been overlooked.
- *Encourage learning and development by building creative working environments.* This principle has been almost forgotten, the current emphasis being upon squeezing more out of people and working them harder, rather than improving the quality of working life and working smarter.
- *Work should be 'broadened' without sacrificing 'depth' of expertise in strategic areas.* The latter consideration tends to be overlooked today.
- *Avoid oversophistication.* People are losing sight of this principle under a growing assault from suppliers of modelling and other BPR support tools that can encourage the collection and input of data at the expense of creative thinking.

- *Build both learning and renewal, and short feedback loops into processes.* Where cursory attention is paid to this and the next principle, a 're-engineered' solution can quickly become either commonplace, and hence no longer be a 'differentiator', or be overtaken by competitors.
- *Ensure that continuous improvement is built into implemented solutions.* Experience of BPR can re-awaken interest in TQM, the two being natural complements.

Given that these and other factors are either overlooked or insufficiently addressed, it is not surprising that critics and critiques have started to emerge. Re-engineering is now regularly described as 'hype', a triumph of packaging, or as a 'cover' for downsizing or other forms of restructuring.[14] Already the term BPR sends a shiver down the spines of many of those who learn they are about to be 're-engineered'.

Current perceptions of quality

While quality may not have aroused such strong negative reactions as quickly as BPR seems to have done, people rarely come to quality as a 'blank sheet'. They tend each to bring their memories, attitudes, values and general approach to life along with them. Less prescribed approaches to quality allow for individual interpretation. Thus one person could apply 'continuous improvement' to 'what is', while it might encourage another person to reflect upon 'what ought to be'.

Very different images or perceptions of quality may be found within the same team. To some it conjures up images of scarcity, luxury or status, while colleagues may relate it to mass-produced consumer goods. 'Quality' may be seen as lavish or plush, while to others it may be associated with cost-cutting or avoiding waste.

Perceptions and misperceptions of quality are likely to reflect the context. In a manufacturing environment quality might well be accepted as a fact of life. It is in the services sector, the world of the knowledge worker, where apprehension is more likely to arise. In many areas, there has been little or no increase in white-collar productivity and the fear of a 'shake out' can trigger defensive behaviour.

To the naive, quality sometimes appears as a panacea, the ingredient that will lead to breakthrough. Outstanding business success is more likely to be the result of such factors as product or technology innovation, changing the 'rules' of the marketplace, strong relationships or dramatic differentiation than of quality *per se*. Care needs to be taken to ensure that preoccupation with the internal implementation of quality does not distract people from innovation and the external customer.[9]

Although some might argue that the current preoccupation with productivity is driving out the time or 'space' to build incremental quality and is encouraging the cutting of corners, an Anderson Consulting study has found that 'world-class plants' are 'simultaneously able to achieve outstanding levels of productivity and quality'.[15]

Liberation or control

Whether or not quality is perceived as a liberating force may determine the nature and extent of its use as a springboard into the future. Alongside the rhetoric of empowerment and delegation, quality is frequently perceived as about control and checking rather than as an enabler or liberator.

In many companies the 'inspection', 'audit', 'checking' and 'control' heritage of quality has determined its location and role within the corporate organisation. For example, the Norwegian oil company Saga Petroleum brought 'safety, quality assurance and internal audits' into a 'new department' which 'reports directly to Saga's president'.

Some view the 'checking' role as essentially negative. According to one director of quality: 'Our role is to look for what is wrong rather than to improve.' Another confided: 'I have to prevent us from slipping back rather than help us to move forward.' A third pointed out: 'To distinguish TQM from quality by stressing continuous improvement is like saying quality of itself is a recipe for stagnation.'

Although the term TQM was designed to embrace 'quality control' and 'quality assurance' and encourage a focus upon activities that deliver value to external customers, the control and assurance heritage has often resulted in a continuing preoccupation with internal product quality and the maintenance of 'quality standards' independently of the external customer.

Peter Blackmore, a director of Compaq Europe, believes that a new paradigm is needed to manage in a state of permanent change:

> Facilitation rather than automation is needed ... design, appeal and finding new ways rather than safety, reliability, and measurability; we need to manage change rather than the balance between input and output; the 'cost of quality' needs to be seen in terms of opportunity rather than resource; we need to evaluate, understand and enhance rather than monitor, control and improve.

The French COGEMA Group recognises the 'two faces' of quality, both of which are important in the nuclear facilities field. Its quality policy is 'based on two complementary orientations': 'quality action plans aimed at improving efficiency of company operations' and 'quality assurance in accordance with industrial and regulatory standards'.

In the nuclear energy sector, with catastrophic risks in the event of 'failure', a high priority is still placed upon assurance and control. According to COGEMA Chairman and CEO Jean Syrota, the company's

Quality and Progress programme 'involves all personnel in meeting the twin objectives of control and quality in every service rendered.'

Reactions to quality

The very word quality evokes a variety of responses, ranging from the zeal of its proselytising missionaries, through scepticism and cynicism to annoyance and derision. It can demonstrate a commitment to improvement or the adoption of a cosmetic. It can divide the core of full-time staff who have been 'quality trained' from 'peripheral' temporary and part-time workers who feel 'excluded from quality'.

If anything, views of quality may have moderated as a result of even more extreme reactions to BPR which now appears widely associated with 'delayering', 'headcount reduction' and cost-cutting.[9] As a consequence, certain companies are purposely avoiding the use of the term 're-engineering' and are placing their 'process' initiatives under a TQM umbrella.[14]

Expectations of quality range from the naively optimistic to the sceptical and cautious. If anything, the more experience people accumulate, and the more they think through the realities of implementation, the more cautious they become. One banker mused that rival Lloyds bank had it about right when they called their customer service and satisfaction drive the 'service challenge'.

The Economist Intelligence Unit study concluded that: 'Two out of three quality management programmes in place for more than a couple of years are stalled: they no longer meet the CEO's expectations for tangible improvement of service quality, customer satisfaction, and operating performance.'[6]

Regarding quality as a programme, or as an initiative, can lead to disappointment as both programmes and initiatives tend to come and go in major companies. Where quality is regarded as a set of principles or business philosophy it is more likely to stand the test of time, albeit at the risk of being taken for granted.

The most sceptical and disappointed tend to be those who uncritically adopt a standard rather than a customised approach, or use quality for a particular purpose without thinking through the extent to which the aspects of quality employed are relevant. For example, those aiming primarily at 'culture change' should develop a culture change programme rather than assume quality will 'do the trick'. Many elements of quality could be irrelevant, even destructive, in a particular context.

Maturity and quality

An encouraging sign is that the quality community has become more ready and willing to face criticism, and a more balanced assessment of quality is emerging. While future economic growth could not be taken for granted, people recognised that where quality is 'for real' it claims victims, both people and organisations:

- There is real fear in the eyes of middle managers in many corporations who, as one quality director confided, 'are expected to self-destruct'. Removing the cost of quality could involve a significant reduction in headcount.
- There is the disappointment, frustration or anger felt by the staff of 'traditional suppliers' who are no longer able to satisfy the exacting quality standards of companies such as Ford, and which as a result are axed.

Even the quality specialists, who will tell you that they are paid to be enthusiasts and champions, may also give a 'knowing look' and say: 'Of course between you and me it's all really a question of ...', before identifying what they really believe to be the root cause of success or failure.

The 1990s started with companies in Germany and Japan, as well as elsewhere, struggling to cope with economic adversity. Advocates and champions of quality have made painful adjustments along with those who have not given it 'house room'. Florida Power and Light, a winner of the Deming Award, is among organisations that has questioned its commitment to quality. As one quality manager put it: 'At least we know quality is not a sausage machine, with a programme going in at one end and improvements coming out at the other.'

Some people do not know how to react, as their quality programmes are too amorphous, and lack focus and clear objectives. Diffuse abstractions, bland sentiments and obscure generalisations are unlikely to impact upon corporate reality.

Those who raise objections and concerns about the direction, implementation and impact of quality should not be written off as 'barriers' or people who are not team players. Their views may have substance. The confident invite feedback and make it easy for people to complain. We will return to certain areas of concern in the next chapter. Understanding and confronting them will help to prepare us for the journey to come.

Checklist

Does your organisation adopt a balanced approach to modern approaches to management?

What does quality mean to you and your colleagues? Is there substance beneath the rhetoric?

Does quality mean different things to different people?

Is there agreement as to the essence of quality?

Is interest in it waxing or waning?

How is quality perceived in your organisation?

What are the reactions to it in different areas?

Is it regarded as a phenomenon of yesterday or for tomorrow?

Is it viewed as a liberator or a constraint?

Is it taken for granted?

What has quality contributed? What is its legacy?

How is BPR perceived?

Is BPR regarded as a complement of quality or as a substitute for it?

How open to challenge is your organisation's senior management team?

Is critical questioning of quality regarded as healthy or disloyal?

Is the quality programme set in concrete, or periodically reviewed?

Is the timescale for its full implementation realistic?

At this stage, where do you or your colleagues feel quality is headed?

Could your organisation's experience of quality be used as the foundation for a broader philosophy of business and management?

References

1. Colin Coulson-Thomas, *Transforming the Company: Bridging the Gap Between Management Myth and Corporate Reality*, London, Kogan Page, 1992, p 200.
2. Colin Coulson-Thomas, *Transforming the Company: Bridging the Gap Between Management Myth and Corporate Reality*, London, Kogan Page, 1992.
3. Colin Coulson-Thomas, *Creating Excellence in the Boardroom* and *Developing Directors: Building an Effective Boardroom Team*, both London, McGraw-Hill, 1993.
4. Robert Heller, 'Putting the Total into Total Quality', *Management Today*, August 1994, pp 56–60.
5. Colin Coulson-Thomas and Richard Brown, *Beyond Quality: Managing the Relationship with the Customer*, Corby, BIM, 1990, p 1.
6. George Binney, *Making Quality Work: Lessons from Europe's Leading Companies*, Special Report No P655, London, Economist Intelligence Unit, 1992.
7. John Cottrell, 'Favourable Recipe', *The TQM Magazine*, February 1992, pp 17–20.
8. Chris Voss and Rita Cruise O'Brien, *In Search of Quality*, London, London Business School, 1992.
9. Colin Coulson-Thomas (ed), *Business Process Re-engineering: Myth and Reality*, London, Kogan Page, 1994.
10. Gary Hamel and C K Prahalad, *Competing for the Future: Breakthrough Strategies for Seizing Control of Your Industry and Creating the Markets of Tomorrow*, Cambridge, Mass, Harvard Business School Press, 1994.
11. Donald Petersen and John Hillkirk, *Teamwork: New Management Ideas for the 90s*, London, Victor Gollancz, 1991.
12. Charles Handy, *The Age of Unreason*, London, Arrow Books, 1990, p 115.
13. Jurgen Hintz, 'Message to Shareholders', *CMB Packaging 1991 Annual Report*, Paris, 1992, p 5.

14. Colin Coulson-Thomas (executive ed), *The Responsive Organisation: Re-engineering New Patterns of Work*, London, Policy Publications, 1995.
15. Michael Ward, Peter Cheese, Betty Thayer, Ichiro Sakuda, Daniel Jones, Rick Delbridge, James Lowe and Nick Oliver, *The Lean Enterprise Benchmarking Project Report*, London, Andersen Consulting, 1993.

Issues and concerns

When cobwebs are plenty, kisses are scarce.

Unwelcome or unintended consequences such as redundancies for some and longer hours of work for others suggest that all is not well. While inner doubts remain, many management approaches are likely to be tolerated or grudgingly accepted rather than welcomed with open arms.

If, arguably, the most widespread management phenomenon, namely 'quality' in its various guises, is to form the background against which we need to go forward into a new age, it is important that we are frank and objective in addressing major areas of concern. Where this is not done we will be building upon foundations of sand.

Contemporary perceptions of quality, and the various reactions to it we encountered in the last chapter, suggest that the concept should not be taken for granted either in formulation or in application. What are the areas of critical concern that need to be addressed? One obvious place to begin is with the question of certification.

Quality certification

A craftsman producing individual products to order could be wise to focus upon quality of product, but for those engaged in repetitive sequences of activities the emphasis tends to be upon the quality of process. This leads to the consideration of some means by which process quality might be assured.

Quality certification appears to have polarised opinions in many organisations. It is regarded as costly and bureaucratic. Cries of: 'Can a small company afford it?' are matched by: 'Can you afford not to have it, especially when suppliers demand it?' Critics suggest standards set existing approaches in concrete, and that quality procedures should follow rather than precede an approach to quality. Advocates argue that in the absence of quality standards some companies might feel it necessary to carry out audits of potential suppliers before placing orders.

IBM Consulting have concluded after examining 202 manufacturing sites across the UK that the possession of quality standard BS 5750 of itself did not have a beneficial impact. Performance only improves when the achievement and maintenance of a standard is an element of a broader approach to quality.

A 1993 survey of 647 UK BS 5750 registered companies reported mixed results: 'BS 5750 falls short of excellence as a contribution to improving performance. This is not to say that BS 5750 has been a total failure; some companies claimed considerable success from implementing the standard.' However, 'Only 27 per cent of the organisations sampled report the standard to have added significant value to their business' and the survey suggests: 'For the last 15 years British business has pursued a quality management standard that seems to have neither captured the imagination of our organisations nor produced outstanding results.'[1]

The Economist Intelligence Unit study concluded that:

> For most organisations the ISO 9000 standards are not the best place to start Total Quality. The quality systems which they codify are important but only part of TQ. Starting TQ with ISO 9000 is beginning a process of change with the bureaucracy of quality: it puts the cart before the horse.[2]

Many small companies appear particularly alarmed. They perceive themselves as facing 'a choice between the devil and the deep blue sea'. They fear they either face exclusion from opportunities to supply larger companies through non-possession of a quality certification, or they face a bureaucratic burden if they seek one which some question whether they can afford.[3]

If 'implementation' is the issue, what is there about quality that makes it so difficult to implement? Given that the UK's BS 5750 grew out of the Ministry of Defence's 'Def Stan 0521' which was designed for defence manufacturers on 'cost plus' contracts, one should not assume it would be easy to apply, or be necessarily relevant, to non-manufacturing environments in very different market conditions.

On occasion there is heat where there could be light. Against the background of a succession of survey reports critical of quality, one survey of the small firm sector, which tends to be especially vocal in respect of quality, found there are benefits to be had when implementation is supported by experienced counsellors who have their feet on the ground.[4]

Quality certification is relatively widespread in many sectors in the UK, but in other countries is relatively rare. Cynics question its value when overseas customers regard it as irrelevant and, in any event, an organisation can select any standards of performance it wishes to achieve. It has been used to create barriers to entry, delay 'contracting out', coerce suppliers and as an instrument of 'economic blackmail'.

Quality registration according to one CEO 'demonstrates that one has a quality system and sticks to it. Of itself it does not mean that what is being done maximises customer benefits. There is a danger that we will cite our registration in our proposals, and delude ourselves that we have "done quality".'

Another argument is the extent to which the public can be misled. How many people take the trouble to investigate whether BS 5750 or ISO 9001/2 applies to the whole or one part of an organisation? Certification does not, as some unwary customers assume, 'guarantee quality'. Rank Xerox and other organisations have addressed this issue by adopting customer quality guarantees, and much of the UK public sector has been required by government to establish 'customer charters'.

Certification, flexibility and the *ad hoc*

So far as the future of certification is concerned, should the focus continue to be upon the processes that produce products? Where more products and services are tailored and the delivery of value to each customer may require a different network of paths and connections across and through an organisation according to whose inputs are considered relevant, would it make more sense to concentrate upon the quality of the framework within which such flexible responses need to occur?

At a number of points in the book we will encounter the view that the repetitive is likely to become less common. More attention needs to be paid to the quality of attitudes and values in relation to innovation, creativity, sensitivity and responsiveness. How does one certify the extent to which a community is adaptive and learns, as opposed to following procedures? Is certification of investment in people the issue? The UK's Investor in People award represents such an approach. Will the concept of certification spread to new areas, or will it pass away?

Jim Havard, a director who has been responsible for quality at Rank Xerox (UK) considers 'learning' to be as important as 'customer focus'. He points out that: 'The requirement to have a repetitive process in order to produce a procedure, can present real problems in fast moving and creative environments.' Companies such as 3M and Honda challenge and question what they are good at and the relevance of what many other corporate cultures accept as the planks or fundamentals of their success.

In spite of much rhetoric concerning the 'learning organisation' few companies are setting out to re-engineer learning processes. One exception is Attitudes, Skills and Knowledge whose corporate purpose, organisation design and processes are all concerned with the support and facilitation of learning.[5]

If continuous improvement is to occur, there must be a degree of dissatisfaction with the status quo. 3M is not a recent convert to quality. It was the first company headquartered outside of Europe to be admitted to the European Foundation for Quality Management, and is committed to continuous improvement. In 1990 a five-year improvement programme was completed which had reduced the company's cost of quality by 40 per cent. In the same year a new international programme was launched, focused upon everything the corporation does to satisfy customers.

Other quality issues

Certification is a pressing agenda item for many companies, but it is not the only area of concern. The participants in the *Quality: The Next Steps* survey[6], undertaken by Adaptation, were asked to indicate the extent of their agreement with 15 'quality issues'.

Their responses suggest that, in spite of reservations, many boards may feel they have little option but to implement a quality programme. The statement most agreed with, in terms of 'strongly agree' replies, is that 'quality is a critical success factor', followed by 'quality is not a question of choice, it is a necessary requirement of being a supplier' (Table 2.1).

What can be learned from the overall pattern of the responses summarised in Table 2.1? In general terms:

- Greater importance is attached to the contribution of quality to 'marketing type' management issues such as competition, customers, suppliers

Table 2.1 *Quality issue statements*
(ranked in order of 'strongly agree' replies

Quality is a critical success factor	81%
Quality is not a question of choice, it is a necessary requirement of being a supplier	72%
An organisation should periodically reassess its approach to quality	47%
A broader and more comprehensive approach to quality is needed	46%
Quality has resulted in more demanding customers	38%
Each organisation's approach to quality should reflect its own circumstances	37%
Customer satisfaction matters, not internal quality measures	33%
Quality needs to embrace less tangible factors such as feelings or values	26%
Quality too often consists of 'motherhood' statements	19%
Quality improvement projects can lead to people trying to find better ways of doing things that perhaps shouldn't be done in the first place	13%
After a couple of years a quality programme can run out of steam	8%
Customer satisfaction should be measured by an independent, objective third party	8%
Quality has caused pressure upon prices	4%
Quality has increased operating costs	1%
When all competitors have quality processes these cease to be a source of competitive advantage	1%

Source: Colin and Susan Coulson-Thomas, *Quality: The Next Steps*, Adaptation Ltd, 1991.

and added value opportunities, and relatively less importance is attached to its contribution to human resource type management issues such as remuneration, relationships and the flexible organisation.

- Quality is considered most relevant to those issues concerning 'ends' or desired outcomes (eg competitive advantage and closer relationships with customers and suppliers), and it is thought less relevant to the issues concerning 'means' or how these outcomes might be achieved (eg remuneration issues).
- The *Quality: The Next Steps* survey confirms that the focus of quality is shifting from 'internal' and 'product' quality to attitudes, values, approaches and perspectives, and the creation of quality networks embracing customers, suppliers and business partners.[6]

These findings are consistent with more recent evidence which suggests that insufficient attention is being paid to employee satisfaction and the quality of working life, a theme to which we will return. Trends such as outsourcing, delayering, raising productivity and 'driving down costs' are collectively subjecting people to such pressures that many feel themselves to be the victims rather than the beneficiaries of change.[7]

Quality, with its focus upon the customer, may have served the company of yesterday, but what about the customer of tomorrow? The RSA enquiry, *Tomorrow's Company*,[8] argues that corporate management needs to give greater priority to the aspirations, interests and requirements of a wider range of stakeholders.

Highly respected companies such as Marks & Spencer tend already to practise the advice which the RSA is giving out. In 1992 The BIS Group undertook its: 'second "Quality for People" survey, asking all 2,000 people in ... 35 locations in 20 countries for their feedback on what it is like to work for BIS.' Others have yet to ask: What about the people of the organisation, its employees, associates and partners? What could or should quality offer them?

Death by cloning

A 'quality culture' might or might not be desirable according to its nature and relevance. A strong and deeply entrenched culture could be too rigid to cope with a changing context. The emphasis should be upon flexibility, and the experience of a company such as 3M suggests this is not necessarily incompatible with scale.

Liberal democracies put a high value upon individualism, initiative, youth and rights. Other cultures put greater stress upon communitarianism, conformity, deference to authority and to age, and obligations. This difference of approach is manifest in the resort to litigation on the one hand, and the search for 'face saving' and consensus on the other. It is also evident in attitudes to quality in different parts of the world.

It is sometimes too easy to assume that some companies and countries are naturals for quality, just as perpetual competitive advantage should not be taken for granted. Who would have foreseen that as a result of quality improvements US cars might begin to outrank their Japanese rivals in terms of customer satisfaction? How quality is implemented, indeed what it is, should reflect conditions, circumstances, needs and priorities.

Can one have too much quality? The Japanese car manufacturer Mazda has found that its commitment to adding extra features in the search for ever more 'quality' resulted in products that were regarded as too expensive by increasingly cost-conscious customers. Relevance or balance could be more suggestive concepts.

In many business sectors there are companies that have considered quality and rejected it as inappropriate for their needs. The rate of rejection appears higher in individualistic cultures. To some the terminology, even the basic premises of traditional approaches to quality, seem foreign or alien.

When in doubt, it can pay to be cautious. There are companies that clutch at phenomena such as quality and BPR in order to avoid thinking through a series of steps that might be more appropriate to their situation and circumstances.

Given the speed with which the jargon of quality has spread around the world, one sceptical director expressed the view: 'Quality must be one of the fastest growing religions. There is a tremendous appeal to faith, and salvation is always around the next corner.' Some enthusiasts press on in an unquestioning way, as if their single-minded devotion is evidence of the true faith.

Groupe EMC 'considerably expanded' its TQM programme in 1991, and 'for most subsidiaries, an overriding objective is to meet ISO international standards.' EMC customers are increasingly seeking certification of their suppliers' output. However, 'seeking accreditation is not EMC's sole concern' and the company's approach includes quality action group, quality process and quality technique initiatives.

The Masco Corporation byline 'Where Quality Finds a Home' sums up the reality that quality often visits without putting down roots. Too often it exists in the form of the bureaucratic requirements of the quality manual, rather than lives in 'hearts and minds'. The establishment of a 'quality culture' may require more than merely equipping people with quality tools. Thus quality processes may need to be established and quality attitudes and behaviours encouraged and rewarded (see Figure 2.1 on page 54).

The encouragement and development of qualities rather than quality may be the issue. Jorge Gonçalves, Chairman of the Board of the Banco

Comercial Português, cites the importance his organisation places upon the qualities of its people: 'Five centuries ago, our sailors crossed the seas in search of new worlds. Today, the same qualities, the courage, initiative and innovation, will allow us to play our role in our changing world.'

Variety and diversity

The 'lowest common denominator' aspect of quality enables its language and tools to be used by a wide range of people. Almost everyone can be involved in quality, and this is often the basis of its appeal. However, given the variety of people and personalities one finds in many organisations, this universal sharing of quality is both an advantage and a disadvantage.

Vibrant corporate cultures thrive on variety and diversity. The interplay of different and complementary cultures, perspectives, approaches and personalities can result in the consideration of a wider range of options, the taking of 'bigger steps' and, in general terms, a more productive learning environment.[9]

It is therefore surprising that many corporate quality programmes result in so much financial and human resource being devoted to wiping out diversity, and the imposition of a standard or corporate way of doing things. As one European director of quality put it: 'We now speak a common language, or at least we think we do. This has some benefits ... but these ... have been obtained at enormous cost. We have alienated, even excluded, many people.'

IBM recognises three principles, namely that:

1. The achievement of quality is for the customer rather than the supplier to decide.
2. Quality needs to embrace a range of services beyond 'the product'.
3. Quality is not an absolute, but relative to the situation and the alternatives that are available.

Rodolphe Greif, Chairman of the Executive Board of EMC, considers the group's quality drive to be: 'a pragmatic program custom tailored to the unique features of each group business'. It is considered 'vital to earnings and to improving working conditions'.

We are all different. While the use of common approaches can enable us to share a 'common language' in group situations, at the same time people should be encouraged to understand and develop what works for them in terms of enabling them to think, problem solve or make a contribution. Quality should be concerned with enhancing competence and contribution, and should not result in proven and relevant techniques and approaches being replaced by those which are less relevant or productive.

The future lies with 'designer quality'. Organisations such as ASK Europe use whatever pattern of work, quality and other processes and supporting technology are relevant to the particular task and how those involved prefer to work and learn.

Matching the corporate culture

Quality needs to both support and contribute to the values that distinguish one company from another. This may preclude the pursuit of efficiency and profitability to the point that these conflict with core values of the organisation.

Value led corporations exist whose conduct and commercial decisions reflect ethical considerations. For example, Levi Strauss has withdrawn from relatively profitable foreign arrangements for the production of garments because of how certain suppliers have treated their staff. Those seeking to become Levi Strauss suppliers have to satisfy strict health and safety, employment and environmental criteria.

The quality environment or culture, as pointed out already, consists of quality attitudes and behaviours, quality processes and quality tools. These need to be mutually supporting and could be perceived as overlapping circles (Figure 2.1)

The quality gap

There are other problem areas that need to be addressed against a background of quality expectations that may continue to rise. When the

Figure 2.1 Quality environment/culture

possession of registration to an external and recognised quality standard has become the norm in certain sectors and people may feel they have 'done quality', a quality gap between expected and delivered quality, along the lines of Figure 1.1 in the previous chapter, may further increase.

A significant imbalance already exists in certain sectors. Thus while information technology (IT) hardware performance continues to improve and more systems are expected to become safety-critical, software quality problems persist. Over time, if a 'care and maintenance' approach to quality is adopted, it will prove increasingly difficult to bridge the quality gap by falling back upon either rhetoric or 'small print'.

In the case of many companies, it should be assumed that the gap between customer expectation and delivery will continue to grow unless:

- more holistic approaches to 'delivered' quality are adopted;
- continuous and incremental improvements are complemented by fundamental or 'step' changes in certain areas, as appropriate;
- a greater commitment to learning and sharing is introduced into corporate cultures; and
- the arena of quality is extended to embrace the supply chain and market innovation.

There is a pressing need in many organisations to deliver higher quality, realistically manage customer expectations, become more innovative, adaptable and flexible, and build more open 'partnership' relationships with customers in order to:

- differentiate them from their competitors, and competitor quality guarantees;
- break out of declining spirals of cost-cutting that can lead to commodity supplier status;
- secure opportunities for higher margin work and market development.

As we will see in the next chapter, organisations that adopt a short-term, defensive, narrow, bureaucratic and 'protective' view of quality are more likely to position themselves for a diet largely made up of commodity work, which will result in continuing pressure upon margins and profitability.

Commissars or counsellors

In time a quality team can itself become an obstacle to change. Constituted as a functional group, and composed of those who 'enjoy doing quality', the quality team can find the prospect of the fluid, multi-skilled and multifunctional network organisation as threatening as do other occupational groups and functional specialists.

There are quality assurance teams that check and audit, that police standards and test the extent to which quality systems and procedures are complied with. Of itself, this activity may do little to improve the quality of goods and services that are delivered to end customers. The impact is intangible, if it exists at all, and is indirect. In these circumstances, the demands of the quality system may be seen as a bureaucratic requirement.

The 'control' approach to quality can attract certain personality types, the purists who aim at theoretical perfection and those who like to remain detached and uninvolved. Standing back may be perceived as necessary in order to retain objectivity and independence. The quality team are guardians of the system, and may want to avoid 'falling prey' to 'compromises' or a 'trimming' of the system to suit particular circumstances.

Other approaches to quality concentrate upon the provision of a range of counselling, advisory, mentoring and facilitating services to those engaged in line activities. Successful quality practitioners are those who 'roll up their sleeves', who understand and share business unit objectives, and who can build relationships and 'add value'.

A supporting role requires involvement, empathy and sensitivity to others. Flexibility and a willingness to take a contextual rather than an absolutist approach are viewed in a positive light, rather than as evidence of a slipping of standards. Someone who has grown up in a 'checking' environment may find it difficult to adjust to such a change of role.

Avoiding the plateaus

Quality programmes have a tendency to plateau (Figure 2.2). For example, having obtained a quality standard an initiative may be put upon a care and maintenance basis. The winning of an award or the implementation of a new system can have a similar effect. People may stand back and feel 'we've done quality', while to the quality specialist the issue is: 'What next?'

A period upon a plateau can be an enjoyable experience. There may be some respite in workload as things 'settle down', accompanied by a sense of satisfaction with what has been achieved. However, a quality team that basks for too long may lose its edge.

The plateau that has been reached may afford but one perspective on quality. There will be those who get accustomed to the view. Accomplishments can become eroded by boredom, neglect and a lack of vigilance. Initiatives sometimes become rituals, and processes become slack as a result of familiarity.

Quality does not exist in a vacuum. Within a company there are likely to be other preoccupations and priorities. Without a sense of direction and a certain commitment to treading water, an initiative may drift off course or even sink.

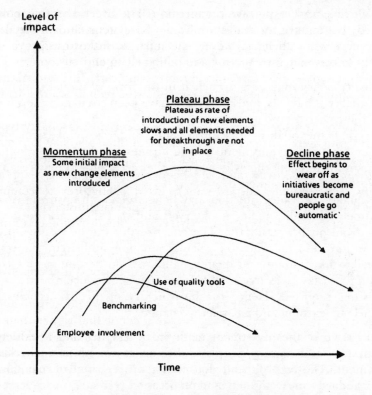

Figure 2.2 The quality plateau

Success has its costs. When quality becomes a way of life, it may be taken for granted. More pressing and novel matters may come to the fore.

There may be further mountains and additional peaks to climb. A situation, circumstances or the context can change. While looking back, a quality team may fail to notice the way ahead.

It is important to understand why a corporate programme, whether quality or BPR, runs out of steam. Were initial expectations too high? Does the organisation even know that momentum is being lost? Is 'bad news' being concealed? Many do not seek appropriate feedback, or if they do they fail to learn from it. Perhaps the requirements in terms of time, cost and commitment to break through were underestimated. Possibly incentives and motivation were lacking.

The bureaucracy of quality

One of the paradoxes of quality is that it is often adopted by companies either as a means in itself or as a complement to other initiatives to create a more flexible and responsive organisation. The overriding desire of a board may be to make the transition from a bureaucratic to a more fluid network or organic form. However, the introduction of quality can of itself help to entrench bureaucracy and inhibit change:

- A quality policy may be entrenched in the form of a quality manual and quality standards, and once these have been circulated there may be a reluctance to update them.
- Over time the quality procedures and standards in place may no longer meet the requirements of the business, and yet not adopting them and producing the evidence that they are followed may result in the loss of a quality standard.
- The quality assurance function may be charged with ensuring that a documented quality policy is observed and that there are no deviations from quality standards. The effect of this can be to discourage innovation and a tailoring to particular situations and circumstances.
- A review and updating of quality standards can become a time-consuming and costly exercise, and there may be a reluctance to spend the sums required. Hence the bureaucracy of quality becomes an obstacle to learning and a barrier to change.

The very scale of the investment made in developing and installing a quality system, and training people how to use it can inhibit change and development. The controls and documentation required to maintain a quality standard can strengthen, and on occasion recreates, bureaucracy.

The reality is that in a large company it may take several months, if not years, to communicate a change of goals or objectives throughout a corporate organisation. While changes are in the process of being communicated, different parts of the organisation may be pursuing their own priorities. The problems involved can act as a deterrent to incremental improvements and 'fine tuning' to match the dynamics of the marketplace and evolving corporate capability.

Confronting reality

The author has written elsewhere of the 'curse of professionalism'.[10] As a consequence of the existence of professional associations – over 400 in the UK alone – people are trained, in some cases over years, at a receptive period of their life to deal with selected aspects of business reality. Furthermore, this partial reality is viewed through the distorting lens of a particular functional specialism.

There are some who argue that quality can help us to better understand reality. For one CEO: 'The key to it from my point of view is root cause analysis. I encourage my people to keep asking why until they have cut through the symptoms and reached the heart of the problem.'

Others are not so sanguine, as using the tools of quality can become an end in itself. People can develop a quality view of reality. According to one director: 'Instead of just looking at the world we are always trying to rearrange it in quality terms. Sometimes we miss the essence of what is there.'

Quality can be a cosmetic. A marketing manager explained: 'We start with what we want to do and then we have to dress it up in the language of quality. This may help communication, but sometimes it just seems a game.' One quality manager took a more cynical view: 'We find things that work in practice and then try to show that they work in terms of quality theory.'

For various reasons a company may underplay or exaggerate the contribution of quality. A personnel manager's view in one company is: 'While quality is the "blue-eyed boy", it gets the credit for everything. Any good that happens is put down to quality. I've been asked to find evidence in my area ... We are desperate to show some returns on our huge investment in quality. I'll be quoting things that are really nothing to do with quality.'

Assumptions about reality need to be confronted and a process for doing this is shown in Figure 2.3. However, corporate experience is rarely as straightforward as we would wish.

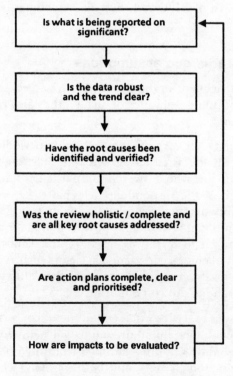

Figure 2.3 Confronting reality

Where are we with BPR?

Endeavouring to understand 'what is going on with BPR' is like operating in a sea of fog. Confusion is widespread.[7] Many early applications of BPR have been functional rather than cross-functional. Until recently there were few independently validated and cross-functional examples of BPR that had run the full course from initiation to implementation and subsequent assessment.

In any event, validation presents its own challenges in a dynamic organisational and market context. When various other corporate initiatives are being undertaken in parallel, how does one distinguish the distinct contribution of BPR or quality?

Suppliers of IT and consultancy services have a vested interest in publicising and exaggerating re-engineering success. Measures are carefully selected. For example, response time, or 'competing on speed', is often stressed as this is something people feel that BPR can deliver.

The extremes are often hidden. Success that results in clear competitive advantage is kept under wraps, while the embarrassment of failure is also hidden. The carefully packaged and self-contained 'case studies' that have emerged often cover initiatives that were started before those involved had heard of BPR, and they can sometimes be used to support arguments both for and against BPR.

Confronting status quo assumptions

Although the participants in the *Quality: The Next Steps* survey cited earlier perceive the continuing relevance of quality, they also recognise the need for a reassessment:[6]

- The statement 'an organisation should periodically reassess its approach to quality' is either agreed with or strongly agreed with by all the respondents who answered this particular question.
- Six out of ten of the respondents felt that their organisation should 'carry out a fundamental review of its quality process'.
- Over nine out of ten respondents believe 'a broader and more comprehensive approach to quality is needed', and almost as many believe 'quality needs to embrace less tangible factors such as feelings or values'.
- Some eight out of ten respondents agree that 'after a couple of years a quality programme can run out of steam'.

These are all issues and views that should be of concern to directors and senior management. The initial drive for quality in most companies may well have started with a 'top down' initiative of the board. Within many corporate organisations it is an approach or policy of the board that is being called into question.

We need to challenge deep-rooted assumptions. For example, is enough attention being paid to the trade-offs between quality and cost or speed? What are the social consequences of an obsession with cost and speed? In the 1995 French Presidential elections the rival candidates were each given 60 seconds of state television time to get their messages across.

The relevance of speed needs to be thought through. Rapid prototyping by reducing product development times can enable a company to win the race to market. Where technologies are developing quickly and relentlessly, companies value their membership of 'The Time to Market Association'.

'Just in time' is a way of life for producers such as Nissan and ICL and retailers like Asda and Sainsbury. One Japanese bank invested £15 million in new technology in order to gain a two second advantage over its competitors, a move which paid off within a month. But response times vary greatly across business sectors. An information service may need to provide the appearance of an instantaneous response whereas a power station may take a generation to come on stream.

Overall, the responses reveal an awareness, and a consensus, that: (a) the successful implementation of a quality programme represents a significant directorial and managerial challenge; and (b) new approaches are needed.

There are various key questions with which any 'first principles' review needs to be concerned. For example:

- What are the quality expectations of management, customers, employees and other stakeholders?
- Does the organisation's approach to quality meet its business needs and corporate objectives, represent best practice, and match its corporate culture?
- What are the obstacles, barriers, hindrances and missing elements?
- What needs to be done to bridge the gap between aspiration and achievement?
- Beyond today's activities, what new requirements or markets need to be created if the organisation is to have a longer-term future?

It is hoped that as a result of reflecting upon the issues raised in this book the reader will be better equipped to address these and related questions.

Quality in perspective

Those who question what quality 'adds up to' are in good company. It has taken quality rather a long time to secure respectability in certain circles. In the case of one alma mater of the author, the Graduate School of Business of the University of Chicago, it was only in 1991 that 'the business school recognized total quality management as a formal field of study at the school.'

Many concerns that are expressed about quality reflect people's approach to it. Quality can be used timidly or imaginatively. The focus could be upon incremental improvements to 'what is' or dramatic steps to what 'should be'. The aim could be to 'attain quality', 'do enough' and reach an absolute level of performance, or to encourage the ongoing striving for improvement. There are people who regard quality as 'obvious' or 'common sense'. Alternatively, it may be regarded as an aspiration that requires a change of attitudes, values and perspective to become a reality.

Loik Le Floch-Prigent, Chairman, President and CEO of Elf Aquitaine, refers to the 'quality and balance' of the group's business mix. Since the initial discovery of a small oil field in the South of France in 1941 the Elf Aquitaine Group has grown to include over 770 subsidiaries around the world. The vision of quality embraces the total enterprise, and the activities of Foundation Elf reveal a concern for a quality of life beyond the company, its customers, suppliers and business partners. Hence the support of humanitarian and artistic programmes and environmental projects in Africa and Antarctica.

Cast the net more widely – a whole business sector can commit to action to improve environmental quality. A US example is the Responsible Care programme of the Chemical Manufacturers Association. Individual companies such as Du Pont have ambitious initiatives to reduce harmful emissions and impacts. Merck has planned to reduce toxic waste by 90 per cent over a three-year period.

The purpose of quality

The rationale or purpose of quality may need to be reassessed. As a result of the emergence of a fundamentally changed business environment, organisations are having to make more radical changes in order to establish new forms and patterns of activities and processes to which continuous improvement should be applied. A challenge for quality and quality people is the extent to which those used to the steady evolution of continuous improvement can adjust to the requirements for frame-breaking change. Revolution rather than evolution is more talked about than achieved.[5]

Can people and organisations change quickly enough? Can they face up to the scale of what needs to be done, and the variety of areas in which change has simultaneously to occur? Many support the traditional organisation and power structure by clinging to, documenting and controlling the formal processes according to the dictates of the quality procedures manual rather than facilitating and supporting the informal network that may actually be the means of getting things done.

In the author's experience:

- There is often little correlation between the formality of procedures and the quality of output. Access to relevant resource and capability, as and when needed, is often a more significant determinant than procedural purity.
- Proceduralism can result in excessive emphasis upon the 'technical' rather than 'people' aspects. The informal networks thrive on inter-personal contacts, sensitivity, skills and awareness.
- In many sectors the problem areas are interpersonal rather than technical or procedural. This can be true of 'high tech' areas such as software development.
- The value of informal networks needs to be better recognised, and people should be equipped to project manage paths through them. Fewer repetitive tasks are appearing, which suggests more thought should be given to which process or approach should be used, and less reliance placed upon the 'normal' or 'standard' procedure.
- Attempting to define, document and support particular paths through network forms of organisation can be the equivalent of replacing the flexibility of the human brain with the programmed responses of the robot.[7]

Jack Welch, the Chairman of General Electric, encourages openness, candour and constructive criticism. The company's 'work-out' process enables people to stand up and seek help in challenging the way things are done or when floating radical ideas. Welch recognises that to wage war against conservatism and bureaucracy requires the active participation of people throughout the organisation.

People do not shed their inhibitions and prejudices overnight. Many remain prisoners of preconceptions or generalisations. For example, a manufacturer might assume a product is more difficult to tailor than a service. And yet the French optical company Essilor operates an international network of processing centres that each year will manufacture tens of millions of lenses each of which is customised to an individual prescription.

In the optical sector, few customers would be satisfied with wearing a 'standard category' of lens, say one which might generally benefit the average short-sighted person. Individual diagnosis and treatment is the norm, and so it could be with many categories of product that are acquired in order to provide a service.

A company needs to consider the extent to which it is competing on quality (Figure 2.4) and the form which this takes. Performance in the marketplace can reflect relative performance against both competitors and changing customer requirements. Interest in benchmarking is often

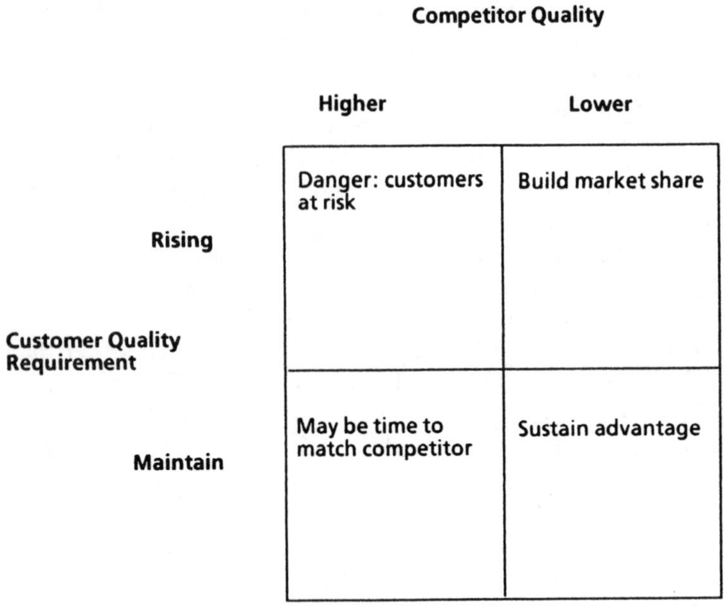

Competitor Quality

	Higher	Lower
Rising	Danger: customers at risk	Build market share
Maintain	May be time to match competitor	Sustain advantage

Customer Quality Requirement (label at left, rows: Rising, Maintain)

Figure 2.4 Competing on quality

the result of organisations wishing to match their own performance against the best, while issue monitoring and management should enable marketplace and broader social and economic trends to be tracked.

Selling a management approach

While some believe that insufficient attention has been given to selling the 'benefits' of quality, others question whether quality has been over-sold or should be sold at all. Perhaps quality should be marketed rather than sold. Consider the following comments:

> We assume quality is a good thing and badger, persuade and cajole. What we should be doing is helping people to understand when and where particular approaches to quality and quality considerations may be relevant.

> To market quality the focus should be upon the context ... Do we understand the situation and what is going on? Rather than sell a standard package, we should help people tackle the problems they face.

It is rarely desirable, and may not be necessary, to sell quality. Instead, the initial emphasis should be upon listening and learning. Sufficient time should be spent examining the context to allow an assessment to be made of the extent to which the introduction of elements of quality might be able to make a contribution.

In the author's experience the most satisfied and productive groups tend to be those that are focused upon customer-related objectives, rather than preoccupied with internal processes (Figure 2.5). Many BPR project teams are losing sight of customer-related goals and becoming 'introverted groups'.[7]

In some situations, people may need to be helped to understand the potential contribution of that which is unfamiliar. Rather than subject them to one–way messages of persuasion, it may be preferable to facilitate their assessment of the obstacles and barriers they face and whether or not quality or BPR can make a significant and cost-effective impact.

Tests to apply

A key test of the impact of quality is the extent to which it enhances the capabilities of individuals and groups to make a distinct contribution. Some approaches increase the degree to which individuals feel impotent to make a difference. As one manager put it: 'Now that we seem to have a standard group view on everything, what is the point in me thinking about these things?'

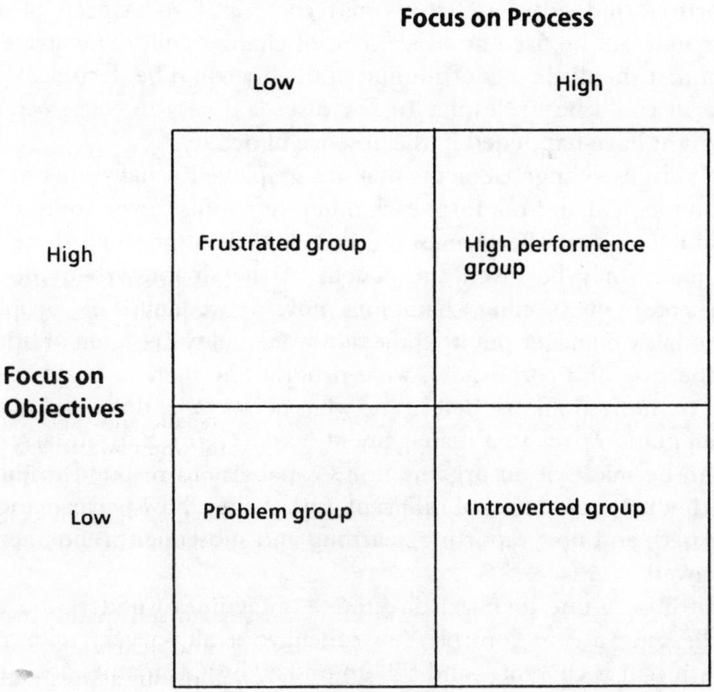

Focus on Process

	Low	High
High	Frustrated group	High performance group
Low	Problem group	Introverted group

Focus on Objectives

Figure 2.5 The focus of groups and teams

Another test for quality is the extent to which it enables an organisation to issue a public commitment along the lines of the Rank Xerox customer satisfaction guarantee or a customer charter. London Electricity offers a Business Charter and Guaranteed Service Standard. The charter draws upon the results of an independent survey of customer requirements which involved over 5,000 respondents.

Many people are cynical. Others have developed a degree of resistance to hype. It is usually counter-productive to attempt to 'hard sell' quality where, on the face of it, it does not seem to be relevant. Encouraging the adoption of a tool, technique, approach or perspective just because it is a corporate requirement can encourage people to go automatic and not to think.

To successfully manage change it is usually necessary to change the attitudes of managers. The scale of a company's investment in quality is less significant than the nature, and particularly the relevance, of its approach which should be dynamic, evolving, changing as new elements are added, while others may need to be dropped.

Quality as an element or solution?

Many companies operate a portfolio of change programmes, and within the portfolio individual initiatives may come and go. Aspects of quality may or may not be used as an element of change policy and strategy. In one context the distinct contribution of quality could be decisive, while in another it could be irrelevant. In few cases is it easy to assess *post quality* what might have happened in the absence of quality.

The various change elements that are employed usually interact. They may complement and reinforce each other, or confuse, even contradict and thus inhibit mutual effectiveness. In the early days, or when there is success, quality may be given the benefit of the doubt. When the mood becomes more questioning, champions move or are moved on, people may as one quality manager put it, 'come down on quality like a ton of bricks'.

In the case of a corporation-wide programme such as quality a board should do more than just determine what needs to be done and hand the implementation over to a management team (Figure 2.6). An assessment needs to be made of an organisation's capability to respond to different goals, the 'pros and cons' of different approaches, how performance is to be assessed, and how reporting, learning and subsequent refinement is to be achieved.

According to one financial director: 'I sometimes wonder who among my colleagues are in control. You can have it all – every management approach that is current – and still go under. Big companies are a bit like the dinosaurs. We are all dying and not sure why.' The disadvantage of size, the vulnerability of such giants as AEG or PanAm, is a recurring theme

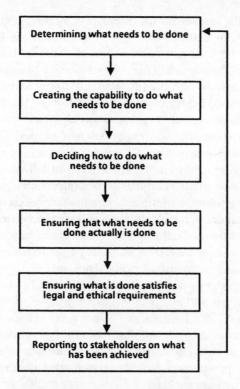

Figure 2.6 The board review process

Source: Colin Coulson-Thomas, *Transforming the Company*, Kogan Page, 1992.

of discussions with today's industrial leaders. The larger an organisation, the more it is likely to need thinking and tailored local implementation.

As we journey through different landscapes we may need to vary the change elements in our armoury. I report in my book *Transforming the Company* of multinationals: 'As the endangered herd tramps through the bleak desert of trial and tribulation only a few are "sensing the presence of water"'.[11] We need to maintain a sense of balance and keep our eyes and ears open.

Maintaining a sense of balance

Quality appears to be 'in the dock' and the onus is upon advocates of quality to demonstrate its relevance. The UK minister for further and higher education, Tim Boswell MP, has suggested that, while some approaches to quality have proved controversial, quality remains valid as an aspiration and that a balanced view needs to be taken:

> Quality assessment has had a turbulent history. But, for all the storm and stress above the surface, there is much evidence that real progress is being

made; that quality assessment has already had a salutary, stimulating effect in department after department, more than outweighing the alleged bureaucratic burden. The processes of quality assurance are negotiable but not the objectives.

A similar sense of balance needs to be maintained about BPR. In appropriate circumstances, where inspired by a vision of the future and when properly used, BPR can represent a useful element of a corporate transformation programme or 'business excellence' model. There is a danger that reaction against simplistic packaging and excessive hype and a focus upon what BPR is not may blind us to what it actually is and can do.[7]

Although most companies appear to be concerned about the impact of their quality programmes, there are organisations such as ICL, Motorola and Xerox that believe quality has made a significant contribution to a turnaround in their business performance. Another example is Landrover. In the mid-1980s the company's performance dipped under the impact of strong competition from new Japanese suppliers.

Following the introduction of TQM in the late 1980s Landrover's use of discussion groups and suggestion schemes has risen over five years to 'best in class'. By 1992 Landrover's 'Discovery' vehicle achieved world-class product status. Significant improvements in customer satisfaction, large increases in sales in Europe, North America and Australia, and record levels of production have been achieved during an era of economic recession in key markets.

The 'Rover Tomorrow' programme has embraced culture, people and process. Terry Morgan, Managing Director of Landrover Vehicles, believes the TQM process encourages people to focus upon quality, productivity and flexibility and the continuous improvement of quality and reliability.

Alone or in combination with other elements, depending upon how broadly it is defined, the approaches and tools of quality appear to have made a substantial contribution to Landrover's performance. As with Xerox, one could debate whether the company might have survived, let alone achieve benchmark status, without the distinct contribution of quality. The experience of these and other companies suggest that when the circumstances are appropriate elements of quality may play a significant role within a corporate transformation programme.

The challenge

Quality has its advocates and its detractors. In many of its guises, quality deserves to be put to rest. It is too often a source of confusion and self-deception. However, whether it will be replaced with anything more appropriate is a moot point.

On balance, we may be advised to create a transformed variety of quality rather than 'jump horses'. We have seen in this chapter that while certain problem areas do exist, recognition of them, and a willingness to address them, is growing. Additionally, we have begun to identify some of the factors, such as a wider view, sensitivity to diversity and context, and a focus upon feelings, values, relationships and learning, that could be used to revitalise current approaches.

What is needed is not a re-engineering of the corporate machine, but an enlivening of the corporate organism and a re-awakening of the corporate spirit.[10] Too many managers are on metaphorical treadmills behind prison bars of their own creation. They need to be freed to dream again, and to dream of a life that will be better than before.

The experience of companies like ASK Europe shows that working and learning can be fun. Models of operation are needed that can cope effortlessly with harsh conditions like the seagull which soars over rugged cliffs and stormy seas. Life, meaning and purpose, and the will and instincts to survive, adapt and develop in order to continue to add value, need to be breathed into the communities of human beings we treat as organisational machines to be re-engineered.

Checklist

What worries you most about quality and BPR? What are the main issues and concerns within your organisation?

Does implementation reflect the degree of diversity that exists?

Are the 'softer' areas such as experiences, feelings, values and relationships addressed?

Are those with concerns listened to?

Who is most concerned? What are their particular preoccupations?

Are the concerns concealed, or are they explicit?

Have the root causes of these concerns been identified?

Have they been recognised by those who can do something about them?

Who is most affected by the issues which have been raised or otherwise identified?

Have their impacts been assessed?

What new or missing elements have been identified?

Are quality issues and concerns being addressed?

Have action programmes been put in place to deal with them?

At this stage, do you consider that your organisation's approach to quality could be revitalised?

References

1. John Seddon, 'Debating the Case for Quality', *Professional Manager*, May 1994, pp 23–24.
2. George Binney, *Making Quality Work: Lessons from Europe's Leading Companies*, Special Report No P655, London, Economist Intelligence Unit, 1992.
3. Small Business Research Trust, *National Westminster Bank Quarterly Survey of Small Business*, Milton Keynes, School of Management, Open University, August 1992.
4. PERA International and Salford University Business Services Ltd, *A Survey of Quality Consultancy Scheme Clients 1988–1990*, The Enterprise Initiative, 1992.
5. Colin Coulson-Thomas (executive ed), *The Responsive Organisation: Re-engineering New Patterns of Work*, London, Policy Publications, 1995.
6. Colin and Susan Coulson-Thomas, *Quality: The Next Steps*, an Adaptation Ltd survey for ODI, London, Adaptation Ltd, 1991; executive summary available from ODI Europe, 1991.
7. Colin Coulson-Thomas (ed), *Business Process Re-engineering: Myth and Reality*, London, Kogan Page, 1994.
8. *RSA Enquiry: Tomorrow's Company*, London, The Royal Society for the Encouragement of Arts, Manufacturers and Commerce, 6 June 1995.
9. Colin Coulson-Thomas, *Creating the Global Company: Successful Internationalisation*, London, McGraw-Hill, 1992.
10. Colin Coulson-Thomas, *Transforming the Company: Bridging the Gap Between Management Myth and Corporate Reality*, London, Kogan Page, 1992.
11. Colin Coulson-Thomas, *Transforming the Company: Bridging the Gap Between Management Myth and Corporate Reality*, London, Kogan Page, 1992, p 102.

3

Relevance of contemporary preoccupations in a changing world

In debt and in dirt.

In a changing world, organisations that are not able to learn and continuously adapt to their environment by reassessing and renewing their purpose, relevance and capability are unlikely to survive. In particular corporate situations sets of either positive or negative symptoms tend to occur together and to reinforce each other. In the contemporary business and market environment too many companies have trapped themselves into negative and reactive spirals of descent into pits of cost-cutting and despair. They are both 'in debt and in dirt' and they need urgently to become proactive and break out.

The management and directorial challenge

What needs to be done is shown diagrammatically in Figure 3.1. The management and directorial challenge is to understand the business and market environment, identify or create an opportunity to generate value, agree a compelling and distinctive vision, establish relevant goals and values, and bring together the people, organisation, technology and finance, and the management, business and support processes that will enable the body or enterprise to satisfy the needs of its various stakeholders.[1]

Many organisations have extensive resources and capabilities which cannot be harnessed as required in order to deliver value to customers or achieve business objectives. Hence the potential relevance of a focus upon processes within: a broad approach to quality; the framework of a business excellence model; or as a consequence of the adoption of process improvement or re-engineering.

Do all that which is suggested by Figure 3.1 and you may have a

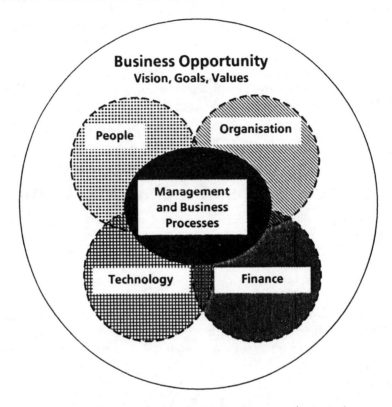

Figure 3.1   Adapting to the business environment

Source: Colin Coulson-Thomas, *Creating the Global Company*, McGraw-Hill, 1992.

potentially viable business concept. Put some ethos, excitement, motivation and drive into the equation and it may fly. How might an existing 'framework' such as a corporate quality programme help us to introduce these ingredients into existing organisations whose people may well be distributed over many locations?

We will address in subsequent chapters what needs to be done to establish a new quality vision and fresh, more people-centred priorities, goals, objectives and strategy. In this chapter, our concern is with understanding the implications for the future relevance of a management approach such as quality of contemporary developments in the business and market environment.

Ephemeral preoccupations

Do, or should, current management preoccupations such as quality have a future? There are enthusiasts and advocates for whom quality is an 'absolute', an approach that is capable of transcending and embracing a variety of conditions and circumstances. Another view is that the slavish following of what is held to be immutable has the potential to result in disaster.

The following are some comments encountered in the course of the author's surveys from those who believe that the onus is upon a concept such as quality to demonstrate continuing relevance:

> Quality has to be organic. It must evolve and adapt as situations change.

Whatever it is known as, an approach to management should leave its mark. Those 'touched' by quality should view things differently, and the consequences of this could be revealed through emphasis, perspective or priorities.

> The culture says fill in the paperwork and you are OK. It's nothing to do with the quality of what is delivered to the customer. Our customers don't come to us because our paperwork is in order ... they come because they believe we can help.

> Quality is a bit like eating your greens at school. People hate doing it, and we try to persuade them that it is doing them some good.

> We paid to obtain a quality registration and now we have to pay to maintain it. Someone is making a lot of money out of quality and it is not us. For us it's a cost all the way, including the cost of all those records that we only keep in order to keep our registration.

> The system has become so onerous that no one has time to review or improve it. They are doing ... busy ... busy ... rushing about. But are they thinking, learning and improving?

Quality should be all about making tomorrow better than today. Where learning and improvement is not occurring the reasons should be investigated.

> I would like to introduce changes, but I am told that this would prejudice our quality registration. I can't introduce the changes that, from my point of view, would improve quality.

> We have a quality system, quality approach, quality manuals, quality reports ... everything but quality tools. We are writing about it, talking about it, reporting on it ... but no one is being equipped to do it.

These quotations suggest an onerous imposition that is causing resistance, rather than an immutable truth. Besides, new management religions are challenging old faiths. The requirement for BPR is in part a consequence of a perceived deficiency of quality, namely its tendency to cause each person in a process to consider the next step, their immediate 'internal customer', rather than processes and supply chains as a whole and the 'external' or end customer.[2]

A commonly encountered sentiment is: 'The world has moved on. Our concept and use of quality is no longer enough.' James Harrington, an authority on business process improvement, believes: 'As we enter the

1990s, our customers and our stockholders are not looking for good quality – they want perfection. Quality is doing the job right every time. Perfection is doing the right job right every time.'[3]

Embracing change

Many critical views of quality are expressed by those who are conscious of the uncertainty, instability and insecurity inherent in contemporary market dynamics. Steve Bull, General Manager of Interox Chemicals, accepts that: 'The only constant is change.' Interox is very conscious of 'the rapid and accelerating pace of change.' Bull's view is that: 'Whilst the future will present us with many challenges they hold no fear for us.'

Not all industrialists are so confident. According to Marc Moret, Chairman and CEO of Sandoz: 'The economic fabric is tearing in all the major industrialized countries, and even companies which were once bywords for organization, efficiency and profitability have been hard hit. In spite – or perhaps because – of their record of success they were too slow in making the necessary adjustments.'

Alex Krauer and Heini Lippuner of Ciba recognise that: 'Changed value systems, new user needs, and greater competition create economic conditions where traditional ways of working are no longer appropriate' and 'not facing these challenges can also lead to unpleasant surprises.' Quality may have been around so long that it is now considered to be a 'traditional' way of working.

No one is immune. Even companies like Unilever and Procter & Gamble with strong brands are struggling to maintain prices and margins. Edwin Artzt, CEO of Procter & Gamble, recognises the challenge: 'We want to take our company apart brick by brick and put it back together again.' America's IBM, Europe's Phillips and Japan's Matsushita are all struggling with bureaucracy.

Alongside the challenges are related opportunities. Thus electronic trading could strengthen the bargaining position of suppliers, or customers, or both, depending upon the assiduity of their responses. Within supply chains, some intermediaries will gain from the arrival of the electronic marketplaces while the less alert will find their competitive positioning has been eroded.[4]

The extent to which changes represent challenges or opportunities will depend upon the relative strengths and weaknesses of an organisation in each of the areas identified in Figure 3.1. The corporate response should address weaknesses and capitalise upon areas of strength (see Figure 3.2). The humbling experiences of such giants as General Motors, Sears Roebuck & Co and IBM illustrate the sad truth that yesterday's strengths may not be relevant to contemporary market conditions.

Companies that anticipate the need for change are more likely to achieve a relatively smooth transition. Planned delayering could be undertaken for

ASPECT	STRENGTHS	WEAKNESSES
Business Environment		
People		
Organisation		
Technology		
Finance		
Management and Business Processes		

Figure 3.2   The corporate response

positive reasons. It can reduce overheads, improve communication and provide more discretion. Just reacting to events often results in negative and traumatic responses, the pain of instant redundancy, brutal downsizing that does permanent damage to morale and trust, not to mention a sudden increase in the workloads of those who remain.

The relevance of quality

The collective language of certain approaches to quality: 'maintaining control', 'procedures', 'standards', 'inspections', 'tests', 'conformity', 'corrective action', 'retention of records', 'manuals', 'audits', etc, can come across as the worst nightmare of someone trying to achieve the vision-led transformation of an organisation. How relevant is quality in the context of the many changes occurring within and around organisations?

The participants in the 1991 survey *Quality: The Next Steps*[5] considered quality to be very relevant (Table 3.1). The priority management issue in terms of 'very important' replies was 'closer relationships with customers', followed by 'securing competitive advantage'. Over eight out of ten respondents considered the contribution of quality to be 'very relevant' to both these issues.

Many of those interviewed indicated that the prioritisation summarised in Table 3.1 reflected corporate priorities to which the distinct contribution of quality was sometimes difficult to assess. More recently, most of the companies surveyed have endured a relatively protracted recession, during which more prosaic and shorter-term concerns such as cutting costs in order to survive have become more pressing. Most of those who have subsequently been reinterviewed have found quality less rather than more relevant in an era of downsizing and retrenchment. Unless action is taken to revitalise it, this widely adopted approach to management could become more of a millstone and less of a life-raft.

Corporate responses

A growing number of companies are seeking to restructure away from a functional form of bureaucratic organisation to a more flexible and responsive one that is based upon the activities and processes that deliver value to customers and achieve corporate objectives. This brings them up against the curse of professionalism and many deeply entrenched attitudes and practices.

Dr Edouard Sakiz, Chairman and CEO of Roussel Uclaf, believes bureaucracy is a cancer within business that has to be fought. In order to increase flexibility, speed of response and the willingness to take risks Ciba is seeking the 'dynamisation' of its organisation, 'flatter hierarchies,

Table 3.1 *The relevance of quality (ranked in order of 'very relevant' replies)*

Closer relationships with customers	82%
Securing competitive advantage	81%
Improved teamwork	65%
Closer relationships with suppliers	60%
Determination of strategy	51%
Tailoring products and/or services	49%
Facilitation of change	47%
Creating a flexible, adaptable organisation	40%
Greater focus upon priorities	37%
Ongoing learning	33%
Tapping new added value opportunities	32%
Linking remuneration to customer satisfaction	31%
Delegation	29%
Relationship between subsidiary and parent	21%
Linking remuneration to tangible output	16%

Source: *Quality: The Next Steps*, 1991.[5]

less bureaucracy, removal of outdated work practices, and the promotion of individual initiative and responsibility'. In Switzerland, the company abolished its system of job titles and replaced them with a new system that better reflected the allocation of responsibilities.

Quality is likely to remain an aspiration where its rhetoric is not matched by the adoption of a structure and processes that enable value to be delivered to customers. Hence many quality frameworks are being extended to embrace these and other 'change elements'. However, just adding extra rooms will not of itself alter the use of a building.

Restructuring can occur quite independently of quality. For example, to enable closer contacts to be established with customers, the spinning systems division of Rieter has been reorganised into business units with responsibilities that embrace the full product development process. Discretion and responsibility has been decentralised to 'smaller, entrepreneurial units'. Rieter believes: 'The integration of product marketing, research and development, assembly and logistics in each of the business units ensures that products are developed and manufactured to meet customers' needs.'

Statoil recognises that 'International competition will become sharper, imposing a strong need for prudent operation and cost-effective solutions.' The group is continuing 'its efforts to reduce costs in response to the challenges facing the industry'. The need to reduce the cost base has become a key priority of many corporations, and yet too often the quality community is, as one quality director put it, 'reluctant to associate quality with cost-cutting'. For another quality director: 'Quality is on trial. Our relevance will be judged by our contribution to the hard decisions when the going gets rough.'

Mikael Lilius, President and CEO of Sweden's Incentive group, accepts the challenge of change: 'Changes are often considered to be messy and troublesome. But changes and the search for new forceful structures constitute a basic mechanism in the development of commerce and industry. With change as the driving wedge, companies can create strong new organisations that are adapted to new conditions.'

For many companies, the creation of a flatter, more flexible and decentralised form of organisation is a matter of necessity rather than of choice. Gösta Wiking, President and CEO of Perstorp, believes that 'extensive decentralisation is essential' as: 'Enterprise and entrepreneurship develop most favourably in companies operating close to the market with a flat organisation and no unnecessary bureaucracy.' Wiking believes that flexibility is a key quality 'during a time characterised by major and rapid change'.

Where were you when we most needed help?

'Quality' is rarely considered a source of relevant insight by those seeking new models of operation during the restructuring phase of corporate responses to market challenges. Rather, it tends to be viewed as an overlay to be added to whatever form of organisation emerges from the transformation process.

Just while quality is under challenge and its contribution has been questioned there has been an unprecedented opportunity for it to play a vital role. The opportunity has been the almost universal preoccupation of major corporations during the late 1980s and early 1990s with 'reducing the cost base' and 'improving productivity'. CEOs felt they knew what they wanted and have been looking for all the help they can get. Yet within the essence and roots of quality few of them appear to have found much to guide them.

It is almost as if quality as experienced to date needs a relatively stable context into which it can be introduced on a planned basis. Quality as implemented in many companies can coexist with a degree of bureaucracy. In some cases, the implementation of a centrally directed and top down corporate approach has helped to consolidate an integrated hierarchy. A central theme of this book is whether there are quality approaches and principles that can accommodate a constantly changing context and perpetual restructuring.

What is occurring is too often perceived as a source of problems rather than as an opportunity. According to one quality manager: 'It's a nightmare for us quality professionals as nothing stands still. The procedures change more quickly than the time it takes for us to update the quality manual.'

Opportunities for quality do exist. At a group level there are but two key strands of the strategy of BP. These are, in the words of former chairman Robert Horton, to 'concentrate our efforts and investment on sectors where BP enjoys competitive advantages' and 'a company-wide drive for enhanced productivity ... All parts of the company are involved in programmes to increase productivity by challenging all expenditures of both capital and revenue to ensure we are competitive.' Quality could help establish the criteria for deciding what should stay and what should go.

Explaining the absence

Many quality practitioners are not responding to the challenge. Perhaps some have been in the dark for so long they are now unaccustomed to the light. One quality manager responded to a question about his contribution to a cost base reduction programme by announcing he was to be made redundant at the end of the month.

The pursuit of incremental improvement can insulate a corporation from the need for fundamental change. While the cumulative effect of continuous improvement can be very significant, the timescale may not be appropriate. Companies such as IBM that face a swift and dramatic change in their competitive positioning need to adjust quickly, hence their interest in process re-engineering, delayering and restructuring with associated empowerment. The aim at IBM appears to be to replace the 'command and control' hierarchy with a network of smaller businesses each with a substantial degree of autonomy.

An emerging complaint during the recent period of economic adversity has been that quality is 'too vague and general' when specific challenges have to be addressed. For example, the priorities of PSA Peugeot Citröen are 'adaptability and flexibility', and 'to make longer and swifter strides to enhance productivity, bolster industrial efficiency, and improve product technology'. In each of these areas specific initiatives are possible.

The focus of companies such as Peugeot suggests some questions:

- Is directed activity preferable to a general quality drive, the relevance and applicability of which may vary according to the context?
- Could quality provide a common base of understanding upon which a family of specific initiatives could be based?
- Are the pressures such that tailored actions in each area of business are preferable to an overall drive that may take a relatively long time to achieve an impact?

Another issue raised in the last chapter is the question of addressing a wide variety of local situations. Some organisations recognise the need for diversity more than others. Within the BSO/Origin group, considerable authority is delegated to individual operating companies. An autonomous Quality Innovation subsidiary provides a coordinating role and offers a range of quality management services, both to other companies within the group and externally.

Cost-cutting

Many quality professionals are contributing little to dramatic cost-cutting programmes. Reducing the cost base has been a priority of most major corporations. In some cases dramatic savings have been achieved.

Forest Oil Corporation in one year, 1991, reduced its general and administrative expenses by 45 per cent. Cutbacks have occurred at all levels of management, the number of senior executives being cut by 75 per cent and the membership of the board reduced from 16 to 11. William Dorn, Chairman of the Board, President and CEO, commenting upon the impact of economic recession, believes that 'adversity spawns opportunity' and explains that: 'We have attempted to structure the company to withstand continued adversity.'

The trick for greenfield operations and young entrepreneurial companies is to avoid the cost base in the first place. The model for the future is the US sportswear supplier Ocean Pacific that, while generating a turnover of $250 million, only employed 13 people. We have entered an era of virtual corporations and other forms of network organisation

(Figure 3.3) for which network quality, embracing customers, suppliers and business partners, rather than organisational quality is the issue.[6]

The network organisation

No one should be surprised by the organisational changes which are occurring. The longstanding nature of the interest which boards have had in building more flexible and responsive organisations has been confirmed by a series of three related questionnaire surveys carried out by the author in the late 1980s and completed in 1989, 1990 and 1991.[7] 'Creating a more flexible and responsive organisation' was consistently the number one issue in all the surveys.

Of itself the network organisation is not a new concept. The community of craftsmen who came together to build the medieval cathedral could be regarded as an early form of both project and 'virtual' organisation. When their task was completed they moved on to the next opportunity, a pattern recognised in today's film industry.

Schindler, the Swiss manufacturer of elevators and escalators, is an example of a company that has actively embraced the network organisation concept. The company's CIE or 'computer integrated enterprise' project aims through 'corporate-wide networking and the computerisation of all activities [to] make it possible to significantly accelerate throughput times, increase the operational availability of elevator systems and globally improve the quality of ... products and services.'

The bringing together of complementary capability regardless of location, function, nationality and ownership has become a high priority of a wide range of companies:

● BP encourages networking across departmental and national borders in order to allow the most relevant skills to be focused upon particular tasks and requirements.

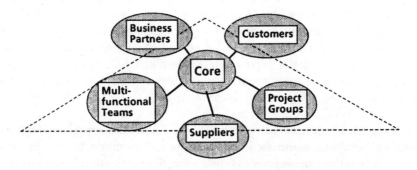

Figure 3.3   The responsive network organisation

Source: Colin Coulson-Thomas and Richard Brown, *Beyond Quality*, BIM, 1990.

- Rieter works closely with a network of specialised engineering firms in developing products to meet specific customers.
- Business units of Hoechst exist as group-wide networks.

With the growth of dual career families and the inexorable rise of relocation and mobility costs, a steady fall in real terms of computing costs means it is becoming increasingly easy to take work to people rather than vice versa. Increasingly, service companies are themselves likely to become nomads, their intellectual centres of gravity moving around the world according to which combinations of people at various locations are networked together to work upon priority projects and tasks.

In the case of Reuters or Thomas Cook one could argue the network is the business. Not surprisingly both companies put a high priority upon the improvement of business processes and their supporting network technology.

Adoption of the network organisation approach with its electronic links between suppliers and customers is itself a source of significant financial savings and improvements in cycle times (Figure 3.3). For example:

- As a result of adopting electronic trading Texas Instruments reduced shipping errors to a twentieth of their previous levels, while 70 per cent of order entry clerks have been released for other activities that add greater value for customers.
- The London Insurance Market Network (LIMNET) links up over 750 organisations and over 30,000 separate terminals are on the network. In the claims area, membership of the network has enabled one broker to achieve staff and service times reductions of one-third and two-thirds respectively.

The creation of 'network packages' and infrastructure by third parties can enable small firms to compete with larger enterprises. Joining the electronic trading network or club is, as one businessman put it, 'like signing up to a latter day cooperative'. An example is the Rodenstock Club which enables the independent opticians to establish direct datalink or faxlink contacts with suppliers. Among the facilities offered are 3D colour graphic images of various product options.

Network operations

Increasingly, competition for customers, suppliers and 'members' is between networks, consortia of cooperating and complementary organisations, rather than between individual enterprises.[4] Membership of a network may embrace very different companies and a number of traditional business sectors. Within a network a company could be both a customer and a supplier. Bringing customers into the network facilitates ongoing and two-way relationships.

A company could belong to a number of networks, aimed at delivering value to customer segments that could be as closely defined as a requirement of a single customer. Each network, perhaps each segment within a network, might require a distinct approach to quality. Those concerned with 'network quality' have to simultaneously determine and deliver what is both desirable and possible in diverse and dynamic situations and contexts.

The use of wireless LAN technology could free the network organisation from the constraints of geography, allowing it to grow organically and continuously change its shape. The organisation itself is a network, its reality lying in the electronic signals and waves that influence the priorities and responses of those that receive them.

The organic network allows people to work alongside customers.[7] It can enter the corporate bodies of customer organisations, taking their shape. Distinguishing the customer and the supplier becomes difficult when both share the same dreams, drives and rewards.

Within a marketplace of network organisations, conglomerates such as BTR or South Korea's Samsung and Hyundai groups have to decide in which areas they wish to specialise. A major proportion of the turnover of Inchcape is made up of services provided for other organisations, from distribution services to motor manufacturers, testing services for a wide range of suppliers, to trade services for governments.

Mikael Lilius of Incentive stresses the value of internal networks in sharing experience and understanding: 'We have to strengthen networks within the Group, promote exchanges of experience and cooperation.' The network organisation needs to become a learning network.[8]

Externally, some companies are openly searching for network partners. For example, Israel's Teva Pharmaceutical Industries went public about seeking a 'suitable partner to join' the company 'in creating an intricate, strategic marketing network' for its products.

Advantages of network operation

Networks can span continents and cultures. The network organisation can bridge the private–public divide and embrace governments and government-owned organisations. A good example is Volvo's network of relationships which has embraced the strategic alliance the company concluded with the government-owned Renault and its Volvo Car BV relationship with the Dutch government. In December 1991 the latter relationship changed with a third of NedCar becoming owned by three partners, the Dutch government, Volvo and Mitsubishi Motors Corporation.

The network organisation can offer significant advantages in terms of speed over bureaucratic forms. The healthcare division of French pharmaceutical company Roussel Uclaf has set up 'a new management organisation ... with the main objective of reducing time to market'. In order to speed up clinical trials the division's 'units in advanced technology countries have been organised into an international network'.

By operating as a 'virtual company' a network can bring together sufficient partners, each of whom specialises according to capability, interest and comparative advantage, to compete successfully with traditional bureaucracies. The rapid growth of Kingston Technology Corporation from a Californian start-up to international operator is based upon a network of relationships based upon trust and a shared vision. The relationships between partners are much closer than one would expect from the traditional customer–subcontractor roles. Mercury Communications is seeking to reinvent itself through a portfolio of network relationships.

Work can be relocated to any location that is accessible by telephone, fax and electronic mail. Distance working is now international in scope. Insurance companies such as Great Western Life and Massachusetts Mutual process claims, McGraw-Hill renews magazine subscriptions and Dell Computers provides technical and sales support from 'offshore locations' in the Republic of Ireland.

Timescales and time horizons vary by sector and activity. A financial institution may be able to implement a change of interest rate almost simultaneously with the decision. In other areas, response and lead times may be far longer. An industrial group such as Saab-Scania has to balance flexibility with perseverance and consistency. According to Lars Kylberg, President and CEO, the group's 'operations are characterised by long-term projects, large investments, high development costs and sometimes considerable risks.'

Currently the application of IT is a priority of those seeking to create network organisations. As technology becomes more pervasive and invisible, and the emphasis is upon knowing, learning, thinking and sharing rather than just communicating, attitudes, interests and motives will assume greater significance. Networks consisting of a shifting community of 'micro units', 'molecular entities', autonomous and self-managing teams and individual gurus who could be located almost anywhere.

Issue monitoring and management

A consideration of trends and developments relating to an existing corporate programme such as quality could be integrated into an organisation's approach to planning, strategic analysis or issue monitoring and management. Let us consider the latter.

The purpose of an issue monitoring and management process is to alert management to important changes and developments in the external operating or business environment (eg political, regulatory, economic, social and technological) and ensure that major trends and forces that are likely to impact upon the organisation's operations or business are identified, understood, taken account of in annual operational or business planning and monitored, and that appropriate action is taken in response and outcomes evaluated (Figure 3.4).

The major functions and components of an organisation should be encouraged to participate. Receiving all inputs in a common format eases analysis, consolidation and feedback. A summary of all inputs received should be examined by means of a formal issue monitoring and management review at which the implications for an organisation's approach to quality could be considered.

Participants should identify the priority issues, trends or developments that are likely to have an impact on the organisation's operations or business over the next 2–5 years (or beyond) either as a risk or as an opportunity. Issues should be ranked in order of priority (preferably no more than ten issues), the aim being to focus on key issues.

An issue could be political (eg policy towards sector or changes of policy with implications for customers), regulatory (eg a 'compensation' issue), economic (eg trade cycle), social (eg attitudes, demographic

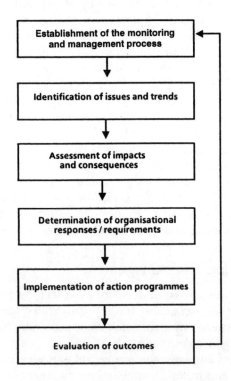

Figure 3.4   The issue monitoring and management process

changes, new patterns of family or work, etc), or technological (eg expert system to provide 'most relevant solution' for customers). It should be remembered that changes and trends can occur at the national, regional (eg European) and international levels.

For each issue, the following should be provided:

- *Issue statement.* A statement of what the issue, trend or development is. Where possible, give the timing and direction of expected changes and any key indicators that could be used to track a trend.
- *Impact assessment.* A description and an assessment of the impact upon the organisation (eg + or – x per cent change in market share or revenue). Comment on whether any current or planned corporate initiatives or policies are consistent or inconsistent with the change or trend.
- *Implications analysis.* An examination of the consequences and implications for quality. The analysis should consider whether or not current approaches are supportive of, or inhibiting, favourable developments and the nature and extent of changes that are thought necessary.
- *Recommended action.* State what actions are underway, and / or what new actions should be taken, when and by whom in response. Distinguish between actions that should be taken at: (a) a local / functional level; (b) organisation unit level; and (c) a wider group level or above (eg 'industry' response). Any relevant information from benchmarking studies or competitor analysis about how other organisations are responding to the issue could also be given.

Try to be concise. A page may be sufficient to cover an issue. Should sufficient responses be received, their consolidation could represent a corporate 'view of the world'. Such a 'view of the world' would allow annual planning to take place against a shared understanding of what may happen in the operational or business environment over the next 2–5 years.

The customer

A key consideration when assessing external developments is their impact upon the customer, suppliers and business partners (Figure 3.5). Helping them to cope could represent a business opportunity. Too many companies appear almost exclusively concerned with the direct impact of changes upon themselves. More attention needs to be devoted to supply chain and network issues.

3M is an example of a company that examines not just the impact of trends and factors in the business environment upon its own operations, but also how its customers might be affected and the opportunities this might create. Retailers who stock the company's consumer products are offered electronic ordering, direct-to-store shipping and in-store marketing

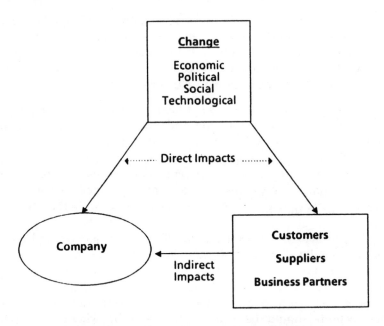

Figure 3.5 The impact of external changes

Source: Colin Coulson-Thomas, *Creating the Global Company*, McGraw-Hill, 1992.

assistance. The focus is upon helping 'customers' profitability by reducing their inventories and increasing turnover of merchandise'.

The Swiss industrial company Rieter Holding considers that 'price and quality are the decisive factors in the struggle for market share.' In itself, this is an unremarkable view. However, Rieter and other companies are having to change how they operate and the nature of their relationships with customers in order to satisfy their more demanding requirements.

The aim of Rieter, according to its chairman, Dr Heinz Kundert, is to 'provide the customer with ideal, specifically tailored solutions.' Rieter 'regards its customers as partners with whom individually tailored solutions are developed to meet specific objectives.' An example of 'the close cooperative relationship between the customer and Rieter' is a 'state of the art technical centre at Grossostheim, where customer-specific spinning trials are performed.'

Review findings

Issue monitoring reviews undertaken by the author in recent years to match current approaches to changing requirements reveal a prevailing sense of unease with existing quality practice. There is also a lack of consensus about what quality actually is. Desires and concerns tend to be translated into procedures rather than adopted as attitudes. Participants invariably stress the need to change attitudes and behaviour, there being many references to 'hearts and minds'.

Implementation is described as mechanical and thought to contribute little to learning. People are documenting rather than thinking. Problems are not being regarded as opportunities to learn, and the means by which they are overcome are not being shared with peers. The quality heritage is associated more with 'negative' concerns such as the avoidance of legal and quality audit problems rather than innovation and creativity.

Overall, existing quality systems are thought to be costly and bureaucratic. They make an insufficient contribution to 'delivered' quality and have little impact upon attitudes and behaviours. They slow response times in bid and opportunistic situations, when speed of reaction can be particularly critical. Quality is often imposed rather than voluntarily accepted. The focus is also too often 'internal' rather than upon the client relationship.

New and broader approaches to cope with today's corporate priorities are called for, a combination of encouraging more relevant attitudes, improving processes and introducing more appropriate tools (Figure 3.6). It was sometimes suggested that any new and holistic approach be called something other than 'quality' in order to differentiate it from what has gone before.

While every context has distinctive features, fundamental issues invariably emerge when organisations think through the implications for their

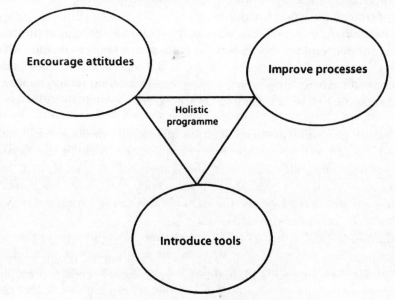

Figure 3.6   Building the quality culture

approach to quality of various contemporary trends and developments. Let us now turn our attention to the implications for quality professionals themselves.

Implications for quality professionals

In general, quality professionals are thought to act as 'policemen' rather than as business advisers. They are perceived as 'bystanders', people 'on the sidelines' who identify deficiencies but do not help to solve them. They 'chase paper' rather than 'add value'. Where line management 'leaves quality to the specialists', their involvement can make matters worse by encouraging an abdication of responsibility for 'delivered quality'.

Where quality teams are staffed by 'brought in specialists' rather than by people on assignment from the line, existing systems and approaches may be 'maintained' and 'defended', rather than 'challenged' by 'new blood'. In many companies there are few career development opportunities for quality specialists. Some observed that quality tends to become an 'unloved child' unless sold or marketed.

Differences of viewpoint are often apparent at different levels within corporate organisations. While quality specialists may wish to do more, many pragmatists at a senior level are understandably cautious and have little enthusiasm for, or confidence in, broader approaches due to concerns about both the capability to implement and the possible costs of major changes. There are widespread doubts concerning the practicalities of changing corporate cultures.

Elsewhere in organisations, while there is often a desire to improve the quality of deliverables, the responsibility for action tends to be somewhere else, eg 'this is a line matter' or 'those at the top must lead'. Also, those whose involvement is necessary for implementation rarely have a shared understanding of what quality is, or are agreed on what its focus should be.

Quality professionals themselves are questioning the vague and unfocused use of the term quality. For example, John Nicholls has 'become increasingly uncomfortable with the variety of meanings that have become attached to TQM.' He believes quality has become 'a portmanteau word' and has advocated the use of 'Value to the Customer' or VTC rather than 'customer-driven TQM'.[9]

If attitudes and approaches do not change, it would appear that as a consequence of limited vision, short-termism, etc, many companies face the prospect of the falling profitability that is commonly associated with a spiral of descent to the status of a low margin supplier of 'commodity' work (Figure 3.7).

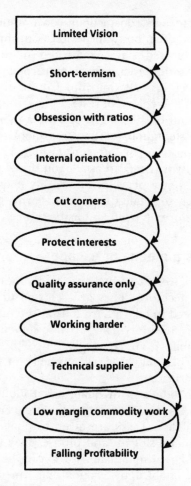

Figure 3.7 The spiral of descent

Given such a situation, how should one 'kick start' a broader approach? What should be the catalyst for action? A crisis or major disaster can do the trick, but when they occur it is sometimes too late.

Management as conspicuous consumption

The possibility that such management approaches as quality may be beyond redemption should not be overlooked. Thorstein Veblen in his classic study of the 'leisure class' identified various forms of conspicuous consumption, such as the deer park around the country house, that were used to demonstrate wealth.[10] Being able to afford waste and unproductive resources becomes a symbol of corporate as well as social standing.

Symbols of waste and conspicuous consumption abounded in large corporations during the postwar period. Corporate head offices were characterised by bloated staffs comprised of anaemic schemers with inflated job titles padding their way along carpets with deep pile en route to meaningless meetings. The murmur from their offices resembled discrete conversations in a chapel of rest.

Quality should not be allowed to become a more recent manifestation of trappings, an ostentatious corporate symbol and expensive cosmetic designed to demonstrate in 'me too' fashion that something is being done. Where quality is regarded as a 'good thing' that can do little harm, it may be perceived as a placebo. The reality may be different. An inappropriate approach to quality can cause harm, while the avoidance of 'real' issues could store up troubles for the future.

Management as a means of escape

Quality, BPR and 'restructuring' are sometimes used as a device for avoiding difficult decisions. They are resorted to as a general means of escape from the need to take a hard look at the fundamental problems of individual parts of a business. They are also sometimes used as a means of avoiding responsibility. For example, once the total quality drive is launched, quality becomes the responsibility of 'everyone', which may mean no one in particular.

Because the introduction of quality or BPR is frequently associated with the use of groups and teams they can provide opportunities to evade personal accountability. Tasks are given to quality improvement teams, and the use of general slogans and phrases may replace a concentration upon the particular. Immediate issues can be postponed while the emphasis is upon establishing groups that can operate effectively, and individual insights and perspectives can become blurred as a consequence of the imposition of a common 'quality jargon'.

Consolidation or development

A corporate programme that stays still for too long runs the same risks as a ship in harbour – it can become encrusted with barnacles. From time to time an initiative may have to be re-energised if it is not to run out of steam.

Change for change's sake should be avoided. A succession of unrelated initiatives can lead to a bemused and punch-drunk management team. Change a corporate programme too often and confusion may result. Particular aspects may come to be seen as a 'flavour of the month'. Where impacts and consequences take some time to work through, certain changes might also be premature.

There is an understandable reluctance to change what has become familiar. There will be those who stress the value of consolidation rather than further development, especially when there has been a considerable investment in training and documentation. Thus the quality manual can set a programme in concrete.

A programme that does not evolve in response to experience and changing circumstances and objectives, can become out of date. After some time its relevance and contribution may be questioned. An original purpose may have been forgotten, and what remains may be regarded as an imposition or distraction.

Quality and other programmes can wander off track like a badly tuned radio. Their implementation needs to be sharp and clearly matched to the 'needs of the business'. In a turbulent and demanding business environment those who 'rest on their laurels' can quickly become a headcount reduction opportunity.

The perils of complacency

Some governments have sought to influence and broaden corporate perspectives. A number of countries are likely to follow the lead given by EFQM and introduce awards that encourage organisations to aspire beyond traditional quality assurance. The UK initiative which has led to the development of a new quality award taps the feeling that past approaches have been too narrow in focus. The responsible Secretary of State has expressed the view: 'It is important to obtain total commitment to quality in every aspect of a company's activities.'

Christer Zetterberg, President and CEO of Volvo, recognises that: 'It is not enough that our end-products be of traditionally high Volvo quality.' He believes that all aspects of Volvo's operations and activities need to be addressed.

The desire to change is frequently a product of dissatisfaction with the status quo. Success can be a curse when it leads to self-satisfied complacency. In a market environment in which customer requirements and competitor capabilities are continually evolving or changing, the positions of those who are not aware and awake face the threat of continual erosion.

An established company may not recognise the need to change. The senior management may be preoccupied with receiving awards based upon past achievements, or reading in books and journals about their corporate accomplishments and strengths. The documented circumstances giving rise to the awards may have moved on, while the 'favourable mention' in the book may have been written eighteen months before. In the meantime, the competitive positioning of the company may have slipped.

Confronting reality

Within organisations with a culture of success, there will be many who are reluctant to question or 'prick the balloon'. Those who bring bad news may be perceived as negative. Efforts may be made to explain away or avoid confronting what may appear to be disturbing facts. Reports may conceal rather than highlight danger areas.

A company should guard against a natural tendency to rationalise and be selective in the use and assessment of information. Facts and other evidence that support an established view may be exaggerated, while those that could bring it into question may be overlooked or downplayed. Disturbing signs may be explained away as 'exceptions' that are not relevant. There will be those who counsel waiting for a few months in case what has been observed turns out to be a temporary phenomenon or 'blip'. By the time a trend has been firmly established it may be too late.

Sometimes complacency is born out of satisfaction with one's positioning in relation to other firms in the same industry. The threat may actually arise from outside of the cosy club of current competitors. A technological revolution or new entrant adopting new approaches may have the potential to sweep away all those existing players that are not able to quickly adapt.

Some 95 per cent of the output of the French steel industry comes from Usinor Sacilor, the second largest producer of crude steel in the world and an active user of total quality, defined by Claude Barbier, its former director of total quality, as: 'a collection of principles and methods, set out as an overall strategy, which aims to mobilise the whole organisation in order to obtain the greatest customer satisfaction at the lowest cost'. To achieve more significant changes the company adopted its own approach to process improvement but elsewhere the adoption of mini mills resulted in its established plants being out-performed by 'greenfield' start-ups. According to Matthias Maier who has examined the Usinor Sacilor experience: 'Incremental change even when successful can be overtaken by fundamental innovation and radical breakthroughs'.[11]

The relevance of BPR

We are in an era of transition between models of organisation with their attendant values and priorities. This ought to have set the stage for the successful application of BPR.

An examination of organisational innovation across Europe suggests that virtually all the new models of more flexible organisation (and of different ways of working and learning) which are emerging have been conceived and, in many cases, implemented quite independently of BPR.[12] It would not have occurred to their creators to 'build in' most of the features and deficiencies of organisations (eg 'vertical' functions) that BPR has been packaged to tackle.[2]

Those offering tailored products and services and 'organised by project' may not have repetitive processes to re-engineer. The opportunity to use BPR is often the least where the most progress has been made in challenging and breaking down a functional form of organisation. It is paradoxical that most manifestations of BPR, with its rhetoric of radical change, depend for their survival upon the continuing existence of traditional 'bureaucratic pyramids'. BPR may be fighting yesterday's battles rather than preparing us for tomorrow.

No one should feel compelled to undertake BPR. In deciding whether to seek incremental improvements or a 'step change' in performance, the following could feature among the factors to be considered:[2]

- How well is the organisation performing, and how big is the gap between where it is and where it would like to be? Could the gap be bridged by improving or building upon what already exists? Alternatively, is the gap so large that the organisation needs to 'throw away and start again'?
- What else is happening? Have customers suddenly become more demanding? Are other similar organisations performing significantly better? Has an innovatory development occurred which is revolutionising existing ways of operating? Is there a need to respond to a radically different direction and strategy?
- How stable is the environment, or framework, within which the organisation operates? Where the environment is relatively static or unchanged from one year to the next, a management team may not feel under any particular imperative to change. However, it might still opt to undertake some 'blue skies' thinking about different ways in which an existing product or service might be delivered.
- Is the model of organisation and mode of operation appropriate in the situation and circumstances? Does organisational capability match both organisational vision and customer requirements? If the answer to these questions is 'no', then a radical transformation may be required. If, however, an organisation is thought to be broadly appropriate, then all that may be required is fine tuning in areas of relative deficiency.

Even where radical change is needed, activities such as creative thinking, benchmarking, corporate transformation, culture change, innovation, etc, can be undertaken quite independently of BPR. Many other frameworks and approaches exist, and these may or may not include the use of certain change elements which have been 'claimed' by advocates of both quality and BPR.

Situation analysis

The extent to which people are motivated to change may depend upon the form of situation analysis used. Typically, such an analysis will involve defining a desired state, examining a current state, and then comparing the two in order to assess the extent to which there is a gap. The next step is usually to agree the actions that are necessary to bridge the gap between where the company is and where its board and management team would like it to be.

This brings us back to an approach described earlier in this chapter. A first step for many companies is to establish a process for identifying relevant developments in the external business environment, assessing their impacts and determining the nature of the corporate response (see Figure 3.4 earlier).

The nature of the desired state will depend upon the ambitions and perceptions of those undertaking the analysis. There are some who find it difficult to handle more than incremental changes, while others may be drawn to all sorts of 'interesting' scenarios, some of which may be fantastic or unreal.

Similarly, some people will deceive and delude themselves when assessing a current situation, while others are realistic, perhaps painfully so. Those doing the 'staff work' may 'paint a picture' to correspond with a prevailing corporate view of reality.

Those eager for challenge may 'play up' the nature and extent of the gap between the existing and the desired in order to galvanise and gain attention. At the same time, those with a preference for 'coasting' or a 'quiet life' may seek to minimise the scale of the adjustment that needs to be made.

What needs to be done will reflect the rigour with which obstacles and barriers are identified. The analysis should get down to root causes. Necessary actions may or may not be expressed in clear terms, and roles and responsibilities for their achievement could be confusing and incomplete in one context and appropriate and comprehensive in another.

In some companies, the actions needed to bridge a gulf between an actual and desired state may represent little more than a wish list. In others, for example, Rank Xerox, each 'vital few' programme may be accompanied by a PERT chart setting out the means by which outcomes can be achieved and progress monitored.

The strait-jacket of standards

The issue of 'standards' raised in the last chapter does represent a dilemma in uncertain, dynamic and shifting contexts:

- Some form of recognised quality system may be seen as an entrance ticket required by those seeking to become players in a particular marketplace. It is a mandatory requirement of some customers and without it an organisation may not be invited to tender.

- However, a quality system and standards that inhibit, discourage or frustrate flexibility can put an organisation at a competitive disadvantage. Quite apart from the burden of their cost, those who staff the quality assurance function may actively seek out all those deviations from standards that people within the organisation might wish to introduce in order to meet the requirements of individual customers.

The imposition of standard approaches and requirements is least destructive, and is sometimes helpful, where activity is repetitive and numbers of standard products are produced. However, the greater the need for diversity, variety and a tailoring to the needs of individual customers, the more quality standards can frustrate.

In many sectors, customers are increasingly demanding individually tailored products and services. Because of the rhetoric of quality, customers may assume that suppliers will achieve a basic level of quality. The incremental business is likely to go to the supplier that is flexible in meeting the unique needs of particular customers.

Customer requirements can also be diverse and fleeting, or may evolve in response to the interaction between customer and supplier. To enable a supplier to respond, its approach to quality may need to be flexible and evolutionary. It must be capable of learning and adaptation.

An exclusive and introverted focus upon the quality of today's products can blind an organisation to broader developments in the business environment that suggest major 'discontinuities' are about to occur. Effort may be devoted to perfecting a product that is doomed, while little is done to develop the capability to cope with new areas of opportunities. Those who insist upon awaiting the amendment of the quality manual before acting will surely be too late.

Reaching the person within

The standards that are relevant in today's world are those within us rather than in the procedures – standards of thought and intention, standards of integrity and commitment. Network organisations operate and survive upon the basis of their values and, particularly, shared assumptions about respect, honesty and trust.

To break free from mechanical approaches we need to reach 'the person within', the collective soul of organisations. A process of reconciliation is required. Reconciliation, balance and harmony are frequently stressed during conversations with thoughtful quality practitioners. People need to be reconciled with technology and organisations, and more of a balance achieved between the interests of different stakeholders.

Do we need to move beyond quality, or merely change the emphasis or focus within a quality framework? Views differ:

- Some argue a break with the past is needed to achieve the degree of impact required. Arno Penzias believes that just as the age of quantity was replaced by the age of quality, so quality in turn will be replaced by the age of harmony in which technology is in harmony with itself, with those who use it, and with the environment and context within which it operates.[13]
- Others advocate building upon existing foundations. Thus within MashreqBank the concept of harmony has become an important value within the bank's approach to quality. A corporate vice-president, Nader Haghighat, stresses the need for harmony within people as well as between them.
- At 3M the focus is upon the harmony of the relationship between quality and innovation. Both quality and innovation are regarded as 'everyone's job'.

In general, a new vision is required if weary and frayed people are to be once again reconciled to the organisations that wish to use their talents. A new balance has to be struck between the requirements of each in a way that will give both a better prospect of continuing relevance in an uncertain world in which we have electronic contact with many and yet close relationships with but a few. We turn in the next chapter to the question of formulating a new vision, the constraints and inhibitors that hold us back and the clouds that obscure our views of desired futures.

Checklist

Does your organisation have an issue monitoring and management system to assess the impacts of developments in the external environment?

Are the implications for current approaches such as quality or BPR assessed?

How are external developments affecting your organisation's quality, BPR and transformation programmes?

When were they last reviewed?

What expectations do various stakeholders have? What are their current perceptions?

Who are the supporters of quality, and who are the critics?

How relevant are quality, BPR and transformation to the achievement of your organisation's purpose, vision, values and goals?

What roles do they actually play?

Is there a future for them within your organisation?

How could they make a more significant contribution?

What is missing? Are more holistic approaches needed?

How might the constraints be removed?

References

1. Colin Coulson-Thomas, *Creating the Global Company*, London, McGraw-Hill, 1992.
2. Colin Coulson-Thomas (ed), *Business Process Re-engineering: Myth and Reality*, London, Kogan Page, 1994.
3. H James Harrington, *Business Process Improvement: The Breakthrough Strategy for Total Quality, Productivity, and Competitiveness*, New York, McGraw-Hill, 1991, p viii.
4. Peter Bartram, *The Competitive Network*, London, Policy Publications, 1996.
5. Colin and Susan Coulson-Thomas, *Quality: The Next Steps*, an Adaptation Ltd survey for ODI, London, Adaptation Ltd, 1991; executive summary available from ODI Europe, 1991.
6. Colin Coulson-Thomas and Richard Brown, *Beyond Quality: Managing the Relationship with the Customer*, Corby, British Institute of Management, 1990.
7. Colin Coulson-Thomas, *Transforming the Company: Bridging the Gap Between Management Myth and Corporate Reality*, London, Kogan Page, 1992.
8. Colin Coulson-Thomas, 'Building Europe's Learning Foundations, The European Learning Network', *IT in Europe Journal*, February 1990, pp 14-19; and 'Breaking Through the Information Barrier: Management Development and IT', *International Journal of Computer Applications in Technology*, Vol 3, No 4, 1990, pp 269–71.
9. John Nicholls, 'Value to the Customer', *Total Quality Management*, April 1990, pp 85–7.
10. Thorstein Veblen, *The Theory of the Leisure Class: An Economic Study of Institutions*, London, George Allen & Unwin, Third Impression, 1957.
11. Matthias Maier, 'Change Management in the French Steel Industry', in Colin Coulson-Thomas (ed), *Business Process Re-engineering, Myth and Reality*, London, Kogan Page, 1994.
12. Colin Coulson-Thomas, *The Responsive Organisation: Re-engineering New Patterns of Work*, London, Policy Publications, 1995.
13. Arno Penzias, *Harmony: Business, Technology and Life after Paperwork*, New York, HarperCollins, 1995.

4

Corporate vision: the rhetoric, the reality and the barriers

Vows made in storms are forgotten in calms.

While some managers recall their past words with the remorse of a Scrooge, others change their minds as often as their socks, and in so doing pride themselves on their pragmatism and flexibility. Crisis resolutions made while commercial realities are stark and clear are soon forgotten as the pressures ease or people become accustomed to the pain. In turbulent times we need to search for visions that are more profound, more able to reach our inner selves and stand the test of time.

Corporate priorities often appear rather like the Victorian notion of progress. The future is described in terms of more of this, extra that, additional and onerous requirements, greater demands from customers – all seen in almost treadmill terms as inevitably involving ever harder and harder work. Pressure and long hours are regarded as challenging and virtuous and as a visible demonstration of commitment.

Few corporate visions use terms such as less, easier, slower or simpler – even though these might well be the keys to the extra balance, reflection, learning, creativity and focus that could result in greater customer and employee satisfaction.

We should not always expect clear-cut answers. As Charles Handy has pointed out, we need to venture beyond the certainties of the past towards new forms of organisation, that, while demanding, different forms of contribution can also support new roles and lifestyles.[1]

We have seen that there is widespread concern about the contribution of certain widely adopted management approaches. In this chapter we will continue to question and probe by taking a closer look at the emerging gulf between the rhetoric of quality and the reality of its application, and at the obstacles and barriers that might be causing the gap to widen.

Activity or progress?

Amidst the frenetic activity associated with the work of re-engineering, restructuring, quality improvement and other teams it is sometimes difficult to identify a sense of direction. In a large corporation there may be hundreds, if not thousands, of such groups at work. But what does it all mean? Is anything fundamental being achieved?

Virtually all the big steps taken by the innovative organisations examined by the author resulted from flashes of insight, connections made and ideas developed outside of normal work. Doing something different on holidays or at weekends, chance encounters, playing with children, backing a band on a bass guitar or just mooching about, all of these appeared more likely to be sources of inspirational thinking than formal approaches such as the use of re-engineering methodologies.

The high-pressure work environment may be associated with working harder rather than smarter, along with the attendant risks of 'burning out' and legal actions for 'stress damages'. A balance has to be struck between thought and action, energy and relevance, commitment and focus. Honda's philosophy is that: 'Action without philosophy is a lethal weapon; philosophy without action is worthless.'

Just living in a society, one is constantly exposed to a growth in articulated concern for quality and the customer while at the same time experiencing a daily sense of unease that actual standards of service may be slipping. For example, with all the talk of quality, do railways or London Transport offer a better level of service than was the case ten, twenty or thirty years ago? Whatever the carefully selected figures show, was travel more or less enjoyable then as compared with today?

Many police authorities are showing great interest in 'quality' and the building of closer relationships with the customer. But has the quality of policing risen, or is it falling? Are people more or less inclined to feel secure or to 'lock up' when leaving home than was the case a generation ago? Are we more or less willing to walk the streets at night? A concern for quality is no substitute for being competent at one's core business.

In the case of the police, less crime and more security is sought by the public, not customer relations campaigns. The latter may be a means to an end in encouraging greater vigilance and cooperation, but they should not be allowed to become an end in themselves. The quality or 'communications' programme should not 'take over' and become a distracting substitute for what an organisation should really be about.

The tendency to regress

Disturbed systems have a tendency to return to a point of equilibrium. Strong corporate cultures may have the capacity to absorb, shake off or deflect a succession of well meaning corporate initiatives. Programmes come and go, and very often once they have passed through the body corporate, little evidence of their previous existence may remain.

Clive Holtham has suggested a five-stage lifecycle of management innovations running from initial research and conception, through packaging into consultancy products, subsequent adoption and the emergence of negative experiences and conceptual problems to growing disappointment as dramatic benefits fail to emerge and eventual disrepute and disuse. Already Holtham positions BPR at the 'negative experiences and conceptual problems' stage of the cycle.[2]

Corporate organisations may regress to a previous situation or return to a longer-term evolutionary trend once the disturbance caused by a particular initiative has ebbed. During the early stages when a programme is perceived as novel, considerable effort is often devoted to its promotion, and people may feel they must be seen to be supportive of it. The activity that is evident should not be automatically equated with progress, as there may be little longer-term impact.

To deflect the course of corporate evolution it may be necessary to administer a succession of 'shocks' to the system, and deploy a combination of change elements that is more extensive than the constituents of traditional approaches to quality.[3] The various approaches used should be complementary and mutually supportive. If not, their use may cause confusion, rather than reinforcement.

Where is quality in the management lifecycle?

Compared with other management innovations quality has experienced a relatively long lifecycle. Perhaps it is different in kind. Maybe it is experiencing a slow decline into marginalisation rather than sudden rejection. Or, chameleon like, it might be regularly and opportunistically shifting its ground and prolonging its life by claiming and absorbing a succession of other concepts, of which BPR is but one of the latest. Let us examine some comments made by participants in the author's surveys:

Quality is about covering your behind. It's protective. It's about us, and not about them. It's damage limitation. It enables us to demonstrate to a court that all reasonable steps were taken.

Our quality system is internally focused. It was developed during a time of growth when we could afford to give priority to our own needs. Things are different now, but the system and the perspective and priorities of those who operate it are still internal.

If quality travels more easily in some cultures than in others, the approach to quality is at fault. If the emphasis is upon harnessing talent and delivering value, then what is used or advocated should depend upon the circumstances and a high degree of tailoring may be required.

Depending on the extent of the differences, it may be advisable to encourage people to 'do their own thing'.

> We are avoiding the 'big bang' and 'sheep dip' approaches. Each group is expected to meet the needs of its own situation within an overall framework that seeks to support local initiatives.
>
> Over-elaboration, over-engineering ... elegance for the sake of it ... chasing absolutes ... can be the enemy of getting the job done. What does the customer actually want?
>
> Our quality system seems designed to alert us to every imaginable pitfall, but it doesn't tell us how to win. It tells us what to avoid but not what to do.
>
> Quality is an attitude of mind, and attitudes of mind are deeply personal. Each person has to find their own way. Blast them with quality training and a lot of them turn off, or retreat into themselves. We are imposing rather than encouraging and growing quality.
>
> What value is added by quality? There is no point in it if it does not help. Our dilemma is knowing whether to repackage and relaunch quality or to quietly bury it.

To address the issues raised in such quotations it is necessary for an organisation to understand where it really stands with quality. Sensitive listening to informal networks can be of considerable value in assessing what is actually happening in terms of perceptions and feelings. Formal reporting can sometimes systematically screen out evidence that is perceived as negative or unwelcome.

Approaches to management innovations

Companies exhibit a variety of approaches to management innovations, and varying levels of commitment to them. Some of the approaches which have been identified by the author are shown in Figure 4.1 and each might have distinct advantages and disadvantages in the context of a particular situation:[4]

- The dabbler could dip into a quality or re-engineering toolkit for particular purposes and use selected elements within some units of an organisation but not in others. By experimenting and being prepared to move on the dabbler can both 'skim the cream' and avoid becoming locked into particular approaches.
- The wader becomes more involved but not too deeply. They avoid total commitment but may acquire sufficient experience to develop a degree of expertise in certain aspects of quality or re-engineering.
- The diver is the most selective and when the right opportunity comes along is prepared to act decisively and with total commitment. The quality or other programme is launched with a fanfare and while the commitment lasts there is no going back.

APPROACH	ADVANTAGES	DISADVANTAGES
Dabbler		
Wader		
Diver		
Flocker		
Cuckoo		

Figure 4.1 Approaches to management innovations

Source: Colin Coulson-Thomas, *Creating the Global Company*, McGraw-Hill, 1992.

- The flocker is less independent, more risk averse and a follower of fashion. Flockers will go along with a management concept when others adopt it and can be flexible in order to fit in with whatever is current among supply chain partners.
- The cuckoo achieves results through the activities of others. For example, by subterfuge or the imposition of onerous quality requirements upon suppliers, cuckoos improve the quality of their own goods and services.

Many organisations employ a combination of the above approaches and their relative advantages and disadvantages can change over time. Thus what is perceived as a lack of commitment during the growth phase of the lifecycle of a management fad can come to be rationalised as prudence during the decline phase.

Corporate activity can sometimes give an appearance of progress. People may be inspired by the thought that 'something is happening' or that 'someone cares'. Ultimately, a 'bread and circuses' approach to management can be a cruel deception. Role models may emerge who are actors rather than contributors, adept at the use of words rather than deeds. People should be offered the reality rather than the illusion of achievement.

An approach to management should achieve an appropriate balance between collectivism and individualism. Organisations are communities of individuals. While groups and teams come and go, individual people, hopefully, live on and continue to work and learn. Too often quality as perceived, articulated and implemented is excessively collectivist. The strong drive towards individualism in many cultures must be addressed.

On occasion, while ostensibly designed to 'involve' everyone or be 'owned' by everyone, a management concept falls into the hands of an inner 'party'. This 'new elite' may see itself as the champions of change or as the 'vanguard of the revolution'. Such an approach could be divisive as some people come to be regarded as 'not one of us' while others seek advantage by playing up their adoption of the cosmetics or trappings of whatever management notions happen to be in fashion.

The management vision

The great variety of approaches to quality and re-engineering that are encountered raise the question of what if any vision of these and other approaches many companies have. A vision is a picture of a better future. The behaviours of many boards during the recent period of economic slowdown and recession suggested they have had little to guide them by way of objectives and goals beyond a desire for survival for a further 12 months.[5]

A simple, compelling and shared vision can sustain the commitment needed to overcome technical and organisational barriers that reach to the limits of what is known or beyond. President Kennedy's vision of a man on the moon is a much quoted example. One interviewee lamented: 'The CEO is always telling us about Kennedy's man on the moon vision. Unfortunately we don't have NASA's budget. The rhetoric doesn't really help.'

Eberhard v. Kuenheim, chairman of the board of management of BMW, believes that: 'Visions are indispensable. These are targets from which a company can take its long-term bearings and which may not be sacrificed to short-term goals. Every company must define its own way.'

People within corporations too can articulate and share visions. For example, within Boeing the vision of air travel 'within a room' led to the 747 family of 'jumbo jets'. What once appeared a huge gamble turned out to be a major commercial success.[6] TNT expanded its operations to cover the globe because its vision of a distribution network was without territorial limitation.

The corporate vision

A corporate vision can be broad and fundamental. For example:

- The mission of the Lyonnaise des Eaux-Dumez group is to improve the lives of people and the communities in which they live by solving the problems of their environment ... By coordinating and controlling the comprehensive range of services it offers, the group pursues two objectives: improving living conditions and enhancing the quality of life.' To do this demands 'firm commitments over very long periods of time'.

- A 'guiding principle' of Hoechst includes a broad view of the 'market requirements' that are met by its products: 'The aim of these products is to meet people's basic needs and improve the quality of life while also safeguarding and raising living standards.'

Organisations of widely differing scale can have similar visions: For example:

- The vision of Matsushita is to contribute to human happiness by means of material affluence afforded by quality and inexpensive products.
- The proprietor of a beach cafe for many years in Cornwall sought to 'brighten up the day of people ... Rain or shine, people knew there was at least one friendly face on the beach. Although I'm retired visitors still drop by ... I might have only sold them a cup of tea.'

A corporate vision could be as profound as preserving diversity and options for mankind. Eckart Wintzen, President and CEO of BSO/Beheer in his company's 1991 Annual Report mourns the loss of wisdom and cultures associated with the forecast loss of half of the world's languages and the threat to biological diversity: 'If we carry on much longer as we are doing now, the party will soon be over.'

Assessing visions

Visions that are broad and long term can sometimes seem remote, and designed for public consumption rather than internal motivation. Employees sympathise with the lofty sentiments but wonder what if anything they can do about them.

Excitement and preoccupations about the future should not be allowed to lure people's attention away from current realities. A vision should also be regularly reassessed, not necessarily to change the goalposts but to ensure that any previous fundamental reassessment was not unduly influenced by a combination of factors that were present at one moment in time. Some of the considerations that were most influential at the time may appear less pressing with hindsight.

A vision should relate to the essence of what it takes to be successful in relation to what represents value for customers. It could be as prosaic as delivering a pizza within ten minutes.

A balance needs to be maintained between inspiration and the potential for achievement. However, practicality should not be taken to the point that a vision becomes anaemic and fails to inspire.

A vision could seek to embrace markets that have yet to be created. The means by which a community of people could collectively enhance their capacity to be innovative and cope with an uncertain but challenging environment could become the subject of a vision.

To be successful, a vision needs to be distinctive, compelling and inspirational. At the end of the day it needs to motivate people to take the first steps towards bringing it about. Many corporate visions fail this acid test. They are perceived to be about the organisation and its survival rather than about the interests of customers, employees and other stakeholders.

Rhetoric versus reality

In many organisations there is a considerable gulf between words and deeds, to the extent that some statements are taken with a large pinch of salt or are just not believed.[3] People, particularly at a senior level, say one thing but may be perceived as doing something quite different. For example, a board might use the rhetoric of empowerment while withholding trust and retaining a firm hold upon the leading reins of power. This aspect of reality is recognised when people stress the importance of 'walking the talk'.

While network organisations thrive on trust the foundations of quality assurance are deeply rooted in distrust. Audits, controls, contracts, quality manuals all thrive where there is distrust. Suspicion can breed distrust. Workplace surveillance practices such as hidden microphones and video cameras or the monitoring of electronic mail messages that are becoming widespread in the US are evidence of lack of trust.

The emphasis is shifting to outputs and outcomes. Quality and BPR no longer have an exclusive claim upon them. One financial director posed the question: 'When aware auditors and accountants are shifting the emphasis from checking inputs ... to such factors as the implications of learning and sharing for outcomes ... what is the the distinct contribution of our quality colleagues? Their message is old news.' However, measures of outcomes too can sometimes become constraints.

While naivety should be avoided, controls and checks can be expensive and may reduce speed and flexibility of response. Investment in the building of trust and encouraging people to take responsibility can pay dividends. One of Southern California's most rapidly growing companies operates as a network based upon trust. Deliveries are made in response to telephone calls and distribution arrangements around the world are based upon handshakes rather than contracts.

In one survey, while the tenets of quality appear to have been taken on board by the participating managers, it was recognised that on occasion financial pressures can result in compromise when applying values. Where corporate values were found to interfere with the short-term commercial

gain, over twice as many of those under 40 considered financial imperatives would take priority as felt values would come first.

In many companies different policies and priorities are in obvious conflict. British Airways puts its staff through extensive customer relations
and 'smile' training. A cynic might argue they need all the preparation
they can get to deal with the victims of a 10 per cent overbooking policy
when all their customers turn up.

There are sophisticates who will justify a degree of deception or delu-
sion. Concealing the truth is rationalised as responsible behaviour to protect the interests of certain stakeholders. The author has encountered
many comments along the lines of: 'If we revealed the full extent of
future job cuts, morale would drop through the floor'. A 'form of words'
might be thought necessary until such times as people have been prepared to face the truth. These attempts can prove self-defeating. When
the word is out people can feel misled or deceived.

Appearance may be preferred to reality. An ability to present, draft
documents and give reports that obscure or avoid reality is a skill that is
highly prized in some organisations. More attention is devoted to concealment than to the identification of root causes.

Taking expectations into account

A corporate vision needs to take account of stakeholder expectations. On
occasion these may vary. Consider quality:

- Externally, expectations are thought to be high. According to Peter
  Smith who leads a quality and service initiative within Coopers &
  Lybrand: 'Quality is now a boardroom topic in most organisations,
  and clients' expectations are rising correspondingly. However good
  we think we are today we must be better tomorrow; if we aren't, there
  will always be another firm happy to go the extra mile.'
- But what about the 'internal' quality expectations of colleagues, fellow
  employees, the people 'on the ground'. According to surveys recently
  undertaken by the author for a variety of organisations, these are
  often very different from what one might expect upon the basis of
  articulated quality visions and the rhetoric of quality.

Rarely do agreed expectations or definitions of quality emerge. Overall,
and on reflection, expectations appear to be modest. Few believe that
quality of itself, and as understood and practised within their companies,
could have much further impact upon the 'delivered' quality of goods
and services. The focus is too often upon the quality system and its
requirements, and not upon those of external customers.

In general, people feel 'quality' may help, but it is thought unlikely to
prove significant, let alone decisive. Big steps will require something else
over and above today's approaches to quality.

The management challenge

Given the different internal and external expectations, one could ask: why should a company's customer be satisfied? In many cases the main reason appears to be the extent to which suppliers are often prepared, at their own expense, 'to put things right'. This would not be needed if output of the right quality were delivered on time. Hence criticism of what quality is can highlight an opportunity for introducing what quality ought to be. The question is the extent to which quality is up to the challenge.

Good quality, excellent, even world-class products in themselves may no longer be enough. Canada's Telus Corporation aims 'to be a leader at enriching people's lives through reliable information and telecommunications services that are accessible wherever, whenever and however our customers want.'

Hal Nelder, President and CEO of Telus, explains: 'Enriching means our products and services have to add to the well-being of people and organisations.' This is a potential acid test of managment concepts. On balance, while their use and application may well keep people busy, sustain the illusion of progress and generate income for consultants, do they enhance and enrich or impoverish and frustrate?

Those most concerned with making concepts such as quality or empowerment work are particularly aware of the scale of the challenge at the leading edge. Jim Havard of Rank Xerox (UK): 'Developing and implementing the skills and processes to negotiate relationships with multiple partners and meet their changing requirements is tough. You ask yourself how much will it cost to satisfy everyone and how will this be shared among the parties?'

Closing the vision and reality gap

Reference was also made in earlier chapters to the existence of a gulf between rhetoric and reality. The rhetoric of quality and the claims that have been made about the growing capability of technology have raised expectations to such an extent that where quality plateaus or is put on a 'care and maintenance' basis, a growing gap is likely to be encountered between expectation and achievement (Figure 4.2).

Expectation and delivery may continue to diverge unless specific action is taken. Various sets of responses are being employed within organisations to re-establish the relevance of certain management concepts. These include:

- Redoubling efforts, perhaps by identifying and tackling obstacles, pitfalls and barriers, or relaunching an initiative in a new form.
- Reaching for new tools, methods and concepts, or extending the quality framework to embrace developments such as re-engineering rather than just improving processes.

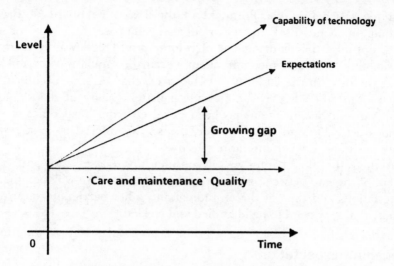

Figure 4.2 The expectation/delivery gap

- Seeking to introduce a new element into the corporate culture such as 'innovation' or a greater commitment to learning.
- Looking for new arenas, for example emerging environmental concerns, in which to apply and practise certain principles such as those of quality.
- Confronting reality by acting to modify or balance expectations.
- Recourse to a further round of corporate restructuring, justified by a pretext such as 'getting closer to the customer'.

The BSO/Beheer concern with the environment is more than just words slipped in at the suggestion of the public relations team. For example, in addition to conventional accounts the 1991 Annual Report also contains a set of 'environmental accounts' designed to quantify the impact of its activities upon the environment and an essay by anthropologist Professor David Maybury-Lewis.

The difficult business environment of the late 1980s and early 1990s has given rise to a new realism. According to Pierre Dauzier, Chairman and CEO of the French media and communications group Havas: 'Overall, the communications sector is now labouring to shake free of the rosy views prevailing in the past, when excessive media coverage helped sustain the impression that the business was a source of easy profits. That bubble has now been pricked and it is clear that a period of more moderate but steadier growth lies ahead.'

The context in which the term 'quality', whether as an adjective or noun, is used may or may not help to clarify what is being sought. For example, Michel Prada, President of the Executive Board of Crédit d'Equipement des PME, refers to efforts to improve the quality of services, optimise the management of resources and significantly increase profitability. Such statements frequently occur in annual reports and are often rhetoric. In the CEPME case, however, changes have occurred. As part of the CEPME drive to provide a better quality of service, loan approval and management has been devolved from head office to the regions as: 'Closer to the customer, the service offered is, as a result, more personal, quicker and more effective.'

In the rest of this chapter we will consider how to assess the nature and extent of the gap between expectations and delivery. We will look first at expectations and then at the attitudinal and other barriers to improved quality that may need to be identified and tackled.

Managing expectations

Too many management initiatives have raised expectations to unrealistic levels. Hype and rhetoric have contributed to the growing gap between aspiration and achievement. While competitors persist in making extravagant claims it may not be easy to reduce expectations, but, at minimum, an effort should be made to prevent the gap from growing.

Management should be about bridging the gap between expectation and achievement. In a quality relationship based upon openness and mutual trust, only what can be delivered should be promised. The exaggerated claim may win some incremental business at the expense of undermining trust and prejudicing a longer-term relationship.

Care needs to be taken to test customer understanding and expectation in order to judge the extent to which these are realistic. Certain customers may not like being 'brought down to earth', but some disappointment now is usually preferable to anger and possibly the involvement of lawyers at a later date.

Particular attitudes and forms of behaviour may not occur if steps are not taken to help bring them about. Observation of what it takes to 'get ahead' or the consequence of performance measures or reward criteria could undermine a drive to instil greater honesty in business relationships.

New style management values and role model conduct should be made explicit. They should be defined and practised. Reward, remuneration, objectives and priorities should be supportive of them. Communications should be fair, responsible and balanced. It is possible to attract interest without making wild and unsupportable claims.

Internal communications that exaggerate achievements and conceal 'bad news' are not treating the people of the organisation with respect. In a mature and responsible organisation people should tell the truth.

Problems should be brought into the open so that they can be discussed and tackled.

Listen to the voice of experience. According to one main board director: 'We have become so cautious these days. Our hype ... the smoke and music at year start meetings ... all these things have resulted in tremendous cynicism. They don't believe us, and why should they? ... To recover this situation you need to tread carefully. You need to promise a little and deliver a lot.'

The gap between rhetoric and reality is particularly acute in the area of corporate values. Customers, and the public generally, often do not see a perceptible change in conduct following the adoption of a statement of values or ethical guidelines. Too many newspaper headlines focus upon conduct that suggests many directors and managers 'sail close to the wind' in their headlong pursuit of results.

Many boards and chief executives do little more than pay lip service to statements of values. Are such statements perceived as a 'luxury' or as essential? Are they monitored and enforced? When was the last time someone was fired for a breach of ethical guidelines rather than inadequate financial performance? Is the understanding and trust such that managers will sacrifice profit in order to observe corporate values when there is a perceived conflict?

Management practice as a person

Some people find it easier to express their views of quality, or other corporate programmes, when encouraged to draw an analogy with an animal, car or person. For example, if BPR were a person how would he or she be perceived? As exciting or as a bore? As a helper or a mugger? As someone to positively seek out, to generally associate with or to shun and avoid?

The author has posed these sorts of question in a diversity of organisations. Tracking the responses in particular organisations over time suggests perceptions and expectations are changing. For example:

- In terms of personal attributes quality used to be portrayed across one group of companies as rather cold and narrowly focused, and with a drive to win attention and acceptance.
- More recently, quality appears to be growing up. Along with the shift of emphasis from engineering concerns, statistics and product quality to the quality of relationships, quality is thought to have become more mature and reflective.

Approaching middle age, quality finds that all its youthful plans have not been realised, and some suggest a form of 'mid-life crisis' is occurring with quality losing its way. At the same time it is portrayed as having become more self-aware and willing to accept that other approaches and techniques have value.

In time, it is suggested, quality is likely to become reconciled to its place in the corporate scheme of things. In so doing, it may dwell more on feelings, attitudes, values and perceptions, areas in which it may be possible to make a longer-term impact. This is the sort of quality we could pick up and run with.

It is easy to dismiss the findings of such exercises as anecdotal, subjective and impressionistic, but a similar pattern over time recurs in very different contexts. They also appear to match the lifecycle of management concepts suggested earlier in this chapter.[2]

Success stories

The results of 'quality as a person' exercises suggest that not all organisations are experiencing, let alone succumbing to, mid-life crises. There are well documented examples of quality success stories. Rank Xerox, winner of the 1992 European Quality Award, is an example, although its approach to total quality embraces a wide range of elements.[3]

Many companies retain their faith. BICC is 'dedicated to total quality, technical excellence and the satisfaction of customer need'. Its commitment to these areas is made explicit on the front cover of its 1991 Annual Report and Accounts. Within many parts of BICC, for example its North American operations, the focus upon total quality is increasing.

Smiths Industries chalked up two years of record profits during 1990–91, a period of economic recession. According to Sir Alex Jarratt, the Chairman of the company: 'Once again the Company demonstrated its ability to react flexibly and quickly to shorter term market influences whilst laying secure foundations for longer term business development.'

The reasons for the success of Smiths Industries include 'a commitment to research and development, investment in advanced manufacturing and closely focused marketing'. Sir Alex Jarratt considers quality also played a pivotal role: 'I believe the key to this lies in quality – quality of the people, quality of the products and quality of the earnings that they generate between them.'

Within Smiths Industries process improvements 'enable the company to meet customers' needs for high variety and short lead times efficiently.' 'Quality and value' have enabled the company to win new business from British Rail and other customers around the world. Many of the company's products have become brand leaders as a result of their quality and this gives 'the power to command a premium price'.

Consistency of corporate and brand image and reputation in the case of Smiths Industries results from the 'common goal' of always presenting 'quality, integrity and technological leadership' through products. In demanding markets, as one Rank Xerox manager put it, the 'products don't lie'.

Corporate barriers

Let us turn now to the factors that are inhibiting the implementation of corporate goals and values. General concerns, such as those relating to board credibility and confidence, must have an influence upon a company-wide commitment such as the path to total quality.

In corporate reviews of quality facilitated by the author multiple barriers to implementation are usually identified, and fishbone diagrams inevitably come to resemble an octopus as links between them are established. Once root causes are established a number of core obstacles generally emerge and very often these existed or were latent at the outset of a quality drive or initiative.

The participants in the *Quality: The Next Steps*[8] survey were asked to attach varying degrees of significance to selected barriers to the successful implementation of a quality process. The overall ranking of the barriers in terms of 'very significant' replies is given in Table 4.1.

The main barrier, by a large margin, in terms of 'very significant' replies is 'top management commitment'. Over nine out of ten respondents consider this to be a very significant barrier to the successful implementation of a quality process.

Many of those interviewed 'pointed a finger' at the board, citing directors that were not thought to be 'serious' about quality, or who do not 'really believe in it' or are 'not doing it'. Directors themselves acknowledged that some colleagues were 'not good ambassadors' or

Table 4.1 *Quality barriers (ranked in order of 'very significant' replies)*

Lack of top management commitment	92%
Too narrow an understanding of quality	38%
Horizontal boundaries between functions and specialisms	31%
Vested interests	29%
Organisational politics	28%
Cynicism	28%
Organisational structure	27%
Customer expectations	26%
Speed of corporate action	24%
Too general an approach	18%
Loss of momentum	17%
Boredom	15%
Gap between management expectation and process achievement	15%
Vendors'/suppliers' capabilities	15%
Subsidiary/parent relationships	9%
Cost	6%

'role models'. One director of quality referred to fellow directors as: 'passengers on the quality journey, who would "get off at the first stop" if they were able to do so.'

In general, problems with implementation are usually portrayed as someone else's fault. Responses in many companies could be summed up along the lines of: 'The hole is not in my part of the boat.' Many organisations appear to be populated by people who are either powerless or reluctant to assume responsibility in that they are waiting for someone else to do something before they themselves act. The insecurity associated with widespread headcount reduction programmes also encourages people to 'keep their heads down'.

Many corporate programmes seem to have their Achilles' heels. The video may say one thing while remuneration practice suggests something else. Responsibility is abdicated to specialists. People are alienated by the hyping of fads. The programme is over-complex or perceived as irrelevant. Its payoff may appear as too remote. As one CEO put it: 'I talk to other CEOs. We've all got something wrong or missing. It's not always the same, but a common cause is not thinking it through.'

Barriers should not be taken for granted, wished away or hidden in the small print. One of the key distinguishers of the successful management team is the rigour with which it identifies and tackles the root causes of obstacles and barriers.[3]

Managerial attitudes

The root causes of many barriers to implementation, for example 'top management commitment', are attitudinal. But behaviours and attitudes reinforce each other. If attitudes are to be changed, they and the 'behaviours' associated with them need first to be identified and understood.

Managerial or directorial attitudes are often subjective and dependent upon the context. A selection of managerial attitudes identified by one corporate-wide exercise are given by way of illustration in Table 4.2. We will look at directorial attitudes in a moment.

The attitudes listed in Table 4.2 are taken at random from a larger selection of responses. Those selected ought to cause some concern in the boardroom if expressed by a significant number of people. For example, such responses could indicate that in terms of behaviours and other factors:

- the role of the manager is not understood;
- there is a gap between the 'words' of the board and its 'deeds';
- directors are not acting as role models;
- vision, goals, values and objectives have not been communicated and shared;
- roles and responsibilities are not clear;
- individuals and teams do not know what is expected of them;

- they have not been motivated to achieve or equipped to act;
- adequate resources have not been provided;
- facilitating processes or supporting technology are inadequate;
- reward and remuneration is not objective and fair;
- managers are not involved and empowered.

It is increasingly common for companies to undertake customer satisfaction and employee attitude surveys, but surveys of attitudes towards the board remain rare. The expectations that people have of a board and what they think about the board can highlight deficiencies that may need to be addressed. References to doubts, divisions and uncertainties could reveal that the board is not perceived to be working effectively as a team.

Table 4.2 *Managerial attitudes*

'I work in the . . . department. You won't know me, but you may have heard of the company.'

'We are being worked harder and harder.'

'Whatever I do, they will want the same again and more.'

'I have a vision. It's somewhere in my drawer.'

'My boss always wants it tomorrow. Why is speed so important?'

'I want to do well and be successful, but how?'

'I want to make an impact and be noticed.'

'It doesn't make sense, but if that's what they want I'll do it.'

'To get ahead you just use the words and slogans.'

'If they don't believe it, why should I?'

'The only vision around here is how to get more blood out of a stone.'

'Whatever I do I won't necessarily be any better off.'

'Others are earning more than me. Why?'

'If you query that your commitment is questioned.'

'I cannot afford to make a mistake, they come down on you like a ton of bricks.'

'To get on you need to give an impressive presentation.'

'I aim to keep on the right side of people and to fit in.'

'I would love to get it right but the procedures get in the way.'

'In this company, you've got to look after yourself.'

'People pinch your ideas.'

'I can't remember when anyone last said thank you.'

'I don't have time to think.'

'We don't know what the board are up to.'

'At the end of the day it is the ratios that count.'

Within any group there are likely to be some whose views have become affected by factors such as disappointment, unrealistic expectations or either unfair or unsound judgements. Too much should not be written into anecdotal evidence. However, the directors should be prepared to 'listen and learn'. A board needs to: (a) take a balanced view based upon the total sample and pattern of responses; and (b) distinguish between symptoms and underlying causes.

Directorial attitudes

Let us now turn to the attitudes of directors, and to what they might suggest about the relationship between managers and directors. A selection of directorial attitudes is given by way of illustration in Table 4.3.

The list of attitudes in Table 4.3. (unlike those in Table 4.2) intentionally mixes some that are positive, or 'help', and others that are negative, or 'hinder'. This is likely to be the case with most lists of attitudes expressed by the members of a typical board.

Relatively few boards undertake surveys of directorial attitudes. The views in Table 4.3 are extracted from a handful of such exercises undertaken by the author and hence represent a compilation. The pattern of directorial responses could reveal a group problem or that certain individuals are 'out of step' with colleagues, where the attitudes of one or more directors are distinct from those of the rest of the board.

It is sometimes possible to map where individual directors might be expected to stand on particular issues from what is known about their attitudes. Information concerning directorial attitudes should not be ostensibly obtained for one purpose and subsequently used for another.

Directors are sometimes more willing to express views and attitudes that could be construed as 'critical' or 'negative' when responses are collated by an independent third party and confidentiality is guaranteed. Where trust is forthcoming, its betrayal can make it difficult for a counselling or facilitation role to be sustained.

Acknowledging and confronting attitudes

Where members of a board appear to be exhibiting a managerial rather than a directorial approach to its business, it might be a good idea to list expressed attitudes, such as those in Table 4.3, and ask the board to: (a) identify which are 'helps' and which are 'hindrances' in relation to, say, improving quality and why; and then (b) assemble and prioritise those directorial attitudes thought most appropriate to closing the organisation's expectations and delivery gap.

Within some boards, directors tend to keep their relationships relatively formal and their attitudes to themselves. Where a board is reluctant

Table 4.3 *Directorial attitudes*

'We are held responsible for the company, but management let us down.'

'All the advice we had pointed in this direction.'

'We must get it right by next year.'

'They are an important group, but unreasonable.'

'The press are a pain, I just refuse to talk to them.'

'I like to use my experience for the benefit of others.'

'The status of being a director is important for me.'

'I want to feel that I'm genuinely making a contribution.'

'A great process, but what did we achieve?'

'We have made it clear, they just don't listen.'

'Financial stability helps me to be independent and objective.'

'At the end of the day what the chief executive says goes.'

'I'm here mainly because I'm a balanced person.'

'Life has given me a sense of perspective.'

'I'm not an expert but I keep things in proportion.'

'We don't always agree, but we respect each other's opinions.'

'You run your department and I'll run mine.'

'If you have to always prove yourself in the boardroom you shouldn't be there.'

'Being respected for honesty is more important than being liked.'

'At the end of the day what value do we add?'

'Perhaps our contribution is what we haven't done but could have done.'

'The organisation, its values and its processes are what we make of it.'

'I aim to be comfortable with a decision, otherwise why do it?'

'We really are committed, but they don't know or believe it.'

'Doing the right thing can sometimes be tough.'

'As a board, ultimately we stand or fall together.'

'We try to get to the heart of the matter but it is sometimes concealed by too much jargon and data.'

'Having all the reports makes you feel good, but I'm often none the wiser having read them.'

'I'm paid to think, not to sweat.'

'We have too much information, what we need is more understanding.'

'What I offer is judgement, but I could do with more opportunity to use it.'

to confront its own attitudes directly, it could be invited to consider the lists of attitudes presented in Tables 4.2 and 4.3, and how they might be used as the basis for an informal discussion of directorial attitudes in relation to a particular corporate programme. Questions could be posed along the lines of:

● Which of the managerial attitudes in Table 4.2 are likely to be, or could be, the fault of the board, and what could the board do about them?
● Which of the directorial attitudes in Table 4.3 are likely to be, or could be, the fault of: (a) an individual director; or (b) that of the board as a whole?
● Which of the directorial attitudes in Table 4.3 are likely to be, or could be, undesirable and which should be encouraged?
● What other attitudes are particularly desirable in directors?
● What are the top ten attitudes that would be possessed by a 'role model' director?

Once desirable directorial attitudes have been identified, the next step is to encourage the members of a board to examine both individually and collectively how closely their own attitudes match what is considered ideal. Deficiencies that are revealed can then be addressed by appropriate counselling and development support.

Why is there a corporate problem?

Each organisation should examine its own situation and the extent to which and why it has a problem with a particular corporate programme. Factors such as 'commitment' and 'attitudes' have already been highlighted, but there are likely to be others. It is important that all major problem areas are identified and categorised in a way that allows them to be addressed.

By way of an example, the results of one analysis are summarised in Figure 4.3. It was recognised that despite 'flexibility' and 'relevance' aspirations not all of the work produced, and as delivered, was meeting the customer's current business requirements at the time of delivery. Various explanations were given for this which suggested the following questions needed to be addressed:

● *Cultural*:
  – Does acceptance of the current levels of performance suggest a degree of complacency? Where is the evidence of tangible commitment to improvement action and role model behaviour to be found?
  – Is there an obsession with the 'bottom line' rather than with incremental and repeat business? Why is there not a greater incentive to raise and tackle problems?

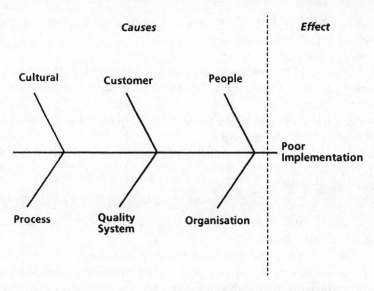

Figure 4.3   Why is there an implementation problem?

- *Customer*:
  – Given that customers may be uncertain and sometimes change their minds, why haven't the systems and processes been developed to cope with this?
  – Is there a need for more open and 'partnership' relationships with clients? Are individual projects being managed rather than the client relationship, or the whole portfolio of projects involving a particular client?
  – Why is it felt that customers are reluctant to pay for higher quality? Would clients pay more for extra quality if it could be delivered?
- *People*:
  – Why is it so difficult to identify the 'right person for the job'? Is the focus upon utilisation of staff rather than value added?
  – Is the recruitment and skill base too narrow in certain areas? What could be done to develop and broaden people?
  – Does the reward system stress technical excellence rather than customer focus? Is sufficient recognition given to effective project management?
- *Process*:
  – Is there an excessive focus upon internal procedures rather than an external customer focus?
  – Is there a trade-off between rigour and speed? If so, should this be discussed with the customer?
  – Why have internal company ways of doing things not kept pace with

changing external customer requirements? Why are process improvement projects not underway?

● *Quality system*:
   – Is the quality system project and organisation rather than client based? Should it embrace various customers and suppliers within the supply chain?
   – Does the emphasis upon technical quality increase the risk of over-elaborate or irrelevant work?
   – Why isn't the current approach to quality reaching people's 'hearts and minds'?

● *Organisation*:
   – Why is line ownership of corporate 'flexibility' and 'relevance' aspirations so limited? How might mutual understanding between line and staff roles be increased?
   – How could the dialogue with training be improved? Why are there no initiatives under way to equip those responsible for delivering corporate programmes with relevant tools?
   – Why when there is a desire to improve are more holistic and coordinated approaches not adopted?

To help prioritise the areas that need to be tackled, each of the factors identified could be taken and an assessment made of the extent to which a particular corporate initiative or drive has had a helpful or unhelpful impact upon the achievement of business objectives. Figure 4.4 is an example of a checklist that could be used to assess 'helps' and 'hinders' resulting from the impact of an organisation's current approaches upon its corporate objectives.

Striving for 'technical' excellence while at the same time meeting the growing demands of individual customers and satisfying a supplier's own commercial requirements puts a heavy burden upon the people of an organisation if it is thought these multiple objectives can be achieved by some simplistic solution such as 'cutting out waste' or 'working longer hours'. The keys to their achievement are more likely to be in areas such as changing attitudes and values, and introducing improved account and project management processes.

Introducing more holistic frameworks

The many questions raised by the analysis the above company has undertaken suggest it could benefit from adopting a broader approach to implementation that addresses each of the areas in Figure 4.3.

Solutions as well as problems can be interdependent. Thus, given that many customers are insecure and do not always know what they want,

Name of programme:	Helpful features	Unhelpful features
Corporate objective 1		
Corporate objective 2		
Corporate objective 3		
Corporate objective 4		

Figure 4.4 How your current approaches help or hinder corporate objectives

changes to account and project management processes could also aim to create opportunities to build closer relationships with customers.

Given the diversity of expectations and requirements of the various parties with an interest in quality, many approaches to quality are fragmented, incomplete and costly. Assessments vary as to the cost of enforcing quality systems and frameworks, but between 10 and 25 per cent of management time is not unusual. In spite of bearing costs of this order, these organisations are not free of mistakes. 'Screw ups' still occur, with quality assurance giving a 'clean bill of health' to activities that result in significant problems.

There is a need in many organisations for more holistic approaches that can get at and address the root causes of multiple problems. Some are responding more imaginatively than others. Thus a project-based organisation could bring a combination of elements together at critical points in the project management process. To introduce an element of independence and objectivity into the review process, use could be made of a peer review system or of specialists at overcoming certain problems. Such an approach could also facilitate organisational learning.

Organisational responses

An uncertain and turbulent decade could be good news for innovators. Attitudinal and behavioural barriers are often easier to confront in crisis situations. At Xerox, according to Vern Zelmer, Managing Director of Rank Xerox (UK), the crisis caused by the entry of a clutch of formidable Japanese competitors into the marketplace which 'the company thought it owned' was 'rather like hanging, it concentrated the mind.' As more boards accept that muddling through and hoping things will improve won't work, there is a greater willingness to consider 'blank sheets of paper solutions'.

British Airways, when building a new maintenance facility at Cardiff, took advantage of the 'greenfield' opportunity to begin with a new approach to working relationships and practices. People are regarded as 'company members' rather than 'staff', and are represented by a single union. Traditional and visible marks of status have been removed, demarcations between categories of skilled staff have been broken down, and everyone, even the managing director, has to spend some time working on the facility's central activity of aircraft maintenance. All non-core tasks have been subcontracted out.

The quality vision

It is usually difficult to take the 'big step' that could close a gap between quality expectation and quality delivery without a compelling vision of an alternative to the present situation. The lack of a 'clear vision' is inhibiting the implementation of more holistic and balanced total quality programmes. Interviewees in the *Quality: The Next Steps*[8] survey stressed the importance of a quality vision. The survey reveals that:

- Many organisations do not have a 'quality vision'. There is a lack of both a common understanding of what quality is, and a shared 'quality vision' of what it ought to be.
- In general, the 'quality message' is not being effectively communicated. Approaching three-quarters of respondents agree that 'quality too often consists of "motherhood" statements.'

We will consider the aspiration to establish more holistic and comprehensive approaches to quality in the next chapter. Let us conclude this chapter by reflecting upon the sort of quality vision that would portray a desirable and achievable future that would be demonstratively better than the present.

Reversing polarity

Quality should be the opposite of what it has become in many organisations. It should liberate rather than constrain, help rather than hinder. Quality has become a set of procedures and a portfolio of standards that constrict and prescribe.

The essence of quality should be freedom:

- Freedom to dream, aspire, build and create.
- Freedom to enter into mutually beneficial relationships.
- Freedom to do what is necessary to deliver value and satisfaction to customers.
- Freedom as a customer to seek new sources of benefit and value.
- Freedom to initiate debates, explore, question, challenge, innovate and learn.
- Freedom to understand one's self, be true to one's self, and to develop and build upon natural strengths.
- Freedom to work at a time, location and mode that best contributes to desired outputs.
- Freedom to use the most relevant technology, tools and processes depending upon what it is that needs to be done.
- Freedom to confront reality.
- Freedom to identify root causes and tackle obstacles and barriers.
- Freedom to learn according to one's individual learning potential.

The means to achieve all of these freedoms exist. The technical barriers have all but been removed. In the main all that is needed is to release the potential within ourselves. This is too often feared rather than encouraged.

An approach to quality could be designed to tackle threats and risks to these freedoms, and encourage and strengthen the relevant enablers. The various freedoms that are available to the different stakeholders in the enterprise should be set out in the form of a new contract or charter. The hard protective shell of the company should become an open arena of opportunity.

Checklist

Does your organisation have a corporate quality or re-engineering vision?

Is this communicated and shared?

What do people actually think about corporate goals, quality or re-engineering?

Is there a gap between rhetoric and reality?

Is it recognised? What is being done to bridge it?

Why the gulf between rhetoric and reality? A failure to address reality? The lure of appearance? The desire for speed? Naivety and innocence? Intolerance of diversity? A reluctance to question and learn?

Do managerial and directorial attitudes help or hinder?

Are attitudes and behaviours changing?

How would you describe where your organisation is with the implementation of corporate drives and initiatives?

Is there an 'official line'? How do your views compare with the official line?

Why are corporate change or transformation programmes not having more impact upon attitudes and behaviours? A failure of leadership? The lack of a holistic perspective? Missing change elements? A failure to identify and tackle obstacles and barriers?

Is the reality accepted? Is it being confronted or avoided?

What are the main barriers to quality, re-engineering and transformation?

Are they being energetically identified and tackled?

References

1. Charles Handy, *Beyond Certainty: The Changing World of Organisations*, London, Hutchinson, 1995.
2. Clive Holtham, 'Business Process Re-engineering – Contrasting What It Is with What It Is Not', in Colin Coulson-Thomas (ed), *Business Process Re-engineering: Myth and Reality*, London, Kogan Page, 1994.
3. Colin Coulson-Thomas, *Transforming the Company: Bridging the Gap Between Management Myth and Corporate Reality*, London, Kogan Page, 1992.
4. Colin Coulson-Thomas, *Creating the Global Company: Successful Internationalisation*, London, McGraw-Hill, 1992.
5. Colin Coulson-Thomas, *Creating Excellence in the Boardroom*, London, McGraw-Hill, 1993.
6. Clive Irving, *Wide-Body: The Making of the 747*, London, Hodder & Stoughton, 1993.
7. John Humble and Alan Thompson, *Corporate Values: The Bottom Line Contribution*, Management Council and Digital Equipment Company, 1993.
8. Colin and Susan Coulson-Thomas, *Quality: The Next Steps*, an Adaptation Ltd survey for ODI, London, Adaptation Ltd, 1991; executive summary available from ODI Europe, 1991.

5

Priorities and aspirations

Depend on the moonlight or light a lamp.

A few companies are swept along by favourable circumstances to desired destinations but most encounter pitfalls and obstacles in their path and need to concentrate on the way ahead. They chose to light lamps rather than rely upon the moonlight.

Just as there are almost as many views of what quality is as there are organisations, so each of these entities will have its own priorities and pre-occupations. The aim may be general such as 'improve customer focus', 'capitalise upon the energies of people' or 'enhance competitiveness' or it could be slightly more specific, for example to 'reduce the cost base', 'simplify the business' or 'reduce time to market'.

Many BPR exercises are concerned with cost and headcount reduction and speeding up response times, often to the exclusion of just about everything else and with a blind eye to the consequences. Quality, re-engineering and other corporate programmes should be reassessed in relation to contemporary aspirations and aims. One former quality director confided: 'What usually triggers a reassessment is a key issue or big development. With us nothing triggered one until it was too late.'

Situations change. For some organisations, obtaining a quality kitemark acted as a catalyst for adopting quality. But after the celebration associated with getting it, what's new and what next? Andrew Given, Financial Director of Logica plc, believes: 'ISO 9000 is like passing your driving test: it means you know the rules of the road, but it doesn't mean you drive well everywhere, all the time.'

Others seek to become more effective in their use of resources. A focus upon cost and efficiency may be a necessary, but not sufficient, condition for improved productivity. The Norwegian company Kvaerner has become Europe's largest shipbuilder with yards in Germany, Finland,

Norway and Scotland. The company takes a holistic and long-term approach to productivity improvement that amounts to a transformation of attitudes and practices as well as of processes and organisation.

One reason for reassessment is growing recognition of the resistance of attitudes and behaviours to change. As one chief executive officer (CEO) put it: 'Quality has become too much of an "external thing", posters on the walls and people meeting in groups. It is what happens inside us that counts.' What is needed are quality feelings, quality attitudes and a quality perspective.

Symbols and substance

There is much articulating and flaunting of the symbols and language of quality rather than feeling or being it. Perhaps the 'real' role of certain programmes is to provide a vehicle through which individuals and groups can visibly demonstrate commitment to the corporate club. In most organisations there is already an excessive bias towards public activity, almost for the sake of it.

Perhaps the substance of quality is now no longer needed because quality has 'done its job' and need only live on in symbolic form. The 1990 survey report *Beyond Quality*[1] suggests that traditional quality is no longer a priority area for many CEOs. The report was based upon a questionnaire and interview survey of 100 organisations employing over two million people. It suggested that:

- Customers were increasingly assuming quality and reliability at a time when many 'early' corporate quality programmes appeared to be 'running out of steam'. Many companies have created a gap between customer expectation and their ability to 'deliver'. 'Quality' has also increased the bargaining power of customers.
- Quality of itself may no longer differentiate between alternative suppliers. Many CEOs were looking beyond 'traditional', 'internal' and 'product' quality, and towards the need to empathise with attitudes and values, use less tangible factors such as 'look or feel' to 'distinguish' or differentiate, and improve the quality of external supply chain relationships.

A study of the sources of success of 100 of the best UK companies suggests that as a strategy for competitive advantage quality is more of a 'qualifier' than a 'differentiator'.[2] 'Quality' was the most cited 'qualifier', but the list of differentiating factors was headed by 'innovative product'.

Qualifiers should not be taken for granted. Howard Davies, while Director General of the Confederation of British Industry, pointed out: 'A reputation for poor quality is harder to lose than one for good quality is to acquire.'

Questions to be addressed

Questions raised by *Beyond Quality* interviewees included: 'How does quality break out of the procedural ghetto and into the world of real people?' and 'What about the quality of information and understanding?' In spite of the concerns, the 1990 survey[1] revealed that quality was still felt to be important. 'Customer satisfaction' and 'quality' were ranked as the top two 'customer issues'. Nine out of ten of the participants in the survey considered them to be 'very important'.

'How to change' is the issue rather than 'whether to change'. The *Beyond Quality* report suggested some specific questions concerning quality that need to be addressed:

- Quality may be a necessary condition for success, but is it of itself sufficient? Do companies need to move beyond quality?
- Is a new approach to quality needed, or greater commitment to a broader concept of total quality?
- Is implementation the issue? What are the 'quality barriers' that are being encountered, and what needs to be done about them? What are the quality priorities?

In some organisations these issues and questions have been addressed, while in others they remain to be put onto the agenda. Recently, the author revisited some of the survey interviewees to assess what has changed in five years. If anything, the underlying concerns have become more pronounced. The main differences which emerged were the evident 'discovery' of BPR and the growing realisation that the interests of investors, the customer and organisations themselves have often been pursued to such an extent that those of employees have suffered.

BPR: a new star in the management firmament?

Evidence suggests the phenomenon of BPR may have compounded rather than resolved problems.[3] Common drivers of BPR include headcount and cost reduction rather than 'value to customers', and in this it matches recent preoccupations. However, a 'negative' focus upon cost-cutting or 'squeezing more out of people' is causing widespread alienation. Employees are too often victims rather than beneficiaries.

In the last chapter we saw that many companies are trapped in a vicious cycle of descent towards commodity supplier status. The employment of a more powerful technique such as BPR can speed up progress along this path.

To break out of the 'commodity supplier trap' we need to establish the sort of virtuous spiral shown in Figure 5.1. The longer-term view and a focus upon satisfying the external customer and the building of capability,

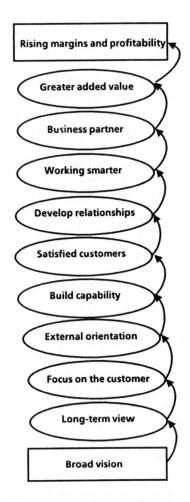

Figure 5.1 The virtuous spiral

especially in terms of developing relationships and 'working smarter', is the route to establishing the partnerships that result in greater added value and rising margins and profitability.

In itself, BPR is a neutral instrument. We determine whether it turns out to be a 'help' or a 'hinder'. Whether or not BPR is of central or marginal importance will depend upon what it is applied to, how it is used and the goals that are set.[3]

More 'positive' BPR goals are called for. Improving learning or the quality of working life are key drivers of far too few BPR initiatives. For example, BPR could enable us to obtain far greater control over our lives. Existing approaches to BPR could be complemented and supplemented to help ensure that issues and opportunities relating to new patterns of working and learning are taken more fully into account during the course of BPR exercises.[4]

Management priorities

Let us now turn our attention to what management priorities ought to be. The participants in the *Quality: The Next Steps*[5] survey were asked to indicate the priority they felt would be placed upon certain areas of quality over the next five years. The overall ranking of priorities in terms of 'higher priority' replies is given in Table 5.1.

The responses reflect concerns that have been expressed about skills and attitudes. 'Quality of management' was considered to be the area of highest priority demanding increased attention (Table 5.1). Over eight out of ten of the respondents expected 'quality of management' and 'quality behaviour, attitudes and values' to be given a 'higher priority'. We saw in the last chapter that the root causes of many barriers to progress lie in managerial and directorial attitudes.

Those interviewed considered 'quality of management' to be a responsibility of the board. Reference was made to personal qualities such as 'adaptability', 'attitudes', 'awareness', 'sensitivity', 'perspective', 'empathy', etc, rather than technical skills when discussing how the 'quality of management' might be improved. Several interviewees made the point that 'skills training' *per se* might not lead to improved customer satisfaction in companies that are not able to: (a) identify the priority tasks that added value for customers; or (b) empower and motivate their employees to act.

Management attention tends to be applied to those things that can be

Table 5.1 *Quality priorities (ranked in order of 'higher priority' replies)*

Quality of management	85%
Quality behaviour, attitudes and values	81%
Vendor/supplier quality	73%
External customers	73%
Technical quality of products and services	65%
Quality of information	63%
Environmental quality	63%
Quality implementation/change processes	61%
Quality strategy	60%
Internal customers	60%
Quality of understanding	58%
Incremental quality improvements	56%
Speed of corporate action in response to challenges and opportunities	54%
Quality along value chains	50%
Fundamental quality steps	46%

Source: *Quality: The Next Steps*, 1991.[5]

easily measured on the grounds that: 'If you can't measure it, you can't control it.' There is a continuing reluctance to come to terms with subjective but important areas such as the quality of information, and all too rarely are attitudes and values mapped.

Users of information often have opinions on what is important to them in terms of such factors as accuracy, timeliness or consistency. They may also have strong views on trade-offs, perhaps preferring a quick 'ball park' response to the authoritative and detailed report that arrives too late. Avoidance of the unfamiliar often results in opportunities to improve relevance being missed.

In an unrelated survey of CEOs the 'quality of management' emerged as the key determinant of corporate success. Over eight out of ten considered it 'most important', compared with 15 per cent for 'quality of products' and 2 per cent for 'quality of marketing'.[6]

Quality of management

What is 'quality of management'? Some further clues as to what is meant by the 'quality of management' emerge from the BIM's *Flat Organisation* survey.[7] Participants were asked to rank in importance the management qualities which will enable organisations to implement the changes that are desired in order to respond more effectively to challenges and opportunities within the business environment. When these were ranked in order of 'very important' replies, the 'ability to communicate' came top. Two-thirds of the respondents considered it to be 'very important'. Next in order of 'very important' replies came 'flexibility', 'adaptability' and 'the ability to handle uncertainty and surprise'.

Quality of attitudes, approach, principles, values and conduct in public and business life have become a topic of debate in societies as far apart as Italy and Japan, and are likely to rise in corporate priorities. Some companies already make them explicit:

- The chairman of Banco Bilbao Vizcaya, Emilio Ybarra, has publicly committed the bank to 'professional ethics', the 'scrupulous observance of ethical standards', and to becoming 'a leader in these aspects'.
- In the BBV Group 'Style Code' which covers 'all relationships with staff, customers and shareholders', principles are ranked first and ahead of missions and values.

There are those who view questions of morality and social responsibility as 'vague and woolly'. Milton Friedman has argued that a board best discharges its 'social responsibility' by ensuring the company satisfies its customers in voluntary exchanges in the marketplace,[8] while Albert Carr has raised the question of whether a corporate conscience can be afforded.[9]

Even a narrow focus upon satisfying investors can benefit from supportive values. A statement of values for Cadbury Schweppes drafted by Sir Adrian Cadbury links quality with integrity:

> The key characteristic we aim for in every aspect of the company's activities is quality ... We must always be searching to improve quality and to add measurable value to the goods and services we market. But quality applies to people and to relationships, as well as to our working lives. We should set high standards and expect to be judged by them. The quality we aim for in all our dealings is that of integrity; the word integrity means straight dealing but it also means completeness. Both meanings are relevant in this context, because the quality standard cannot be applied in part; it must be consistently applied to everything which bears the Company's name.[10]

Quality of management does not just occur as we will see in Chapter 9. For Rank Xerox:

> The most sustainable competitive edge for any company is the quality of its management. Quality of management is the practice of developing competitive advantage by making the most effective use of a company's most valuable asset – its management – through the implementation of the most appropriate methods and structures to support the business.

Quality of direction

Another related question is that of quality in the boardroom, the value added by the board. The distinction between direction and management and the building of more competent directors and more effective boards is the subject of two other books by the author.[11,12]

Returning to the questions of directorial attitudes and top management commitment which emerged in the last chapter as significant barriers to quality:

> If a company had a heart or a soul it would be found in the boardroom. Intelligence and strength might be discovered in greater measure elsewhere within the corporate organisation, but whether or not the company will live and grow, or wither and die, will depend upon the purpose established by the board. It will depend upon the values, the sense of will to generate customer satisfaction, and the drive to achieve excellence and quality that emanates from the board.
>
> The vision, which is the essence of the purpose of the company, is articulated by the board. It is communicated by the directors, and will influence attitudes and behaviours to the extent that the board is visibly committed to its achievement.
>
> If commitment is lacking in the boardroom, or if there are divisions among the boardroom team, this is likely to be detected elsewhere. A company can be cramped and stunted by a lack of vision among members of the board.[13]

The author has concluded:

> Most boards face the daunting challenge of turning aspiration into achievement, and in the context of a turbulent and demanding business environment. The key to success is to ensure that: (i) the board is united, committed, and focused; (ii) 'every element of the corporate transformation jigsaw puzzle is in place'; and (iii) the 'vital few' actions are in place to tackle the major barriers to the attainment of a shared corporate vision.[11]

Boards should be challenged on the questions of their attitudes, priorities and commitment.

Quality in relation to other priorities

Quality should not exist in a vacuum. While quality of itself may not be enough to achieve the degree of impact that is sought, it may form a useful element of a broader approach to change. Thus Scania Trucks and Buses has initiated a long-term action programme of which quality is one of four key elements, the others being efficiency, work organisation and wage structures. The company's use of quality is to complement and support the delegation of responsibility and associated building of capability.

Although product quality may be assumed it should never be taken for granted, especially, as we have seen, because standards and expectations can rise. Product quality may be immediately visible. In the case of the broadcast media it has to be renewed and maintained every second of air time.

In 1991 the Swedish packaging company ASSI Karlsborg received its ISO 9001 certification. In the same year, the company established the guidelines for a broader approach to quality to encourage 'all departments within the company' to 'propose quality-improving measures within their particular areas'. The hope was that the initiative would 'engage all employees in improving company performance'.

Alain Levy, President of music producer and publisher PolyGram, believes: 'As in everything, there is a yardstick of quality in entertainment, and PolyGram aims for all-round excellence – of product, marketing, delivery and performance.' More and more companies are developing 'business excellence' frameworks that embrace all the elements needed to deliver certain sets of objectives, in place of reliance upon a single panacea.

One interviewee likened management priorities to 'chinese boxes', while another talked of concentric circles. By this they mean that one priority can exist within another. For example, within an environmental quality programme one could find an initiative to secure ISO 9000 accreditation of an environmental testing process.

Selection of corporate priorities

Prior to taking 'next steps', it is important to both understand and be sensitive to the situation that you are in. Claes Dahlback, President of the Swedish industrial holding company Investor, believes 'conditions are an unavoidable ingredient in all business. The "stars have to be right".'

A dilemma for many companies is how long to wait for 'it to come right' or for 'benefits to appear'. Rank Xerox lists 'controlled patience' alongside top management commitment, employee involvement, pervasiveness and process orientation as the keys to successful quality implementation. In terms of its own experience, the company has concluded: 'We were a little too patient.' While premature action should be avoided, nettles need to be grasped.

A matrix along the lines of Figure 5.2 could be used to rank priorities in terms of factors that are judged to be particularly significant in the context in question. Thus in the example shown the management team desires to make a visible impact in a relatively short period of time.

A priority could lie outside the formal boundary of the corporate organisation. For SCPA, within France's Groupe EMC, 'quality programmes have

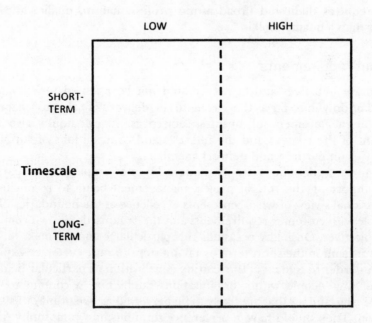

Degree of Visible Impact

Figure 5.2 Selection of management priorities

focused on adapting suppliers' quality systems to the ISO 9002 "model for quality assurance in manufacturing".' The first priority was to 'set goals for quality-procedure certification for selected product lines, initially with ... two main suppliers.'

Next steps should address both strategic and tactical issues. A company has to deliver its business objectives from one year to the next, while at the same time concentrating upon the achievement of longer-term goals. While he was chairman of BP, Robert Horton pointed out that: 'The distinction between my role as Chief Executive Officer and that of David Simon as Chief Operating Officer recognises that BP's performance needs to be considered against different timescales.'

Business acumen is required to identify which combination of complementary factors, when subjected to management attention, might lead to success. Thus in North America, Essroc's performance improvements in the cement business required traditional quality control, but also specific actions in the areas of industrial processes, truck fleet management, and product line extension. Action areas are often interdependent, progress in one field requiring the support of developments elsewhere.

According to Chairman André Rousselet and CEO Pierre Lescure, CANAL+: 'is constantly seeking to optimise its core business both by constantly striving to improve the quality of programming, as a key differentiating factor, and by setting new standards of customer satisfaction, leading to renewal rates far above the average for the pay-TV industry.' This requires dedicated broadcasting professionalism, quality attitudes rather than a quality toolkit.

Output requirements

Corporate initiatives and activity should not be pursued for their own sake, but only in so far as they relate to the delivery of value to customers and the achievement of business objectives. They should also take account of the context and the interests and contributions of suppliers, supply chain partners and network members.

Figure 5.3 identifies outputs thought by one company to be particularly important, the role of project management being to reconcile the professional's view of what represents excellence at the boundaries of the possible with customer requirements and the organisation's own commercial objectives. On many occasions this particular company makes its life more difficult in the short term by taking steps to raise customer expectations in order to remain at the 'cutting edge' within its particular field.

Thinking people within organisations ought not to commit to 'cosmetic' programmes that are likely to be perceived as irrelevant or as a distraction. They should have a preference for a business philosophy that is shared rather than imposed, allows a flexible response according to the

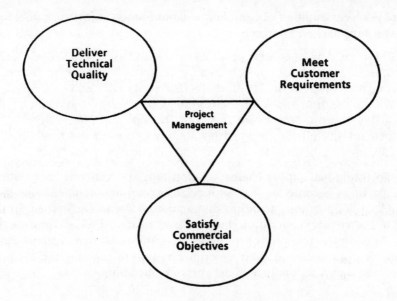

Figure 5.3   Output requirements

local situation and circumstances, and which has been thought through in terms of its application within a particular corporate context.

Eberhard v. Kuenheim, Chairman of the Board of Management of BMW, acknowledges that after a period of recession: 'We had to stop talking in generalisations and, thus, in over-simplifications of our sector of industry. It is no longer possible to generalise about "the industry" or individual regions. The picture is now far more complex ... It was always superficial to talk about "the" American, "the" Japanese or "the" European car industry.'

According to Kuenheim: 'The quest for panaceas, which in any case was doomed to failure, has ended. Strategies that proved successful in one country, or for one company, cannot be imposed upon another ... In this situation, each company must define, and then hold to, its own way.'

Within the European Union small and medium-sized enterprises have been identified as 'the key sector for generating employment opportunities and growth'.[14] Collectively they employ some 60 million people, or seven out of ten of those employed. For the small company the fixed cost of securing and maintaining a recognised quality registration can represent a competitive burden. Some larger organisations are not sensitive to the problems which their standard and 'big company' approaches can cause.

Within certain companies and sectors, the management perspective already embraces the supply chain. For example, in the motor industry there is a long tradition of a division of labour among a network of collaborating suppliers and partners:

- BMW has developed new products on a joint basis for many years, and expects its suppliers to take increasing responsibility for their distinctive contribution to the quality of what is delivered to the 'end customer'.
- Within the framework of their strategic cooperation agreement, the quality control programmes of both Renault and Volvo were being 'structured similarly', and in 1992 an announcement was made that: 'A joint organization will be set up to deal with quality-control matters.'

Within traditional supply chains, relationships are relatively long lasting. The partners become familiar with relative roles and contributions, and have some opportunity to adjust and accommodate to each other. In the age of the virtual corporation, linkages and relationships are more fleeting. Already its champions are questioning the relevance of many management approaches to their emerging requirements and the shifting, diverse and transient nature of network membership.

Changing quality perspectives

We have seen in earlier chapters that perspectives on quality are changing (Table 5.2), and this will have an impact upon relative priorities.[15] In particular, more emphasis is being placed upon relationships, joint action with network partners and supply chain quality.

Supply chain and network partners may be sufficiently interdependent to stand or fall together. Thus a drive by a company such as Volkswagen to reduce costs has a very significant impact upon Robert Bosch and other automotive industry suppliers. In the early 1990s Bosch reduced its labour force by between five and ten thousand per annum as a result of problems experienced by its supply chain customers.

A broader view of quality creates new partnerships with shared interests.

Table 5.2 *Changing quality perspective*

Old	New
Product quality	Quality attitudes and values
Quality as distinct programme	Quality as integral process
Use of statistical tools	Focus on relationships
Quality as a cost	Quality as an investment
Quality a choice	Quality essential
Achieve quality standard	Move beyond quality to business excellence
Corporate focus	Supply chain focus

Source: *Transforming the Company*, 1992.[15]

For example, both insurance companies and their clients have a joint interest in reducing the risk of harm to customers or the environment. Biotechnology and cosmetics company Elf Sanofi sees itself as 'a company working for life'. Its global strategy is 'in the service of life'.

For some companies the achievement of world-class levels of performance and productivity may require adjustment on a massive scale. Data General halved its workforce over a five-year period. BT has worked on a single programme to reduce its core staff by some 70,000 people. A similar reduction has already been achieved over a similar timescale. This is change on a massive scale that is being actioned at the same time as a drive to enhance quality and customer service.

With change occurring on the scale of that in BT, it is not surprising that participants in the *Quality: The Next Steps* survey[5] put such stress upon 'adaptability', 'empathy' and 'sensitivity'. Various surveys undertaken by the author and others since the late 1980s (eg for BIM[16]) have consistently shown the creation of a flexible and responsive organisation to be the 'number one' human resource issue.[15]

While greater openness, flexibility and willingness to change have been advocated for a decade in larger organisations, re-engineering, restructuring and delayering have put people on to the defensive. They are often more inclined to batten down the hatches than to break out. Rosabeth Moss Kanter's theme that giant corporations are not supple or nimble is still valid.[17] Yet in places the spirit could still be alive. Once we cut through their thick hides, we may find potential cheetahs and gazelles waiting to be set free.

Sadly, the short-term actions taken by many boards in times of economic adversity are not encouraging the longer-term shifts of attitude needed to achieve the flexibility that is desired.[15] Many people are becoming more wary rather than more open. They are turning off and inward, withdrawing into their shells.

Those who manage need to become more aware of the longer-term implications of today's trade-offs. For example, the approaches being used to bond today's workgroups and build closely knit teams may need modification to cope with tomorrow's members of the virtual corporation or network organisation who may be widely scattered, and many of whom may work as independent contractors. The replacement of relatively homogeneous, permanent and contiguous groups with changing networks and communities of diverse and diffuse individuals raises new management challenges.

The individual and the team

An emerging priority is the achievement of a balance between the individual and the team. According to Dr Edouard Sakiz, chairman and CEO of the French healthcare company Roussel Uclaf: 'An enterprise is a group of people, who individually assume responsibility and take the initiative, but nonetheless act as one, working within an overall corporate plan rooted in values and goals.'

In the case of the Swiss Roche Group, a twin-track strategy has been adopted of simultaneously seeking to give individuals greater scope for initiative, while at the same time encouraging greater horizontal cooperation. Thus 'one of the goals of divisionalising and decentralising' has been 'the creation of flatter, more open hierarchies which encourage the delegation of responsibility and help mobilise the initiative, performance and professional competence of all employees'.

Roche recognises that 'these changes have created new opportunities for entrepreneurial attitudes and personal initiatives at all corporate levels. As a result appropriate, function-related staff training and development have assumed even greater importance.'

At the same time, the company acknowledges that: 'Two heads are better than one ... Success takes teamwork at the departmental level, between disciplines and across national boundaries. Each and every one of us has an important contribution to make. It is only by pulling together that we can get all the different jobs we do at Roche into a single dynamic effort.'

The individual and the organisation

Another priority is to reconcile the individual with the organisation. For example, companies need to achieve both economies of scale and operate on a human scale. Means of obtaining this vary, but the extent of achievement appears to reflect management focus and commitment rather than technology factors:

- In the food processing sector, the Ochsenfurt plant of Gervais Danone, a German subsidiary of the French company BSN, a flexible workshop approach to production has been adopted. This unit 'is capable of handling small production runs on an economically viable basis, since different products can be produced by the same machines.'
- Asea Brown Boveri's approach to decentralisation and the flattening of the organisation has resulted in no fewer than some 5,000 profit centres. Percy Barnevik, President and CEO, explains: 'The Group's seemingly "contradictory" structure of being big and small, global and local, all at the same time, is now well established and has proven to be successful in a highly competitive marketplace ... People in our many small units live closer to the customer, are more sensitive to customer needs, and are faster in decision making.'

The application of BPR can shift power away from individuals and back to the corporation. Boards are undertaking BPR exercises in order to reassert managerial and directorial control and drive through objectives such as cost reduction and 'downsizing', the purposes of which are being perceived as primarily beneficial to organisations rather than to the individuals who work within them.[3]

Relationships

Survey evidence suggests that a higher priority is being given to the quality of relationships within the supply chain and between the members of the network organisation.[5] John Kay has expressed the view that corporate success depends very much upon the structure of a company's relationships with employees, customers and suppliers, and that these need to be sustained if there is to be a flexible and cooperative response to change.[18]

Achieving supply chain quality can be a formidable undertaking, especially for those struggling to introduce the concept into their own organisation. IBM has over 20,000 business partners, and their combined activities represent approaching a half of the corporation's turnover. The challenge for IBM is to learn from rather than dominate such a large number of partners many of which are minute in comparison with its own size, and yet in their creativity, enterprise, imagination, approaches and understanding they might hold the keys to the corporation's future.

Recognising the need for supply chain quality does not of itself bring it about. BMW enters into long-term contracts with its suppliers at an early stage in product development in order to create a framework within which cooperation, the sharing of know-how and the development of joint approaches and procedures is encouraged. Supply chain partners are able to plan ahead, and a shared vision, the open exchange of knowledge and the interlinking of systems allow a more integrated and flexible production chain to be established.

Building closer relationships with other supply chain members can be demanding of management time. Hence companies such as ABB are linking a drive for a greater depth of cooperation with a rationalisation of suppliers. Percy Barnevik, President and CEO of ABB, believes the two are linked: 'As we reduce the number of our suppliers and increase volume per supplier, we work more closely with them to optimise the whole chain from supplier to customer.'

Supply chain relationships are not the only ones that need to be addressed. The importance of satisfactory relationships with other stakeholders has been stressed by Dhanin Chearavanont, Chairman of the C P Pokphand Co Ltd which operates in China, Thailand, Indonesia, Turkey and Hong Kong:

> It is one of our business philosophies that our activities must not only contribute to the Group's profit but also seek to improve the living standards in

the economies in which we operate and to foster businesses complementary to our own. This will remain central to all our business plans, for it is through this philosophy that we believe we can establish steady and mutually profitable relationships in the areas in which we operate and can contribute to the long-term success of these societies.[19]

Preoccupation with internal 'results', change and quality implementation sometimes 'crowds out' less apparent and tangible activities such as external relationships. Many managers will need to change their attitudes and approaches in order to build relationships with new publics.

Environmental Impact

Public and governmental concerns about environmental quality give rise to significant new areas of business opportunity. While the 'knee jerk' reaction may be to send in the lobbyists to protect a position, more consideration allows business development options to be identified. For some the 'environment' is a public relations opportunity, for others it is a source of longer-term inspiration:

- Anders Scharp and Leif Johansson of Electrolux view environmental issues as potential opportunities. They: 'regard environmental activities as a long-term requirement for survival and as a tool for additional improvement of our positions.'
- The Japanese company Toray Industries invests heavily in environmental initiatives and sees 'promoting business activities and contributing to society as two sides of the same coin.'
- For Heinz Schimmelbusch, Chairman of the Executive Board of Metallgescellschaft AG, growing environmental concerns have become significant commercial opportunities: 'Our pro-environment services ... have become a central core of our business activities.'

Many major companies appear to stress the importance of both quality of service and environmental quality. For example, Rodolphe Greif, Chairman of the Executive Board of Groupe EMC, believes his group: 'will pay special attention to problems of quality and environmental protection.'

Carlsberg's environmental perspective embraces both the working environment and the external physical environment, and various programmes are undertaken to improve the quality of both. For a company such as Statoil environmental protection and health and safety are more important than quality *per se*.

The environment represents an arena in which crises can occur. If managers are to make a contribution to protecting the environment they will have to focus more upon the external physical environment. Paradoxically, in view of the statistical and engineering origins of quality, there are many quality professionals who ought to be more at home operating in a scientific or systems environment, for example assessing the risks of pollution, than they might be expected to be when focusing internally upon attitude change. However, for significant changes in environmental quality to occur changes in the attitudes, perceptions and values of the stakeholders of many companies will be required.

As a producer of building materials the French company Lafarge Coppée is placing increasing importance upon quality of the environment. Chairman and CEO, Bertrand Collomb, recognises that 'to be truly effective, we will have to broaden our technical expertise and develop relationships with all parties concerned – local people and their elected representatives, government departments, international associations, and so on.'

Mutually rewarding relationships

The focus of management thinking and strategy should be upon creating the conditions that will allow mutually beneficial and rewarding relationships to occur. If the benefits of relationships accrue disproportionately to one party they are unlikely to last. Relative strengths within supply chains can change over time, a dramatic example being the relationship of IBM with Microsoft and Intel.

Not only must the customer benefit, but the people of the organisation should be encouraged and enabled to be true to themselves. Customers should be satisfied, and employees and business partners fulfilled. People, and the members of network communities, should be allowed to play to their strengths.

Many management teams are putting such effort into defining and communicating their core values and beliefs that they forget that other people and organisations have values and beliefs as well. The French bank BFCE believes that 'it is quality service that wins client loyalty, and increases market share' and is dedicated to 'quality, security, speed and clarity'. While BFCE wishes to share its values, ambitions and successes, it also recognises the importance of 'making our clients' values our own.'

People and organisations are held together by the values they share. Michel Freyche, the bank's Chairman, explains that BFCE has 'concentrated on promoting the values we share with our customers, with a view to shaping our future development.'

Shared values are a natural complement of free markets. Voluntary and mutually rewarding exchanges are possible when competition is free and fair. Such transactions are unlikely to occur when one party is in a protected or advantageous position *vis-à-vis* the other unless values prevent capitalising upon the opportunity to exploit.

Board members should be in the business of facilitating and supporting patterns and networks of relationships that deliver benefits to the various stakeholders in an enterprise. A holistic view of management should embrace all the elements that enable relationships to be more rewarding and productive.

To improve the outcomes of relationships, interactions and games, the attributes, motivations and requirements of the various players and participants need to be understood. Senior management may have the power to decide who participates and plays, or when someone is ready to participate and play. This is a considerable responsibility as it embraces both actual and potential participants.

Allowing someone who is not equipped, motivated and enabled to play to the expected standard to participate in a network, community or relationship can reduce the benefits of participation to other players. At the same time, someone with the potential to both participate and contribute should not be unfairly or unreasonably excluded.

Incremental or radical approaches?

So what needs to be done to set priorities? First, one must determine the extent to which an existing corporate approach can be improved, or whether a new or more comprehensive approach is needed. For example, if a review results in the conclusion that 'quality' has 'had its day', quality in a form that has clearly proved inadequate and ineffective should be laid to rest. A 'blue skies' approach should be adopted.

An improvement strategy could be perfectly valid in a particular context. For example, one company's priorities were to maintain its quality registration at minimum cost, while maximising 'delivered' quality to customers and encouraging thinking and learning in order to adapt and survive (see Figure 5.4). A range of suggestions were made for improving the current quality system. These included actions to:

- articulate a broader vision and goals that embrace learning and the supply chain;
- establish measurable learning and capability development objectives;
- put a higher priority upon attitudes, approaches, relationships and new ways of working and learning;
- develop a learning toolkit and promote the use of root cause and help and hindrance analyses, problem-solving techniques, visioning and other tools;
- develop an integrated project management approach and support environment focused upon risk reduction and shared learning.

Many corporate programmes employ the surface trappings of activities without embracing underlying attitudes and values. 'Western' companies

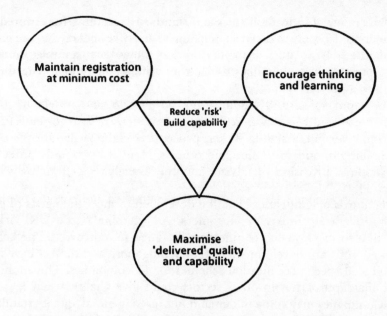

Figure 5.4 Quality and learning system requirements

sometimes misinterpret Japanese experience by failing to distinguish between symptoms or outcomes and root causes.[20] More stress may need to be put upon identifying the root causes of obstacles, pitfalls and barriers.

In many organisations people do not appear to be equipped with the tools that would enable them to make a significant improvement in their performance. Advice on the relevance of learning, diagnostic and problem-solving tools and alternative approaches to particular projects and tasks would be welcome.

Central staff teams are often hesitant to undertake a fundamental review of their own operation. If they were hived off or became a profit centre, and business units were able to seek equivalent services outside of the corporation, many head office quality teams would not survive the competitive challenge.

Improving or junking rules and standards

In the light of new priorities a current portfolio of rules and standards may be viewed as a constraint. In a world of diversity, empowerment, supply chains, restructuring, downsizing, process redesign and new patterns of work they may need to be abandoned or consolidated, rationalised and simplified.

The review of individual rules and standards and the areas covered by them should be undertaken in relation to the whole. Are the essentials highlighted? How much flexibility do they allow? For example, do they recognise that it is sometimes difficult to write a quality plan before getting into a project?

For rapid access and guidance on 'how to do' and 'where to find', greater use could be made in many organisations of a 'front end' to an electronic version of standards and procedures and a facility for the electronic filing of documentation and reports. Many users would appreciate the 'hotline' provision of advice, and the availability of training when required.

Standards or guidelines could be developed to meet the needs of particular sectors, contexts or customers. An example is the UK TickIT award, a form of quality certification designed to improve the processes used for software development. Sweden, Singapore and the US have also introduced special certification schemes for IT companies. The adoption of similar approaches in other sectors could give quality a new lease of life. Companies may come to demand not just a 'general' quality standard from their suppliers, but a form of certification that is perceived as relevant and appropriate to the business they are in.

New specialisms

In time, distinct areas of quality specialisation could well emerge, each with their professionals, consultants, measures, approaches, literature and standards. The field of environmental quality has already emerged as a distinct arena for practitioners and experts.

Pearson, with interests spanning newspapers, books, entertainment, oil services, investment banking and fine china, aims to 'build environmental considerations into all relevant decisions'. All Pearson-owned businesses conduct environmental audits and are required to implement a wide-ranging group policy which recognises the need to establish appropriate measures, maintain records and 'provide training where necessary on environmental matters' if objectives are to be achieved.

Opportunities can also be translated into problems through inappropriate responses. In time, a creeping bureaucratisation and proceduralisation of priority areas like environmental quality could occur. Already companies are having to plan for the EC Eco-Management and Audit Regulation, and standards such as the UK's BS 7750 which requires companies to have an environmental policy including a commitment to continual improvement of environmental performance and to establish management systems to assure policy is met. This is good news for tickers and checkers. Concerns about relevance and cost, awarding bodies and the 'threat' of being excluded from tender shortlists may spread to a family of specialist quality certificates.

Business excellence

A business excellence model can provide an agreed process for regularly reviewing priorities in relation to those factors thought critical for business success. The most successful companies appear to be those that adopt a holistic approach that embraces all the areas that need to be addressed to both satisfy current stakeholders and ensure continuing viability. They identify and overcome the major barriers to 'making it happen' in the context of their own situation and circumstances. For larger companies, this requires a high degree of integration between long-term transformation goals and medium-term business planning.

To illustrate the range of priorities that may need to be taken into account by a board intent upon corporate transformation, let us examine what can be learned from the experience of Rank Xerox (and its parent Xerox) whose approach is outlined in the author's book *Transforming the Company*.[15] The company's comprehensive business excellence model contained no fewer than 45 discrete elements ranging from tools and techniques to the encouragement of values such as integrity, openness and trust.

The Rank Xerox approach embraces a clear, compelling, articulated and shared vision that is rooted in customer value and requirements and supported by top management commitment and role model behaviour. The company recognises that 'good financials' result from 'customer satisfaction' and 'employee involvement and satisfaction'. Go straight for the 'financials' and they can prove as elusive as the end of a rainbow.

Fact-based management, supportive reward and remuneration, policy deployment, empowerment, self-managed teams and benchmarking are all practised within Rank Xerox. New approaches to working and learning have also been tried, and training programmes are in place to equip people to work and learn in new ways. However, the company's experience as an early champion of teleworking illustrates that pioneers, just as much as laggards, need to continually assess where they are in order to ensure they remain up to date.[4]

The achievement of 'network' or supply chain quality demands closer and partnership relationships between internal departments and external organisations. At the local level, Rank Xerox staff in former functions such as sales, service and administration now work together in 'partnerships' that can harness the resources of the company to meet the requirements of individual customers.

There comes a point when a company should become a producer rather than a consumer of management techniques. Rather than 'make do' with inadequate or 'standard' approaches, a benchmark company should be prepared to think through its problems and devise its own solutions. Rank Xerox has developed many of its own tools and techniques in order to address the distinctive features of its own situation and circumstances.[21]

Rank Xerox and Xerox have together won many quality awards, including the Malcolm Baldrige award in the USA, the Deming award in Japan, and the first European Quality Award of the European Foundation for Quality Management. While the company is in no position to rest on its laurels and has missed strategic business development opportunities, dramatic improvements have been made in many areas of its business in the face of intense competition from formidable players in a demanding marketplace. Rank Xerox has moved from crisis, through quality and is now aspiring to business excellence.

To remain a benchmark company, it is necessary to adopt ambitious priorities and aspirations that push out the boundaries of what can be achieved. Rank Xerox reviews annually and sets its own, and progressively more demanding, standards of achievement. The company has moved some way beyond generally accepted, or 'official', standards in such areas as 'environmental' quality.

Achieving business excellence

The experience of a 'benchmark' company such as Rank Xerox suggests that significant culture change can be achieved, but it requires total commitment. Boardroom resolutions, however perceptive and incisive, are not enough. The onus is upon the board to be absolutely tenacious in confronting and overcoming obstacles and barriers.

In many organisations, there is a need for a more holistic approach to corporate transformation. Only a minority of major companies appear to have entered the 1990s with 'a formal management of change programme'.[22] Only about one in six had 'a formal management of change programme' linked to a systems strategy.[22]

A process along the lines of that shown in Figure 5.5 could be used to move towards a more comprehensive and learning-centred approach to business excellence . This embraces a number of areas that are examined in more detail in later chapters of this book, namely transformation leadership (Chapter 6), a focus upon customers and supply chain partners (Chapter 7), people and people management factors (Chapters 8 and 9) and the need for more appropriate quality and BPR tools (Chapters 10 and 11), which together build capability and deliver customer value hence ensuring business results (Chapter 12) and continuing relevance (Chapters 13 and 14).

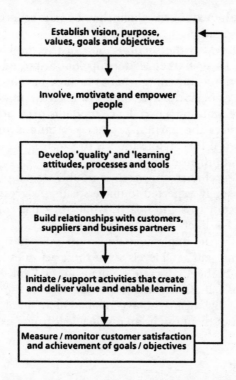

Figure 5.5   Business excellence process

Diversity and comparability when measuring progress

A 'world-class', 'next phase' or 'business excellence' approach should recognise the reality of diversity by allowing individual business units or subsidiary or operating companies to tailor it to their own local needs, priorities and circumstances. This allows each entity to set its own priorities and measure itself against an external standard such as 'best in class' on its list of factors in order to assess by how much it needs to improve in each of the areas selected.

The scales of measurement used by different companies typically varies from 1 to 5 to 1 to 10, with 'no action to assess' etc at one end and 'world-class' performance at the other. Each priority is likely to be assessed on appropriate and hence different criteria, and guides and checklists are often circulated which describe each element or factor to be taken into account, along with suggested or mandated measures of performance and progress.

Even more so than with quality assurance, a business excellence review can separate the cosmetic from the committed. For a few companies, completion of the assessment may represent a 'ticking exercise', while others find that the extent to which they benefit reflects the amount of effort and thought put in.

The key to success is the identification of the combination of factors likely to lead to local market leadership. Sophisticated advocates allow some local discretion concerning what to include beyond the core list that permits a degree of performance comparison across units.

An overview of a business excellence model is presented in Figure 5.6. The vision embraces the parties, processes, attitudes and tools that are collectively needed if the organisation is to survive and thrive in relation to its rationale and purpose.

The business excellence approach is doubly demanding in that: (a) a business unit is usually expected to make steady progress towards 'best in class' performance across the board, while (b) what constitutes 'best in class' performance is likely to continue to improve.

Self-assessment is the implementation route selected by companies such as Rank Xerox, and staff at all levels assess those activities for which they are responsible. Each of the 45 discrete elements in the Rank Xerox model represents an area of self-assessment. Inspection of how the process is implemented could be by means of a combination of local and head office inspectors. Self-assessment can be an invaluable learning experience.

Figure 5.6 Business excellence model

Very often the use of a 'peer review' system is the best option, as this can broaden the perspectives of those involved and facilitates cross-unit learning. Assessments of structure, processes, procedures and policies should be from the perspective of the customer. Areas in which gaps between current and 'best in class' are especially large suggest themselves as the 'vital few' priorities by which subsequent management performance will be judged.

Getting started

A sense of what needs to be done to develop new approaches to management may be found at many points within an organisation. Sometimes the members of the board are the source of insight or drive, which they may or may not be able to communicate to management colleagues. On other occasions, the board may feel the responsibility is 'someone else's', whether 'learning' specialists or the transformation committee. Its focus is upon the 'financials' and, particularly, the 'bottom line'.

Awareness of the need for new priorities and aspirations could originate at the level of the subsidiary, business unit or operating company. Some may have seen the light, while others remain in darkness. Across a number of units there may be a variety of viewpoints and little consensus.

The point of awareness could be buried deep within a part of the corporate organisation. Those intent upon encouraging a new approach may need to seek them out in order to recruit them as allies, confidants or conspirators.

Awakening the need

When told of achievements and ranking on league tables, or the results of self-assessments in a business excellence exercise, the immediate response should be: success in relation to what? Aspirations that are modest and prevent few challenges may be easy to reach. A company may be a leader in a sector that has lost its way, or in a market protected by barriers that are about to be swept away.

Benchmarking can be used to raise expectations, especially if those undertaking a benchmarking exercise look beyond the confines of market and geography to identify those who are most capable at the activities in question. An effective benchmarking programme may reveal opportunities to make significant or 'step' improvements. Looking ahead, an organisation should be concerned with both maintaining a differentiated position *vis-à-vis* its competitors and matching customer expectations.

According to one CEO: 'We thought we were great until we started looking at other industries. In our sector we do things one way and take it for granted. Elsewhere they do things differently. They do it in a tenth of the time, at less cost, and take that for granted. You realise there are other worlds.'

The recognition that there may be very different ways of doing something can of itself be a spur to raising aspirations. The opportunity becomes a challenge and a threat when it is recognised that other companies may have access to the same data. Companies may find themselves competing in terms of the desire and will to change. While the lure of competitive advantage may represent a spur, the thought that the 'investments' needed to change could put a company at a cost disadvantage may inhibit and constrain.

Views differ on what represents an effective organisation. Some stress commonality and common tools, reliability and predictability, while others are drawn to evidence of differences, variety and flexibility. Many approaches to management have concentrated upon the former at the expense of the latter which relate more to such emerging priorities as change, learning and creativity.

Moving from the discipline, rules, standards and structure of the bureaucratic organisation to the organic network in order to create a more flexible and creative culture, a higher degree of shared values and objectives may be required.[15] Some transitioning organisations have suffered a degree of disintegration, confusion and chaos which can be unsettling to those who are uncertain as to where they are.

Crisis

A problem of crisis proportions can sometimes be an opportunity. Thus a sense of crisis can awaken a management team to the need for action, while a crisis situation can also broaden a company's aspirations – for example, to embrace the quality of life or the environment. Thus in the US the 1989 *Exxon Valdez* oil spill in Alaska gave rise to the Coalition for Environmentally Responsible Economies' CERES Principles. Fundamental reviews are difficult to initiate when people are satisfied and complacent.

Xerox faced the focused onslaughts of a clutch of determined corporations. The company's renaissance stemmed in large part from an awareness of how far the corporation had fallen behind its Japanese competitors. If the various levels of board within the Xerox/Rank Xerox family of companies had not made such a sustained commitment in recent years to learning and innovating across a 'broad front', it is likely that the enterprise would have been 'wiped out'.

The Choice

Let us conclude this chapter by returning to a central theme of the book. We have a choice. Rather than grasp at straws in the wind as management ideas come and go we could opt to think and learn, and then put some heart and soul into what we have.

Reebok is one of a growing number of companies that believes in the value of a sense of moral purpose. Chairman Paul Fireman stresses his company's 'desire to make a difference in the larger world'. Reebok has tried to further the cause of human rights through its Human Rights Awards Programme.

South Korean company Lucky-Goldstar sees a sense of humanity as an integrating element across its very diverse businesses: 'It is this human quality that drives us to enhance everyday living, making life healthier and more comfortable by creating everything from petrochemical products to antibiotics and pioneering research into genetic engineering.'

In an age of uncertainty and insecurity, the challenge is to remain flexible while at the same time thinking longer term. We need 'big ideas', priorities and aspirations that grip our imagination and demand our continuing allegiance. Turnarounds such as that which has occurred at SGS-Thomson in the competitive microelectronics sector do not occur overnight.

Staying put may be more important than rushing about, remaining in one place long enough to think something through or make an impact. The time spent by Bhudda sitting under a tree or by Nelson Mandela in jail or Guglielmo Marconi in a hut on the Cornish cliffs was used for reflection. Personal time and space are precious and should be safeguarded. Greater priority needs to be given to actions and developments within ourselves, especially to the quality of thinking and learning.

Checklist

What is your organisation contributing to the world? Where is it going?

What are its priorities and aspirations?

Are they sufficiently stretching? Do they touch the soul? Can they be achieved?

Are the priorities and aspirations agreed and shared?

How relevant to the achievement of business goals and objectives are the management priorities which have been established?

Do these extend to a broader business excellence drive?

Do they embrace feelings, values, relationships, learning and the supply chain?

Do they reflect the situation and circumstances of the company?

Have all the elements needed to succeed been identified?

Is the approach sufficiently flexible to accommodate the distinct requirements of different parts of the organisation?

Does the interest, commitment and momentum exist to move forward?

References

1. Colin Coulson-Thomas and Richard Brown, *Beyond Quality: Managing the Relationship with the Customer*, Corby, British Institute of Management (BIM), 1990.
2. Department of Trade and Industry and Confederation of British Industry, *Competitiveness – How the Best UK Companies Are Winning*, London, DTI/CBI, 1994.
3. Colin Coulson-Thomas (ed), *Business Process Re-engineering: Myth and Reality*, London, Kogan Page, 1994
4. Colin Coulson-Thomas (executive ed), *The Responsive Organisation: Re-engineering New Patterns of Work*, London, Policy Publications, 1995.
5. Colin and Susan Coulson-Thomas, *Quality: The Next Steps*, an Adaptation Ltd survey for ODI, London, Adaptation, 1991; executive summary available from ODI Europe, Wimbledon, ODI Europe, 1991.
6. Henley Centre, *Tomorrow's Business Priorities*, a survey undertaken for Apple Computer (UK) Ltd, Henley, Henley Centre for Forecasting, February 1991.
7. Colin Coulson-Thomas and Trudy Coe, *The Flat Organisation: Philosophy and Practice*, Corby, British Institute of Management (BIM), 1991.
8. Milton Friedman, *Capitalism and Freedom*, Chicago, Ill, University of Chicago Press, 1962.
9. Albert Z Carr, 'Can an Executive Afford a Conscience?', *Harvard Business Review*, July–August 1970, pp 58–74.
10. Sir Adrian Cadbury, *The Company Chairman*, London, Director Books, 1990, p 216.
11. Colin Coulson-Thomas, *Creating Excellence in the Boardroom*, London, McGraw-Hill, 1993.
12. Colin Coulson-Thomas, *Developing Directors: Building an Effective Boardroom Team*, London, McGraw-Hill, 1993.
13. Colin Coulson-Thomas, *Creating Excellence in the Boardroom*, London, McGraw-Hill, 1993, pp 1 and 2.
14. Commission of the European Communities, *Maximising European SMEs' Full Potential For Employment, Growth and Competitiveness*, Brussels, Commission of the European Communities, 20 March 1996, p 1.
15. Colin Coulson-Thomas, *Transforming the Company: Bridging the Gap Between Management Myth and Corporate Reality*, London, Kogan Page, 1992.
16. Colin Coulson-Thomas and Richard Brown, *The Responsive Organisation, People Management, the Challenge of the 1990s*, Corby, British Institute of Management (BIM), 1989.
17. Rosabeth Moss Kanter, *When Giants Learn to Dance*, New York, Simon & Schuster, 1989.
18. John Kay, *Foundations of Corporate Success: How Business Strategies Add Value*, Oxford, Oxford University Press, 1993.
19. Dhanin Chearavanont, *Chairman's Statement*, C P Pokphand Co Ltd Annual Report 1991, Hong Kong, May 1992, p 13.
20. Tim Jackson, *Turning Japanese: The Fight for Industrial Control of the New Europe*, London, HarperCollins, 1993.
21. Robert C Camp, *Benchmarking, The Search for Industry Best Practices that Lead to Superior Performance*, Milwaukee, Wis., Quality Press, 1989.
22. Colin and Susan Coulson-Thomas, *Communicating for Change*, an Adaptation Ltd survey for Granada Business Services, London, Adaptation, 1991.

6

Corporate leadership

Promises like pie-crusts are made to be broken.

If achievement fails to meet aspiration, or even expectation, who is to blame? According to Sir John Harvey-Jones: 'If a company is successful it is due to the efforts of everyone in it, but if it fails it is because of the failure of the board. If the board fails it is the responsibility of the chairman, not withstanding the collective responsibility of everyone.'[1]

A company needs a source of will, purpose and drive, and it was suggested in the last chapter that this spring of essence, relevance and commitment should be located in the boardroom.[2] Without it, the company, even the largest corporation, can become Sir Winston Churchill's vivid image of the cut flower that is beautiful to look at but doomed to die.

Too many boards do not provide a sense of will, purpose and inspiration. If people do not understand what their companies stand for then the board is at fault. Many outputs from off-site 'away-days' seem more like evidence that the expense of fine food and wine was not entirely wasted rather than goals and objectives which have been formulated to be implemented. Like promises, they are made to be broken.

Directors and senior managers should not expect others to do more than the bare minimum for something they do not themselves believe in. A directorial comment sometimes encountered is: 'How do you expect people to get excited about widgets?' Those who ask this question should give way to someone else who is able to create a sense of excitement, challenge and purpose. What happens to widgets? What are they used for? What do they lead to?

Expectations for the future

In the last chapter we examined expectations and aspirations. Many companies do not have a compelling and distinctive rationale for existence. If they ceased to exist, the world would lose very little. Their customers would go elsewhere and buy something very similar from someone else. Their own people probably know in their hearts that their longer-term future is insecure.

To differentiate, just a 'me too' approach to aspects of corporate life such as quality may not be enough. The expectations of realists for the future are contingent upon such factors as clarity of vision, demonstrable top management commitment and appropriate action to improve the quality of management.

To significantly raise expectations and persuade people that change is likely to occur, senior management may need to provide some evidence that it has thought through the implications of corporate aspirations and has assembled an appropriate combination of elements to 'make it happen'.[3] When all the elements of the jigsaw are clearly in place, the slick corporate videos and Tina Turner singing 'Simply the Best' at year-start meetings may not be necessary.

Initiating a more holistic approach to management, perhaps along the lines of a 'business excellence' type portfolio of complementary actions as discussed in the last chapter, can demonstrate visible commitment. People could look through the elements of the model itself for evidence that certain sensitive and pressing issues have been considered. For example, the following were among questions of particular concern in one large group:

- Whether the reward and recognition system encourages openness, learning and a focus on implementation obstacles.
- How 'role model behaviour' and 'personal development' might be defined and assessed in relation to promotions.
- Whether each subsidiary or business unit should be asked to appoint a board member with specific responsibility for learning, undertake regular customer satisfaction and supply chain reviews, and carry out a comprehensive annual 'business excellence' assessment.
- How people might be equipped with the approaches, tools and techniques to enable them to better identify and overcome obstacles and barriers to learning and the delivery of 'output' quality.

By including these issues, and many others, within the framework of a business excellence model the board sent out a clear signal that it had registered various proposals which had been put to it, had identified some missing change elements that now needed to be put into place, and that this was to be done through a vehicle that would involve the appropriate people in the organisation in assessing themselves against best practice.

Corporate direction

Winning companies, according to an authoritative UK study, are led by visionary, enthusiastic champions who encourage innovation, learning and customer focus and are committed to unlocking the potential of their people.[4] They also embrace quality. However, many of us do not work for winning companies.

There is considerable uncertainty as to where many organisations are going. If they exist, the following have either not been communicated and shared, or because people have not been equipped to action them, they are perceived as 'words on paper':

- a framework of relevant and inspiring values;
- a compelling and distinctive vision;
- a clear strategic direction;
- a shared sense of will, purpose, drive and focus;
- measurable business and learning or 'capability development' objectives.

In the absence of a framework of values and a clear sense of purpose and direction, people can feel insecure and 'at sea', particularly in an environment of discontinuous change. As one senior director put it: 'Goals and objectives are being agreed for individual BPR projects within a corporate vacuum. So many major issues are up in the air. Depending upon how they come down, some of my projects could be rendered irrelevant overnight.'

Younger and newer staff, external contractors and network partners in particular, may not always be clear as to what an organisation personifies or stands for. According to one pragmatic CEO:

> Clear direction through business excellence is expensive first time around, but so is establishing a consistent and strong set of company messages through a variety of communications campaigns. Just changing a visual image across our publications, buildings and work environments can cost a fortune and might not be understood. With business excellence and self-assessment people are involved, thinking and learning.

Indeed, the main cost of business excellence reviews is people's time. Because this is precious, elements in models should be prioritised and chosen with care.

Corporate values

The essence or nature of an organisation may find expression in terms of its values and aspects of corporate culture. Very different situations can be encountered. For example:

- Some years of downsizing and early retirement has denuded one company of a whole generation of people that had been guardians of a proud tradition and distinctive approaches and values. All that remains are younger, and generally insecure, managers whose prime loyalty is to their own careers and who are finding it very difficult to offer other than 'me too' responses.

- In another company, there is an almost religious deference to the circumstances in which the organisation had its origins and the values of its past to the extent that changes to match a rapidly evolving market context have not occurred. Continual corporate renewal is needed in order to survive in a competitive and demanding business sector.

In both cases, none of those interviewed described their organisation in terms of either values or a vision for the future. Neither did anyone appear to attach any particular significance to a heavy investment over many years in quality. The questions on many people's lips were: 'What next?', or 'Where do we go from here?' On occasion a lack of direction and purpose, or an absence of corporate values, vision and philosophy, can appear to be an industry or sector as much as a company issue.

Corporate vision

Many organisations need a 'big idea', a 'challenge' that will capture people's imagination, galvanise them, excite them and cause them to want to move forward together. They are existing rather than living. Possible futures are not being visibly explored. The 'great debates' are absent.

We saw in Chapter 4 that quality may also need a vision of where it is going. As one manager put it: 'Who is the keeper of the quality vision around here? Is it everyone or no one? Where are the small voices that tell us when we start to diverge or go off track?'

In the *Communicating for Change* survey,[5] the two key requirements for the achievement of change were 'clear vision and strategy' and 'top management commitment' (Table 6.1). The two were related in that interviewees stressed that the existence of a clear vision and strategy was prima facie evidence of management commitment. Also evident in Table 6.1 is the importance attached to 'sharing the vision' and 'communicating the purpose of change'.

A distinctive and compelling vision may not be easy to achieve. Where one exists, it could be an organisation's most valuable asset. While some fundamental thinking might appear to be called for, a few 'words of caution':

- No vision is often better than the wrong vision. As one director explained: 'Some of our competitors have gone off in the wrong direction. They did their visioning ahead of us and now wish that they hadn't.'
- A strategy, however superbly crafted, is 'academic' unless the requirements for implementation are assembled. One CEO confessed: 'It

looks good ... It's all in the brochures, posters, tapes and videos. The printing would win an award, but people are not taking it on board.' Too much of the essence of quality is imprisoned in lifeless documents and manuals, like a rare insect trapped in amber and waiting to be discovered.

Both consistency and flexibility are needed. While avoiding being locked into a course of action that loses credibility, attention and focus needs to be sustained over whatever timescale is necessary for effective implementation.

While a vision may be long term, a sense of urgency may need to be engendered. In the absence of relatively early and tangible benefits, attention and commitment may be difficult to maintain. As another director put it: 'Some wins early in the season really pulls a team together and gives it a buzz.'

Those intent upon radical change should take to heart the following comment on innovation by Akio Morita, Chairman of the Board of the Sony Corporation:

> The innovation process begins with a mandate which must be set at the highest levels of the corporation by identifying goals and priorities: and once identified, these must be communicated all the way down the line. The targets you set must be clear and challenging because you cannot wait for innovation to just show up at your company one day.[6]

Akio Morita also acknowledges that: 'The innovation mandate, as determined by top management, can only succeed in an environment which nurtures it.'[6] However, too many boards, in attempting to move from a 'directing' to 'empowering and involving through TQM' management style, follow the contemporary trend of establishing a framework, delegating, empowering, equipping people with tools and supporting them with

Table 6.1 *Change requirements (in order of 'very important' replies)*

Clear vision and strategy	86%
Top management commitment	86%
Sharing the vision	71%
Employee involvement and commitment	65%
Communicating the purpose of change	65%
An effective communications network	54%
Communicating the expected results of change	44%
Understanding the contributions required to the achievement of change	42%
Communicating the timing of change	38%
Linking a company's systems strategy with its management of change	38%
Project management of change	27%
Ongoing management education and development programmes	23%
One-off management education and development programmes	8%

Source: *Communicating for Change*, Adaptation Ltd, 1991.[5]

processes, etc, but fail to provide any sense of direction, drive and purpose. These missing elements could be provided by a corporate or business philosophy.

Corporate and quality philosophy

Quality should be a philosophy of business, and CEOs should be prepared to share their philosophies of business with immediate colleagues and the wider team. Where a philosophy of business does not exist, one should not be created in haste and without serious thought. A first step might be to initiate a general debate.

People should not assume the ability to question and think is limited to those along executive suites or expensive consultants and gurus. The distinguishing skill of many of the latter lies in packaging and marketing contemporary insights, concepts and developments that may already be emerging simultaneously at several levels in a variety of locations. For example, BPR in different forms was practised for several years in certain companies before particular aspects of it were collected and packaged for public consumption.

There are often many questions to explore and priorities are likely to vary between companies. Views on an issue such as 'complexity versus simplicity' could be sought throughout an organisation. Thus Brother has focused upon reducing unnecessary product variety while Xerox is seeking to simplify its organisation as part of its 'Vision 2000' strategy.

People should be at the heart of a corporate philosophy. It should enable them to understand themselves and each other, and do both with greater confidence. Without an understanding of self and others it is difficult to establish and build relationships, match people to tasks and opportunities, and be sure that what is really driving a purchase decision is identified.

A corporate philosophy should accept and accommodate the reality that people sometimes want to be alone. Being by oneself may be good for understanding, thinking and learning. So much emphasis is now placed upon teamwork that it is sometimes easy to forget how productive individuals can be, and how satisfying individual achievement can be. A profusion of groups, teams, procedures and standard tools could indicate a failed philosophy of quality.

Balance and the avoidance of extremes are also important. Thus a balance may need to be maintained between individual and group time. The nature of such a balance may vary according to the situation and circumstances.

A 'clear vision and mission' is also a vital element of any attempt to create a new philosophy of management according to another survey (Table 6.2).[7] It was regarded as more significant than both 'customer focus' and

Table 6.2 *Factors for creating a new philosophy of management (in order of 'very important' replies)*

Clear vision and mission	74%
Customer focus	66%
Harnessing human potential	66%
Attitudes, values and behaviour	52%
Personal integrity and ethics	40%
Individual learning and development	29%
Processes for ongoing adaptation and change	29%
Turbulence and uncertainty	19%
Organisational learning	14%
Management techniques	5%
Others	3%

Source: BIM report, *The Flat Organisation*, 1991.[7]

'harnessing human potential' but related to them. As one interviewee explained: 'What an organisation is about determines who it forms relationships with and for what purpose, while at the same time the philosophy may evolve to reflect the requirements of those with whom it deals.'

Responsibility for quality, learning and transformation

Clear roles and responsibilities for quality, learning and transformation are required. A third of respondents in the *Quality: The Next Steps*[8] survey consider it to be the responsibility of the chairman or chief executive. Over two-thirds believe that responsibility for quality should be at director or board level.

However, we have seen that 'top management commitment' has been questioned, and many of those interviewed in surveys feel that the boards of their companies remain sceptical.[3,8,9] Due to a lack of collective leadership, quality and learning are too often part of the furniture in a back room rather than a spirit which pervades the whole house.

In the case of a fundamental transformation or 're-engineering' of a business, responsibility at a senior level needs to matched by the allocation of sufficient time to maintain attention and tackle the many obstacles and barriers that are likely to emerge. Some companies have appointed board directors with specific responsibilities for corporate transformation while their colleagues concentrate upon sustaining customer, supplier and business partner relationships within the changing framework.

Where a significant change of a corporate culture is required, it may be advisable for the 'champion' or 'sponsor' to be the CEO. Those at the top who have attempted to drive radical changes through their organisations include David Kearns and Paul Allaire of Xerox, David O'Brien at the National & Provincial Building Society, and Iain Vallance at BT.

Formal and actual authority and responsibility

A distinction needs to be drawn between nominal or formal and exercised responsibility. Accountability and responsibility may only exist 'on paper'. Consider the following representative comments:

> In theory the board is responsible. In practice this means that no one at this level is either interested or accountable ... They tend to rubber stamp, and we put up what is uncontroversial and likely to go through.

> The manual says the chief executive, but we in the quality department are left to get on with it. We are supposed to be the experts at maintaining registration ... we keep a tight grip on it.

In the case of Saga Petroleum, and 'in conformity with international quality-assurance standards, senior management holds the principle responsibility for quality.' Saga believes that: 'Practical measures implemented by the management have demonstrated its commitment.'

Many CEOs have accumulated considerable power and find themselves the primary advocates and champions of change. For programmes requiring a relatively long timescale for implementation, this can be a severe disadvantage. As such cases as John Akers at IBM, Robert Horton at BP, Robert Stempel at General Motors or Akio Tanii at Matsushita have demonstrated, the need for change can outlast the tenuous and temporary hold that a CEO can have upon an organisation.

Implementation requires followers, indeed champions, throughout an organisation. In the case of Xerox, the quality policy established in 1983 makes responsibility for quality quite clear:

> Rank Xerox is a quality company. Quality is the basic business principle for Rank Xerox. Quality means providing our external and internal customers with innovative products and services that fully satisfy their requirements. Quality improvement is the job of every Rank Xerox employee.

Line responsibility for quality is the basis of one of 'six guiding principles' formulated by Xerox: 'Quality is "on the line by the line". Line management must lead quality improvement. Quality is now an integrated part of our management process – not a staff responsibility, but a line responsibility.'

Does the problem lie in the boardroom?

The questions of top management commitment and clear vision, mission or strategy repeatedly 'top the charts' in management surveys. Their continuance suggests urgent action is needed to improve the competence of directors and the effectiveness of boards. Evidence provided by surveys of directors and boards suggest that neither should be assumed.[2,10]

An IOD discussion document *The Effective Board* suggests the board itself may be partly to blame for the disillusionment found in many companies.[11] The participants in a survey upon which the document is based are not satisfied with the overall performance of their boards. Three-quarters of them felt the effectiveness of their boards could be improved.

Board members should periodically revisit the role of the director, the function of the board and the distinction between direction and management. The following questions are among those which could be posed:[2,10]

- Is there a formal statement of the function of the board, and is it agreed, understood and periodically reviewed by the board and brought to the attention of all new directors?
- Are all members of the board aware of their general legal and fiduciary duties and responsibilities, and of the contents of the memorandum and articles of association of the particular company?
- Are all members of the board aware of the circumstances that can give rise to legal penalties and, in particular, wrongful or fraudulent trading?
- Are legal developments relevant to directors and boards brought to the attention of all the directors?
- Are all directors aware of the circumstances in which they might experience a conflict of interest, and are such conflicts of interest declared?
- Does the board act as an independent check upon the executive, or to what extent is it 'in the pocket' of the CEO?
- Does it understand the distinct interests, needs and requirements of each group of stakeholders?
- Has the board established and communicated a framework of corporate philosophy and values which is observed? Do all members of the board themselves behave as 'role models' in respect of all aspects of their conduct?
- Who ensures that the board learns and acts in a responsible, competent, prudent and ethical manner in respect of its various accountabilities?

Once it is has been established that the above issues have been addressed, it ought to be possible to progress to: (a) defining the requirements for effective boards and competent directors, and (b) drawing up a comprehensive board and director development programme to achieve them, depending upon the nature, situation and circumstances of the particular board.[2,10]

The effective board

The following questions address board effectiveness:[2,10]

- Does the board of your company operate effectively as a team and discharge its various accountabilities and responsibilities?
- How regularly and systematically does the board assess its own effectiveness?
- Are 'output' measures used, and what other indicators of effectiveness could be used?

- Does the board operate as a board or as a corporate management committee?
- Do individual members of the board feel a sense of 'challenge', and do they share a common challenge?
- Does the board listen, reflect and learn?
- Does the board probe and endeavour to uncover what is hidden?
- Has an assessment been made of the factors that help or hinder the effectiveness of the board?
- How much 'politics' is going on within the boardroom?
- Does the board act as a role model in terms of its own conduct?
- Are its actions consistent with its rhetoric?
- Are the priorities of the board appropriate to the vision, values, goals and objectives of the company?
- Has the board focused upon, and reviewed the processes that identify and deliver the value that is sought by customers and enable learning?
- If so, have the results led to an examination of whether additional or different cross-functional processes might be required?
- Does the board have an adequate understanding of direction, management, business, support and learning processes, and what needs to (and might) be done to increase this understanding?
- Is the board equipped to stimulate learning and capability development, and to bring about a fundamental transformation of the company?
- Has the board articulated, agreed, communicated and shared a distinctive and compelling vision, and are its actions and conduct consistent with it, and supportive of it?

As we saw in Chapter 4, under pressure to perform and survive, the focus of many boards has become visibly internal and short term. At the same time, corporate messages communicated to managers have encouraged them to develop longer-term relationships with external customers (Figure 6.1). Misunderstanding and distrust occurs in many companies when 'actions do not match words'.[9,10,11]

People who once started to believe in quality have now lived through an era of recession during which short-termism and the sacrifice of cherished beliefs became commonplace. Some feel tricked, conned and betrayed. Many corporate leaders could benefit from DHL's slogan of 'not only delivering your package but your promise'.

Responses and reactions

Given the mixed experience of quality and transformation, it is not surprising that boards vary in their attitudes and approaches. Some appear to have given up on success and seem more concerned with avoiding

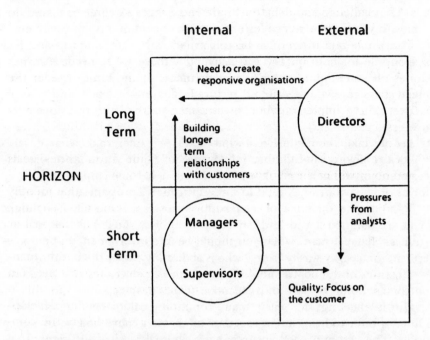

FOCUS

Figure 6.1 Apparent contradictions in focus and horizon
Source: Colin Coulson-Thomas and Alan Wakelam, *The Effective Board*, IOD, 1991.

further failure. As one manager put it: 'We are keeping it alive because of what has been written about it in the annual report ... In practice, a "ring fence" has been put around quality to limit the harm it can do, while I'm charged with the task of coming up with "show case" projects to demonstrate we weren't fools to adopt it in the first place.'

Leaders should think things through, be selective, make judgements and anticipate. Too many boards, in desperation for results, fall for the latest fad or hyped up panacea without considering their relevance, suitability or implementation requirements.

Tensions, differences, contradictions and apparent paradoxes are a fact of life in a vibrant corporate culture. A board needs to be able to reconcile contradictory and contending forces and viewpoints. The incompatibility of focus and horizon that can give rise to arenas of conflict is evident in Figure 6.1. If trade-offs and accommodations are needed, at least they should be made explicit, explained and justified in public rather than rationalised in private.

Peace and harmony of itself does not necessarily create an effective working environment. Its existence might be evidence of complacency or a lack of challenge and debate. Honda encourages a degree of dissatisfaction with what is in order to foster a culture of continuous improvement.

The whole board needs to be concerned with, committed to and feel responsible for both quality and learning if these are to become cornerstones of a new philosophy of management. At the same time, it may make sense to give individual directors facilitating or leadership roles in respect of the implementation of certain aspects of the transformation process.

People take their cue from what they see rather than what is said. Political lobbying, in-fighting, intolerance of failure, avoidance or concealment of difficult or risky problems soon become apparent and, as forms of behaviour, they tend to spread through an organisation rapidly.

Tackling the dilemma of leadership is not easy. One CEO confided: 'You are damned if you lead, and damned if you don't. You are either a ruthless "hatchet man" when you should be into involvement and empowerment, or a wishy-washy "softy" who is abdicating rather than leading.'

Meetings of the board should focus upon key objectives and 'vital few' outcomes. Some boards and executive teams have separate monthly or quarterly meetings for each main common goal of the organisation. Others prefer to bring them together to enable a more holistic review to occur. The first approach ensures that each goal receives sufficient attention, but the latter approach may be advisable when and where goals are closely interrelated.

Looking ahead

A major problem is the lack of reflection and 'first principles' thinking about how organisations of today, let alone the future, should be governed and led. Future leaders of 'virtual corporations' need to be identified and prepared. The parties involved need to agree what leadership of a 'network organisation' means. The corporate governance debate, such as it is, is overly concerned with checking on the executive directors rather than corporate transformation.

The following questions could also be considered by a board during the course of a fundamental review of its nature, evolution and relevance in relation to the situation and context and identified trends and developments:[2,10]

- What is the nature of the board in terms of category and form, and does it reflect the type of company and its situation and circumstances?
- Why is the board the way it is? (Make sure the reasons are really understood.)

- When did the last significant change in the nature of the board occur and why?
- Does the board 'benchmark' itself against other 'representative' boards of 'similar' or 'equivalent' companies?
- What other models of corporate governance and boards might be appropriate, and what are their advantages and disadvantages?

The governance of a network organisation requires a range of political and relationship skills that may not be possessed by those who have climbed bureaucratic ladders as a result of obediently receiving directives from above and issuing orders to those below. If they are not satisfied, network partners and people whose skills and experience are in demand can 'vote with their feet' and go elsewhere.

Considerable skill may be needed to hold the network together. Network partners have to be listened to. Their allegiance can never be taken for granted. Coordination and accountability has to be preserved in the context of what may appear to those involved to be an unprecedented degree of delegation and empowerment.

The listening, reflective and learning board

An aware board should be alert to the existence of arenas of conflict within the corporate organisation. The effective board is a listening board.[12] As one CEO put it: 'At least we know we have a problem.'

Top management needs to consider how to express its commitment. The members of a sales oriented culture may require strong direction and driving leadership while in other contexts it may be more appropriate to concentrate upon listening, counselling and the sharing of goals and values in order to give people some 'space' to 'buy in'. 'Buy in' may be helped by sharing an understanding of the 'situation' or 'problem' and encouraging others to draw the conclusion that a particular approach or tools might be appropriate.

In many organisations those at the top feel they have to 'know it all' and work out and impose a solution, when it may be more important that they are receptive to suggestions from others and willing to reflect and learn. It may be more sensible to initiate a debate and encourage people to develop their own responses according to their particular roles and responsibilities. People should be encouraged to challenge, question and learn, and to refine and continuously improve in the light of experience.

Increasingly the 'leader' is expected to listen, learn, advise, counsel and mentor. This is fine, but in respect of a narrow or inappropriate corporate philosophy, mentoring can result in the 'blind leading the blind' and the spread of bad habits. Mentoring can also entrench a deference for authority and position, and encourage the more senior to 'tell' rather than to question and learn. It can be destructive in some contexts where people follow 'hints', 'tips' and 'short-cuts' that undermine the 'right' corporate values, while in other situations this can help to break down barriers and practices that have outlived their usefulness.

Reviewing corporate philosophy in the boardroom

Fundamental change is inevitably an act of faith. Yet in contemporary economic conditions, the stakeholders in many organisations generally acknowledge that in order to survive radical change may well be required. The issue is how rather than whether to change.

According to Sir Adrian Cadbury: 'If shareholders are to have the long-term confidence of owners in their investments, they need to assure themselves that their companies are directed by competent boards, who will keep their shareholders regularly informed about their future plans, as well as their present progress.'[13] A corporate, quality or business excellence plan could set out the various elements of a change agenda and could be used with various stakeholders as a form of manifesto.

We saw in Chapter 4 that 'top management commitment' is considered overwhelmingly to be the main barrier to the achievement of total quality. Over nine out of ten respondents consider it to be a very significant barrier to the successful implementation of a quality process.[8] A first principles review in the boardroom could itself be a means of demonstrating interest and commitment.

Directors should demonstrate leadership by raising and addressing fundamental questions concerning their companies' business philosophies and approaches to management. A board could compare and contrast its own views and reactions with those suggested by 'general views'. For example:

- Is there a problem with the company's approach to management? (Consider Chapter 1.)
- What are the priority management issues and concerns? (Consider Chapter 2.)
- Is a fundamental review of the company's quality, transformation or learning strategies, approaches and processes needed?
- How relevant are contemporary preoccupations? (Consider Chapter 3.) How do they relate to the vision, goals, values and objectives of the company?
- In the areas of greatest desired or potential relevance, are current approaches, initiatives and programmes 'living up to their promise'?
- Does the company have a clear vision in relation to quality, transformation, learning and supply chain partners? (Consider Chapter 4.)
- Does the board face a 'credibility' or 'relevance' challenge?

- What are the main quality, transformation, learning and relationship barriers? (Consider Chapter 4.) How might they be overcome?
- What are the quality, transformation, learning and relationship priorities? (Consider Chapter 5.)
- What is the board doing to improve the quality of the company's management? (See Chapter 9.)
- What actions (if any) of the board are likely to have a significant influence upon attitudes, values and behaviour?
- What 'next steps' are needed to implement or achieve corporate priorities?
- To what extent is the board responsible for progress (or lack of progress)?
- Within the boardroom, who is, and who should be, responsible for selected aspects of implementation? (Chapter 6.)

Some boards have discovered key 'missing elements' as a result of undertaking a holistic review along the lines suggested in Chapters 5 and 13. With hindsight, they could not have succeeded in changing attitudes and behaviour while some pieces of the jigsaw puzzle were missing and until certain obstacles and barriers had been identified and tackled.[3,9]

Corporate strategy

A business philosophy, quality, transformation or learning review should lead on to strategy formulation. Adopted approaches and initiatives should in large part derive from, and be strongly related to, a company's strategic purpose and intent.

Corporate leadership should communicate and share a concise understanding of goals, objectives and strategy. The 'strategy' of TI Group, according to the Chairman and Chief Executive, Sir Christopher Lewinton, is 'to be an international engineering group concentrating on specialised engineering businesses, operating in selected niches on a global basis. Key businesses must be able to command positions of sustainable technological and market share leadership.'

While focusing upon today's customer requirements, the pursuit of the fashionable and the preoccupations of the moment, people should not lose sight of what is distinctive and special about an enterprise. Confidence can result from self-knowledge and being true to one's roots. Guido Hanselmann, Chairman of the Board of Directors of Finter Bank Zurich, points out: 'We simply need to remain aware of our strengths, use them to our advantage and not allow ourselves to be deterred by the unusual signs of inner insecurity which are manifesting themselves in certain spheres within our own country.'

Role model leadership

Strategy, philosophy, vision and values can seem empty, lifeless or mean-ingless when they are not evident in the daily conduct of directors and senior managers. Rank Xerox defines role model behaviour and all managers are assessed by their subordinates on role model criteria. Only those assessed as role models in formal reviews are promoted.

What is a role model leader? Let us look at the comments of two CEOs:

- *Being the role model manager is all about how one does things – it's not about outcomes.* Individual outputs can shrink to insignificance over time, but how individuals generally behave, and how they treat people, may be remembered. Examples of noble conduct, expressions of values and principles, even in the context of failure and tragedy, can outlive generations of admirers.
- *Why are we doing this? Is it really about customers or about us? Are managers trying to show that they are doing something?* Energy and activity without purpose or consequence may be registered without being respected or admired.

We will return to some issues raised by these comments in a moment, but first a further example. The Belgian insurance company Fortis and its parents AG Group and NV AMEV believe leadership is about being inno-vative and imaginative, breaking new ground and taking the customer by the hand into the future. They have used a variety of images and analo-gies to share with their stakeholders their view of what it takes to be a 'trail blazer'. The role model 'trail blazer':

- has to make choices to reach his goal;
- decides which is the best course, and then goes ahead at full speed;
- motivates and inspires with the enthusiasm of his approach;
- contributes to success through his own efforts and initiatives;
- applies his energies now, but his eye is on the future;
- knows where he wants to go and has his own understanding of the objective;
- makes the road his own, even when others have been there before him;
- overcomes obstacles, determined to forge ahead;
- knows he needs the support of a strong team;
- puts know-how and experience to work together and allocates the responsibilities as appropriate;
- uses the strength of diversity to move together in a shared direction;
- directs combined forces to a shared constructive purpose;
- is persevering and tenacious, climbing higher with each little step;
- records successes along his path and looks ahead to fresh challenges; and
- looks past the successes of today to the potential of the future.[14]

If that seems a long list, the board of the Dutch trading company SHV identified four key elements of the method suggested for implementing its 'strategy for the nineties' of investing for growth in the next century, going for market share or niche, investing in people and managing change, namely: 'look for the unusual; motivate people; listen, learn and react; keep things simple.'

Walking the talk

Whatever the points, judgements are made on the basis of what leaders do rather than say. Certain decisions and activities can have both a direct impact and a significant indirect and symbolic influence. For example:

- Ford shutting a newer plant and keeping an older one open because the latter had a greater commitment to quality and had chalked up a better quality record sent a strong signal through the organisation.
- At the Scottish engineering company Barr and Stroud the directors join managers and shopfloor workers as members of project groups and multi-disciplinary teams.

A definition of role model behaviour should reflect current priorities. Thus to support an empowerment drive openness, giving information, sharing, encouraging both self-expression and cooperation and providing feedback might all be encouraged. Self-awareness, understanding oneself in relation to others and a commitment to one's own learning and development encourage self-empowerment within the management community.

Top management can set the tone. If they do things to give the appearance of action, or to mislead, others will follow. Thus much talk of innovation is mere rhetoric. If it actually occurred it would be regarded as a threat to status quo positions and interests, and to past goodwill valuations and investments.

The role model board creates a culture that encourages learning and innovation (Figure 6.2). Too often, innovations that occur within one project or part of an organisation are not shared and do not spread:[3]

- Why did it take so long for the transformation lessons of the experience of pioneering units within General Electric to be learned elsewhere in the corporation?
- Why did General Motors in the US struggle to change while a significant turnaround in the performance of Opel in Europe occurred?
- Within a multinational company (MNC) such as Rank Xerox how can one national operating company have twenty times as many core processes as another?

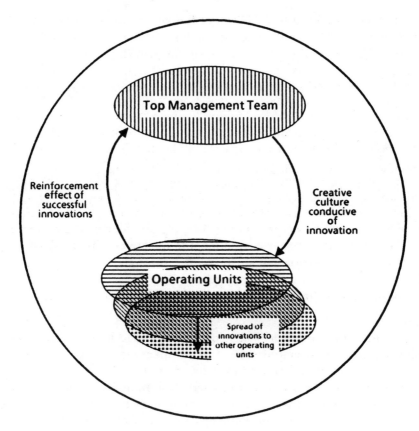

Figure 6.2   The innovative culture

Source: Colin Coulson-Thomas, *Transforming the Company*, Kogan Page, 1992.

'Walking the talk' may have a short-term impact upon the bottom line. Companies such as Nike and Sears are prepared to put the support of corporate values ahead of profitability when selecting suppliers. The damaging 1993 media coverage of British Airways' 'dirty tricks' activities illustrates the potential long-term damage to image and reputation that may be done when some people within an organisation are prepared to compromise on corporate values.

Heroes as symbols

Quality has made an impact upon certain companies because committed chief executives like David Kearns at Xerox or John Neil at Unipart have driven it through their organisations. We need now to agree a new generation of corporate programmes and philosophies, negotiate the terms on which people are to be involved with them, and learn how to exert leadership throughout a network of diverse 'partners'. We will examine involvement, empowerment and the quality of management generally in Chapter 9.

In some companies excessive status, recognition and reward goes to those occupying various levels of management, while frustration and the weight of bureaucracy tends to fall disproportionately upon the key value generators. These are the people who ought to be heroes rather than 'beasts of burden'. The focus of a corporate programme should be upon them, and the extent to which it helps them is an acid test of its contribution.

In airforces around the world it is the pilots, those who 'do the business', who are the heroes, not the desk-bound at 'headquarters' who may be their superiors in terms of formal rank. The purpose of the organisation is to maintain the processes, systems and logistics to support those in the 'front line'. Most of the 'supply tail' has no other reason for existing, and so it should be with many other organisations.

Conformists or radicals

Some corporate organisations need to be subverted rather than supported. There is sometimes a tendency to put new initiatives into the hands of reliable conformists, those who are 'safe' company people, those who can be trusted and who 'know what it is all about'. What may be needed is to put them into the hands of radicals, those likely to act as instigators and catalysts of change.

There are various conventions that operate in many corporate hierarchies, for example every effort may be made to be polite and to avoid confrontation. Although not designed to avoid grasping the nettles of reality, they may have this effect.

Friendship and team spirit may be feigned by those who hate each other, rivals for the next promotion smiling at each other while silently and subtly 'putting in the knife'. Ploys are sometimes used by certain groups to protect their positions and preserve an existing distribution of status. The compliant transformation team may support rather than challenge the status quo.

Where fundamental change is desired a more aggressive approach may be required. Instead of compliant 'smoothies', there may be a need for those who are likely to be more robust in attacking entrenched interests. To the complacent they may appear abrasive and threatening, but complacency is the enemy of progress.

The emphasis should be upon confronting reality and what is important rather than playing the game. Peaceful harmony is sometimes the result of naivety. It may be difficult to bring about significant change without causing a degree of angst and disruption.

Hidden dangers

Among users of the seemingly innocuous term 'role model behaviour' are the disturbing portents of some insidious practices and the prospect of much injustice and bitter disputes. Already, as a result of an eagerness to transform cultures, people are at work whose job is to 'finger' those who are not conforming to the role model specification. Known variously as 'shadows' or 'enforcers' and less kindly as 'informers', 'spies' and the 'thought police', they seek out examples of 'non-role model conduct'.

Within some companies there is the prospect of 'shadow' or 'enforcer' roles being made explicit. In one case, the 'role of the manager' is likely to be broadened to include reporting the conduct of others, whether of those 'above' or 'below' one in what remains of the corporate hierarchy or of lateral colleagues. No one is likely to be safe.

Imagine what a 'field day' this will provide to certain personality types and the 'alternative reporting networks' likely to emerge. Organisational politics and rivalry will take on a new dimension. Consider the impact upon innovation and creativity. As one director confided: 'The quality team already checks what we do to the last form. Now people are going to start questioning what we say and think.'

Obsession with activity

Many react against the concept of role model behaviour. Either it conjures up images of 'thought police' or it is feared that the subjectivity of its measurement offers a 'field day' for the slick and the smooth, for favouritism and for boot-licking and crawling. There is inevitably the risk of bias and selective perception, and effective appraisal should not be assumed in the absence of effective preparation. How does one compare thought with action?

In many corporate cultures, perhaps most noticeably in US MNCs, there is a strong bias in favour of action. Very often inaction is preferable to an excess of activity and plethora of initiatives that leave everyone bewildered and confused. At least people can get on with whatever it is they are expected to do free of the diversions of the latest initiatives.

Activity of itself is a poor indicator of impact. People may be busy tackling the unimportant, the symptom rather than the root cause. Are they thinking or going automatic? They should focus internally only in so far as this concerns factors that help or hinder learning or the delivery of value to external customers.

The problem with thinking, according to one manager, is: 'Like silent brainstorming no one knows that you're doing it. You could be daydreaming.' In some cultures those with clear desks and who are thinking rather than acting make themselves headcount reduction opportunities.

A vicious and destructive circle of distraction can result from either a surfeit of zeal or a penchant for fads. Those at the top initiate and cavort in order to 'feel good' and 'justify their keep'. Further down the organisation, within structures that still exist and having long lost sight of any sense of priority, people attempt to appear visibly committed to the latest initiative rather than tackle those things which they know are more related to the underlying reality of the business.

Policy deployment

Having determined a learning, re-engineering or transformation strategy, established the required commitment and identified appropriate behaviours, some mechanism needs to be found for agreeing and communicating each person's role in implementation. Let us move on to the question of 'policy deployment'.

Reference has already been made earlier in this chapter to one of the 'guiding principles' formulated by Xerox. Another is that: 'Management develops, articulates and deploys clear direction and objectives ... Every Xerox person must know what their personal objectives are and how they relate to the corporate objectives.' The management process has been revised and policy deployment implemented throughout Xerox.

Within Xerox, policy deployment is defined as 'the cascade mechanism that drives an organisation towards the achievement of its goals. It is a translation of a vision or strategic intent, set at corporate level, into operational plans throughout the entire organisation.'

Policies and plans need to be deployed throughout an organisation if they are to impact upon behaviour. When significant changes are sought, this almost always takes more time and effort than is initially assumed. A typical policy deployment process is shown in Figure 6.3. The process involves the examination and review of corporate purpose, vision, mission, values, goals and vital few priorities, followed by a cascade with iterative loops that results in the formulation and agreement of roles, responsibilities, support and implementation plans throughout the organisation.

The art in using such a process is to ensure that input, involvement, participation and debate occur at every stage. Where these are short-changed in the interests of speed or because of insecurity, and priorities and tasks are imposed from above, 'buy-in' is less likely to occur and the top-down approach adopted could reinforce command and control structures and undermine attempts at genuine empowerment. Badly used, as with many management approaches and techniques, it can do more harm than good.

Within some groups considerable discretion in respect of how to deploy policy is given to business and other units. BSO/Origin aims to give as much authority as possible to separate operating companies. It is 'strongly decentralised' and 'operates in small and highly autonomous

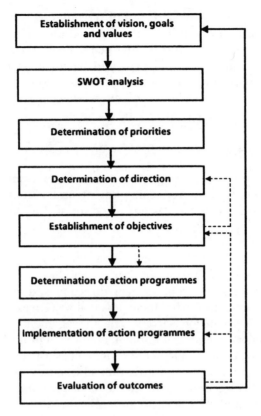

Figure 6.3 The policy deployment process

units': 'these operating companies or cells are given as few rules from the top down as possible, carrying out their own policy within the framework of a number of (quality) standards drawn up centrally.'

In the case of BSO/Origin, it is only for funding that operating companies are 'dependent' on the holding company. Thus corporate standards and procedures are not regarded as a strait-jacket or imposition, but as an important element of the framework that allows local empowerment to become an operational reality.

Policy deployment continues a management by objectives tradition and many companies still use 'MBO' terminology. For example, for the Swedish mining company LKAB management by objectives is a key element of personnel strategy and 'requires that the employees be familiar with the goals and the action plan to attain them. Management by objectives – MBO – and competence development are interlinked processes.'

Early approaches to policy deployment have tended to be largely top down. Lack of experience with the process, and the pressure of timing, have tended to prevent people from contributing to issues already addressed 'above them'. Future priorities typically include encouraging feedback by 'closing loops' or making the process circular. A common inhibitor is reluctance to change an approach that, after two or three years, operational managers have become familiar with.

Communicating new philosophies and strategies

Unless vision, values, goals and objectives are communicated and shared, their impact if any is likely to be limited to those who formulated them. According to the prospectus for the 1993 Wharton-IBM Executive Management Conference: 'Many companies claim to be "market driven", "customer focused", and "quality conscious", but the difference between those who just talk about success and those who succeed is usually senior leadership and unparalleled implementation of a vision of quality which is communicated at every level of the organisation.'

Top-down communication is necessary at some stage to share a holistic perspective of what needs to be done, but without horizontal communication, what is sought may not be achieved.

Charity fundraisers worth their salt would not dream of soliciting contributions without putting much effort into drafting a compelling case for support. Yet many boards expect the people of their organisations to commit their time – indeed their careers – to a fundamental initiative without feeling the need to put the case for why change is needed. Why is change needed? What is wrong with the present? A clear and succinct summary of why action is needed should be communicated along with a compelling vision of a desired state and an honest analysis of what the consequences of inaction are likely to be.

How does one communicate the need for change to bright people who feel they are doing excellent work within a successful company? One CEO voiced a dilemma shared by his equivalents in other sectors: 'I say we should perhaps be doing even better, given the scope ... given the opportunity. All I get is "come on – we are number one, aren't we? How come no one else is grabbing all those extra opportunities? We are OK." It's tough, trying to interest people that feel pretty good about themselves.'

To establish the need, it is necessary to get people to think. For example, do the customers know how much has been done? According to Peter Smith, the partner responsible for quality at Coopers & Lybrand: 'Much of the effort we put into our work is invisible to the client and it is extremely difficult for them to determine whether the calibre of the work is outstanding or merely competent.'

Operational requirements

The overhead costs of a new initiative will depend upon the extent to which it complements, adds to or replaces other activities. Thus a policy deployment process might be considered as a significant bureaucratic requirement. However, once set up, and people are familiar with it, no more than one person may be required to coordinate the process at the time of an annual planning cycle.

Where the roles and responsibilities that emerge from a policy deployment process replace traditional job descriptions, a company may find that it no longer needs to undertake other forms of formal appraisal. The procedures needed to review and update job descriptions and maintain the organisational chart may no longer be required. Instead, the organisation is recreated each year in terms of roles and responsibilities to implement a set of vital few tasks and achieve business objectives.

Old habits die hard. The implementation of policy deployment can lead to the unthinking application of what comes from above, with inputs being taken as 'orders' rather than an invitation to participate by reflecting upon and discussing the next stage. For example, rather than a corporate drive towards distinct business units or 'self-managed workgroups' being automatically adopted, questions could be asked, such as whether fragmentation will result in groups that are introverted or too small to think broadly or assemble the capability to cope. Networks of relationships across the organisation might be a better recipe for success in certain sectors than relatively self-contained units.

Involvement and empowerment for implementation

It is important that those at the top are open and honest about the reasons for introducing change and the likely risks. People should not be expected to be committed where they either do not understand or agree with the reasoning behind a course of action. If change is to occur, people need to be empowered, motivated and equipped with the skills, processes and supporting technology they will need to bring it about.

Rolf Börjesson, President and CEO of PLM Plastics, believes that:

> Leadership does not just entail performing the role of a manager by following given instructions in a businesslike and creative manner. It is also about explaining to one's fellow workers what targets are to be attained and indicating ways of doing this. It is about motivating, stimulating and being receptive to the views of others, showing understanding and paying attention, in a nutshell, creating in every respect a good work climate.

The network model of organisation is a source of considerable anxiety for those who are wary, cynical and reluctant to trust. When project groups and task forces come together and disband with growing frequency, and their memberships are in a constant state of flux and drawn from many locations and functions, so many people have alibis. Never before have so many people had such an opportunity to engage in frenetic activity and multiple communication. New means need to be found to ensure it is coordinated, harnessed and focused.

Retaining customer focus

Restless and demanding customers can keep an organisation on its toes. Uncertainty, challenge, surprises, failures and competitive losses should be accepted as facts of organisational life. In response, people within organisations need to be encouraged to establish whatever relationships inside and outside of the corporate network allow them to learn and respond appropriately.

A changing corporate culture should be compatible with and preferably match and complement the evolving cultures of network partners and particularly of customers.[3] For example, an international company with a differentiated corporate culture and differentiated customers would need to encourage its subsidiaries to tailor and match at a local level (Figure 6.4).

Cultural and organisational change appears to be widely associated with decentralisation and delayering.[15] The discretion that is given to people needs to be used to focus upon those things that deliver value to customers and achieve business objectives. According to Gerard Cottet, Chairman and CEO of the optical supplier Essilor: 'Our aim must be to encourage initiative and responsibility at all levels of the company, which means making sure that our objectives are clearly defined and well understood, internally and externally.' We will examine some of the requirements for effective delegation in Chapter 9.

Excessive diversity, diversification and delegation can create problems of management and group effectiveness. When Incentive was formed in July 1991 through the division of Asea it inherited a 'conglomerate' of 'industrial and trading companies offering both consumer and capital goods' and two development companies. For the President and CEO Mikael Lilius: 'The broad, difficult-to-oversee structure has negative consequences at all levels. As far as the companies are concerned, it means that the group offers scant added value. Synergies are limited. It is difficult to manage and control a group with businesses of many varied types.'

Maintaining control

Some boards become carried away with the rhetoric of empowerment and the propaganda of advocates of the process approach. The appeal is

International Corporate Culture

	Differentiated	Undifferentiated/ Common
Differentiated	Encourage diversity, tailoring and matching at the local level [Build on `strength`]	Build links with local partners able to tailor locally [Need help]
Undifferentiated/ Common	Build global awareness/brand through use of international agencies [Need help]	Encourage common global approach [Build on `strength`]

International Customer Culture (row label, left side)

Figure 6.4 Matching corporate and customer culture

Source: Colin Coulson-Thomas, *Transforming the Company*, Kogan Page, 1992.

seductive. All the board has to do is establish a framework of vision, goals, values, objectives, processes and empowerments, and the results will emerge.

In reality, not much may happen unless and until the board takes steps to support and facilitate the implementation process. For example, a vision is likely to remain as 'words on paper' unless it is communicated and shared. If this is not done, when delegation and empowerment occurs an organisation may fragment as people 'rush off' in all directions.

The network organisation is held together by shared vision, values, goals and objectives. The challenge for those responsible for governing the network is to formulate and agree a framework of values and goals that can embrace a community of partners. This requires a different perspective from that which may have been acquired providing strategic direction for a single enterprise.

A learning network or culture that focuses upon the customer is composed of a number of elements. Complementary and shared attitudes, processes, tools and technologies are especially important (Figure 6.5). Within a group, network or an international or diversified organisation, each of these may need to be tailored to a degree to local situations and

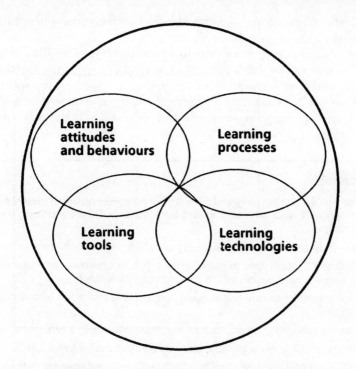

Figure 6.5 The learning network or culture

circumstances. A balance needs to be struck between the benefits of diversity and the advantages of common approaches.

Innovation

As an organisation makes the transition to a more flexible form, a board needs to find new ways of ensuring that activities, corporate capability and individual energies and potential are focused upon learning, the delivery of value to customers and the achievement of business objectives. It also needs to watch for unintended consequences. For example, the empowerment of self-managed workgroups along with the use of groupware might result in a mushrooming of information that threatens to clog up corporate and network systems.

While running with the herd can reduce short-term risk, it impedes differentiation. On occasion doing the opposite or standing a concept on its head can sow the seeds of an alternative approach. For example, against the general trend of 'outsourcing' or moving activities out of offices and factories into competitors' premises, what about its reverse 'insourcing'. In order to develop closer attention to its requirements and build closer relationships, General Motors has invited suppliers to set up operations within its own factories.

Some groups devote more time to allocating blame, avoiding responsibility and passing the buck than to moving ahead. A 'can do' attitude is required, and a willingness to tackle problems together, irrespective of their source. Challenge and change, creativity and innovation, shared learning and working imaginatively with business and network partners can all be fun.

Checklist

How committed to learning and to establishing a new business philosophy and renewed sense of meaning and purpose is the board and top management?

Is this commitment shared by all members of the senior management team?

Is sufficient attention paid to the external business environment, networks and supply chains within which the company operates?

Have the implementation, relationship and learning strategies been thought through?

Have all the elements needed to turn intention into reality been assembled?

Do members of the management team exhibit role model behaviour?

Do they listen and invite feedback, reflect and learn and then share the results?

What steps are taken to involve customers, suppliers and business partners and to seek stakeholder and network 'partner' opinions?

Do corporate leaders 'live' the organisation's vision, values, philosophy and goals? Do their actions match the words?

Is there an effective policy deployment process in action?

Have clear and measurable objectives been established and deployed?

Have roles and responsibilities relating to their achievement been agreed and communicated?

Do other people understand what they are expected to achieve and contribute?

References

1. Sir John Harvey-Jones, foreword to Sir Adrian Cadbury, *The Company Chairman*, London, Director Books, 1990, p x.
2. Colin Coulson-Thomas, *Creating Excellence in the Boardroom*, London, McGraw-Hill, 1993.
3. Colin Coulson-Thomas, *Transforming the Company: Bridging the Gap Between Management Myth and Corporate Reality*, London, Kogan Page, 1992.
4. Department of Trade and Industry and Confederation of British Industry, *Competitiveness – How the Best UK Companies Are Winning*, London, DTI/CBI, 1994.

5. Colin and Susan Coulson-Thomas, *Communicating for Change*, an Adaptation Ltd survey for Granada Business Services, London, Adaptation Ltd, 1991.
6. Akio Morita, *The UK Innovation Lecture*, 6 February 1992, London, DTI – The Department for Enterprise, 1992, pp 5 and 6.
7. Colin Coulson-Thomas and Trudy Coe, *The Flat Organisation: Philosophy and Practice*, Corby, British Institute of Management (BIM), 1991.
8. Colin and Susan Coulson-Thomas, *Quality: The Next Steps*, an Adaptation Ltd survey for ODI, London, Adaptation, 1991; executive summary available from ODI Europe, Wimbledon, ODI Europe, 1991.
9. Colin Coulson-Thomas, 'Strategic Vision or Strategic Con? Rhetoric or Reality?', *Long Range Planning*, Vol 25, No 1, 1992, pp 81–89.
10. Colin Coulson-Thomas, *Developing Directors: Building an Effective Boardroom Team*, London, McGraw-Hill, 1993.
11. Colin Coulson-Thomas and Alan Wakelam, *The Effective Board: Current Practice, Myths and Realities*, an Institute of Directors (IOD) discussion document, London, IOD, 1991.
12. Tom Peters, *Thriving on Chaos: Handbook for a Management Revolution*, New York, Alfred A Knopf, 1987; and Andrew Kakabadse, *The Wealth Creators: Top People, Top Teams and Executive Best Practice*, London, Kogan Page, 1991.
13. Sir Adrian Cadbury, *The Company Chairman*, London, Director Books, 1990, p 204.
14. Fortis, AG Group and NV AMEV, Annual Reports 1992, Brussels, 1993.
15. BDO Consulting, *Vision into Action: A Study of Corporate Culture*, London, BDO Binder Hamlyn, January 1992.

7

The customer: relationship management and the supply chain

Even a fool has his luck.

Some companies appear to succeed in spite of themselves. They have the luck of fools. However, most us us have to 'watch the customer'. The first CEO of Xerox Corporation, Joseph Wilson, was in no doubt about where the customer stands as a 'stakeholder': 'It is the customer and the customer alone who will ultimately determine whether we succeed or fail as a company. Serving the customer is the responsibility of every Xerox employee.'

'The source of commercial meaning, purpose and reality is the customer. Commercial survival requires understanding and supplying what constitutes value to customers.'[1] So begins the conclusions of a 1990 survey concerning managing the relationship with customers. However, it should not have been necessary to make this point.

Management and the customer

Quality and BPR should be all about the customer, but much management effort is departmental or functional and related to activities that may or may not be on a path that generates value for an end customer. Too many BPR teams quickly lose sight of the end customer as their exercises unfold, and become almost exclusively focused upon the internal processes that are being re-engineered.

Regardless of both rhetoric and genuine concern it is so easy to lose sight of the customer. At the conclusion of one COBRA workshop exercise when a group of leading BPR authorities and practitioners had finished discussing a range of prioritised issues concerning the implementation of BPR and reporting back their recommendations, someone noticed that two rather lonely looking 'Post-It' notes remained 'left over'. On examination, the word 'customer' was found written on both slips.

Impacts and attention

Having an impact, even where it occurs, may not be enough. Creeping improvements can go unnoticed by regular customers, especially when their cumulative effects are matched by competitors. At the same time, the enthusiastic drive for excessive variety and frequent changes of models that cause perceived obsolescence can alienate and annoy.

Customers can also resent the forced attentions of those who have undergone 'smile training'. One of the five key values articulated by Richard Goswell, Managing Director of Mercury One-to-One, is to treat people as both individuals and adults. The customer calling with a query is neither a prospect or punter nor a team, but an individual person who will wish to be treated with respect.

A company should not expect dramatic improvements in customer satisfaction if it has not identified the points of leverage, breakthrough or breakout at which the application of effort and initiatives can result in a disproportionate increase in the customer's perception of value. Visible improvements in such considerations as relevance, speed, service, quality or cost or any combination of them could be sufficient to 'register' with the customer.

Marketing and the customer

Like quality, marketing is variously viewed in terms of attitudes, approach and perspective; tools and techniques; processes; or as a philosophy of business. To one person it could be a management function within a departmental organisation, while another might regard it as a total focus on, and commitment to, the customer.

If the marketing community had succeeded in focusing themselves upon identifying and meeting customer requirements, and persuading colleagues to do likewise, it might not have been necessary for so many companies to embrace quality. The failure of the marketing community created the need to adopt other approaches to making people 'customer orientated'.

Marketing turned its back on the writings and insights of the disciplines of its pioneers. Like so many other functional groups, it lost its objectivity, independence and focus in order to serve the short-term and organisational requirements of the bureaucratic corporation. In particular, marketing professionals sold their skills to create ever more sophisticated and costly ways of persuading the customer to buy what companies thought they were good at producing.

Protected by various barriers to entry, too many companies regarded customers as 'product fodder', to be zapped by one-way direct mail and advertising messages. Relatively little, if any, effort was made to enter into a dialogue with customers or to listen to them.

Key questions to address are: What do you do to learn from the customer? Are your communications with the customer about you or the customer? How porous is the corporate shell? Who initiates contacts? How open and receptive is the organisation? Is communication 'one-way' or 'two-way'? Are customers outsiders, targets for 'ads' and 'mailshots', or are they business partners, colleagues or part of the network organisation?

Attitudes and beliefs

The rhetoric of corporate transformation is revealing. Giving people cross-functional or end-to-end accountability with a 'clear line of sight' to the customer, or the arrows in diagrams aiming all the people of the hard, lean and 'aligned' organisation at the customer, all suggest a continuation of the perception of the customer as a target.

Marketing roles and responsibilities and marketing initiatives rarely embrace the factors that are most conducive of the relationships that deliver value to the customer and result in profits for the supplier. The sources of real impact often lie within us. Customer approaches should not be contrived. As Beth Bronner, a Vice President of AT&T points out: 'You gotta have heart.'

Mike Quinlan of McDonald's believes his colleagues have a 'genuine love' of serving customers. He has likened respect for the customer to a religion. In Moscow McDonald's has attracted queues of people who were fed up with shoddy treatment elsewhere and who pay premium prices in the local context.

The factors identified as important by one company and summarised in Figure 7.1 span the responsibilities of a number of departments. Many concerned attitudes and values rather than programmes and initiatives. In this particular exercise, the efforts of some so-called 'customer oriented' and 'creative' groups were found to have little impact upon the customer, while others, for example those who sent out the bills and who were regarded as just 'administrators', could be a significant source of dissatisfaction.

Although the literature of marketing stressed the strategic importance of creating a marketing culture and market-centred form of organisation, a group that largely confined its attention and the major part of its budget to the external communication of the company's needs would soon be

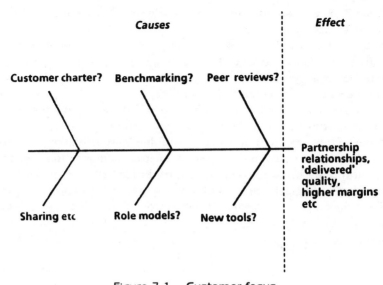

Figure 7.1   Customer focus

perceived as having little to offer in terms of helping to change internal attitudes.

Relationship management

The perceived deficiencies of marketing, greater recognition of the customer as the source of all value, more focus upon identifying, understanding and delivering what represents value to the customer, and concern with customer satisfaction have all stimulated interest in quality. More recently, with growing awareness of the customer as colleague and business partner, and interest in establishing, building and sustaining mutually beneficial relationships with customers, the term 'relationship management' has come into vogue.

As employed in many companies relationship marketing means little more than a return to the roots of marketing and a focus on what ought to be. However, it is often being approached via a desire to extend quality to embrace the relationship with the customer rather than by stressing the value of a return to the basics or essentials of marketing.

Let us examine some views of where we are. Those interviewed have made the following observations about their companies' relationships with customers:

- 'Customers are excluded rather than involved. A hard protective and defensive shell lies between the company and its customers.'

- 'The focus is upon protecting our positions *vis-à-vis* the client and avoiding claims rather than satisfying customers.'
- '"Legalism" should be a rare safety net, rather than a common crutch or alibi. Defensiveness and a reliance upon "small print", results in more commodity work than is desirable.'
- 'The focus of quality procedures is on "safety first" rather than success. They cover every pitfall and problem to watch out for, but not how to win business or deliver value.'
- 'The company is too often seen as a supplier rather than a trusted colleague. Why are company people so keen to remain distanced from the customer, uninvolved and as outsiders? Are staff on customer premises "out of sight and out of mind"?'
- 'There is a need to initiate earlier relationships with clients – how early the company is involved could be a measure of the quality of these relationships. Higher margins come from more open partnership relationships based upon empathy, flexibility and trust.'
- 'The company appears reluctant to listen to the customer. It has a tendency to believe it "knows best". There is no quality feedback loop from the customer, and no systematic follow-up after delivery.'
- 'Account reviews are "internal" and from a company perspective. Changing customer requirements are seen as a source of hassle rather than as incremental revenue opportunities.'

Many organisations would benefit from considering questions such as the following: What do you do to build and sustain a relationship with the customer? Is the customer a part of your organisation? Who in your organisation is responsible for the customer? Who in your organisation adds value for customers? Who could or should add value for customers? How much time and resource is devoted to the customer? Why do you need the rest?

The processes used to enter into a more open and interactive relationship with customers in order to explore and better understand their requirements would hardly have been a 'revelation' to those who were true to the essence of marketing. Those for whom it is a discovery, the purveyors of one-way messages who have 'grown up' in a fast-moving consumer goods environment, may well lack the orientation, empathy and interpersonal skills to make a contribution to building closer relationships with customers.

Quality and the customer

From a customer perspective, who needs quality? Isn't either customer service or customer value the issue, and isn't this quite different from quality? It is possible to examine and tackle gaps between sought, expected, perceived and delivered service or value without any reference to 'quality'. It is possible for those who have never been quality trained to question, reflect upon and define what represents 'service' or 'value' in a particular context.

Quality programmes often fare little better than marketing in terms of actually focusing upon the customer. *The Economist* has estimated that: 'Of those quality programmes that have been in place in western firms for more than two years two-thirds simply grind to a halt because of their failure to produce the hoped for results.' *The Economist* believes the 'crux' of what it terms the 'quality crisis' is the 'apparent inability' of programmes to 'aim their efforts at the right target – The Customer.'[2]

While people may be focused upon the customer, they may not be 'aligned'. That is they may not be working together in a cooperative and complementary way in order to deliver value to the customer. Organisations need to be both focused and aligned, but not to such a degree that alternative orientations and possibilities are not spotted.

BPR can align effort and activity by identifying, documenting and supporting certain, and hopefully more direct, paths through an organisation that deliver value to customers. However, in certain contexts the super-efficient but prescribed process could reduce responsiveness where customers seek tailored solutions, and perhaps those involved should devise a unique process to cope with each case rather than 'go automatic' with a standard approach.[3]

A comment received during one interview summarised a common reaction: 'We haven't been sitting around waiting for quality or BPR to help us discover the importance of the customer, and now that they're here we mustn't let them distract us from the customer.' Too often quality and BPR seem to develop a rationale of their own that is 'semi-detached' from the customer.

JCB avoided the name 'total quality', and instead uses the term 'customer quality' to reflect the company's long-standing focus upon the customer. Customer delight and customer obsession have become watchwords of major US corporations. A manager from one US MNC commented: 'Where are all these people who should be wowed and walking on air? With all this talk of staggering or amazing the customer it ought to be unsafe to step outside ... If it became a reality, could we handle it?'

The small print of many customer obsession programmes suggests the driver is usually internal, for example to increase customer loyalty and retention. By the time initiatives reach people in the field, they are likely to be expressed in terms of such measurable activities as call frequencies and response times which are easy to chart and manage. Listening to, awareness of, empathy with and thinking about each individual customer is more difficult to track.

Customer issues

Eastman Kodak acknowledges at the beginning of its *Quality Leadership Process Guidebook* that: 'Quality is defined by current and future customers.' This is not an unusual statement, but what does it mean? Customers are perceived as often uncertain and with changing requirements. This is sometimes regarded as an operational problem rather than as a business partnership opportunity. By the time certain customers 'know' and are able to define their requirements, the 'job' concerned may emerge as a 'commodity' that is put out to tender.

The approach to business of many companies and their systems and processes need to evolve to match new ways of working with customers. For example, younger interviewees in software companies referred to the use of 'object orientation' and the shift from third to fourth generation languages as possible opportunities for iterative refinement and interaction with clients, as well as 'prototyping' to close gaps between expectation and delivery.

A state of mind may be more important than a product. Thus people may be buying confidence from a company and this could be a question of listening, empathy, understanding requirements and business relevance as much as technical competence. As one CEO put it: 'Relationships are crucial. We're in this together. Who really knows what they want, or what to do? Aren't we all confused by variety and choice? There are so many different things that could be done. This confusion should be seen as an opportunity rather than a problem.'

Learning

Many companies need to be more selective in determining which areas of need to address. Yoshikazu Kawana, a Managing Director of Nissan, has admitted that his company has attempted to meet too many different requirements. A failure to focus and prioritise resulted in an excessively wide product range and uneconomic production runs.

Hunter Plastics had focused upon price and quality until it set out to find what clients really wanted. It emerged that customers were seeking an opportunity to make a profit and profitability was often the result of 'service' factors such as availability and speed of delivery as and when needed rather than 'price'. In response the company initiated a programme to establish, build and support 'partnership sourcing' relationships with its major customers.

Hunter Plastics now competes on whichever of a broad range of factors are of concern to particular customers. The important thing is to be flexible and focused on today's issues. Rover's approach to quality puts primary stress upon creating a sensitive and learning organisation.

Nothing should be taken for granted. So much depends upon the context. It has become almost part of the mythology of quality that one should not compete on price. But assumptions exist to be challenged. Japan's NEC struggled to respond to Compaq's assault upon the personal computer market in Japan. The US computer supplier came into the market with prices 40–50 per cent below those of NEC, the market leader.

A common failure within organisations is the lack of learning that occurs across departmental and unit boundaries. Economies of scale that result from sharing each other's experiences do not occur. Black & Decker tackles this problem by employing staff in coaching and liaison roles whose purpose is to encourage the adoption and spread of new ideas, not just within organisational units but across their boundaries.

The 'goal' of Xerox is: 'To become one of the most productive companies in the world and to work in partnership with our customers to enhance their business productivity and help them create new value for *their* customers.' Learning about changing customer needs, requirements and aspirations is built into the corporation's integrated operating and planning processes and there are 'feedback loops' into product and service refinements, organisation and process redesign, and research and development. The evolution and emergence of the underlying core technologies with which the company works is customer led.

Understanding where you are

To establish a perspective on where you are it helps to understand what customers, staff and business partners think of each other (Figure 7.2). Many people and organisations are not sufficiently self-aware to see themselves as others see them. Different groups could be asked to independently set out, and then to come together and discuss, the expectations or stereotypes they have of each other.

Perspective can also vary according to where one is located within an organisation or supply chain. A head of a function in a large organisation and with a budget to spend might be irritated by 'calls from little suppliers about their invoices'. However, a CEO 'owning a bottom line' might well view such callers as peers, business-like entrepreneurs with a healthy concern for their cash flows. Ultimately, the key perspectives are those of the customers and the people who deal with them and deliver value to them.

We saw in Chapter 2 that out-of-date corporate rules and policies can act as a barrier, inhibitor or constraint. Many companies find on investigation that a significant proportion of those they employ are working to frustrate rather than further current priorities. Within Rank Xerox, hundreds of redundant policies were swept away as a result of a 'first principles' review. According to Vern Zelmar, formerly Managing Director and

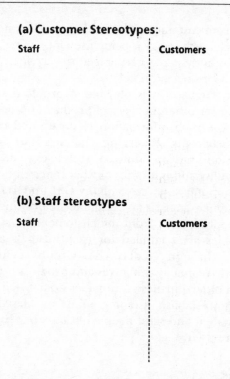

(a) Customer Stereotypes:

Staff	Customers

(b) Staff stereotypes

Staff	Customers

Figure 7.2   What do customers and staff think of each other?

later Chief Coach of Rank Xerox (UK) Ltd: 'One in five people used to turn up every day to work against us.'

Account management needs a fundamental reassessment in many organisations: Is there a single or multiple point of contact? Who owns the customer? Who listens to the customer? Are account teams departmental or cross-functional? Would self-managed workgroups help? Are the required empowerments in place? Is there open access to the information required? Are there account development plans? What about those who should be customers? Are the organisation's processes and is its technology supportive?

How open, porous and receptive is the company to those outside? Many organisations appear to be surrounded by a hard shell and are unwelcoming from the perspective of a first contact. France's leading TV channel Canal+ 'has made a service-orientated commitment to keeping in constant touch with subscriber expectations, thanks to direct and practical paths for feedback.' Its switchboard alone is staffed by over 240 people who handle over 2,500,000 calls each year.

In both the public and private sectors, many 'one-stop-shop' or 'front-end' applications of emerging technologies allow immediate and individual responses to and from customers. Thus in Europe, North America and the Far East touch-screen technology is being used for 'voting', recording views and comments, or otherwise registering feedback at either the point of consumption or at an accessible location.[4]

From customer databases it is possible to profile customers and estimate their demand for different types of product and service. Expert systems allow us to use such information to create and cost product and delivery package concepts. Emerging channels such as the Internet, interactive television and multimedia technology make it easier to demonstrate the utility and relevance of what is new and unfamiliar.

The French computer services company GSI undertakes a continuing 'Voice of the Customer' analysis and maintains a prioritised and weighted list of areas for improvement from the customer's perspective. 'Voice of the Customer' tables are compiled for each business activity, and customers themselves through 'Quality User Groups' define improvement objectives. These drive quality initiatives and progress is monitored.

Matsushita and other Japanese companies do not wait for customers to come to them. They establish 'listening points' or 'lifestyle centres' where customers are situated, and send people out to experience the context in which products are used.

Customer focus

A 'return to basics' might help many organisations to become more customer focused: Is customer satisfaction the number one business objective? Are people equipped, empowered and motivated to add value?

Companies such as Xerox and Perstorp have reorganised upon the basis of market need. Customer focus could itself become a key driver of corporate priorities:

- The Cyprus Minerals Company of the US has won a number of quality awards from its customers: 'Customer focus at Cyprus means satisfying customer needs; asking what customers want; listening to them and anticipating their needs; and building long-term, mutually beneficial relationships.'
- Asea Brown Boveri has initiated a corporation-wide customer focus drive. 'Customer Focus' programmes throughout the group 'are resulting in better quality, shorter development and manufacturing cycle times, lower costs, and a more adaptable, customer-oriented organisation.' Their main aim is to increase value. Associated with the programmes are linked initiatives to increase decentralisation and enhance the competence of employees.

Percy Barnevik, President and CEO of ABB, considers the 'Customer Focus Program is an effort to permanently change our value system and orient every employee towards the customer. A fundamental goal is to increase operational excellence and to create better value for the customer by reducing cycle times and raising quality and service levels.'

Perhaps a frank assessment should be made of where the organisation stands in terms of strengths and weaknesses in relation to selected indicators of customer focus. Those identified as especially important in one exercise are shown in Figure 7.3.

Following the customer

Political scientists are aware of how in the political marketplace 'followership' can contribute to 'leadership'. Many companies pay insufficient attention to the trends and developments affecting their customers. The more enlightened adopt a different approach: 'They are embracing the customer. They are establishing meaning, drawing essence of purpose, and deriving values and missions, from customers.'[5]

ASPECT	STRENGTHS	WEAKNESSES
Accessibility		
Communication		
Attitudes		
Shared Values		
Listening		
Awareness and Understanding		
Shared Learning		
Commitment		

Figure 7.3 Customer focus

Consider the following examples:

- Xerox has drawn up six guiding principles 'to help us intensify quality as we move through the 1990s'. Top of the list comes: 'First, customers define our business. We must continue to systematically gather and use information to understand customers' problems, requirements and needs.'

- The financial services company Allied Dunbar undertook an extensive customer satisfaction survey *before* embarking on an expansion strategy to double its business. Roger Swan, the company's Customer Service Director explains: 'The research outlined the company's strengths and weaknesses and was the basis for a substantial increase in Allied Dunbar's business.'

- GSI enters into a direct dialogue with its customers through its Quality User Groups, and, as has been mentioned, they are involved in the formulation of improvement objectives. Its policy is to share competencies as it builds customer relationships.

- According its Director General Tony Hagström, the 'strategic point of departure' of the Swedish telecom group Televerket is: 'to offer customers the best possible choice, no matter where they are located. One important aspect of this strategy will thus be to follow Swedish customers out into the world.'

In order to 'follow its customers', Televerket has built up its representation, affiliations and joint venture arrangements abroad. An example was the formation of Unisource, a jointly owned company with PTT Telecom Netherlands. In commenting on the joint venture, Ben Verwaayen, CEO of PTT Telecom, stressed that 'internationalisation, cooperation, quality and long-term commitment will be the main spearheads of the services' that are provided.

Some companies experience a wave effect. They compete on price until one or more competitors differentiate on quality. Price may then become less significant in purchase decisions. However, when all suppliers are able to supply a high quality product, price may again become important. The search is then on for new areas of differentiation such as service or tailoring.

Who is the customer?

The flexible and adaptable organisation, moving this way and that in response to myriad changes and forces, should sometimes take stock of where it is. As one quality manager put it: 'I'm too busy responding and empowering to think.' In some companies, the use of sophisticated tools and strategies exists alongside a reluctance to ask such basic questions as: Who or where is the customer?

Too many suppliers fail to establish a direct relationship with the end users of their products and services. To them the 'customer' is the next link in the supply chain. Such an approach limits the opportunities to learn about ways of generating extra value.

A company needs to understand the full value chain if it is to avoid becoming boxed into the role of a commodity supplier by positioning itself where the competition is the most intense and margins are the slimmest.[6] This phenomenon is encountered in many sectors, Figure 7.4 summarising an information technology (IT) supplier example.

Users vary in their involvement and commitment. A supplier needs to ensure that understanding of customer requirements is based upon contact with a reasonable cross-section of users. To overcome this problem in sectors such as IT, user groups are established. Insurance company Legal & General uses regular meetings of customer advisory groups and panels of brokers and agents to establish a better dialogue and as a forum within which suggestions for improvements and developments can be discussed.

It may be that relationships have to be established with a range of users, decision-makers, sponsors and influencers. Thus a school in understanding its 'customers' needs to pay attention to pupils and their parents, and to employers and other groups in the community.

Where is the customer?

Typically, traditional organisation diagrams take the form of a pyramid, the position of the customer being at the bottom, or off the page. The

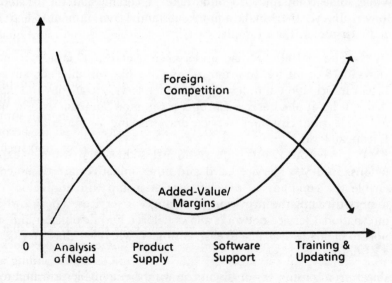

Figure 7.4 The added value curve

Source: Colin Coulson-Thomas, *Creating the Global Company*, McGraw-Hill, 1992.

corporate bureaucracy can appear remote, impenetrable and intimidating from the perspective of the 'worm's eye view' of the individual customer.

Attempts to turn the organisational pyramid upside down, with the customer on top, can help to make a point at a meeting without fundamentally altering people's perspectives. Getting ahead, or moving on, is still usually associated with acquiring the status associated with climbing 'through the ranks' in search of scarce and visible positions at the top of the pyramid.

Those with ambitions often aim to get as far away from the customer as they can while they steadily climb the organisational hierarchy. According to one personnel director: 'The world of teams and self-managed workgroups can appear a swamp. Once in there you can be lost for years. Other than your colleagues and your immediate customers, who knows whether you are alive or dead?' Not surprisingly, those with ambitions seek to escape as soon as possible from the quagmire of serving customers and delivering value in order to concentrate upon self-promotion and career progression.

Measuring customer satisfaction

Until recently in many organisations, customer satisfaction was not measured, and no mechanisms were in place to enable it to be tracked. Customer satisfaction was hoped for rather than assumed, and possible rather than probable.

While some companies do undertake or commission the occasional customer survey, others make a more substantial commitment to learning from the customer. For example:

- By the end of 1991 3M had undertaken over 18,000 customer interviews in 16 countries. In order to compare 'like with like', obtain consistent information and develop customer service strategies and tactics that can be applied across Europe, a common language is now used for measuring customer service and tracking is undertaken on a European basis.
- BMW carries out regular surveys to assess changing customer expectations. Its BMW Service Card and other initiatives are designed to enable the company to develop a relationship with individual customers through the provision of a range of services. The growth of international service networks allows tailored and flexible on-line support to be made available to each customer, wherever they may be, on a 24-hour-a-day basis.

Feedback from customers or discussion with them enables a company to assess whether or not it is delivering value. One quality director confided: 'Why should any of this improve the quality of service when there are no feedback loops from the customer? The quality system does not reach into the customer.' Response mechanisms should be built into loyalty card type schemes.

After over 30 years of living up to its slogan 'We try harder' Avis uses a variety of survey instruments to understand both its visible and invisible customers. The results are used to draw up a Customer Care Balance Sheet that assesses the cost of customer dissatisfaction and to feed a Market Damage Simulation Model. Lesley Colyer, Director of Personnel, Avis Europe, explains the latter is used to undertake sensitivity analysis to 'identify the sources of greatest dissatisfaction and pinpoint the major areas of concentration that will bring the most return.'

Managing customer satisfaction

Continuous cycles of refinement and review are required, that in Figure 7.5 being at the level of the whole organisation, but cycles can also exist for products and even individual customers.[6] Rank Xerox builds feedback from customers into certain of its products. By means of 'Remote Interactive Communications' a fault that could result in a breakdown can be identified and fixed without the customer being aware of the potential problem.

As with other aspects of management, there is often a wide gap between the rhetoric and the reality of customer satisfaction.

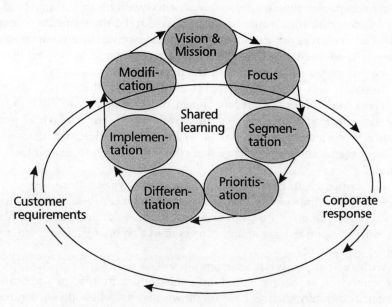

Figure 7.5   Continuous cycle of refinement and review

Source: Colin Coulson-Thomas, *Creating the Global Company*, McGraw-Hill, 1992.

Relationships between many companies and their clients are still fundamentally sale or project based. Longer-term account management may occur, but it often appears to be the exception rather than the rule. Many sales or project teams do not feel responsible for customer satisfaction.

Little appears to be done in other organisations to significantly improve customer satisfaction. One looks in vain for action teams, task forces, benchmarking exercises, improvement initiatives, shared learning and vital few programmes. When these are absent, it could well be that 'lip service is paid to the customer'.

Among those interviewed at all levels there was a willingness, in many cases a desire, to challenge assumptions and to change. However, many companies do not have comprehensive and agreed change programmes.[7] Improvement initiatives often appear to peter out, while in many contexts various suggestions that have been put seem to be either ignored or to be on hold.

In certain situations, there could well be good reasons for caution. For example, suggestions may not have been thought through, while the initiatives advocated may be incomplete. However, responsible reflection and reassessment may be perceived as indecisiveness or inaction, and a feeling may persist that 'something needs to be done'.

Quality assurance and the customer

Many companies that are relatively new to quality adopt a quality assurance and certification route because, increasingly, their customers expect this. For example, the Esab Group, a supplier of welding equipment and materials, adopted a quality assurance programme in large part because of the recognition that 'certification is important to customers'.

Empathy with customers requires an awareness of customer attitudes, concerns and values. When launching British Standard 7750 concerning the demonstration of continual improvement in environmental performance, President of the Board of Trade Michael Heseltine stressed the value of certification as 'evidence that companies are in tune with their customers'.[8]

The approach to quality assurance of many organisations is concerned with the reduction of the risk of non-conformance. Risk and margin are often related (Figure 7.6), but focusing excessively, in some cases almost exclusively, upon risk avoidance can result in a company missing out on the 'big opportunities'.

With certain products, for example software or Intel's microchips, the consequences of failure could be catastrophic in certain applications. Hence a company such as IBM might withdraw a whole product range in the face of what could appear a miniscule risk of failure. Prudent organisations need to remember that customers want systems that work, not

Level of Margin or Profitability

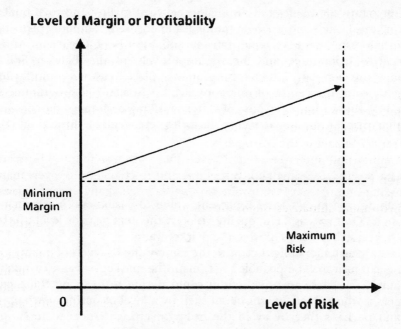

Figure 7.6 Risk management

'small print' mentality, although this requirement, of course, should be reconciled with both commercial caution and a commitment to harnessing collective, as well as individual, creativity in order to add value for customers.

The Saudi Basic Industries Corporation accepts that its 'business success depends upon the recognised quality of its products as well as the quality of service commitment to its customers.' SABIC's priorities are fast and effective technical support, cooperation with others, decentralisation to get closer to the customer and to be more sensitive to their needs, and the encouragement of 'participation responsibility'. While recognising the importance of 'internationally certified product quality assurances', SABIC believes it is 'more important ' to 'make certain this commitment to quality is maintained'. SABIC is using TQM to support longer-term customer–supplier relationships.

In Chapters 1 and 2, in particular, we examined some criticisms of an excessive reliance upon standards at the expense of other aspects of quality. However, some customers may demand them. A recognised quality standard is a basic entrance ticket for those who wish to play in a growing number of markets. Statoil acknowledges that: 'The European market increasingly demands that suppliers have quality assurance systems certificated to the international ISO 9000 standard.'

For many companies the distinction between quality and total quality lies in the latter's more single-minded and focused commitment to the external customer. For Daniel Janssen and Yves Boel, Chairmen of the Executive Committee and Board respectively of the Belgian Solvay group, the company's TQM programme 'places customer satisfaction ever more at the centre of our approach.' A 'structured programme of Total Quality with the purpose of better satisfying customers' has 'become a high priority' of departments, factories and centres throughout the Solvay group.

When have we done enough?

Assuming one knows what represents value to customers, how much is enough? One view is: 'The quality vision is the next gear or level up. It's the next notch in terms of what the market wants.'

Not all customers might require the same value or levels of quality. To some extent it may be possible to segment the market by value or quality (Figure 7.7). Thus an organisation could decide to focus on those customers a whose needs might be satisfied by a level of performance up to b, and perhaps thereby avoid the heavy investments needed to supply those demanding higher levels of achievement. GSI discusses and defines quality expectations with its customers. Their requirements find expression in formal Quality Charters.

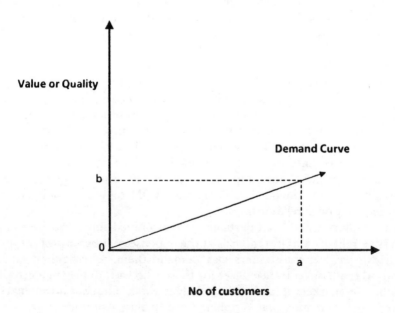

Figure 7.7   Segmentation and value

All the quality procedures in the world provide little defence against a lack of business acumen or poor judgement. Promise too little in a competitive market and the customers will look elsewhere. Promise too much and the hype may return to haunt. Many companies win business by overselling or undercharging. The elation of success may be short-lived. Additions to the order book can sometimes stretch a capability to deliver to breaking point and deal a longer-term blow to credibility.

Nothing is more frustrating than to achieve a significant improvement in quality only to find that, however genuine a company's intentions, its promises are not believed. An established image or reputation and entrenched perceptions can take a long time to change. The opportunity may be long gone before a sufficient shift of attitudes and expectations occurs.

Value, quality and the competition

When serving its customers, a company could, in certain circumstances, aim to do enough to differentiate itself from the competition without going overboard. The value or quality battleground needs to be understood (Figure 7.8). Thus emphasis and strategy could depend upon both the relative effectiveness of competition and the extent to which customers

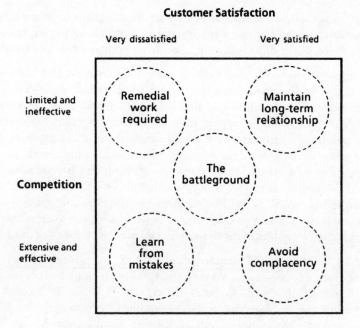

Figure 7.8   Identifying the battleground

are satisfied. For example, an organisation with very satisfied customers and limited and ineffective competition might pursue a 'maintenance' strategy.

A sense of balance is crucial. Do too little and the business may go to a competitor. Do too much, or overreach, and delivery could result in slim margins, or even a loss. Knowing when to stop is important. The trick is sometimes to be up front, but not so far out ahead as to risk running out of steam.

A company's value or quality may have to be significantly better than that of a competitor if it is to, of itself, become a differentiator:

- A value or quality advantage that is not perceived or understood may not work in a company's favour when buying decisions are made.
- When a level of value or quality is either what was expected or assumed, a customer may not be motivated to speak positively about a supplier to other people.

Given the growing enthusiasm for benchmarking, such advantages over a competitor as may be achieved can also be difficult to sustain when they are visible to competitors. 'Windows of opportunity' in some sectors are becoming so narrow that perhaps they should be referred to as 'slits of edge'.

Effective differentiation

'Quality' is sometimes added, almost as an afterthought or something that is expected, to complement some other factor which an organisation feels is really the essence of its differentiation from competitors. For example:

- Companies owned by the Swiss company Electrowatt Ltd 'concentrate on the manufacture of products and the provision of services featuring advanced technology and high quality.' The reference to 'advanced technology' rather than to 'quality' explains the essence of the company's business. Few would claim to supply low quality goods, but some customers might have a preference for simple technology.
- The focus of Reebok International, according to Chairman and CEO Paul Fireman, is upon 'quality, comfort, performance and style'. Identifying with its athlete customers, the Reebok team consider themselves 'ordinary people who seek to achieve extraordinary things' and share 'a commitment to peak performance as a way of life'.

Edward Whitacre, Chairman and CEO of Southwestern Bell Corporation, expresses one view of the quality challenge: 'It is no longer enough simply to meet customer expectations. We must exceed them with quality, personal service and dependability beyond compare.'

A company that is perceived as offering significantly higher quality than competitors may well be able to take advantage of this by seeking to raise its prices, or by driving for market share at existing prices. Care needs to be taken to ensure than any temporary quality advantage is sufficient to differentiate.

Customers may be prepared to trade off price and quality between certain floors and ceilings. Within acceptable price limits, customer buying decisions in a market usually reflect relative differences of quality between suppliers, although an overall increase in absolute quality can increase a total market. Hence, there may be both positive-sum and zero-sum games that could be played,[9] without incurring the high risks of collusion.

Mike Harris, Chief Executive of Mercury Communications plc, recognises that:

> Mercury has been competing, not just on price, but on quality of service and customer responsiveness ... Communications operators will have to shift emphasis from purely building and operating networks to adding customised services based on software, and also to marketing and account management. Competition will increasingly be based on understanding exactly what customers want and delivering it rapidly.[10]

The search for convenience continues to have a strong impact upon shopping habits, and the technology of communications can itself revolutionise retailing. For example, the US-based Home Shopping Network allows people to buy a wide range of goods from their homes or any other convenient location.

For many customers the convenience of electronic and home shopping is causing them to change their habits. The consequences for traditional shops are, as one retailer put it: 'on the wall and plain to see. Why should people come here when all I do when I get a question is to call a help desk they can access from home. Increasingly we get in the way without adding any value.'

Improving product quality

The approach of many organisations to quality assurance focuses excessively upon internal procedures that miss the full range of factors which increase the risk of outputs not meeting customer requirements. If appropriate action is to be taken, the major and likely risks to product quality must be understood.

The sources of potential quality problems identified in one international exercise were categorised under the headings shown in Figure 7.9. Even at this highest level of generalisation it is clear that there were diverse issues to be addressed. Suggestions made for improving product quality included:

- achieving closer relationships with customers and suppliers by adopting a broader approach to quality and extending it to embrace customers

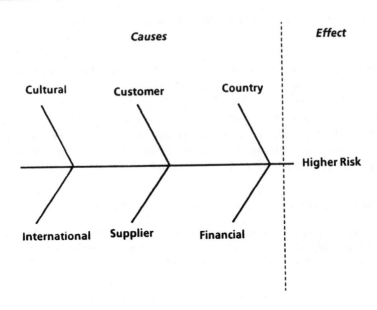

Figure 7.9   Why is there a quality risk problem?

and other organisations in the international supply chain or 'quality network';
- clearer objectives that were also shared by all supply chain members;
- an understanding of account management, shared learning, project management and product development processes that could cope with cultural and financial diversity.

Those interviewed, in this case, did not believe that a continuation of previous practices would lead to significant improvements. They called instead for the fundamental review of assumptions, roles, competencies and processes, and the adoption of a more integrated and holistic approach to management that embraced: attitudes and behaviours; the tools, techniques and methodologies used both internally and by suppliers and business partners; and counselling in shared learning, relationship management and project management.

The establishment of agreed approaches that embrace a supply chain or network organisation appears to be an increasingly common outcome of first principles review exercises. ICL and other companies have vendor accreditation programmes which encourage suppliers to bring their own quality assurance standards up to approved levels. Direct electronic links between network partners may also be encouraged in an age of network competition.[11]

A focus upon the supply chain is difficult to avoid once the emphasis is upon the end customer. As Joe Gantly, the customer operations manager of Apple Computer's factory in County Cork, explains: 'Like any chain, a supply chain is only as strong as its weakest link. The poorest performer drags us all down. We need to work together.'

The Japanese concept Kansei recognises the oneness of customer and product and the importance of such intangibles as look and feel. Too many companies persist in regarding the product as an entity in its own right and distinct from the relationship with the user. It is use that gives the product meaning and value.

Individual tailoring

All customers are to some extent unique, and increasingly they seek and expect a degree of tailoring to their particular requirements. The Cyprus Minerals Company recognises that: 'Assuming customers want the same product they have been getting, or the same thing that the competition has been providing, can be a costly mistake. As technologies and applications change, customer needs change, offering opportunities for product and service improvements.'

Innovative managers confront rather than accept trade-offs. For example, tailoring to individual customer requirements need not be incompatible with economies of scale. Companies as varied as Ford with its 'world car' programme and Blue Circle with condensing boilers are trying to secure both production economies and the flexibility to tailor to local market requirements:

- Flexible manufacturing is enabling companies like BMW to produce cars to meet the needs of individual customers. Process industries are likewise able to combine flexibility with the economies of large-scale production.
- In the pharmaceutical field the age of the 'designer drug' has arrived. Fritz Gerber, Chairman and CEO of Roche, believes his company's sales and profits have benefited from 'a consistent policy of tailoring products to customers' needs'. The flexibility and independent decision-making such an approach requires has been helped in Roche by a 'continued process of divisionalization'.

Having the potential to adapt, introduce additional features or enhance the sophistication of a product is one thing, but the desirability of doing so and the implications for quality can depend upon both the product and the customer (Figure 7.10). Thus supplying commodity products to homogeneous customers allows more prescriptive approaches to be adopted than would be the case with diverse customers demanding highly tailored products. If we compare the mass produced garment with

Customers

	Homogeneous	Diverse
Commodity	High volume Low margin?	Product: * adaptation * tailoring
Tailored	High volume Standard products	Low volume High margin?

Product (axis label on left)

Figure 7.10   Adaptation and tailoring

the designer dress, in the former case quality might be largely built into the work processes and supporting technology operated by relatively low skilled staff, while for the more creative people producing the latter, quality could be largely an attitude of mind associated with the ethos of the particular house.

Excessive diversity

Some companies appear to have pursued variety almost for the sake of it, with the result that customers have become confused. Delighting the customer can be carried too far. A little can be delicious, while too much can result in people 'throwing up'. Has any one customer ever used all the buttons on some electronic gadgets?

Diversity can also impose extra costs which customers may be reluctant to cover once their basic requirements are met. Toyota has sought to reduce the range of choice it offers its customers in order to control costs at lower levels of demand.

What is perceived as excessive diversity or complexity can result from 'customer pull' as well as from 'supplier push'. Individual customers can become so demanding as to cause their suppliers to question whether it is worth continuing a relationship with them. There are relationship lifecycles (eg Figure 7.11), and some companies find that sustaining a particular connection imposes relationship costs that outweigh the gains.

In the example shown in Figure 7.11 excessive attention to the customer becomes a source of concern. Is the supplier 'making enough out of it' to survive and hence be able to continue the relationship? For similar reasons, relatively low bids are sometimes rightly viewed with suspicion. While no one might want a building contractor to go into liquidation just before the 'busy season' and with their hotel only 80 per cent complete, such an eventuality is not unknown.

The answer to a genuine and growing desire for tailoring could be innovation, taking a 'big step', a conceptual leap that offers the prospect of turning a problem into an opportunity. Thus IBM and Blockbuster Entertainment are developing the technology that will allow each customer to chose a personal selection of tracks for inclusion upon a personalised CD. Already publishers are using electronic printing technology to print on demand rather than estimate demand, produce and then hold stock until items are sold or pulped. This approach maximises consumer choice, while minimising waste.

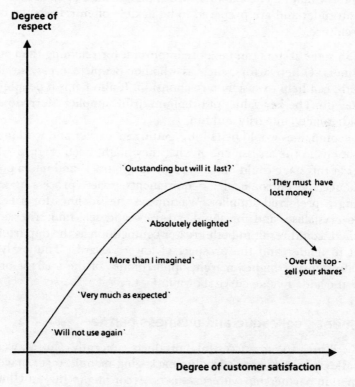

Figure 7.11 Sustaining relationships

The customer-supplier relationship

By themselves, many companies cannot deliver the value sought by their customers. They are forced to work with suppliers, customers and business partners. In this case, quality and learning cannot stop at the front door. They must embrace the supply chain, including the customers themselves.

What a customer is seeking from a supplier is likely to vary at different stages of a relationship, for example whether one is shortlisting potential suppliers, selecting or working with a chosen supplier:

- A reputation for quality and tangible symbols of quality such as an ISO 9001 certificate might be one criterion for shortlisting.
- Once a shortlist is drawn up of those who satisfy the basic criteria, price can be an important factor in final selection, particularly in the absence of any other obvious means of differentiation. Where a preoccupation with price is not apparent, this could be because a broader view of value for money is the deciding factor.
- Having established a relationship, relevant attitudes and processes can help to sustain it. The extent to which people have open and cooperative attitudes and are prepared to be flexible often reflects the corporate culture.

Quality in some sectors can be more important for retaining than attracting business. Other factors, such as whether people are easy or fun to work with, can help to sustain a relationship. It also helps if people enjoy what they do. The key values of premium drink supplier Merrydown are threefold: quality, integrity and fun.

Some companies would benefit by 'getting in' earlier and working with organisations in the assessment of what they might need (Figure 7.12). A supplier at this stage could move onto an 'inside track' and into a position to influence the outcome of a requirements review process as well as becoming a preferred supplier. Waiting on the sidelines for a requirement to crystallise, and for supplier review and selection criteria to be established, could result in both greater competition as the opportunity is put out to tender and the prospect of lower rewards. The 'early bird' might also tap the higher margin opportunities of the analysis of need stage of the added-value curve shown in Figure 7.4.

Customer as colleague and business partner

Nearly all of the successful products recently introduced by CarnaudMetalbox, Europe's leading packaging manufacturer, have been developed in partnership with customers. According to Jürgen Hintz, the company's President and CEO: 'Most of our business growth can be

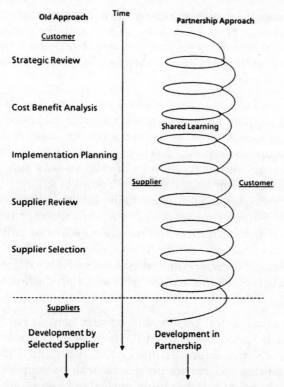

Figure 7.12 Initiating customer relationships

traced to improved customer service, being achieved by better collaboration with our customers.'

In the case of CarnaudMetalbox, Jürgen Hintz believes that process improvement and 'customer partnership' are the twin keys to the company's future: 'We are breaking out of the traditional 'buyer versus seller' contest. We are demonstrating that we serve both interests better by working together cooperatively. It is the way to drive out system costs, to improve service, and to raise the success rate in introducing new products.'

Customers that might sustain a long, maybe a lifetime's, relationship with a particular supplier should be regarded as 'members' of the organisation and treated as such. Members tend to be viewed as privileged insiders to whom people owe a duty of service. Perhaps the benchmark partner should be the sports club, professional body or other membership organisation with its journals and various member benefits. American Express and other companies with newsletters and magazines adopt this approach.

Customers and users of products and services themselves have an important role to play in the quality improvement process. Lazy customers whose approach to quality is limited to checking whether or not an ISO 9000 certificate is held do little to build a supplier's understanding of opportunities to transform the customer–supplier relationship.

The nature of 'supply chain quality' and how it is approached will vary enormously by sector:

- A supermarket chain may establish, impose upon its 'hidden' and 'tied' suppliers in respect of own-label goods and police absolute and detailed quality standards. In contrast, a music producer such as the Dutch company PolyGram has to exercise some flexibility and sensitivity in dealing with its community of creative artist suppliers, many of whom will be better known than the 'record label'.

- The supermarket chain is likely to impose its quality system and 'way of working' upon suppliers, while the 'record company' may respond differently to the practices and moods of each of its artists while maintaining the highest standards of released product. The George Michael case illustrated the consequences of a breakdown in the relationship between an individual artist and a production and marketing team.

Within the retail sector 'relationship management' is hardly a new concept. Marks & Spencer developed the basis of its distinctive approach to working closely with suppliers during the 1920s and 1930s. Today the company initiates and carries out jointly with its suppliers searches for new ways of building and delivering quality and value.

In the case of the network organisation that allows its customers direct access to its services and resources, much of the customer relationship is electronic, silent and unobserved.[11] Quality needs to be built into the systems and processes. These can still allow an unseen but tailored service to be provided.

Within the public sector many BPR exercises are aiming to provide a 'one-stop-shop' type interface with the customer:

- The vision of the Benefits Agency is that one visit of one hour duration to one person in one location should be sufficient to deal with almost any set of client circumstances and problems.

- HMSO operates an electronic catalogue containing details of 25,000 product lines in order to offer its customers one-stop shopping and an electronic ordering service. The system can also provide customers with expenditure and budget information which enables them to better monitor and control their purchasing.

Customers prefer to work at clarifying their requirements with those whom they trust and who share their vision and values. The 'business and learning partner' who is committed rather than 'protected' and who assumes some risk both deserves and is more likely to earn higher margins than the 'commodity supplier' who seeks to avoid risks and takes on narrow and specific briefs (Figure 7.13). A growing number of consultants appear to be prepared to work on a payment-by-results basis in relationships akin to partnership joint ventures.

Mutual interest based relationships

When things go wrong and a number of parties are involved, people may seek scapegoats. The prospect of problems is reduced when all concerned focus upon end-user objectives, the user context or environment is supportive, and there is open interaction and effective coordination, shared learning, support and project management.

It takes two to form a relationship, and in open and competitive markets it is not easy for one party to impose an arrangement or mode of operation upon the other. Suppliers should aim to build the relationships sought by their customers. This needs to be on the basis of mutual interest and trust, requirements we will return to in the next chapter when we consider relationships between people and organisations.

A customer problem is an opportunity to build a closer relationship. Rank Xerox has found that a customer who has had a problem which has subsequently been resolved is five times more likely to buy from the company than a customer who has never had a problem.

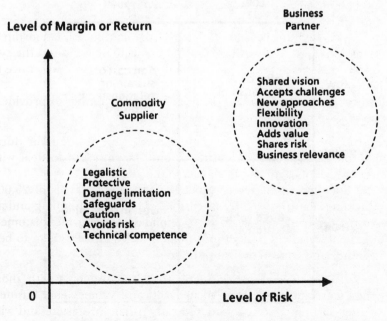

Figure 7.13 Commodity supplier or business partner?

Perhaps, just as those who philosophise about the 'good society' generally consider both the absolute level of wealth and its distribution, so quality of relationships should be viewed in terms of a balanced, just and fair allocation of value and time between the parties involved, including both customers and suppliers where the nature of a relationship still allows such a distinction to be drawn.

If relationships are to last, they must be perceived as mutually beneficial by all parties. Thus both the customer and supplier should derive benefits that clearly exceed a combination of the costs of sustaining the relationship and the possible penalties and opportunity costs (Figure 7.14). The consequences of not being able to put each aspect of a service out to tender and buy at the lowest price could be said to be a penalty for a buyer, while an opportunity cost for a resource-constrained supplier could be a forgone contract that would have been more lucrative.

Sustaining relationships

Relationships are generally easier to sustain when all is well. Recession and hard times can sometimes test them to the limits. Adversity can either

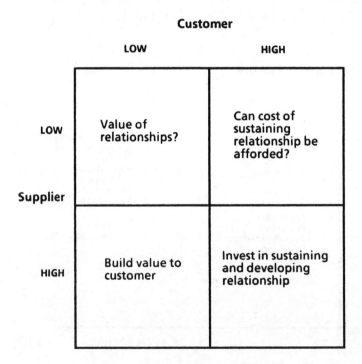

Figure 7.14 Allocation of benefits

bind the various parties to a relationship closer together or cause them to retreat into their own short-term priorities which could cause each to seek to gain some advantage at the expense of the others.

Partnership and supply chain relationships make new demands upon managers. To succeed behaviours may need to change, and dramatically:

- IDV reduced the number of its packaging suppliers by two-thirds in order to concentrate upon a more intense and longer-term relationship with the selected few.
- At the Brazilian company Semco, managers spend over half their time with customers. The St Lukes advertising agency actually organises itself by customer rather than staff specialism, and the decor and equipping of office areas devoted to particular clients reflect the customers' cultures and priorities.

Too many managers still remain remote from their suppliers and customers. Coups occur in the rarefied atmosphere of plate-glass offices. Revolutions occur on the ground, out in the streets.

Checklist

Does the customer come first in terms of vision, values, goals and priorities?

Are customer value and satisfaction the top business objectives?

Does the customer satisfaction system measure what represents value to the customer?

Does your organisation's approach to quality, learning or BPR result in greater value being delivered to external customers? How might they contribute more?

Why should a customer be interested in your organisation's approach to quality, learning or BPR? How involved is the customer?

How much is known about the customer? How appropriate is customer analysis and segmentation?

Is there a 'feedback loop' from the customer or shared learning with the customer? Who listens to, or learns with, the customer?

Are customer queries and complaints encouraged, received and acted upon?

Are customers retained or are they 'turning over'?

What is being done to build closer relationships with customers?

What forms of commitment or guarantee are given to the customer?

Is the customer regarded as an outsider, or as a partner and business colleague?

Does reward and remuneration encourage a focus upon the customer?

Does your organisation's approach to quality, learning, BPR or transformation embrace the supply chain?

What would the customer lose if your organisation's quality, learning, BPR or transformation programme were abolished?

References

1. Colin Coulson-Thomas and Richard Brown, *Beyond Quality: Managing the Relationship with the Customer*, Corby, British Institute of Management (BIM), 1990, p 45.
2. 'The Cracks in Quality', *The Economist*, 18 April, 1992, p 67.
3. Colin Coulson-Thomas (ed), *Business Process Re-engineering: Myth and Reality*, London, Kogan Page, 1994.
4. COBRA (editor and principal author, Colin Coulson-Thomas), *Business Restructuring and Teleworking: Selected Cases*, Report for the Commission of the European Communities, London, Adaptation, 1994.
5. Colin Coulson-Thomas and Richard Brown, *Beyond Quality, Managing the Relationship with the Customer*, Corby, British Institute of Management (BIM), 1990, p 1.
6. Colin Coulson-Thomas, *Creating the Global Company: Successful Internationalisation*, London, McGraw-Hill, 1992.
7. Colin Coulson-Thomas, *Transforming the Company: Bridging the Gap Between Management Myth and Corporate Reality*, London, Kogan Page, 1992.
8. Michael Heseltine, 'BS 7750 will enhance UK competitiveness', speech at launch of British Standard 7750, London, Department for Enterprise, 8 March 1995.
9. Thomas Schelling, *The Strategy of Conflict*, New York, Oxford University Press, 1963.
10. Mike Harris, 'Mercury Communications Report to Pitcom, 26 November 1992', *Information Technology and Public Policy*, Vol 11, No 2, Spring 1993, pp 96–100.
11. Peter Bartram, *The Competitive Network*, London, Policy Publications, 1996.

8

The people dimension: Individuals, groups and teams and the quality of working life

Might as well whistle jigs to a milestone.

It is rare to have a discussion about the implementation of quality, re-engineering or transformation without encountering a range of comments, from the platitudinous to the profound, about the importance of people. For Alain Levy, President of PolyGram: 'The prime factor in all our success is our people and their ability to delight audiences by the exercise of imagination.'

According to Donald Petersen, when quality was being introduced into Ford: 'The real breakthrough occurred at a meeting when someone suggested that our values could be expressed with three *p*s to make them easy to remember: people, products, and profits. The most important element was the sequence, with people first.'[1]

People are remarkably capable and adaptable in supportive environments. Japanese companies such as Toyota are recognising that there are limits to the extent to which work can be automated. At Toyota's Kyushu plant the pendulum is swinging back towards a greater involvement of people in the production process.

At the same time, people can be as unresponsive as milestones when what is advocated carries little conviction or is not to their liking. In the last analysis, when so much can be copied, stolen, inadvertently lost or disposed of, what is special or distinctive about any company other than the corporate culture, the motivation, emotional capability, ethos or spirit of its people?

Paying lip service to people

Evidence suggests that the importance of the 'people factor' is widely understood. For example, in one 1991 survey[2] every respondent agreed that 'human resource is a critical success factor'. In the UK, a growing number of organisations that are concerned about the quality of their people are seeking 'Investor in People' certification. For some, this could complement quality certification, while for others it could be more relevant and rewarding.

While there are some encouraging signs, once again there appears to be a significant gap between aspiration and achievement. For example, inadequate attention is being paid to people issues in BPR exercises.[3] Too many people are becoming victims rather than beneficiaries of BPR as a result of a focus upon working them harder rather than 'smarter'.

Many employees have, or have experienced, cynical reactions towards fashionable terms such as 'multiskilling' and 'empowerment'. A Roffey Park study reveals widespread concern about diminishing job security and limited career prospects and suggests a new range of motivators needs to be devised for those operating in organisations with flatter structures.[4]

An Institute of Management survey of management attitudes in the 'post-recession' economy has found that: 'over 80 per cent of managers reported increased workloads over the past two years, with almost six in ten stating that their workloads had greatly increased', while 'the vast majority of managers find their work stressful.'[5] Security ultimately comes not from overworking but from a willingness to change and an ability to learn more effectively than competitors.

The pressure to conform and achieve can be relentless. It can lead to breakdowns and suicides. Even Japan's Economic Planning Agency has sought to warn Japanese managers of the dangers of not having a purpose in life or social relationships outside of work.

It need not be this way:

> BPR is not out to get us. It is how we use it, to what ends, and to what it is applied that will determine whether or not it bites us. It could be undertaken with the express purpose of improving the quality of working life, introducing new ways of working or learning, or widening job opportunities. There are models of organisations that make it much easier for people to be true to themselves and to work in ways, and at times and places, that enable them to give of their best.[6]

Individuals and organisations need to be reconciled.

Individuals and organisations

Modern management approaches have tended to be viewed by many as 'group phenomena'. For example at a simplistic level, as one interviewee put it: 'Groups and teams are built into the language of quality. A PSG [problem-solving group] of one or a quality improvement team [QIT] of one doesn't sound right.'

Individuals should not be overlooked. Increasingly, policy deployment type exercises allocate tasks to individuals, assessment is based upon individual 'outputs', learning and development is tailored to the individual, delayering and headcount reduction exercises result in greater demands upon individuals, and more work is done by independent contractors, part-time employees and home-based teleworkers.

Approaches to management need to cope with periods of resurgent individualism, for example in China, the US, the UK and across Northern Europe. The balance between emphasis upon the individual and that on the group can change. According to Terry Lunn, Personnel Director of Joshua Tetley and Son:

> Current management thinking is propelling organisations to instinctively assume that team working and multi-disciplinary groups are good things in themselves without thinking through the requirements for their effective operation. In too many companies teams are put together upon the basis of the disciplines of the members, rather than the relevance of their attributes and qualities to effective group operation. Furthermore, care needs to be taken to avoid the team adopting a collectivist approach whereby individual talents are submerged within a group norm. [7]

At the Scottish company W L Gore an environment of freedom has stimulated both team and individual creativity. While people are invited to join one or more groups, they are also encouraged to develop their own ideas and support is provided to enable them to pursue individual projects. After settling into the culture people are allowed to chose their own 'sponsors' and 'leaders'.

Paul Allaire, President of Xerox, recognises that ultimately individuals and organisations depend upon each other: 'Our people provide us with a competitive edge in the global marketplace. They are among the best and the brightest. They understand that their personal success as individuals and the success of Xerox as a business enterprise are commingled.'

The consideration of people issues should be built into the corporate planning process. A typical process for the formulation of business development strategy is shown in Figure 8.1. The company concerned has sought for a number of years to internationalise its business and the great importance it places upon the 'people' factors is evidenced by the various human resource and development (HRD) considerations that are built into the strategy development process.

Individuals may vary greatly, both in different parts of the business and within them. The corporation that tries to be the same everywhere may obtain the advantages of common approaches at the cost of losing the benefits of diversity.[8] Some cultural differences are stark. The US manager subjected to what would be perceived as the grovelling public admission of errors and mistakes by a Japanese colleague and the associated humiliation

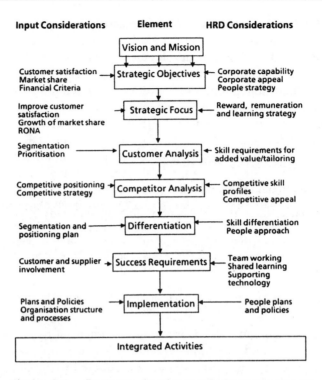

Figure 8.1   Business development strategy process

Source: Colin Coulson-Thomas, *Creating the Global Company*, McGaw-Hill, 1992.

might well react by calling a lawyer. Other differences, while less visible, can be important for particular individuals.

Organisational change and people

We saw in Chapter 3 that organisations are having to become more adaptable in order to cope with more demanding and challenging environments. Companies that are becoming adept at tailoring their products to individual customers may need to become more flexible in their relationships with their own people. Could an organisation have a different face for each of those it wishes to retain? The answer is more likely to be 'yes' where the 'organisation' is perceived as whatever is necessary to support a community of people and enable them individually and collectively to develop and give of their best.

The rhetoric of empowerment and 'delayering' suggests that the dependency of the individual upon the organisation is being reduced as the boundaries of freedom and discretion are widened. At the same time, whether the result of the related 'downsizing', continuous improvement, 'speeding up' of the company, or re-engineering, people are being put under greater pressure.

Companies such as Dow Chemicals that were among the first to flatten their hierarchies have found that new means need to be found of motivating and rewarding people. However, few companies are equipping people to operate within the new paradigm of an organisation that is emerging.[2]

People, organisations and quality

So what needs to be done, and where does quality fit in? Consider the following view expressed by one chairman: 'Quality is all about having the right person in the right place at the right time in order to deliver value and satisfaction. It's about matching people to situations and requirements.' A key question is: from whose perspective?

The last chapter emphasised the desirability of focusing quality and learning upon the customer. However, organisations have a tendency to hijack quality and use it for their own internal purposes and priorities.

While often initially created as a device perhaps to separate ownership from management or provide a framework within which people can come together for some particular collective purpose, organisations tend to develop a momentum of their own. Management teams often struggle to keep organisations alive long after they have ceased to have any distinctive or compelling rationale for existence.

When the survival of an organisation is threatened, its management is likely to focus even more narrowly on short-term and internal preoccupations. Objectives may come to reflect overriding corporate concerns rather than customer requirements. Such a concentration, and associated 'bunker mentality', can be self-defeating when what is actually needed is a renewal of purpose in terms of what the organisation has to offer to those who associate with it.

Organisational death can be short and traumatic, or delayed and painful for all concerned. Companies tend not to grow old gracefully. An orderly winding up is seen as failure. Heroic and futile defences are sometimes staged by hardworking management teams of companies that may have little reason to continue in terms of delivery of value to customers.

In many cases, an appeal to pragmatic organisational self-interest is made in order to sell a quality programme to an executive team. Thus quality might be justified in terms of its contribution to survival and 'bottom line' financial performance, rather than as a 'philosophy' or general approach. One CEO said candidly: 'It has to be about us. I doubt if many people here would be interested in satisfying customers if there wasn't something in it for us. We make people interested in the customer by stressing that our bottom line depends upon satisfied customers. We can't satisfy anyone if we go under.'

In some cases, direct links and benefits are portrayed that may be difficult to attain or measure. Promises are made that may not be delivered within the timescale anticipated. Quality is sometimes distorted and perverted in order to serve ends that cannot be achieved.

There are quality professionals who avoid references to customer requirements in case they might be perceived as not focusing upon the 'commercial realities'. As one director put it: 'Everyone nods and says quality is a good thing. [However] ... when you mention the customer, they say what about us? ... Don't forget the ratios.' According to one quality manager: 'Talk about the customer too much around here, and its "whose side are you on?" or "have you gone native?".

People-centred management

Organisations should be regarded as a means to an end, rather than as ends in themselves. They should exist to develop and harness the potential and capabilities of both individuals and teams, and to apply collective capability and commitment to those activities that deliver value to customers and achieve business objectives.

Organisational performance should derive from both satisfied customers and involved and satisfied employees. The first without the latter becomes increasingly difficult to achieve. The direct impact of quality should be upon individuals, whether as customers or as employees and business partners. Organisational success should be a product of satisfied and fulfilled individuals.

So much stress is laid in many management approaches upon the organisational aspects, the procedures, processes, standards and controls that people, their interests, concerns, attitudes, behaviours, hopes and dreams, are largely forgotten. An alternative approach begins with people – satisfying their requirements. In the case of both customers and employees, this means listening, building relationships and understanding what is important and represents value and opportunity for them.

In essence, management should be organic rather than mechanical.[9] It should be about empathy, flows, openness, trust and tolerance. The quality organisation is concerned with improving the quality of life of those who enter into relationships with it. The organisation that takes, or is seen as 'on the make', tends to be shunned. The one that gives value and provides opportunities will attract the people who can give it life and meaning.

Success requires the matching of individual qualities, competences, experience and motivation with a corporate environment that provides purpose, resources, commitment and support. Either without the other is likely to lead to frustration.

People as victims

The very term 'human resources' suggests a view of people as a factor to be utilised and exploited. In many traditional organisations quality is imposed upon people who are owned – they do not themselves own quality. It is often imposed, like BPR, to improve efficiency or productivity and this can mean putting people under greater pressure. The impact is compounded by downsizing and delayering, and the symptoms are all around us with people working longer hours, suffering stress and not having time for themselves or their families.

As with natural resources, there are those who are tempted to use without replenishing or renewing. In some companies people are burned out and then pushed out. In others, any initial stock of credibility and goodwill is rapidly exhausted by a stream of initiatives that all seem to result in extra claims and demands upon the individual.

The restless search for improvement is unsettling to some. According to one director: 'We constantly undermine achievements by asking for more and better tomorrow. People don't have time to reflect upon and enjoy what they have done.'

There comes a point when the last straw can break the camel's back. Another director confessed: 'What is it all for? That's what people ask me. They are getting cheesed off that we are never satisfied. They see quality as a hassle factor, and don't believe all the constant disruption is in the best interests of customers.'

Change sometimes occurs almost for the sake of it, without having any lasting impact. This can be unsettling as well as irritating. For one interviewee: 'There are no anchors any more. We have gone out of our way to cut them out in order to free things up. We take pride in shaking up the organisation, but our people don't know who or where they are.'

At Xerox the disorientating effect of fundamental change is acknowledged:

> We are in a state of transition where former processes may not work anymore. New roles and responsibilities may not be totally defined or understood. Key interfaces between organisations may not be solidified. This can be a difficult state in which to operate. Many people are uncomfortable with change. They feel anxiety as power bases shift and familiar working patterns are altered. This is a normal outcome of dramatically re-engineering an enterprise.[10]

Corporate restructuring as an opportunity

During periods of transformation and radical change an organisation has an opportunity to become a 'quality employer' and to demonstrate whether or not this concept is just rhetoric. For example, new learning options could be created.

One indicator of the sensitivity and humanity of an organisation's approach to transformation could be the extent to which it adapts to traumatic developments. Many management programmes and procedures would fail this acid test. They generally appear to continue unchanged and unaffected by corporate restructuring, while the latter appears to have become so associated with BPR that a growing number of organisations are consciously avoiding the use of the term re-engineering.[11]

Any attempt at a fundamental change of culture on the scale of BT's 'Operation Sovereign', Philips's 'Operation Centurian' or BP's 'Project 1990' is likely to have a traumatic and unwelcome impact on many people who were broadly happy with the way things were. A vision along the lines of BP's 'continually developing a style and climate which liberates the talents, enthusiasm, and commitment of all our people' should perhaps be extended by '– those who remain, that is.'

Some people make themselves potential targets. The 'drivers' move things forward, while the 'blockers' can prove as destructive as the bad apples in a barrel. One personnel director expressed the view: 'When I don't see any victims, I get worried. The chances are that people are talking rather than acting.'

Not all will survive the transformation journey, and in some situations it may be naive to assume that more than a minority will. At BP, approaching a half of head office staff lost their positions during one lightning strike against corporate bureaucracy. BT shed 40,000 staff in one year, the associated termination payments being a major cause of a drop in profits of £1 billion during the period.

At IBM terminating some 25,000 people in one year was estimated to cost some $6 billion. Rather than being an asset, people are emerging in many companies as a massive contingent liability. Like the insolvent struggling to pay off a growing burden of debt, organisations that are downsizing face a rising tide of termination costs as those retained accumulate extra rights with each month or year that passes. Imagine if such sums were spent on learning, competencies and innovation rather than redundancy obligations increasing over time.

Levelling with people and caring

A quality employer ought to be an honest employer. In many instances, a loss of jobs may appear almost inevitable. In general, one should 'come clean' unless a problem is being concealed long enough to enable it to be quietly tackled. As one CEO put it: 'It is not as straightforward as it might seem. What if an announcement triggered a collapse in share price or resulted in lost orders and jobs? Might not a revelation become a self-ful-filling prophesy?'

In many organisations, people are reluctant to be open. Some compa-nies appear to approach headcount reduction by stealth. It is claimed that improvement initiatives are launched to 'speed up' or 'enhance' ser-vice, when the real reason is to reduce the 'cost base'. It is not surprising that such initiatives are met with a degree of cynicism.

One personnel director expressed the view: 'If our people really understood the situation we are in, and were committed to the achieve-ment of our key objectives, a quarter of them would volunteer for redun-dancy.' Such a proportion should not be regarded as an exaggeration – the Swedish company Euroc, in the hard hit construction industry, reduced the number of its employees by 1,794 or a fifth during the course of 1991 alone.

If a significant reduction in the cost base and manning levels are required, a management team should share its analysis and intentions. It is perfectly legitimate to employ a range of techniques and approaches for this purpose, while deception is rarely, if ever, justified. Open approaches are adopted:

- BP has been through 'the painful process of shedding a large number of jobs', and it has been relatively open about the consequences for its people. Lord Ashburton, the company's Chairman, recognises that while 'without fairly radical surgery, the long-term health of the com-pany might have been in jeopardy ... understanding the need for the cuts is one thing, but it does little to mitigate the pain felt by those affected.'
- Mikael Lilius, President and CEO of Sweden's Incentive group, is committed to open communication: 'Our goals will be clear to each and every person within the Group. No one should have doubts about our course and the demands that are involved. Our information will be straightforward and candid.' Incentive's Annual Report for 1991 announced as a 'highlight' that 'New owners are being sought for seven companies.'
- Another Swedish company MoDo was quite open about the need for cost-cutting and the existence of 'overmanning'. A series of 'special measures to deal with overmanning' were designed, according to CEO Bernt Löf, to reduce the number of employees by 2,000, or approaching one in six, over the five-year period 1989–93.

Some companies appear to care more than others. Thus BSN has encour-aged job sharing as a means of enabling a wider community of people to contribute. Those people who are 'nearing retirement' are 'able to scale down their working week in stages'. Daniel Lefort, BSN's Senior Vice-President Human Resources, acknowledges that: 'Admittedly, implementation of such programmes is not always easy, but BSN is determined to take a fresh approach and examine all practicable options.'

There are often alternatives to redundancy. Thus Ericsson has retrained and relocated whole groups of staff rather than lay them off. Chief Executive Lars Ramqvist believes this approach has enabled the company to carry its people with it during restructuring, while retraining an existing workforce is often a quicker and cheaper course of action than terminating an existing set of employment contracts and recruiting and inducting a replacement group.

BPR and employment

Evidence has shown that re-engineering exercises almost invariably result in less people being required to deliver previous levels of service.[3] However, lower levels of employment are not inevitable. For example, customers may wish to have more direct contact with people providing a personal service and may be prepared to pay for this. Also a focus upon improving the quality of working life could lead to developments such as job sharing or 'learning leave'.

Whether or not, and the extent to which, staffing levels in a particular organisation actually are reduced will depend upon the motivations underlying an individual BPR project:[12]

- If the aim is to find a more cost-effective way of delivering an existing service and to compete on price, then advantage may be taken of the opportunity to achieve a headcount saving, or to move jobs 'off shore' to cheaper locations.
- If the intention is to differentiate by doing more than has hitherto been possible, then staff released from traditional tasks may be redeployed to other activities that generate greater value for customers or create new business opportunities.

Much will depend upon the extent to which an organisation is under pressure to reduce its budget or costs. Where the pressure is intense, an organisation may feel compelled to sacrifice a longer-term competitive advantage in order to achieve a short-term cost saving.

An outcome of BPR could be that such extra value is created for customers that further people need to be recruited to meet the additional demand. Innovation that results in new categories of service can also have this effect. Also, where a BPR exercise helps to distinguish an organisation and improve its competitive positioning, the longer-term consequence could be an increase of staffing levels in a number of areas. Increases in employment (or a slower rate of scaling down) may also be experienced by suppliers and business partners.

Alternative approaches

Top-down initiatives increase the prospect of quality, BPR and change generally being perceived as 'things that are done to people'. At Germany's HYPO-BANK managers at all levels are regarded as 'engines of change' and a new culture is being grown from the roots up. In HYPO-BANK's 'Better Still' programme 'the classical hierarchical pyramid and communications structures are turned upside down. Customer-orientation is no longer initiated in a top-down process, but from the bottom up, ie at the counter.'

Putting the emphasis upon capability, knowledge, and competence can create a more people-focused organisation. The Swedish forest company SCA bases its 'business concept' upon its knowledge. While focusing upon 'end users', the belief within SCA is that: 'Knowledge should benefit the consumer in the form of increased productivity, product quality and product safety, or the quality of life.'

BT has found that its downsizing programme has had a very significant impact upon staff moral. In an uncertain, insecure and transient world the best guarantees of survival are loyalty and trust and commitment to learning and change. Yet these are the very areas that are most undermined by corporate change programmes.

If people are to become beneficiaries rather than victims of change, and the demands of work are to increase upon those remaining in employment, opportunities need to be created for people to fulfil such needs as variety and socialising that have traditionally been met outside of work. Some companies are endeavouring to create more people-centred approaches to management:

- SAS has sought to create a working environment that best enables its people to deliver outputs. This can involve giving them considerable discretion in terms of how they work.
- BMW, through its 'Lernstatt' programme, encourages small groups of employees to discuss working conditions and initiate local improvements.
- Kodak at its chemicals manufacturing plant in Liverpool has integrated quality, health, safety and environmental management into a more holistic approach to the achievement of its business goals.

Operating at the boundaries of knowledge in a number of areas, ASK Europe plc puts enormous emphasis upon the quality of the work experience. Its work environments reflect the interests of its people and appear designed to encourage thinking, learning and development. According to CEO Robert Terry:

> The tropical fish tanks and the workstations, the guitars and the expert systems, are all important to us and natural complements. Together they

encourage balance, reflection, imagination and creativity, and when insights and innovation occur they can be captured, communicated and shared among ourselves and with our customer partners.

Mature and talented people want an environment in which they can grow and develop. Their commitment and contributions need to be focused upon activities that generate value for customers. To ensure this occurs a form of leadership is required that fosters creativity and responsible risk-taking without encouraging dependence or an unhealthy level of organisational politics. Style and ethos are becoming key sources of competitive advantage.

At Rank Xerox (UK) individual employees have ownership of their personal development, 'role model' standards for employee development have been defined and 'employee development' has become a 'vital few' priority. Chief coach Vern Zelmer accepts that: 'Today's reality is that to survive and succeed we must adapt and grow the capability of all employees at a superior pace to our competitors.'

Teamwork: the aspiration

Teamwork is generally assumed to be a 'good thing'. Groups and teams are a basic building block of the new forms of organisation which Rank Xerox and many other companies have been seeking to create. The role of the manager is increasingly described in terms of coaching, counselling, facilitating, motivating and supporting groups and teams.

Teamwork is regarded as a cornerstone of quality. According to participants in *Harnessing the Potential of Groups*, a survey[13] covering 100 organisations with a combined turnover of some £150 billion and employing over one million people:

- The most important uses of groups and teams are to deliver customer satisfaction and achieve total quality, the next most important uses being to overcome departmental barriers, encourage cross-functional cooperation and change the corporate culture (Table 8.1).
- The most important groups and teams are those which are cross-functional. These are necessary to overcome departmental and functional boundaries that inhibit the delivery of value to customers.
- The areas in which the greatest increase in the use of groups and teams is expected to occur are delivering customer satisfaction, achieving total quality and building closer relationships with customers (Table 8.2).
- The highest priority for groupwork and teamwork is making sure groups focus on those things which add value for customers. Other high priorities are ensuring all groups understand the vision, goals and values of the organisation, and building an open, sharing and trusting corporate culture.

Table 8.1 *Team/group working towards corporate objectives (in order of 'very important' replies)*

Delivering customer satisfaction	77%
Achieving total quality	74%
Overcoming departmental barriers	65%
Encouraging cross-functional cooperation	63%
Changing the 'corporate culture'	63%
Involving employees	62%
Increasing speed of response	56%
Building closer relationships with customers	55%
Improving managerial productivity	49%
Harnessing individual talents	48%
Building a learning organisation	44%
Encouraging teamwork in the boardroom	43%
Creating a flat and flexible organisation	36%
To focus on the delivery of outputs	33%
Building closer relationships with suppliers	26%
To internationalise	25%
To allocate roles and responsibilities	21%

Source: *Harnessing the potential of groups*, 1993.[13]

Table 8.2 *Expected group and team contributions towards corporate objectives five years from now (in order of those respondents who considered more use will be made)*

Delivering customer satisfaction	89%
Achieving total quality	81%
Building closer relationships with customers	78%
Encouraging cross-functional cooperation	71%
Overcoming departmental barriers	70%
Increasing speed of response	70%
Improving managerial productivity	61%
Changing the 'corporate culture'	59%
Involving employees	56%
Building closer relationships with suppliers	55%
Harnessing individual talents	51%
To focus on the delivery of outputs	51%
Building a learning organisation	49%
Encouraging teamwork in the boardroom	48%
Creating a flat and flexible organisation	45%
To internationalise	45%
To allocate roles and responsibilities	30%

Source: *Harnessing the potential of groups*, 1993.[13]

While relatively little importance was attached to the contribution of groups and teams to building closer relationships with customers or to focusing on the delivery of outputs (Table 8.1), the importance of the former was expected to increase significantly (Table 8.2) within five years.

There are champions of teamwork. 'Self-management', 'empowerment', 'facilitation', 'involvement', 'flexible' and 'multiskilled' are terms that are widely used in companies like Alcan, Baxi, British Airways, Kimberly-Clark, Lucas, Motorola, Rolls Royce and Rover that have made substantial investments in the creation of team-based organisations or operations.

Visit a modern plant such as that of Bosch in Cardiff and training, appraisal, remuneration and organisation collectively support multifunction teams composed of people who are multiskilled and led by empowered leaders. Use is made of group problem-solving skills, there is a commitment to continuous improvement and, according to Bosch, effective teamwork is a reality.

Teamwork: the reality

In a 'classic' case such as the Brazilian manufacturing company Semco, profitability and growth can rise with each new innovation with teams, and members of the management team even take turns at being CEO. Elsewhere the signs are not so encouraging. Many groups and teams appear to be a hindrance rather than a help. Too many of them are struggling to be effective rather than focusing upon the delivery of outputs.

In another and earlier survey of company chairmen,[14] the improvement of teamwork at all levels emerged as the priority boardroom issue. Why should this be the case when in the 1980s so much rhetoric was devoted to the advocacy of teamwork and teamwork training was a central element of so many corporate training programmes? Is there a problem with the concept or its application?

In many organisations there is a naive faith in groups and groupwork that is not justified on the basis of corporate experience. According to the *Harnessing the Potential of Groups* survey:[13]

- Focusing internally upon the achievement of corporate change and the creation of flatter and more flexible organisations can result in companies losing sight of their customers.
- Few companies assemble the elements needed to significantly improve teamwork. In particular, most of the companies that champion teamwork are taking insufficient steps to equip their people with the skills they need to work or learn effectively in teams.
- The fashionable term 'empowerment' is largely rhetoric. In many organisations neither appropriate empowerments nor the technology

to support teamwork are in place. Groupware is not being effectively used.

- Most groups are given objectives that are not expressed clearly in terms of measurable outputs.
- Many groups are not working upon tasks that deliver value to customers or contribute to the achievement of business goals.
- In general, reward and remuneration does not support effective teamwork.
- Groups and teams still tend to be departmental, rather than cross-functional and inter-organisational. Multilevel teams are rare in many companies.
- Teams are often set up when their use is not appropriate and may even be undesirable. Often, the right individual or a one-off consultation would suffice.
- Many organisations lack teamwork 'role models'. Also, some definitions of 'role model' teamwork can encourage different thinking to be regarded as wrong thinking.

In general, far too many groups and teams appear to be focusing on internal team effectiveness rather than on the external customer. Effective teamwork, involvement and participation are sometimes sought as ends in themselves, regardless of their relevance and contribution to satisfying customers.

Overwhelmingly, the participants believe that more could be done within their organisations to improve the effectiveness of groupwork and teamwork. There is a realisation that much activity within companies may have little to do with the satisfaction of customers or the achievement of business objectives.

Overall, the survey[13] reveals a strong desire to return to the basic purpose of an enterprise which is to profitably serve and satisfy customers. Effective groupwork and teamwork should not be sought for its own sake, but only in so far as it facilitates both the delivery of value to customers today, and the learning and development of capability to deliver it tomorrow.

Improving teamwork

What needs to be done to improve teamwork will depend upon the situation and circumstances of each case. In the *Harnessing the Potential of Groups* survey,[13] clear and measurable objectives followed by personal commitment and management attitudes are considered the most important enablers of more effective groupwork and teamwork (Table 8.3).

The most agreed with attitude towards groupwork and teamwork is that groups need clear objectives (Table 8.4). Other attitudes strongly agreed with are that talking about effective groupwork does not make it happen, the members of groups should have more open access to the information they need, and the board should be a 'role model' in the area of effective groupwork.

While struggling to become a team, a preoccupation with internal dynamics can sometimes lead people to lose sight of purpose and objectives. The focus of concern becomes the creation of an effective team

Table 8.3   *Enablers of more effective groupwork and teamwork (in order of 'very important' responses)*

Clear and measurable objectives	71%
Personal commitment	66%
Management attitudes	63%
Teamworking skills	54%
Accountability	49%
Empowerment	48%
Overcoming departmental barriers	41%
Roles and responsibilities	37%
Project management skills	36%
Supporting software, eg groupware designed to support and foster group collaboration	36%
Supporting hardware technology, eg communication networks	34%
Management processes	33%
Tackling vested interests	30%
Role model behaviour	29%

Source: *Harnessing the potential of groups*, 1993.[13]

Table 8.4   *Attitudes towards groupwork and teamwork (statements in order of 'strongly agree' responses)*

Groups need clear objectives	66%
Talking about effective groupwork does not make it happen	61%
The members of groups should have open access to the information they need	59%
The board should be a 'role model' and work effectively as a group	58%
People need to be equipped to work in groups and teams	52%
Different groups should share a common vision if they are all to move in the same direction	48%
People should be rewarded for working effectively in groups	41%
Groups tend to outperform individuals	26%
Diversity should be encouraged within groups	25%
People learn effectively in groups	22%
Managers are reluctant to give up real authority to groups of subordinates	16%
Most information technology is a barrier to effective groupworking	8%
Workgroups are the flavour of the month	8%
Groupwork slows things up	4%
Responsibility is lost when tasks are given to a group	3%

Source: *Harnessing the potential of groups*, 1993.[13]

rather than the delivery of results. The protracted team-building process needs to be guarded against.

Not surprisingly, the highest priority for groupwork and teamwork, which is consistent with earlier responses, is making sure groups focus on those things which add value for customers (Table 8.5). Other important priorities for groupwork and teamwork are ensuring all groups understand the vision, goals and values of the organisation, and building an open, sharing and trusting corporate culture.

In many organisations, little thought appears to be given to the selection of team members in order to bring together complementary skills, or to the allocation of roles within the team relating to the work of the team itself.[13] Where groups and teams are given specific projects to undertake, care also needs to be taken to ensure that project management and learning skills are available amongst the membership, and too often the distinct nature of these is not understood.

A degree of self-awareness can help people to complement their own strengths and weaknesses when assembling groups and teams. Martin Bartholomew, on taking responsibility for Mercury Communication's government business, put himself and colleagues through the Myers-Briggs Test and encouraged open discussion of the results. In allocating and seeking roles and responsibilities people were encouraged to play to their strengths. Differences and variety came to be perceived as sources of advantage when creative combinations of people were brought together.

Many groups work on only an element of a wider task and are not able to see any tangible results of their efforts. Deere & Company introduced 'cradle-to-grave' project teams to allow mixed function groups to remain involved through to final implementation. At Lucas multidisciplinary taskforces see change projects through to completion.

Table 8.5 *Groupwork and teamwork priorities (ranked in order of 'very important' replies)*

Making sure groups focus on those things which add value for customers	61%
Ensuring all groups understand the vision, goals and values of the organisation	45%
Building an open, sharing and trusting corporate culture	38%
Allocating clear roles and responsibilities	33%
Ensuring the people of the organisation are equipped with the skills they need to work effectively in groups	33%
Empowering groups with the authority to act	26%
Providing people with the technology and supporting groupware to enable them to work effectively in groups	19%
Provide encouragement through reward and remuneration of effective groupwork	15%

Source: *Harnessing the potential of groups*, 1993.[13]

Cross-functional groups

Some organisations are working hard to make teamwork a reality and overcome whatever barriers are inhibiting progress in their particular context. Attitudes across a company may need to be tackled:

- In 1992 the human resources team at the French Telecom subsidiary Cogecom 'made a special effort to focus on Group spirit, with a view to encouraging the sharing of skills and information.' The Chairman of Cogecom, Gerard Eymery, explained: 'In an effort to add further force to our action, it is now time to break down the barriers dividing one job speciality from another.'
- At computer manufacturer Amdahl it was necessary to 'wage war' on departmentalism in order to encourage the emergence of self-managed workgroups. Companies moving in this direction often find the distinction between manager and supervisor increasingly difficult to sustain.

The 'curse of professionalism' is limiting the ease with which people from different specialities and functions can work together.[9] The urban development and environmental services group Lyonnaise des Eaux-Dumez is, according to Chairman Jerome Monod, 'building up the complementary links between professions and the technical and commercial synergies between the group's two principal sectors.'

In many organisations, the infrastructure to support cross-functional and multilocation groups is not in place. For example, effective use is not made of groupware and the value to a learning organisation of a continually updated and shared memory that is open and easily accessible is not appreciated.

Increasingly, organisations are team based, and yet there is a wide gulf between what is and what should be. Effective cross-functional teamwork is advocated but not achieved. Its requirements needs to be better understood. There is an urgent need to take a first principles look at the contribution of groups and teams and how this can be improved.

The potential for networking

One of the most exciting developments of recent years has been the widespread availability of technologies and software specifically designed to improve the effectiveness of multiskilled, multifunctional and interorganisational groups and teams. Yet beyond technical specialists, awareness of the potential contribution of computer-supported work and learning environments appears to be woefully inadequate.[13]

Technology has the capacity to bring an almost infinite number of permutations and combinations of people together within a network organisation framework. By the year 2000 as many as 2 billion people could be working with electronically accessible information. Whatever forms of quality and security are built into networks will influence, and perhaps determine, what approaches will have to be taken by those who use them.

People need to get to know about each others interests, skills, priorities and systems. Opportunity and capability markets and electronic notice-boards are required, and people may also need to be helped to acquire networking and relationship-building skills if they are to embrace the technology rather than seek refuge from it. In the case of Smart Valley in California, the whole community is taking up the gauntlet.[15]

For the Japanese company NEC the challenge of making network and learning organisations and societies a reality is regarded as an epic business opportunity. Tadahiro Sekimoto, President of NEC Corporation, explains his company's vision is to use its know-how 'to help advance societies worldwide toward deepened mutual understanding and the fulfilment of human potential.'

Distinguishing between a group and a team

Encouraging people to reflect upon the difference between a group and a team can enable them to better understand the relevance, benefits and dynamics of each. Too often, those who should constitute a team operate as groups, and many collections or sets of people are only a team in name and intention.

Interviewees in the *Harnessing the Potential of Groups* survey[13] were asked to distinguish between a group and a team. Their responses are summarised in Table 8.6.

The categorisation in Table 8.6 is necessarily crude as in many cases the allocations overlap, and some respondents appeared to regard the distinction between a group and a team as a question of semantics. However, in general:

> The word group tended to be associated with collections or sets of people with certain common characteristics, while the term team tended to be attached to those groups that are cooperating together for some shared purpose. In this sense, a collection of people waiting for a bus is more likely to be considered a group rather than a team, while the reverse would probably be the case of a collection of people of the same side who were playing a competitive game.[16]

Overall, there is a surprising lack of consensus among the participants. In many cases, individuals argued the reverse of the categorisation in Table 8.6, or appeared to use the terms interchangeably. Few organisations appear to have attempted to agree a shared definition of what constitutes either a group or a team, and there is little recognition of the range of options available. Organisations should distinguish between different forms of group in order to evaluate which to apply or use in a given situation.

Customers, shareholders and employee satisfaction

Customers and shareholders are people too. They like to be listened to and to talk about things that interest them. Relationships with customers in particular often involve personal contact and a dialogue with people.

Table 8.6 *The distinction between a group and a team*

Attribute	Group	Team
Nature	Arbitrary, uncoordinated and lacking cohesion	Motivated, tightly knit and managed
Timescale	Ongoing	Specific timescale
Purpose	General, functional or multiple	Specific *ad hoc* task
Objectives	General, multiple or vague	Specific, single and defined
Responsibilities	General or common	Internal allocation of roles and responsibilities
Accountability	Vague and diffuse	Mutual with performance goals
Focus	Broader, various projects	More specific, single project
Approach	Varied	Common and agreed
Communication	Weak	High degree of inter-dependence and interaction
Bonds	Common interests	Shared commitment and objectives
Motivation	Weak	Strong
Vision	Acknowledged	Shared
Common goals	Few	Strongly shared
Membership	Diffuse, diverse, cross-functional and relatively open	Selected and homogeneous or complementary
Size	Relatively large	Comparatively small
Integration of new members	Poor and slow	Good and swift
Agreement	Limited	Shared
Leadership	Multiple or various	Single person

Customer and employee satisfaction are interrelated. Thus people may become frustrated when they are not free and equipped to do whatever is necessary to serve *their* customers. Whenever possible they should be given the discretion and means of taking the initiative within an overall framework of corporate goals and values. We will examine empowerment and delegation in the next chapter.

ABB's 'Customer Focus Program' has resulted in increased employee involvement and competence. According to Percy Barnevik, President and CEO of ABB: 'These efforts do not represent a one-time project but will push ABB in the direction of becoming a "continuously learning" organisation. Skilled and motivated people will give us the only really lasting competitive advantage.'

Virgin puts people first. According to Richard Branson, Founder and Chairman of the Virgin Group of Companies: 'We give top priority to the interests of our staff; we give second priority to the interests of our customers; and third priority goes to the interests of our shareholders.' Branson explained at the 1993 Annual Convention of the IOD that:

> Working backwards, the interests of our shareholders depend upon high levels of customer satisfaction, which enable us to attract and retain passengers in the face of intense competition. We know that the customers' satisfaction, which generates all-important word-of-mouth recommendations and fosters repeat purchase, depends in particular upon high standards of service from our people; and we know that high standards of service depend upon happy staff, who are proud of the company they work for. That is why the interests of our people must come first.[17]

The transportation company CSX Corporation aims to meet and exceed customer expectations by identifying and delivering what represents value to them. To encourage a focus upon value in respect of every delivery, a common mission and shared purpose the company launched 'The CSX Way' initiative in 1991. John Snow, the Chairman and CEO of CSX, believes this initiative will create a corporate culture and framework within which employees can be empowered. The company is also encouraging employee share ownership 'to more closely align' the interests of employees with those of shareholders.

The Canadian mining company Inco also has a philosophy of aligning 'the interests of employees as closely as possible with those of shareholders'. Although attitudes to employee shareholding vary greatly across different countries the Inco chairman and CEO Donald Phillips was able to report in 1992 that over 80 per cent of the company's 18,369 employees in 20 countries were shareholders.

The quality employer

So what else should be done to both enhance employee satisfaction and align their interests with those of other stakeholders? Some general comments can be made based upon the areas we have examined so far, namely that the people of an organisation and its business partners need to understand and share:

- a distinctive and compelling vision, common goals, clear objectives and a focus upon the customer;
- agreed and appropriate values that are seen to influence decisions and personal prospects;
- a commitment to openness, empowerment, involvement, mutual trust and respect, self-development, shared learning and continuing improvement;
- a readiness and ability to work and learn effectively in teams while at the same time respecting, encouraging and developing the individual;
- a willingness to confront reality and a degree of doggedness and persistence in identifying and tackling obstacles and barriers.

To assess the extent to which the above factors are present or need to be developed, it is necessary to understand the corporate context rather than rely upon generalisations. We will consider various aspects of improving the quality of management in the next chapter. But first, let us return to a central theme of this chapter, namely whether so many people must necessarily suffer as a consequence of organisational change rather than benefit from it.

Quality of working life

While the flattening of organisational hierarchies and headcount reduction programmes in many companies appear to have reduced the quality of working life, 'simplifying the organisation and reducing the number of levels in the hierarchy' is regarded by ITT Flygt as one of a 'number of measures' to 'improve working conditions and job satisfaction'. Other 'measures' used include minimising the number of repetitive jobs and the encouragement of job rotation.

In the *Managing the Relationship with the Environment* survey,[18] matters such as health and safety and improving the quality of internal working life were ranked in priority significantly below external and environmental quality. There are, however, companies that recognise the importance of the quality of both working life and the environment. For example:

- Williams Holdings plc acknowledges both the internal and the external aspects. The company 'is committed to the provision of high quality and safe working conditions for the benefit of its employees and the adoption of sound environmental policies in the interests of the community.'
- The Norwegian company Kvaerner makes explicit that: 'Group

companies give a high priority to measures aimed at improving the working environment.' The Kvaerner board monitors the company's impact upon the physical environment and has concluded that: 'Pollution of the external environment by Group companies is almost negligible.'

- Another Norwegian company, Aker, undertook a 'working environment study' among all the group's employees in Norway, Sweden and Denmark. All the companies concerned 'have followed up the study with measures to improve their organisation.'

When improving the quality of working life, a balance has to be kept between the interests of employee and employing organisation. They need not be but sometimes are in conflict. Thus Saab found that while giving teams wider value-added responsibility improves employee satisfaction, it can also lengthen the production cycle of a car. There may be trade-offs to be faced between the interests of employee, employer and customer.

The creative workplace

Offices need not be boring. Some companies have taken specific steps to make the workplace a culturally rich and creative environment in which to work and learn:

- ASK Europe has sought to integrate both the aesthetic and the leisure leanings of its staff into the workplace. The company also pioneers and shares the development and use of relevant learning environments.
- The Bank of Minneapolis allows employees to express their views on works of contemporary art which are positioned within the office according to preferences and taste. In the process, openness is encouraged and individuals are given an opportunity for self-expression.
- The aesthetic vision of Cummins Engine extends beyond the office to the local community. The company has agreed to pay the design fees of public buildings in and around Columbus, Indiana provided the services of architects of the highest standing are employed. Other local companies have adopted similar policies, and over 50 buildings in Columbus have been completed to a higher standard of design than might otherwise have been the case.

Imaginative solutions can be cost-effective. Rank Xerox sponsored a national art competition and a selection of the winning entries were used in its new international headquarters. In any event, new rooms and spaces would have needed to be furnished. As it is, in place of standard and uninspiring office decor, one finds paintings, textiles and sculpture selected by recognised authorities as representing the best work of a generation of young artists.

New ways of organising

There are organisations that have adopted unconventional but successful approaches to people management. Many more people are aware of Ricardo Semler's open and democratic approach to management than could name Semco's products that include pumps and household appliances. Yet its lack of job titles, information sharing and collective decision-making are becoming more common among emerging knowledge-based businesses. For example, at St Lukes, a London based advertising agency, people do not have any personal space and the company is co-owned by all members of staff. Trust and an obvious lack of the visible trappings of status are also apparent.

For some companies the priority is to establish more manageable business units. AT&T believes: 'The best way to take advantage of opportunities is to separate into smaller, more focused enterprises.' ABB has split into some 1,200 separate businesses each employing an average of around 200 employees in an attempt to produce human scale enterprises.

Richard Branson believes 'small is beautiful': 'Being small lets us create new products fast and effectively. Being small allows us to react quickly ...' As his record company grew Richard Branson spun off new companies, led by people with a stake in the enterprise:

> The end result was that we had 50 small record companies around the world, with no more than 60 people working out of any one building. The buildings themselves were intimate buildings, on canals, on rivers and in mews houses ... Doing business should be fun, for our staff, for our customers and for ourselves. All of us spend most of our lives at work, so for goodness sake let us enjoy it.'[17]

With all the emphasis being placed upon groups and teams, the desires of many individuals for identity and 'space' should not be forgotten. Self-sufficiency and 'teamwork' need not be incompatible. The Indian engineering company Telco encourages the 'inner voice' of its employees, self-awareness and self-motivation in support of its policy of empowerment. Hindu swamis give talks to encourage people to think through and develop their own positions on issues.

Those who like 'being in their own space' are sometimes the quiet reflectors organisations cannot afford to be without. Rather than organisation charts, these people may prefer, and should be given, maps which illustrate the contribution expected of them and the extent of the latitude they have in terms of discretion and where it relates to, and may overlap with, the spaces of others.

New ways of working and learning

The questions of where, when, with whom and how people should work and learn is an obvious arena in which organisations could give individuals greater discretion. It happens to be an area in which no generation in history has had such a wide range of choice. In fact, we are almost spoiled for choice.

The challenge is to match the options with requirements, aptitudes and preferences in particular situations and contexts. Britain's Royal Mail has investigated the value of self-managed teams and experimented with applications of both business process re-engineering and new ways of working. Rather than use particular techniques to improve existing practices, it has evaluated how a combination of approaches under the umbrella of total quality could be used to transform the culture of the organisation. The focus is upon people, their roles and attitudes, and how they are developed and rewarded. The aim is to radically change how work is done within branch offices.

Teleworking, with its emphasis upon the use of information technology and telecommunications to overcome barriers of function, organisation, location and time, turns out to be a very good indicator of whether or not a so-called radical change programme is actually reaching down to the roots of an organisation and how it operates. Among the conclusions of one investigation of the link between BPR and new ways of working in general and teleworking in particular,[3] in which information on over 100 European BPR exercises was collected and over 80 of these were subjected to further examination, are that:[11]

- Teleworking with associated telelearning can offer both an organisation and its people a wide range of benefits, but even where it is applicable, appropriate and actually demanded it is either not involved or plays a minor role in many 'solutions' that result from BPR exercises.
- In comparison with the focus upon such factors as cost and speed, the introduction of a new pattern of work such as teleworking or a new approach to learning has too low a priority in many BPR exercises.
- The successful introduction of new patterns of work or ways of learning can, and often does, occur quite independently of BPR, and in some cases it contributes significantly to the transformation of organisations.
- BPR and teleworking may both result from common 'drivers', and there is potential for them to be perceived and used more widely as complements.
- Compared with BPR, teleworking has the more positive image, and is perceived as more likely to offer benefits to both an organisation and the individuals working within it and for it.
- Organisations that adopt a holistic approach to BPR, and put the greatest emphasis upon 'people' and quality of life factors, are more likely to introduce teleworking as a result of undertaking BPR.

- The introduction of teleworking may effectively redefine processes and, on occasion, redefine an organisation's structure and motivation, control, etc. Where its impacts are significant it may appear to imitate BPR.
- Some organisations have used the introduction of a new pattern of work or new approach to learning to achieve more radical and fundamental changes than comparative organisations that have adopted BPR.

There is generally little if any contact between those in 'personnel' and elsewhere who seek to build learning organisations and those undertaking BPR. Each group tends to attract different sorts of people. They usually speak 'different languages' and often 'live in different worlds'. BPR and transformation should enable and support drives to introduce new ways of working and learning.

A new social contract

The Caux Round Table has developed a set of 'Principles for Business' which draw upon different ethical traditions and have been adopted by major European, Japanese and North American companies. They view individuals as important in themselves rather than as merely a means of achieving corporate results.

For many organisations and their people to reap the full benefits of BPR, expectations, attitudes and behaviours will have to be transformed. Fundamental changes need to occur within ourselves before more civilised and liberating living, working and learning environments can be created.

More 'positive' BPR goals are called for. Improving learning or the quality of working life should be key drivers of BPR initiatives. BPR should enable us to obtain far greater control over our lives. One re-engineering methodology is specifically designed to complement and supplement existing approaches to BPR and thus help ensure that issues and opportunities relating to new patterns of work are taken more fully into account during the course of BPR exercises.[11]

A sense of perspective and a new agenda are also needed:

> What is so great about work as compared with working out, or walking in the woods, or listening to the blues, etc? Due to advances in productivity we no longer need so many people to produce a wide range of goods. This offers us the prospect of higher quality lives built around hobbies and interests rather than work. Social attitudes and expectations need to adjust to both the realities and the alternatives.[19]

Checklist

How important are individuals within the culture of your organisation?

Are they victims or beneficiaries of organisational change?

What priority is placed upon reflection, learning and the quality of working life?

Are people treated as colleagues, and with respect?

Do they receive equal treatment and consideration regardless of age, sex, nationality and social, ethnic and cultural background?

Have all the requirements for successful self-development, shared learning and group and teamworking been thought through?

Are obstacles, barriers and 'hindrances' actively identified and prioritised, are root causes diagnosed and are 'vital few' programmes put in place to tackle the key problem areas?

In particular, are people equipped with the tools, techniques and technologies to operate and learn effectively in groups and teams?

Do they have easy and open access to information and appropriate learning environments? Do these increase understanding and improve the quality of work?

Is the working and learning environment conducive of health, safety, satisfaction, creativity and performance?

Are people encouraged and enabled to work and learn at times and locations, in modes and with other people of their choice?

References

1. Donald Petersen and John Hillkirk, *Teamwork: New Management Ideas for the 90s*, London, Victor Gollancz, 1991, p 26.
2. Colin Coulson-Thomas and Trudy Coe, *The Flat Organisation: Philosophy and Practice*, Corby, British Institute of Management (BIM), 1991.
3. Colin Coulson-Thomas (ed), *Business Process Re-engineering: Myth and Reality*, London, Kogan Page, 1994.
4. Linda Holbeche, *Career Development in Flatter Structures*, Horsham, West Sussex, Roffey Park Management Institute, 1995.
5. Neville Benbow, *Survival of the Fittest: A Survey of Managers' Experiences of, and Attitudes to, Work in the Post Recession Economy*, Institute of Management (IM) Research Report, London, IM, November 1995.
6. Colin Coulson-Thomas (ed), *Business Process Re-engineering: Myth and Reality*, London, Kogan Page, 1994, p 38.
7. Colin Coulson-Thomas, *Harnessing the Potential of Groups*, a survey undertaken for Lotus Development, London, Adaptation Ltd, 1993, p 38.
8. Colin Coulson-Thomas, *Creating the Global Company: Successful Internationalisation*, London, McGraw-Hill, 1992.

9. Colin Coulson-Thomas, *Transforming the Company: Bridging the Gap Between Management Myth and Corporate Reality*, London, Kogan Page, 1992.
10. *Xerox 2000: Putting It Together, Building The New Productivity*, November 1992 update, Xerox Corporation, 1992, p 6.
11. Colin Coulson-Thomas (executive ed), *The Responsive Organisation: Re-engineering New Patterns of Work*, London, Policy Publications, 1995.
12. Colin Coulson-Thomas (ed), *Business Process Re-engineering: Myth and Reality*, London, Kogan Page, 1994, p 32.
13. Colin Coulson-Thomas, *Harnessing the Potential of Groups*, a survey undertaken for Lotus Development, London, Adaptation Ltd, 1993.
14. Colin Coulson-Thomas, *Professional Development of and for the Board*, London, Institute of Directors, 1990.
15. Eric Benhamou, 'The Community as an Electronic Proving Ground', in Colin Coulson-Thomas (ed), *Business Process Re-engineering: Myth and Reality*, London, Kogan Page, 1994, pp 183–91.
16. Colin Coulson-Thomas, *Harnessing the Potential of Groups*, a survey undertaken for Lotus Development, London, Adaptation Ltd, 1993, p 38.
17. Richard Branson, 'Growing Bigger while Staying Small', *Director: The 1993 Convention Report*, Special Supplement, May 1993, pp 60–7.
18. Colin and Susan Coulson-Thomas, *Managing the Relationship with the Environment*, a survey undertaken for Rank Xerox, London, Adaptation Ltd, 1990.
19. Colin Coulson-Thomas (ed), *Business Process Re-engineering: Myth and Reality*, London, Kogan Page, 1994, p 37.

The quality of management: learning, involvement, empowerment, reward, recognition and communication

Swear a hole in an iron pot.

In the last chapter we considered the 'people dimension' from the perspective of individuals and the relationship between the individual and the group. Overall, a picture is emerging which suggests our collective lack of imagination is preventing us from achieving the full potential of BPR and other means of 'fundamental change'.

Single-minded or stubborn adherence to a narrow course of action can cut through not only obstacles but the very fabric of an organisation, and much that is valuable may flow through the holes. In many organisations the quality of management is at fault, and in this chapter we will examine the various ways in which it might be improved. But first we need to understand the particular situation we are in.

The corporate context

People's views, perceptions and expectations will reflect their opinions and perspectives on the corporate context within which they are working. Thus any broader approaches to management that are advocated may need to cope with a distinctive 'company way of doing things'.

Corporate cultures, even within the same sector or group, can vary significantly. For example, in one exercise a company was felt to be impatient and arrogant, while a sister organisation was considered laid back, complacent, 'middle aged' and 'set in its ways'.

To identify the salient features of a particular culture, questions along the lines of the following, based upon the issues we considered in the last chapter, could be asked:

- Is it individualistic, even idiosyncratic, and competitive or collaborative and cooperative? Is it compatible with 'collectivist' approaches, for example to quality, or resistant to central initiatives?
- From a customer perspective, are people welcoming, helpful and flexible or defensive, stiff and angular? Is there is a need to reconcile individual creativity with corporate discipline, shared learning and a greater commitment to the customer?
- Do people appreciate and welcome the relative freedom, responsibility and accountability they have? Or do they feel abandoned and left to 'get on with it'? Can people gravitate to roles that suit them, and work and learn in a mode and at a place, time and location that suits them?
- Is it a caring culture? Would 'loyal staff' who are underemployed in terms of 'adding value' from a customer point of view be asked to improve internal processes etc, or would they be pounced upon as 'headcount reduction' opportunities?
- Do employees lead 'protected' or stressful lives? Are certain roles such as testing, documentation and maintenance regarded as boring, even though they may be important from a customer perspective?

The precise questions to ask will depend upon the context, and there are many aspects of corporate culture to consider. Some symptoms of especial significance for the people of an organisation are listed in Table 9.1.

Customers don't exist to give employees interesting things to do. For

Table 9.1 *Symptoms of corporate culture*

Mission statement
Values, concerns and business ethics
Terms of employment
Form of organisation
Importance of network relationships
Approach to decision-making
Location or pattern of authority
Communication practice
Sharing of information
Criteria for assessment
Delegation of responsibility
Emphasis on teamwork
Focus on quality
Degree of specialisation
Tolerance of diversity
Speed of action
Method of control
Extent of mutual trust
Commitment to learning and development
Openness to outsiders
Sensitivity to values and feelings

some companies to develop more of a 'partnership' relationship with their customers, the protective, self-expression culture of certain groups of individuals may need to give way to a more open, sharing culture of groups and teams.

A generation gap or 'previous history' may be evident in responses. In one company the 'oldies' stressed that an activity was an art, and used painting and other 'artistic' analogies. They acted as 'guardians' or 'trustees' of 'the company way'. The younger generation tended to question whether this view represented yesterday's mythology rather than tomorrow's reality. This latter group was more likely to stress the potential value of automated methods, new development tools, re-engineered processes and building block approaches.

In many companies, one particular national culture seems to dominate. Some of the factors that could contribute to the development of a multinational and transnational management team were summarised by one management team under the headings set out in Figure 9.1. Successful internationalisation, the subject of another book by the author,[1] can be an important consideration for multinational, transnational and international companies as some management approaches travel better in some cultures than in others.

The learning culture

During a period of change and uncertainty the attempts of some managers to shield and protect can be mistaken. Charles Heckscher has

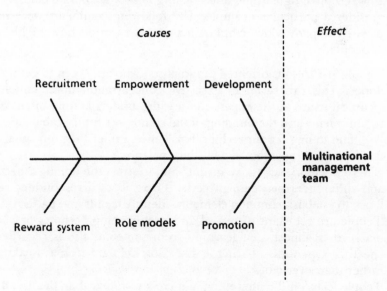

Figure 9.1   Becoming a transnational company

pointed out that the loyalty and commitment many employees display under pressure can be counter-productive when focused upon the past rather than the demands of the future.[2]

Successful transformation often requires people to think differently, ie the focus should be upon the processes of collective thinking, learning and creating rather than the quantity and speed of work. Too few BPR exercises are concerned with the identification and re-engineering of learning processes, or the creation of a learning organisation. Learning cultures are more talked about than achieved.

Bright, creative and talented people will not necessarily come spontaneously together to constitute a learning culture. Learning may need to be actively encouraged and championed. Unipart has invested £3 million in a learning centre at its Oxford location. Learning may need to become a basic drive.[3] For Rover Group 'Corporate Learning' is a 'key business process', while 'an organisation which can learn' is regarded as a 'fundamental principle of quality strategy'.

There are many different approaches to the management and practice of learning. One of the quality teams at British Aerospace went out and examined the approaches of 40 other companies. Unisys examined how 80 other corporations have sought to create a customer service culture before adopting its own approach. However, at some point a mature company becomes a producer and creator of new approaches rather than an absorber, consumer or improver of existing approaches – a leader rather than an imitator.

How receptive to learning and creating is your corporate culture? Let us consider a particular example. The following comments were made about one company which employs many of the world's most highly educated people:

- 'People are "results oriented pragmatists" who are "keen to get the job done". This can result in excessive concentration upon immediate technical issues at the expense of a wider understanding of customer requirements and the building of the company's future capability.'
- 'We tend to market our technical brilliance, rather than our openness, flexibility and capability as a business partner.'
- 'There is a tendency to "re-invent" and to stress the unique aspects of, and differences between, projects. There is a corresponding reluctance to establish common elements, identify trends and patterns.'
- 'People are reluctant to record and re-use, compare notes or benchmark. It is almost as if learning from someone else is regarded as cheating. Openness, sharing and seeking help are seen as weaknesses rather than strengths.'
- 'People focus on the interesting and creative rather than the useful and practical. While technical expertise is respected, people, presentational

and other skills needed to establish and build "partnership" relationships with customers are under-valued.'

● 'Problems tend to be glossed over rather than highlighted, and to be hidden until they become critical. The inclination is to hope for the best, rather than prepare for the worst.'

As frequently happens, during the recession there had been an excessive preoccupation with a short-term and financial orientation, at the expense of building longer-term relationships with customers and preparing for the next 'quantum leap'. The organisation was perceived as hardening or solidifying, and barriers to the mobility of people and ideas between subsidiaries were perceived as growing.

Learning and shared learning across functional, project group and business unit boundaries can be especially important in competitive markets. PSA Peugeot Citroën believes cooperation across its separate car divisions has resulted in significant benefits for its customers.

Do not overlook the 'learning supply chain' or the 'learning network'.[4] Learning across organisational boundaries has enabled BMW to improve 'the efficiency of the entire value-added supply chain'. Rover consciously set out to learn from Honda during their close partnership. London Electricity, Nestlé and Lucas have all actively participated in shared learning projects.

Barriers to learning

To confront a situation such as the one just described we need to explore the various barriers to learning. Overall, communication in the company was predominantly one-way and top-down, rather than two-way and horizontal. There was a noticeable lack of feedback, attitude surveys, etc, while at the same time there appeared to be a latent requirement for internal interest groups and networks.

It was not clear how, and to what extent, organisational learning occurred, or how the company in question managed to obtain 'economies of scale', while its approach to quality appeared on occasion to be a hindrance rather than a help:

● People claimed to be 'busy bees', but few had time to think. People wrote reports to line managers rather than thinking, talking, sharing and learning, either among themselves or with customers.
● The company appeared to collect, but not always to use, information. Learning was unstructured, by the 'grapevine' and through 'individual doing'. There was a noticeable lack of group and organisational learning, and too little sharing across projects and business units.
● Creativity was linked to the solution by individuals of particular technical problems, rather than to the moving forward of collective understanding or 'adding value'.

- The focus was upon the efficient utilisation of people rather than upon their growth and development. One sensed an under-investment in defining and agreeing roles, and in building both individual competences and group capabilities.
- The company's culture appeared 'introverted'. There was limited use of benchmarking and few had considered who or what to benchmark.
- Also, people did not appear to have been equipped with many of the tools, techniques, approaches and technologies that can support learning.
- While a significant amount of time was devoted to writing and reading reports, action only tended to occur when crises arose, by which time it might be too late to do other than 'handle the consequences' or employ a rescue approach.

This relatively long example is given because it is by no means atypical. In many organisations, one should neither assume nor expect learning to occur. This reality suggests certain questions to address:

- How many of those reading quality and other management reports are able to do much to help those writing them? Are the reports 'bureaucratic overhead' or are they adding value? Why are so many people not more productively engaged in analysis, review, improvement and learning activities?
- How should companies learn from experience and reap learning 'economies of scale'? Why is radical thinking and 'first principles' discussion not more actively encouraged? Are there distinct and clear development, reward and status progressions for those who learn? Why should a company expect its processes, ways of doing things, etc, to keep up with those of competitors when it is not taking steps to review and improve them?

In many organisations, the answers to such questions would reveal an urgent need to improve the quality of management.

Quality of management

Over time, one must assume that organisations which are deficient at learning will fall behind benchmark practice. In many companies there is an urgent need to equip people with the attitudes, approaches, tools and techniques to encourage and enable learning and sharing within and between groups.

Opportunities to grow by moving through a progression of roles, and to develop capability and competence, also need to be created to replace vanishing 'career ladders' and the status of job titles if above-average talent is not to be lost. In most organisations there are potential learning

and improvement roles that could both challenge good people and benefit stakeholders.

Given the intrinsic quality of their 'human capital', many organisations
could obtain a relatively high return from investment in improving their
quality of management and learning. The following questions concerning
the role and contribution of management should be addressed:

- What contribution do the various levels of management make either
  to learning or to the value or quality delivered to customers?
- Are line managers meddlers or enablers and facilitators? Are managers actively advising, counselling and coaching, or are they just
  reading, checking, waiting and surviving?
- What vital few programmes are in place to improve working practices,
  learning, project management or account management?
- Who is actually learning, for example by looking for links, patterns
  and relationships? Who is developing the future capabilities that will
  not just 'drop out' of today's projects?
- How are lessons arising out of individual activities and projects learned
  and shared, and is learning occurring and shared across supply chains?

These questions go beyond traditional 'training', which might or might
not be applied to activities that deliver value to customers or achieve business results. In any event, holistic changes of attitudes, approach and perspective may be needed, rather than just particular skills and techniques.

In many companies the management agenda is largely driven by organisational objectives and does not encourage learning in particular, or more
sensitive and people-centred approaches in general. Thus the Institute of
Management and Manpower's fourth annual survey of employment strategies has revealed that: 'Decisions on employment continue to be driven by
the need to reduce costs, improve productivity and increase flexibility.'[5]
Increasing creativity, employee satisfaction, loyalty, commitment and
choice are not priority objectives.

Raising the quality of management

In a particular context, a number of related measures might be needed to
significantly improve the quality of management. To illustrate the range
of issues that may need to be considered, the following were suggested in
one exercise:

- the encouragement of thinking, questioning, networking and sharing
  by means of seminars, workshops and taskforces;
- subjecting certain opinions and assumptions to public debate or testing them against available evidence – opinion and assertion may need
  to be replaced with fact and understanding;
- the introduction of risk analyses, root causes and trends, etc, into

presentations and onto accessible databases to encourage both thinking and understanding;

● articulating, agreeing and communicating definitions or expectations of role model behaviour where appropriate;

● the introduction of 'learning labs' and internal and external benchmarking;

● equipping people with a range of practical approaches, tools and techniques, which would enable them to tackle the problems and situations they face, and review and improve working and learning practices and corporate processes.

In general, more holistic approaches to skill and capability development are required. One such approach is outlined in Figure 9.2.

Many organisations would benefit from an integrated framework of roles which could provide people with optional development paths. Both

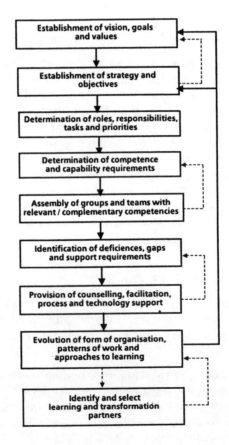

Figure 9.2 Skill and capability development process

the competences of each role and desired behaviours could be agreed with those currently in them, and a framework of assessment and development activities with supporting reward and remuneration could be put in place to encourage them. The assessment and accreditation of prior learning and experience can allow learning support to be directed to where it can have the greatest impact.

Each situation should be considered on its own merits, as standard solutions can do great harm. Let us move on to consider some areas that may require sensitive handling.

Role model behaviour

'Role model' conduct could be encouraged in a number of areas, and in each of these its definition should be honest. One personnel director confided: 'We award brownie points to those who verbally support something we ourselves consider flawed.' Another expressed concern that subjective top-down assessments tended to favour 'pals and cronies'.

Whether or not to define role model behaviour is a dilemma faced by many management teams.

Advantages of definition

On the one hand a definition can help ensure that people 'walk the talk', and common criteria are established to guide reward and promotion decisions. People know what is expected of them.

The definition of role model qualities can help to avoid the incompatibility of different activities. Thus while some are extolling the virtues of empowerment, elsewhere in the organisation promotion and 'fast-streaming' decisions might be taken on the basis of traditional 'command and control' criteria. In such a case, greater compatibility could result from putting more emphasis upon such qualities as openness, trust and willingness to share and delegate as criteria for advancement.

Harvester Restaurants found that introducing shared values was an essential element of its delayering and introduction of a system of self-managing teams. Without supporting values and related reward and recognition changes Operations Director Sue Newton does not believe the necessary changes of attitudes and behaviour would have occurred.

Disadvantages of definition

On the other hand, there are dangers. Too tight a definition of role model behaviour and shared values could result in the 'production' of a community of corporate clones who think and act in similar ways. Meetings could become opportunities for collective exercises in 'groupthink', while ambitious crawlers, bootlickers and toads 'use the words' in order to 'get ahead'.

An organisation that goes out of its way to, or inadvertently does, create a high degree of conformity may deny itself the richness and creativity that can stem from diversity. A culture that is intolerant of differences and exceptions may find it difficult to be flexible in response to the requirements of individual customers.

The absurdity exists of companies that have introduced courses and programmes to encourage creative thinking some time after driving through their organisations, at great expense, a standard approach to quality or some other programme which encourages conformity to certain narrow guidelines and recommended tools rather than a broader and more imaginative search for solutions. Such corrective action can represent a hidden cost of 'mechanical' quality initiatives.

Commitment and ownership

Many management initiatives decrease rather than increase the commitment of people who may regard them as imposed and 'owned' by the CEO or board and not by themselves. They alienate where they should encourage.

Patrick Ricard, Chairman and CEO of Groupe Pernod Ricard, stresses the importance of commitment: 'A business such as ours cannot function without the total commitment of its people, regardless of their tasks.'

Rather than support people and release their enthusiasm and commitment, many change programmes when coupled with corporate imperatives to slim down and, as one manager put it, 'squeeze more blood out of a stone', make their lives harder and less rewarding. The reluctance of some companies to measure employee satisfaction results from an awareness that people are not as happy as they used to be. They might prefer less stress and more time for reflection. They may be working harder, but is it at the right things from a customer perspective?

Commitment, creativity and talent need to be harnessed and applied to tasks and activities that add value to, or for, customers and deliver corporate objectives. Quality ought to have an important role to play in this process, yet the management of talent is frequently considered without first reflecting upon what actually constitutes talent in a particular context.[6]

Sweden's Esab Group regards staff development as a 'strategic necessity'. Training activities 'are designed to give the staff greater job satisfaction, create increased involvement, improve motivation and thereby lead to greater efficiency for operations as a whole.'

The extent of commitment

Some find it difficult to judge the extent of commitment to new corporate programmes. With the injection of new tools and approaches and the adoption of unfamiliar jargon new means of judging understanding and commitment may be needed. Management fads create new opportunities for people to put out misleading signals and climb aboard bandwaggons.

According to one subsidiary CEO: 'I used to have a handle upon how people felt. I knew the signals. Now they are hidden in a layer of fog. With all the new words, how do you judge how really committed people are?'

When a new initiative comes along there will be those who are eager to 'play the game' or 'keep in'. The 'early adopters' of quality or BPR may include crawlers as well as converts. What appears to be commitment may be cosmetic or insincere.

Considerable intuition and judgement is generally needed when taking people decisions. With the benefit of hindsight, CEOs often feel they should have been 'tougher' or 'grasped the nettle' earlier with those whose commitment was lukewarm. According to one: 'I persisted with a few cynical ones in the boardroom. They were not just apathetic, one or two seemed to be actually working against what we were trying to achieve.'

On other occasions, when a chairman or CEO has worried about the commitment of certain boardroom colleagues, investigation has revealed their reservations to be based upon genuine concerns. Perhaps the initiative has not been thought through, or elements are perceived to be missing. At the same time, among the apparent 'team players' may be the courtiers and office politicians who are sensitive to which way the wind is blowing.

Involvement and participation

Although it is rare to find a quality or change programme that does not identify involvement as a key success factor, one survey of corporate practice discovered: 'The relationship between employee involvement and overall corporate performance was found too problematic to make any precise evaluation.'[7] Is this yet another example of packaging and rhetoric triumphing over substance?

According to Tom Irvine of the CBI Education Foundation:

Participation is important, but as an end in itself it misses the point. Too much emphasis on ensuring that everyone is participating can have the net effect that the focus of attention is inwards, retrospective, and not focused on the customer. If, however, emphasis is placed on building a consensus about the organisation's competitive position, the focus of attention moves towards the customer and the needs of the marketplace, and is forward-looking. The involvement of others is essential, but is a consequence of building the consensus, not an end in itself.[8]

Much depends upon the approach to involvement that is adopted. For example, the results of suggestion schemes suggest that many companies have for many years denied themselves the benefit of many ideas and comments from their employees. In 1991 VEBA introduced a company suggestion scheme designed to encourage improvements throughout the group. In the manufacturing companies within the VEBA group over 4,200 suggestions were received during the year, of which 1,700 earned a bonus payment.

So far as corporate transformation is concerned, an extensive European survey involving five sectors across 12 countries found involvement and participation to be essential when fundamental and discontinuous change occurs.[9] It also tends to result in improved understanding, greater openness to new developments and a more satisfying work environment, and these benefits can be obtained without incurring the delays in implementation that some critics of involvement and participation allege.

People can have a major impact upon the largest of corporations. Thus at Ford the Taurus or the 'driver's car' resulted from involving as many people as possible in the product development process, rather than just the 'experts' who in the past had sometimes been those who were furthest removed, and least in touch, with the requirements of the users of the company's products.

Top down or bottom up?

In Chapter 6 we examined policy deployment. In companies such as Xerox policy deployment is based upon the Japanese concept of 'hoshin kanri' or 'management by policy'. Corporate action plans and policies are cascaded down and through organisations gaining detail as they are applied and modified to suit local circumstances. Essentially 'hoshin kanri' is a 'top-down' approach.

Other organisations adopt more of a participative and 'bottom-up' approach. While encouraging people to suggest, question and refine can also lead to challenge and dissent, this is welcomed in some organisations:

- At MashreqBank, the whole management team have participated in a review of vision, mission, goals and priorities, not just the 'Leadership Council' composed of the senior officers of the bank.
- The computer services group EDS involved people at all levels in a fundamental reassessment of its role and purpose in a changing marketplace. In effect a change of strategic direction was charted by the people of the organisation rather than by the board of directors and their immediate network of advisers. Inputs were received from thousands of people, not just from a few.

Sharing responsibility and wider involvement can lead to more tailored approaches where generalised slogans sometimes seem to lack bite:

- Boots has split itself into ten relatively self-contained business units each of which is encouraged to develop a distinct identity and approach to its particular market sector.

● Lew Platt, CEO of Hewlett-Packard, believes decisions should be taken wherever possible by those who are closest to the customer. According to Platt: 'The first rule is to trust and respect all employees.'

The more secure personalities find it easier to share. However, in the case of too many corporate leaders: 'The very people who should be the fount of corporate drive and purpose are frequently plagued by insecurity and doubt'.[10] They avoid confronting reality or involving their people.

Encouraging involvement and learning

Involvement requires confidence and trust. Dennis Keller, Chairman of DeVry, believes corporate leaders should exude, champion and build trust.

Ultimately a business is founded upon trust. It should not be assumed but actively encouraged lest it be choked by the weeds of disappointment and distrust:

● For Dr Hasjim Ning, Chairman of Lippobank, adherence to the principle of trust is 'our overriding strategic vision and mission'. Ning believes: 'Trust will always endure in Lippobank as the nucleus or moral strength that inspires confidence on the part of depositors, shareholders, team members, regulators and potential investors alike.' For Lippobank trust depends upon integrity of management and management integrity.

● John Orange, Chief Executive of BP Oil, also believes in the importance of trust. The company sought the views of its employees around the world ahead of introducing a culture change programme. Their responses suggested a more holistic approach needed to be adopted that embraced structure and processes as well as culture, and related all three to corporate objectives.

Involvement in improvement activities and direct experience of the results can have a significant impact upon attitudes. Michel Boulerne, Director of Total Quality at the Brussels headquarters of Solvay, believes that: 'By operating a pragmatic and systematic process of continuous improvement, the men and women who work for the Group will learn, experience and achieve Total Quality.' At Solvay, TQM is integrated into 'individual and collective work and behaviour'.

The technology of corporate democracy, working and learning

Networking and communications technology offers the prospect of 'electronic democracy'. People could be encouraged to vote on options, seek feedback or canvas opinions. Interest groups and coalitions of people for or against particular corporate developments and practices could emerge. This could help create greater corporate democracy by opening up organisational politics which has been hitherto concealed and allowing a much wider range of viewpoints to be represented.

BMW is examining a number of means by which a combination of new technology, empowerment and training can be used to reduce the barriers between functions and broaden the range of tasks and responsibilities of groups. The aim is bring together the planning and performing of work, and both to improve the attractiveness of the workplace and combine the flexibility of handcrafted production with the cost advantages of large-scale manufacture.

Emerging technologies also create new opportunities to bring together the activities of working and learning which are too often separated:

● Esab believes in the integration of learning and working. During 1991 Esab introduced a new form of manufacturing cell 'known as instructive organisation in which everyone in the Group collaborates to solve problems and complete tasks.' Pilot studies suggest: 'This way of working calls for far greater involvement on the part of every individual and helps to give the staff more in-depth knowledge.'

● ASK Europe and its client partners work with integrated working and learning environments that can not only identify development needs but also how each individual might best build his or her understanding. Both information content and approach to learning are then tailored to both individual and group requirements, offering people in effect personal learning support environments.

The transition to a learning network organisation is not neutral in its impacts upon people. The technology of the network allows some to be accessed and others to be bypassed. A group may feel 'excluded' as a result of considering itself on the periphery of a network. New means have to be found of monitoring and assessing who is contributing to, and who is 'living off', the network.

Empowerment: the concept

Another fashionable but much misunderstood and sometimes controversial concept is empowerment. Without direction, shared vision and common purpose, empowerment can lead to confusion and fragmentation. In a worst case, without some form of cerebral cement to hold it together, the network organisation dissolves or falls apart.

Empowerment is about building local authority, accountability and ownership and creating circumstances in which inhibitors and contraints are removed, thus allowing the former to be responsibly exercised. It is not about giving a general licence to people to do what they please. It should not result in an abdication of responsibility, and however it is accomplished some form of organisational structure is likely to remain.

Xerox recognises that: 'Success depends upon the involvement and empowerment of trained and highly motivated Xerox people.' Paul Allaire envisions 'a Xerox that is seen as one of the best places to work.' To become benchmark for employee motivation and satisfaction the corporation recognises that its people must be 'empowered, trained and work in an environment that reflects the value they represent for Xerox.'

Empowerment is defined within Rank Xerox as: 'The effective delegation of authority and accountability to a level as close as possible to the customer in order to satisfy "customer requirements"'. For those on the receiving end 'empowerment' is 'being energised, committed and enabled to autonomously achieve continuous quality improvement in work processes and outputs.'

Making empowerment a reality

In most contexts, for some to be empowered, others must let go. The manager needs to become a coach, counsellor, enabler, facilitator and 'leader of learning'.

Such terms as 'social engineering' and 'social architect' are used to describe the role of the manager in creating both an environment that is conducive of empowerment and a group of people who match its requirements. Invariably the tighter the definition and the more demanding the nature of the 'society' that is sought, the greater the number of those who do not fit.

Power in terms of the capacity to influence and act is too often seen in 'zero sum' terms. Managers fear that by giving some away their own stock will be reduced. In reality by releasing the latent energies and potential of others, and enabling and supporting their growth, the collective capability of the enterprise is enhanced. Empowerment can be a 'positive sum' game in which both 'giver' and 'receiver' benefit.

The degree of empowerment can range from the level found in the functional departments of traditional bureaucracies which allow a degree of autonomy to the specialist professional to the wide ranging discretion allowed to the semi-autonomous business unit (Figure 9.3). Some companies such as Rank Xerox have made steady progress through self-managed work groups to semi-autonomous business units, learning as they proceed and enabling their people to accommodate gradually to greater freedom of independent operation and a wider range of responsibilities.

Restructuring to support empowerment

A key principle of empowerment is 'subsidiarity', or to locate power and responsibility at the levels at which they can be most effectively exercised.

Level of discretion given to
point of contact with customer

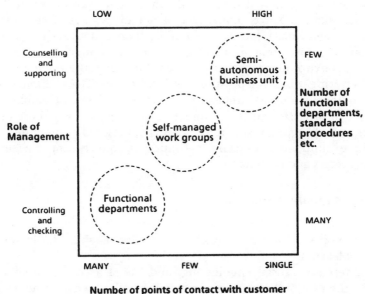

Figure 9.3   Degrees of empowerment

This should be the driver, rather than an obsession, of delayering and delegation.

We saw in the last chapter that organisations are being broken down into more manageable units and reference has been made in this chapter to the restructuring at Boots. Giants such as Royal Dutch Shell that have only started the process more recently may have a long way to go. In Japan there are pressures to loosen the constraints of the web of company relationships of the Keiretsu system in order to give individual enterprises greater freedom and independence.

Cigna, an insurance company, has reorganised six business functions into two basic processes that cover pre-sales and post-sales activities, and significant improvements in throughput time have been achieved. The experience of Cigna emphasises the need for involvement and communication. Bringing groups together in cross-functional teams during the change process was found to be particularly beneficial, and an element of individual remuneration is now linked to team performance.

Linking physically dispersed staff up electronically has encouraged cooperation and sharing in Ericsson and Motorola. Compaq Computer intends to operate largely as a virtual corporation as a result of forging network links with its customers and suppliers.

At the same time the balance can swing too far in favour of decentralisation and 'network operation'. A degree of physical interaction can stimulate creativity and help build a cultural identity. Thus ASK maintains work activity and learning centres, while large companies such as Deere & Co are consolidating by co-location – bringing previously scattered groups of staff together at the same location.

Effective delegation

Delegating responsibilities while withholding the discretion to act can lead to frustration and conflict. Calvin Campbell, Chairman, President and CEO of the Cyprus Minerals Company, recognises that 'the decision-making process must move downward with accountability.' This requires some faith in people's ability to respond.

Trust may need to be nurtured. It grows out of relationships, and can involve risks for the party taking the initiative. Increasingly, managers are being expected to take the first step. Calvin Campbell is an optimist: 'My feeling is that some employees, individually and in groups, could produce even more than they themselves ever envisioned given the proper atmosphere to succeed.'

Delegation, whether irresponsible or in good faith, can sometimes lead to shocks. A balance has to be struck between overstretching people and holding them back. Shell incurred heavy losses on currency dealing which had an impact upon overall group results as a result of allowing the team concerned considerable freedom to act. The experience of the losses of Barings in Singapore has become legendary and led to the acquisition of the company by the Dutch ING Group.

A challenge for senior management is to achieve sufficient cooperation across business unit boundaries to secure the benefits of synergy while at the same time encouraging an entrepreneurial approach and differentiation. For example, according to Roland Darneau, Chairman of the French Moulinex group, the company is seeking 'internal coherence' in order to 'fully benefit from synergies and also result in a decrease in administrative overheads' while at the same time maintaining the identity of its Krups and Moulinex brands.

To build a quality and learning culture it is usually necessary to encourage attitudes, improve processes and introduce tools (Figure 9.4). Learning and supply chain partners may also be involved. Each of these areas should be reviewed, and changes may need to occur during the transformation from a bureaucratic to a network form of organisation. Having examined attitudes, in the next two chapters we will move on to consider processes and tools.

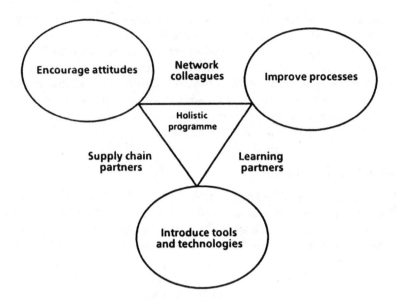

Figure 9.4 Building the quality and learning culture

Barriers to empowerment

Reluctance to let go and concerns about risks and loss of power tend to be related to insecurity. The Swiss pharmaceuticals company Ciba, a champion of empowerment, found that many middle managers in particular are reluctant to delegate authority to their subordinates. These are often the very people who are bearing the brunt of other corporate changes such as downsizing or rightsizing.

The insecure are a threat to empowerment. Encouraging self-empowerment is seen as fomenting or encouraging challenge or trouble. The confident are more willing to empower others and take advantage themselves of opportunities for self-empowerment.

Controls can constrain, and management by shared values and objectives is preferable to bureaucratic approval processes. Those not used to discretion may need to be encouraged by a succession of steps to develop their self-confidence. Too often, empowerment is something that is done to people rather than assumed or grown into. It is imposed upon them by senior management.

Common approaches, the standard toolkit, fitting in, absorbing and assuming a corporate personality and submerging one's individual identity into that of the group are sought-after measures of accommodation and 'cohesion'. Some companies use quality to support this process, while others put more emphasis upon individual responsibility.

The reality is that some people will not want to be empowered, and most, if not all, will need to be carefully prepared for it. However, this should not be used as an excuse for not letting go. Where owners of businesses have been open with their people, the results have sometimes been dramatic:

- Kingston Technology has built its rapid expansion upon the commitment of its President John Tu to openness and trust. The corporation's financial records are open to its people, but many of them do not avail themselves of the opportunity because they are interested in the future rather than the past.
- The experience of Semco in Brazil, where people decide their own salaries and hours, gives some insight into what others might achieve if they were prepared to 'trust the people'. The company which once faced an uncertain future has been turned around under the imaginative leadership of Ricardo Semler.

The organisation of ABB involves both cross-border knowledge transfer, cooperation and coordination and a high degree of decentralisation to local operating units. ABB aims to be both 'big' and 'small'. Being big results in 'economy of scale' and 'economy of scope'. Percy Barnevik believes 'the latter means we can offer our customers "one-stop" shopping.' At the same time, Barnevik explains that decentralisation means that 'flexibility and entrepreneurship are promoted in our many small profit centres and corporate staffs are kept at minimal levels.'

Schlumberger operates as a transnational, with a permanent presence in over 75 countries. Its 53,000 employees are expected to show initiative. A typical view is: 'You're given a problem and expected to solve it. How you solve it is your problem.' The approach is: 'We tell you what you are expected to do, not how to do it.'

According to one Schlumberger employee: 'You're given plenty of rope with which to run ... Of course, that's plenty of rope with which to hang yourself.' The company consciously seeks people who are confident and self-reliant. In the words of a Schlumberger recruiter: 'We look for the independent-minded.' Given its distinctive approach, and the opportunities Schlumberger gives to its people to learn and grow, it rarely needs to recruit from the outside.

Reward and remuneration

Reward and remuneration are the subjects of perennial debate. While one organisation could put great store in particular incentives, another might find they have limited impact. Overall, one study has concluded that there is little evidence to suggest a causal link between individual performance-related pay and increases in productivity.[11] Also, when attitudinal changes occur, they are not always in the right direction.[11]

Korean car maker Daewoo employs 'customer advisers' rather than salespeople. Their role is to assist and provide whatever information is required by the customer. Sales commissions that encourage staff to improve their remuneration at the expense of customers are not paid.

For reward and remuneration to have a positive impact they must be perceived as appropriate, relevant and fair both in the context and for those concerned. Increasingly performance is being measured at the level of the individual or group, and as people move across and between tasks many organisations face a demand for a greater diversity of approaches. The age of the 'designer package' beckons.

The need for personal tailoring is a challenge to some managers steeped in quality who have been reared on the language of 'reducing variation'. A start can be made by recognising the value of reconciling the distinct requirements of different parts of an organisation with the 'social cement' of shared aims:

● Lafarge Coppée employs over 31,000 people. Bertrand Collomb, the group's Chairman and CEO, stresses the importance of 'the variety needed for stimulating career paths' and meeting 'the needs of individual business units', and 'the cohesion that can only come from individual commitment.'

● The 'guiding principles' of Hoechst state: 'Hoechst sees itself as a community of people working together in a lasting union, motivated by shared aims. We impose exacting standards on ourselves, our skills, our willingness to learn and our commitment to performance. Our financial rewards are commensurate with our own performance and the Company's success.'

The proportion of income that is linked to customer satisfaction could be related to the degree of impact upon the customer (Figure 9.5). The approaches of some organisations are so tentative that the schemes they introduce are insufficient or too modest to reach the threshold at which they would begin to have a measurable impact upon the customer. In the case of the Rank Xerox scheme, it was decided at the outset to increase the proportion of income linked to customer satisfaction with seniority to reflect the greater and wider impact upon the customer that more senior managers were expected to have.

When quality is linked to continuous and measurable performance, all employees are given a challenge to improve and have the prospect of being rewarded for achievements. Those at all levels may have an opportunity to 'star' as a result of achieving a significant improvement. In this sense, quality can be relatively democratic and open to participation.

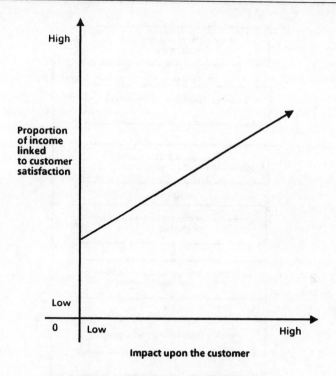

Figure 9.5   Reward and remuneration

For performance review to be effective, a transparent process along the lines of Figure 9.6 may be advisable. The greatest motivation and satisfaction occurs when proper attention is given to all stages of the process. For example, involvement in agreement of performance levels and development objectives is real and support and counselling requirements are actually provided.

Featherbedding versus motivation

A major corporation can have a significant impact upon the lives of many millions of people. It therefore becomes a target for those who wish to place extra social responsibilities upon businesses. Eberhard v. Kuenheim, Chairman of the Board of Management of BMW, has pointed out that the company's 'reserves are not infinite' and that 'excessive demands would weaken the competitiveness of our industry.'

Can people be treated too well? A form of welfare dependency used to be found in certain corporations that were over-protective and shielded their people from market forces. The result can be complacency, with the occasional costly and disruptive reorganisation justified as a means of keeping people on their toes.

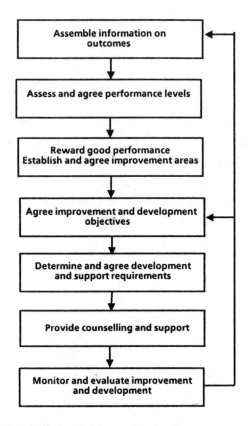

Figure 9.6 Performance review process

IBM and GE are two companies that have put great stress upon looking after their staff to the extent of cocooning them for too long against the realities of the need to change. Devolution, hiving off and empowerment can be particularly tough upon those who have abdicated responsibility for their development and future to the 'planners in personnel'.

Competitive and international pressure upon prices and margins means that a growing number of companies cannot afford to continue to provide the range of benefits that may have hitherto been taken for granted by their employees. Pension, insurance and other benefits, not to mention an expectation of job security, can no longer be taken for granted.

As a consequence of being no longer able to guarantee or promise the provision of a framework of social and psychological support, companies are having to find new ways of securing commitment and loyalty. Those that do not succeed will find themselves 'used' by able nomads who will take whatever development and learning opportunities are available before moving on. The smart will seek temporary refuge in whatever companies happen to be at the cutting edge in terms of their particular interests.

An assessment and support environment that is perceived as fair is more likely to be accepted. The performance review process set out in Figure 9.6 recognises that development opportunities and the support environment are becoming increasingly important to those concerned with ensuring the continuing relevance of their competencies and contribution.

Corporate communications

Many corporate statements are bland and do little to inspire. A vision, mission or strategic intent should enable people to know what to do. The mission of Coca-Cola is simply: 'To put a Coke within arm's reach of everyone in the world.'

Those seeking to bring about fundamental change need to communicate in all directions. John Melo of Thomas Cook spent a period as the group's Director of Performance Engineering. He points out that: 'No one at Thomas Cook has so far ever overestimated the need for communication. Our advice is to continuously and tirelessly sell what you are trying to achieve to every member of the organisation regardless of seniority.'

Earlier in the chapter we considered the growing importance of team-work and the need to make it more effective. According to Roger Young, Director-General of the Institute of Management: 'This calls for new skills and a new type of manager. Qualities needed include the ability to communicate, negotiate and motivate.'[12]

Concepts such as quality are often meaningless outside a particular context. They only have life within the hearts and minds of groups, teams and communities of people. To influence attitudes and behaviour, they must be compatible with ethos and culture. If this is not the case they may be rejected, or linger on as a cosmetic, ritual or 'trapping'. At Xerox two 'key enablers' have been identified: 'open and honest communication' and 'organization reflection and learning.'

Top-down patterns of communication can appear to contradict the messages of empowerment of involvement:

● Alex Krauer, the President and Managing Director of Ciba, and Heini Lippuner, the Chairman of the company's Executive Committee, believe that: 'Active two-way communication is vital to a modern, efficient organisation. It gives our people confidence and improves their ability to adapt to change.'
● Two-way communication does not spontaneously occur. BP Exploration and BP Oil have introduced international 'upward feedback' programmes as a worldwide initiative to encourage 'two-way communication between managers and their staff'.

The communication process should be both logical and integrated into other corporate management processes as shown in Figure 9.7.[4] In particular, before rushing off to make the corporate videos and print the posters it is advisable to analyse the situation the organisation is in, establish the purpose of communication, understand the interests of those to be communicated with, and agree clear objectives before creating messages and selecting channels.

When analysing the situation, a technique such as root cause analysis could be used to ensure people deal with underlying causes rather than surface symptoms. Effective communication can be time consuming, so publics and the channels for reaching them should be selected with care and prioritised. Focused and tailored approaches tend to be the most effective.

Effective communication

The passengers on Emirates Airways flight EK0003 from Dubai are imagining themselves swimming through warm and buoyant water towards

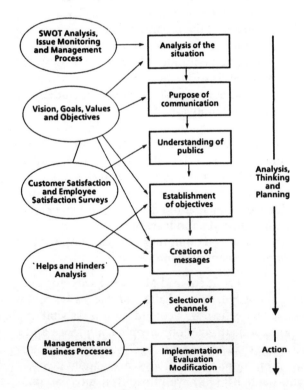

Figure 9.7 The communication process

Source: Colin Coulson-Thomas, *Transforming the Company*, Kogan Page, 1992.

the soft tumbling sound of a waterfall when their relaxation programme is interrupted to inform them that a violent western *The Quick and the Dead* is about to begin on one of the movie channels. So often do conflicting messages negate each other's impact.

We saw in Chapter 6 that there is little point in formulating strategies that are not communicated and shared. Some companies use a list of points to help communicate the essence of what an approach such as quality is thought to be about. Consider the following ten points which were used to communicate Hewlett-Packard's approach to quality:

- Focus on customers, their needs and expectations.
- Regularly check how satisfied they are; establish the dissatisfiers.
- The next person in the process is your customer.
- Strive to remove the basic causes of customer defects; search continually for problems, deviations.
- Have constancy of purpose, continuous innovation and improvement of products and processes in all activities.
- Never fail to standardise to hold gains.
- Build quality in upstream.
- Break down barriers between departments.
- Drive out fear throughout the organisation.
- Continuously educate, train and retrain to realise our full potential.

To communicate effectively, it is necessary to be aware of the main barriers to both internal and external communication. Those uncovered in one survey[13] are shown in Table 9.2. Once again, 'top management commitment' appears, but is closely followed by 'communication skills'. Those interviewed stressed they were not thinking of technical skills, such as how to give an effective presentation or be good at public speaking, but rather attitudes and approaches to communication. For example, are people just passing on messages or are they thinking about them? Are they open and honest and actively trying to share, involve and listen to feedback?

Communication is likely to become more open. As one chairman put it: 'The aim is to remove the places and roles in which people can hide.' Perhaps he should have added: 'and the verbiage and platitudes behind which people conceal their commitment and motives'. In the age of the 'white-board' the writing is literally on the wall, whether assessments of people on the wall at the JC Bamford plant or the business excellence plan in the Rank Xerox control room.

In the open organisation there will be new games to play, and not everyone will be equally adept at making the transition. A prominent advocate of TQM confided: 'Being a positive, team playing role model twenty-four hours a day is tough. You wake up in the middle of the night with the slogans buzzing around in your head.' Those seeking a greater degree of privacy or who like to be 'in their own space' may need to join the peripheral workforce or join networks for people of their own kind.

Table 9.2 *Barriers to effective communication*
(ranked in order of 'very significant' replies)

Internal communication	
Communication skills	**33%**
Top management commitment	**27%**
Employee attitudes	19%
Lack of two-way communication	19%
Organisation structure	13%
Ability to access people when needed	10%
Management processes	8%
Speed of communication	8%
Organisational politics	8%
Cost of communication	6%
Communications technology	2%
External communication	
Communication skills	**19%**
Top management commitment	**13%**
Speed of communication	8%
Employee attitudes	8%
Lack of two-way communication	8%
Ability to access people when needed	6%
Management processes	4%
Communications technology	4%
Cost of communication	2%
Organisational politics	2%
Organisation structure	0%

Source: *Communicating for Change*, Adaptation, 1991.[13]

Contemporary careers

In Chapter 3 we saw that organisations are being transformed into more flexible and responsive network forms. Traditional career ladders do not exist in many of the models of organisation that are emerging. A 1993 survey suggests they may be disappearing among organisations in general.[14] This has implications for quality, re-engineering and new approaches to management.

More frequent changes of job and employer might suggest that staff may move on before a new initiative has a chance to affect their attitudes and values. However, within the network organisation people may move between roles and members of the network, or leave and rejoin the network from time to time according to the availability of relevant projects and tasks. In the latter case, thought needs to be given to ways of ensuring partners, 'associates' and contractors are updated in respect of quality and other developments.

Insecurity influences attitudes. In a recession, people with jobs hang on to them like limpets. Many of the courageous who 'broke' free in order 'do their own thing' have subsequently come to regret their decisions. With hindsight, what once appeared enterprising can seem impetuous and foolhardy.

Yet the 'benefits' of full-time employment may be illusory, and job security may prove short-lived. While corporate life may appear rosy and enticing to the outsider, the reality may be different.[4] For many employees the 'fun' has gone out of management life. Growing gaps between the rhetoric of empowerment and change and a failure of implementation are leading to disillusionment and despair.

The gulf between words and actions results in staff feeling they have been tricked, duped and betrayed. The fine words of senior management in the corporate quality videos and house journals have been swept away by short-termism, downsizing, heavier workloads and other reactions to and consequences of economic adversity. Improving the quality of management involves recognising and addressing this reality, and action to improve the quality of working life along the lines of examples we considered in the last chapter could demonstrate commitment in this area.

The evidence suggests that corporate transformation can occur when all the pieces of the jigsaw puzzle are in place.[4] Benchmark companies are making the transition to a network form of organisation based upon project groups, taskforces and teams. As the transformation occurs the full-time and the part-time, the employed and the contracted, may all be required to develop new attitudes and skills.

There are some very positive aspects. Career ladders within functions leading to dead-end positions are being replaced by opportunities to work upon new projects as existing ones are completed. People can learn and grow by tackling more demanding problems and tasks, accumulating competencies rather than status. CVs consist of projects worked upon and outcomes achieved rather than positions held. The dangers of 'plateauing' and 'glass ceilings' are avoided by those who are open, flexible and willing to learn.

The international opportunity

Increasingly it is possible to access skill across the barriers of function, distance, time and nationality. The international challenge is to form taskforces and teams, and to harness the talents of people and apply them to activities that add value for customers, irrespective of location, function and nationality.[1]

As more suppliers and customers join the 'network organisation', teams and groups will draw their members from a wider variety of backgrounds. Whether or not and how individuals are employed, and by whom, becomes less important than the relevance and availability of skill and the sharing of a vision. It is the common vision, values and goals that hold the network organisation together, not employment status. A management philosophy could help to differentiate one network from another.

The emerging reality suggests that contract working, telecommuting and interim assignments are all likely to grow as people work and learn in whatever ways enable them to give of their best and contribute most to team and project objectives. Approaches to empowerment, involvement, reward and other areas considered in this chapter will have to cope with a growing diversity of situations.

Those who already work flexibly have a head start. As economic upswings gather momentum they will be the winners. Rather than cast envious glances at the full-time employed, whose lot may be less attractive than it appears to an outsider, they should prepare for the inevitable opportunities. The grass is not always greener on the other side of the employment fence.

The very notion of a 'fence' seems dated as boundaries within and between organisations become more porous. Agreed and shared values should embrace all the members of a network regardless of contractual arrangements and how and where they work and learn.

Where an organic or community view of organisations is taken and all individuals are dealt with fairly, then tackling one area should lead to reinforcement rather than envy or difficulty somewhere else. Perhaps looking over one's shoulder at others will become a thing of the past. With quality management each individual might have greater confidence that his or her contribution is both recognised and fairly rewarded by colleagues and peers.

Checklist

How might the quality of management in your organisation be improved?

Are people confident and secure, and equipped, empowered and motivated to act? Is management open and on the basis of fact or opinion?

Are the roles, competencies and qualities needed to seize tommorrow's opportunities agreed and understood, and are the required people being identified or selected, contracted or recruited, and enabled and developed?

Do the people of your organisation share a vision and a philosophy of management? How committed are they to corporate or network goals, values and objectives?

Have measurable objectives been established, and have these been deployed throughout the corporate network? Is everyone clear about what they have to do to contribute towards their achievement?

Is their involvement and participation actively encouraged, and is it measured? Are suggestions encouraged, submitted and implemented?

Are people equipped and motivated to learn from and share their experiences, and to continuously review and improve the processes and capability of the organisation and of the networks to which it belongs?

Should, or has, role model conduct with appropriate behaviours been defined? Does it support learning and the achievement of shared goals and objectives?

Does the reward and remuneration system encourage motivation, responsibility, self-development, shared learning and role model conduct? Does outstanding performance receive sufficient non-financial recognition?

Have the vision, philosophy, goals, values and objectives of the organisation or network, and desired behaviour and conduct, been communicated and shared?

Do people believe in the messages that are being communicated? Is there open and two-way communication?

References

1. Colin Coulson-Thomas, *Creating the Global Company: Successful Internationalisation*, London, McGraw-Hill, 1992.
2. Charles Heckscher, *White Collar Blues: Management Loyalties in an Age of Corporate Restructuring*, New York, HarperCollins, 1995.
3. Robert Howard, *The Learning Imperative: Managing People for Continuous Innovation*, Boston, Mass, Harvard Business Review Books, 1994.
4. Colin Coulson-Thomas, *Transforming the Company: Bridging the Gap between Management Myth and Corporate Reality*, London, Kogan Page, 1992.
5. Institute of Management and Manpower, *Survey of Long-Term Employment Strategies, 1995*, London, Institute of Management and Manpower plc, October 1995.
6. Philip Sadler, *Managing Talent: Making the Best of the Best*, London, Century Business, 1993.
7. Mick Marchington, John Goodman, Adrian Wilkinson and Peter Ackers, *New Developments in Employee Involvement*, Research Series No 2, London, Employment Department, May 1992.
8. Colin Coulson-Thomas, *Harnessing the Potential of Groups*, a survey for Lotus Development, London, Adaptation Ltd, 1993, p 41.
9. European Foundation for the Improvement of Living and Working Conditions, *Roads to Participation in Technological Change: Attitudes and Experiences* and *Issues of Participation in Technological Innovation: Attitudes and Experiences*, both Luxembourg, Office for the Official Publications of the European Commission, 1990.
10. Colin Coulson-Thomas, *Transforming the Company: Bridging the Gap between Management Myth and Corporate Reality*, London, Kogan Page, 1992, p 41.
11. Marc Thompson, *Pay and Performance: The Employer Experience*, IMS Report 218, Brighton, Institute of Manpower Studies, 1992.
12. Colin Coulson-Thomas, *Harnessing the Potential of Groups*, a survey for Lotus Development, London, Adaptation Ltd, 1993, p 22.
13. Colin and Susan Coulson-Thomas, *Communicating for Change*, a survey for Granada Business Services, London, Adaptation Ltd, 1991.
14. Kerr Inkson, *Are Career Ladders Disappearing?*, Corby, Institute of Management, 1993.

10

Re-engineering: the process dimension

Fat hens are poor layers.

Bloated bureaucracies do not deliver for long when faced with more flexible and responsive competitors. We saw in Chapter 3 the extent of the challenge faced by organisations that are engaged in a race against time to remain relevant and effective.

Quality and re-engineering

Throughout the middle and late 1980s various companies engaged in combinations of activities designed to build upon and complement their involvement with quality. And yet these initiatives were often described as differing from quality in that they were designed to achieve dramatic and discontinuous changes rather than incremental and continuous improvements. In the early 1990s selective aspects of this experience were packaged under the umbrella of 're-engineering'.[1]

During the subsequent promotion of the re-engineering concept, a mixture of misunderstanding and hype has created widespread expectations that are difficult to fulfil given that some key elements needed for success were omitted from the initial wave of packaging. In general, far too little attention was given to intangible 'people' factors such as attitudes, behaviour and the importance of learning. Notwithstanding these deficiencies, re-engineering is often described as a substitute for quality or as a successor to it, rather than as the complement to, or element of, a total quality approach as some originally intended.

Should or could re-engineering replace quality? Is it in some way 'better', whether in its nature, for example because of its focus upon 'process', or because of the degree of change it can bring about? The quality purist is likely to respond 'no' to both aspects of this question. Early quality tools arose out of a focus upon the outputs of certain manufacturing processes, while no less an authority than J M Juran wrote in the early 1960s of 'breakthrough' change to achieve a 'dynamic, decisive movement to new higher levels of performance' as a key task of management.[2]

The cross-functional approach is also not exclusive to re-engineering. Quality improvement teams can operate across functions. At Tenneco cross-functional quality teams have achieved savings in the 'cost of quality' that amount to in excess of 10 per cent of corporate revenues.

This chapter examines some issues relating to re-engineering. It draws in particular upon an extensive examination of European experience and practice of re-engineering.[3] There are examples of organisations such as the French steel company Usinor Sacilor with textbook approaches to quality that were overtaken by innovators that 're-engineered'.[1] At the same time, other organisations have undertaken periodic re-engineering exercises to find themselves overtaken some time later by rivals that adopted a continuous improvement approach.

Perceived deficiencies of quality

The question of a 'successor' to quality would not have arisen if it was seen to be achieving the degree of change described by advocates and enthusiasts of re-engineering. Too often quality, with its manuals and procedures, helps to set an existing organisation in concrete rather than facilitate corporate transformation. There is sometimes a reluctance to change when even only minor alterations in working practices are involved where these would necessitate rewriting the 'quality manual'. There are other perceived deficiencies. Consider the following comments:

> The focus of quality is upon activities rather than outcomes. For instance, lots of our staff are giving or going on courses, but are we learning more effectively or developing more capable people?

> Quality is a blunt instrument. You apply it to the whole, and not necessarily where it would be most relevant. You can focus re-engineering like a laser beam.

A focus on process enables quality tools to be used more effectively. In many companies the adoption of quality circles has resulted in confused responsibility, concentration upon trivia and middle management alienation. Circles established their own priorities, and on the whole worked in isolation and without any overall coordination or sense of direction. As one quality manager put it: 'The chance of even two or three circles working simultaneously on key aspects of a cross-functional business process are about one in a million.'

Quality standards tend to concern activities which may or may not translate into delivered quality. As a quality consultant put it: 'It is too indiscriminate. People aim to improve the quality of a whole range of departmental activities that are not on the horizontal paths that deliver value to customers.'

Turning on a PC and walking through a 'process model' of an organisation's processes can enable people to understand the wider significance and contribution of their roles. At Unipart people no longer think in terms of functional quality. Their focus is upon quality along processes and value chains.

Some of those interviewed argued that quality is not sufficiently radical. For example, according to one CEO: '[Quality] operates within an existing framework, whereas re-engineering challenges the framework. With quality the goals are not sufficiently challenging. The questions are not bold enough.' The Financial Director added: 'Improvement is a god, as if any improvement were enough. People are satisfied with too little.'

Rivals or complements?

Many of those consulted see quality and BPR as natural complements. For example, at an automotive works one manager expressed the view: 'Without quality there is the risk of rubbish flowing along our re-engineered processes.' Other comments hint at some further negative attitudes and behaviours that can result from the adoption of quality:

Re-engineering takes a longer term view. It is concerned with fundamentals.

One group picked the quality assurance process for improvement and concluded that quality itself did not have a customer. It is just something we all do as a bureaucratic imposition. It is regarded as part of the overhead cost of being a registered supplier.

Since quality reports were introduced people tend to conceal problems. They don't want to commit things to paper. They keep quiet, muddle on and hope for the best. Before quality, people would seek help if they had problems ... They would ask around until they found someone who could help. In comparison, formal procedures are impersonal.

We used to be individuals ... each with their own way of doing things. People did what worked for them. Now there are standard procedures for everything. Having encouraged everyone to behave like robots, we are now starting a creativity drive to get people thinking again.

Its all too mechanistic and automatic. Using the tools and the processes has almost become an end in itself. People don't worry about the outputs any more.

The sudden growth of interest in business process re-engineering (BPR) during the early 1990s has greatly increased the number of managers who claim to take a process view. It is often said: 'It's all a question of getting the processes right.' At its most extreme, the view is: 'Put in world-class processes and everything will be OK.'

Life is not so simple. There are many other factors to consider. Inadequate or plain wrong information flowing along re-engineered processes operated by those with suspect judgement could result in disaster more quickly than before.

A word of caution is needed as major 'step changes' are easier to talk about than implement. Experience suggests that achieving radical improvements in such outcomes as profitability, service, time, understanding and employee and customer satisfaction by re-designing end-to-end processes alone will prove as elusive as the end of a rainbow for most, if not all, companies. Success will only come to those adopting a holistic perspective that embraces all the change elements that are required in a particular context.[4]

Understanding processes

Many mangers are already familiar with the term 'process' in various guises. They may be directly involved with such quality processes as the 'quality delivery process', 'quality system', 'quality control process', 'quality improvement process', 'problem-solving process', 'benchmarking process' and 'quality management process'. Some of these embrace the whole organisation. More recently, many people will have been introduced to 'cross-functional business processes'.

What is a process? Processes are the sequences and combinations of activities, the paths through the various components of an organisation, that collectively deliver outputs and accomplish tasks. 'Quality' tools such as benchmarking and problem-solving processes can be applied to them, and they can become the subject of quality improvement projects.

Processes can sometimes seem invisible to the casual observer. General Motors thought the relative success of its Japanese competitors lay in what could be seen, for example robots on the factory floor, when in reality it was how they managed the process of 'lean production'. Truth was obscured by the distorting spectacles of past beliefs and expectations.

Where process improvement tools are used will depend upon the prospects and priorities of a business. How they are used will depend upon the degree of change sought. Figure 10.1 illustrates a simple approach to understanding an individual process.

Re-engineering

The rhetoric of re-engineering stresses the degree of change that can be achieved, revolution rather than evolution, as a consequence of posing fundamental questions. However, BPR is not the only, or necessarily the

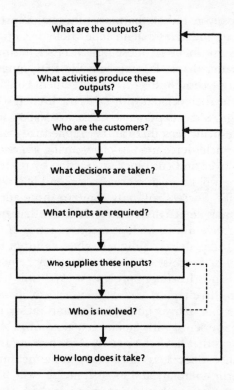

Figure 10.1 Understanding individual processes

easiest, route to radical change. For example, one could evolve to a new model of organisation, introduce a new pattern of work such as teleworking or a new approach to learning, or concentrate upon changing how the organisation interfaces and interrelates with other entities within its marketplace, perhaps by embracing EDI. In the latter case, by focusing upon a whole supply chain there may be greater potential to 'impact' upon an end customer than would result from focusing exclusively upon the internal processes of just one organisation contributing only a proportion of the total value delivered to the customer.[5]

Restructuring can occur with or without re-engineering, and re-engineering may become but one element of a broader change programme. For example, the German company Schering is undergoing a 'transition' and 'restructuring' with a view to focusing on pharmaceuticals and agrochemicals, improving efficiency and profitability and reducing costs. In the pharmaceuticals area a priority is being given to speeding up certain areas of the research and development process.

The most common arena for the application of re-engineering is at the level of the individual process. Often departmental processes or sub-processes are involved rather than cross-functional processes. Relatively few re-engineering exercises extend to a whole organisation. At the level of supply chains and markets most radical changes appear to be occurring by means other than BPR, for example EDI, or through the use of another emerging technology.[5]

Given the rhetoric associated with BPR, the limited scope of its application is surprising. As the experience of 'Smart Valley' in the US demonstrates, there are principles that can be applied to a whole community,[1] while certain countries have used re-engineering at national level.

Types of processes

A business process is an activity, or a combination of sequential or parallel activities, that receive inputs and, as a consequence of one or more people acting upon these, deliver a higher value of output to a 'customer'. In addition to business processes there are also management processes, support processes and learning processes. We will examine learning processes later in this chapter.

It is processes that deliver quality, value and satisfaction to customers, and some past experience with quality can encourage a focus upon those aspects and drivers that have the potential for making the greatest impact upon the customer. Success is more likely to be measured from the perspective of both the company and its customers.

Management processes should not be overlooked. Many continue to be operated for years without being subjected to even a rudimentary review along the lines of Figure 10.2. They may or may not be effective:

● At Pearl Assurance corporate planning is now done by process rather than by function. According to Maria Stafford, General Manager Strategy and Planning: 'Plans that seemed OK in functional terms looked terrible when looked at in process terms. [We found] ... all sorts of problems that did not have activities against them.'
● An international oil company found on reviewing its corporate planning process that the process did not have any customers. Those who had been assumed to be the customers made 'other arrangements' when setting their targets as the planning process information arrived too late. At certain times in the year the planning process absorbed many days of the time of senior managers. As a result of the review the process was abandoned.

A review should start with an organisation's vision, values and goals. Some then prefer to focus upon 'what is' by means of documenting and critiquing existing processes in order to identify deficiencies and areas for improvement, while others concentrate more upon what 'ought to be'. We will return to this distinction in a moment.

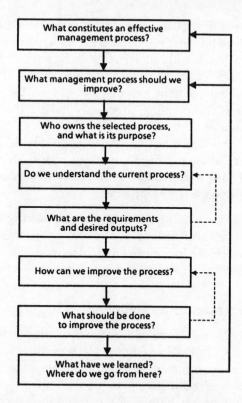

Figure 10.2 Understanding process improvement

Within Rank Xerox a management process is defined as a 'cycle of inter-related specific forums, held at specific frequencies, requiring specific inputs and outputs, that control and review business processes'. In many companies the *ad hoc* and undisciplined 'get togethers' that occur, with each participant having a different view of what it is all about, do not satisfy this requirement.

An effective management process is one that is well integrated with other processes, focuses upon reality and fact, is efficient, flexible and responsive, and promotes learning and understanding. Ideally an integrated management and learning process should exist within a culture that is supportive of individual, group and corporate learning and encourages and rewards role model conduct.

Where to begin?

What sort of process should be subjected to BPR? A key early decision is whether to apply BPR to business, management, support or learning processes:

- With deficient business or support processes a company could lose vital customers while first re-engineering management processes.
- On the other hand, without effective management processes it may not be easy to determine which business processes are the most critical. Effective management processes would enable identification of which business or operating process is having the greatest impact upon the customer.
- Without effective learning an organisation might soon fall so far behind as to be excluded from important relationships and networks. A confident board with a longer-term perspective is more likely to put the emphasis upon learning processes.

One place to start is by 'piggybacking' onto an existing exercise. Thus if some process or area of activity is already under investigation, it can make sense to widen the initial brief and encourage the team to include a process improvement or re-engineering methodology in their toolkit.

Selecting processes to re-engineer

Tackling a relatively self-contained business or management process can enable experience, credibility and tangible benefits to be achieved. Early results can encourage top management buy-in ahead of more widespread use of re-engineering techniques.

Criteria should be established for determining which processes are most critical in terms of impact upon the business and customers. Some business processes, for example the sales process, have a very direct and visible impact upon the customer.

Companies that have re-engineered their sales processes have emerged with a variety of alternatives to the conventional 'sales rep' ranging from electronic trading to taking over customer staff. The productivity of travelling sales staff and response times can be greatly improved by making use of mobile communications and portable computers.

Alternatively, where the securing of senior management commitment is perceived as a vital precondition of implementing substantial change throughout a corporate organisation, beginning with management processes can give those at the top some early experience of the impact of the methodologies that are available. The National & Provincial Building Society opted for a top-down approach, concentrating first upon key management processes involving the board. The society paid particular attention to the encouragement of learning throughout the organisation.

A quality approach could be brought to bear upon a wide range of management processes. Thus in the case of MEPC a range of processes from project management to account management could be involved in providing the company's tenants with 'quality buildings and an outstanding management service'.

One should not lose sight of certain support and production processes:

- Xerox has put a high priority upon speeding up the new product design, development and deployment process.
- The pharmaceuticals division of the Swiss company Sandoz is implementing a long-term plan to 'create the conditions necessary to ensure further improvements in the quality and speed of new drug development.' 'Other objectives' of the plan are 'greater flexibility in getting new research projects under way and increased R & D productivity'.

To achieve a significant improvement in performance, it may be necessary to simultaneously tackle both management and business processes. The biggest potential payoffs in terms of competitive advantage might derive from corporate transformation or the 'root and branch' total redesign of an organisation. However, because of the risks involved, few people undertake such an approach.

Process models

A process model of an organisation can be of value in identifying where processes interact. If crossover points are not identified, fixing one problem can be the cause of unintended consequences elsewhere. Models can also assist the allocation of ownership and the determination of leverage points and skill needs.

Process models of companies can appear complex and unsettling. However, the matrix model of organisation is also frequently complicated, and can cause even greater confusion as to focus and priorities. Hewlett-Packard moved away from a matrix structure and simplified its organisation in order to clarify responsibilities.

The number of distinct cross-functional business processes that can be found within different operating companies of the same multinational corporation or MNC can vary by a factor of 20 or more. When adopting a 'process approach', the opportunity should be taken to prune and simplify, reducing the formal organisation to the minimum necessary to deliver value to customers and achieve business objectives.

In future, some head offices that are always on the look-out for opportunities to both 'add value' and 'justify their existence' might develop standard process models and may then seek to impose these upon business units or subsidiaries. When the latter have similar requirements, this can make sense, depending upon the implementation. However, the more diverse they are, the greater the likelihood that the practice will be insensitive to local requirements.

Rank Xerox is seeking to put seven basic and uniform processes into place within each of its European operating companies, where hitherto each has done 'its own thing'. In another context, such an approach could force diverse entities with distinct requirements into a standard strait-jacket.

From whose perspective should an organisation be modelled? Many organisations begin with the customer. Figure 10.3 presents an example of an improvement model which is driven by 'the customer'. The holistic review of the total organisation and the collective identification of problem areas determines which of these should be subjected to a quality or process improvement exercise and which should become the basis of learning or re-engineering projects.

Where the focus of action should be in any particular company must depend upon the areas of greatest weakness and greatest potential contribution. In one context, systems could be the key issue, while in another structure or attitudes could be seen as the major problem or opportunity.

Improvement or redesign?

The term BPR has been applied to both improvement initiatives and exercises aimed at more radical changes. Improvement activities tend to

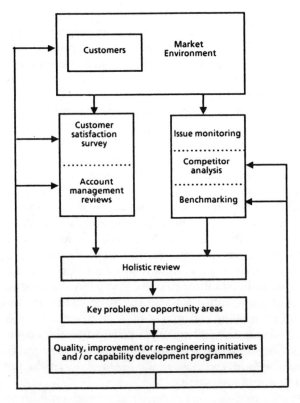

Figure 10.3　Corporate improvement model

concentrate upon squeezing time or cost out of an existing process while re-engineering of the radical change variety assumes that what exists is likely to prove inadequate however improved. It examines instead how people, information and technology might be combined in new ways to design an alternative that delivers a step change in performance.

Simple improvement may not be as risky as more radical approaches. The competencies required to successfully undertake each of them could be very different.[6] Thus improvement can sometimes demand the methodical application of technique, whereas re-engineering might require more emphasis upon imagination and creativity. Most exercises undertaken across Europe have been of the improvement variety.

Rank Xerox draws a distinction between two approaches to process review:

- Business process simplification is defined as 'a structured methodology that reduces time and resource requirements by removing non-value added activities from a business process in order to improve productivity and optimize responsiveness to customer requirements.'
- Business process re-engineering is defined as 'a vision-led, structured methodology for the fundamental rebuilding of business processes through a balanced interaction of processes, people, information and technology.'

Both concepts are not new. The principles and practice of process simplification through standardisation were understood by Henry Ford who revolutionised the productivity of motor car production. Radical innovation and the fundamental review of how goals could be accomplished underlay many of the foundations of the agrarian and industrial revolutions.

Many of those claiming to have undertaken some form of re-engineering exercise are in fact describing a change, downsizing or quality programme that was initiated before the term re-engineering became fashionable. Fundamental redesigns are rare, and in view of the higher risks should not be attempted unless radical change is on the agenda.

In any event, the very concept of 'redesign' can result in the shuffling, changing or juggling of elements. What may be needed is not a 'redesign', but a new organisation altogether, possibly something quite different from what has gone before. In such cases, a paradigm shift is required, and trying to understand what is or to 'document the process' can be a distraction, especially when there is little sense, coherence or logic behind what has evolved.

While the claims of re-engineering can be seductive, many organisations do not need to turn their worlds upside down. They resort instead to less risky and demanding improvement methodologies. For those interested in improvement, guides such as James Harrington's book *Business Process Improvement*[7] are available. A basic improvement cycle is illustrated in Figure 10.4.

A specific focus upon process improvement can release potential time savings that have not been tapped by previous restructuring or change programmes. Few customers who are given the choice opt to wait longer. Percy Barnevik, President and CEO of ABB, has pointed out that: 'It is striking to note that during decades of earlier rationalisation efforts total cycle times were not attacked more efficiently.'

As we will see in Chapter 12, an organisation's approach to re-engineering will depend very much upon such factors as its understanding of stakeholder interests and requirements and whether the board adopts a short- or longer-term perspective. Too many organisations rush too quickly into the activity of re-engineering without first considering a range of stakeholder and contextual issues. The COBRA BPR methodology is designed to correct this imbalance.[3]

Processes in perspective

Just as quality can become an obsession in its own right, so too it is possible to become so preoccupied with 'processes' as to lose touch with the

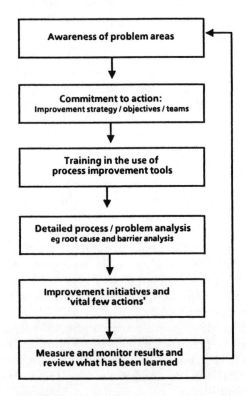

Figure 10.4 The process improvement cycle

realities of a business. Re-engineering processes can become 'avoidance behaviour'. It is often not a satisfactory substitute for taking the right decisions about products, prices or business partners.

Nor should one contrive to create standard processes where they might be inappropriate. Where matters have been routed according to their nature in order to allow a tailored response, the introduction of a prescribed process could be tantamount to replacing the flexibility of the human brain with the programmed responses of a robot.[1]

Lou Gerstner, Chairman of IBM, is in no doubt that processes should not be allowed to become ends in themselves: 'I'm spending a lot of time on customer issues, on technologies, on employees and the economics of the business, and I don't really care what committees we have ... Process is not what we're going to talk about. Performance is what we are going to talk about.'

Efficient business processes should not be a sole end in themselves. They need to be effective at delivering value to customers. Christer Zetterberg, President and CEO of Volvo, points out that: 'Volvo's organisation is being developed and refined with the objective of supporting a more efficient way of working and further increasing our focus on customers.'

Hitting the right level

Corporate life is too uncertain and tenuous to do other than focus upon essentials. Both quality and BPR should reach the 'heart of an organisation'. BPR, like information technology (IT), tends to be a neutral instrument. Whether each is of crucial significance or irrelevant will depend upon where and how it is used, and for what purpose. We determine whether BPR helps or harms us.[1]

Within many companies there are some particular key areas of core competence. Often there are individuals and groups whose work represents the essence of the organisation. These are the activities that contribute most to the delivery of value to customers. In one company project managers might constitute this critical group. In another, account managers could be those who 'pull it together' and make it happen for the individual customer.

A diffuse quality initiative aimed at 'involving everyone' or a specific BPR programme may or may not reach or touch the key people. Much TQM and BPR work of high technical quality is occurring in areas of little strategic significance to the organisations concerned. A top-down initiative could peter out before it gets to the 'front line' or to a crucial level or team. Some approaches to quality will add to their bureaucratic workload rather than help them to add value.

Many of the 'real adders of value' may be found some way down the bureaucratic organisation. Those higher up the organisation chart should assist, guide or counsel them. In some companies, people at certain levels have traditionally done little to facilitate the process of delivering value to customers. Many have been checkers, skimming over reports and identifying problems people already know they have, while doing little to enable difficulties to be overcome or resolved.

There is often little incentive for people to be open in reporting problems to those above them who are regarded as a source of hassle, heat and aggravation rather than help. Messengers still get shot in some cultures. They are more likely to 'tell it as it is' to those who encourage openness and who might be expected to roll up their sleeves and provide some practical assistance. This could include the posing of insightful questions based upon a detached overview.

Those in management roles should add value to colleagues in excess of their cost to the organisation. This could be done by searching for root causes, trends, patterns and relationships and encouraging and facilitating learning rather than nitpicking and worrying about 'status symbols'.

Some processes are 'more equal' than others. Within Rank Xerox cross-functional teams have been given the task of assessing all processes in terms of two dimensions, namely according to the extent to which they are (a) strategic or non-strategic, and (b) mature or immature. Resources are switched from the non-strategic, the things the company chooses rather than needs to do, and the well established and familiar and redeployed on what is new and strategic in terms of 'supporting tomorrow's customer' and achieving current business objectives.

Maintaining a holistic perspective

A sense of balance, strategic perspective and a focus upon essentials should be provided by the board. BPR can enable a board to reassert control and direction and it could be said to be an honest mirror that generally reveals a board's true priorities. Most re-engineering exercises in Europe are concerned with business processes. Few teams are concentrating upon management processes, and hardly any upon learning processes. Working people harder appears a more widespread objective of boards than enabling them to 'work smarter'.

BPR is often distinguished by its emphasis upon cross-functional processes. So much is made of the cross-functional perspective, the horizontal paths through an organisation (Figure 10.5),[4] that people can lose sight of the importance of support processes within single (perhaps even functional) departments. For many small and medium-sized enterprises (SMEs), the financial management process is a critical one. Many SMEs find their survival is threatened by periodic cash flow problems as opposed to 'customer satisfaction issues'.

In many companies key strategic support processes (eg finance, IT) are the responsibility of particular functional departments. Each will have traditionally fed into the boardroom via a particular director who may well have been equipped through experience and training to take a partial view of what needs to be done from the perspective of one function or profession (Figure 10.5). This is the 'curse of professionalism', the viewing of corporate reality through the distorting lens of individual functions and the allocation of selected aspects of a generic problem to specialists.[4]

The board itself sometimes becomes an arena within which various alternative and entrenched approaches are in conflict rather than debated.

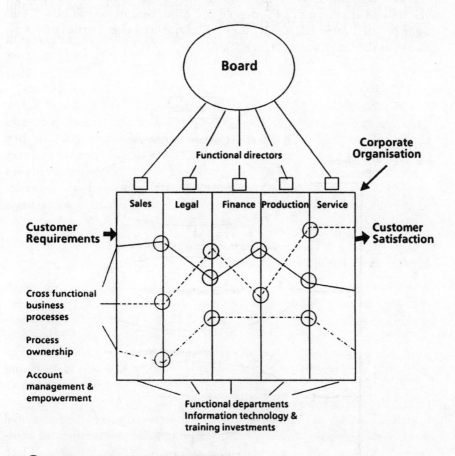

Figure 10.5 The board and cross-functional business processes: shifting from a vertical to a horizontal focus

Source: Colin Coulson-Thomas, *Transforming the Company*, Kogan Page, 1992.

Directors who do not 'fight their corner' and push the departmental view are thought to undermine the standing of their team. Those with the quickest tongue sometimes win over those with the most perceptive insights.

Within a single organisation there may be strategic planning, financial planning, manpower planning, organisational development planning, marketing planning and other self-contained planning activities. When a quality or transformation planning process is introduced there may be further scope for confusion if not division.

Within Rank Xerox (UK) in the middle 1980s the 'quality improvement process' was located within a family of related management processes that successively established where the company was going, what it needed in terms of IT, people and other resources, and how these might be used most effectively, the role of quality being particularly significant at the latter stage (Figure 10.6).

Figure 10.6 Rank Xerox (UK) processes

It is generally advisable to bring the various separate planning processes into one integrated approach along the lines of Figure 10.3. This can enable more people to obtain a holistic and shared overview perspective of the key issues, priorities and what needs to be done. Learning should be built into the process as the most flexible form of planning process is a hybrid of issue monitoring and management and a learning process.

Processes versus messages

A policy development and deployment cycle starting and ending in the boardroom could be an example of an integrated process. When such a cycle with its feedback loops is taken all the way through an organisation, people can appreciate not only their own roles and responsibilities, but what everyone else is supposed to do. As a consequence, departmental and functional barriers are broken down, as are those between the board and the management team.

The means used to communicate a message can subvert it. For example, there are companies that use a centrally directed and top-down cascade to spread a set of messages about empowerment, delegation and the need for cross-functional working. While the rhetoric seeks to break down a corporate bureaucracy, the process of communication can actually reinforce it.

The policy deployment or quality cascade can entrench and give new meaning to hierarchy. It is paradoxical, but corporate change programmes can sometimes shore up creaking bureaucracies. In some cases, the bureaucracy is reinvented, organisation charts being updated or redrawn in order to allow a top-down programme (perhaps BPR) to be implemented.

Management processes should not be taken for granted. As new models of organisations emerge (eg virtual networks) so new forms of management processes and approaches to governance will be needed. It is not easy to design a process for even understanding, let alone coordinating and focusing, a changing population of groups and teams some of which are largely autonomous, or to govern a network of partners over whom one has no line control. Sensitivity to shifting interests and political skills are required.

The cross-functional view and IT

BPR and IT have become inextricably linked. Studies by the OECD and various individuals at, or associated with, the Kobler Unit at Imperial College suggest one should not necessarily expect an organisation to benefit from IT. Lester Thurow, Dean of the Sloane School of Management at MIT, has concluded that, so far as the application of IT is concerned, 'when it comes to the bottom line there is no clear evidence that these new technologies have raised productivity ... or profitability. In fact, precisely the opposite is true.'[8]

Historically, much of IT investment and indeed training has been departmental. Both have helped to set departmental forms of organisation in concrete. Little if any IT has been focused upon those sequences and combinations of activities that deliver value for customers, or employed to tackle the 'hot spots' at the 'vertical' boundaries between functions and departments at which 'handover' problems and delays occur (Figure 10.5).

One exercise at Rank Xerox found that 107 of 112 days required to complete one activity consisted of waiting time at the 'hot spots'. Until IT investments are used to bridge the 'no man's lands' between departmental systems and the responsibilities of departmental managers one should not expect 'investment' in IT to impact significantly upon the customer.

Applying IT to the support of cross-functional processes ought to be more beneficial. IT suppliers have jumped onto the business process re-engineering bandwaggon: 'IT suppliers, with a mixture of cheek and bravado, are now in the business of offering solutions to the many problems their own products have created, suggesting that this or that attachment may yet turn the lead boots they supplied into winged slippers.'[9]

In some cases applications of IT, in the context of re-engineering, are helping to achieve breakthrough levels of performance improvement.[10,11,12] This is particularly so when it is applied to the supply chain or customer relationship.[5] Examples are various electronic commerce applications, telemedicine, home or telebanking and shopping, 'one-stop shops' and electronic services.

IT should be used with care. When employed to facilitate and support new forms of relationships between organisations it can transform a marketplace. In another context there could be too much rather than too little IT. Productivity across a support process of one company was increased threefold by going back to basics and operating a manual card index system, the flexibility and utility of which in the particular context staggered a generation used only to computer screens. Instead of peering into their VDU screens all day people actually started to sit around a table and talk to each other.

Cross-functional roles

Too many managers persist in viewing the company as a hierarchy of job titles rather than as a set of processes. The reasons for this need to be understood. One manager was quite clear: 'Processes deliver benefits to customers, but the hierarchy decides my future.' Another made the comment: 'I want to get on and move up, not just float around "horizontally" for the rest of my life at one level.'

In due course, as process owner responsibilities are assumed at board level, the directorial team will come to consist of process owners rather than heads of traditional functions (Figure 10.5). At the National & Provincial Building Society the director members of a renamed 'direction management team' now assume process leader roles in place of functional responsibilities. Managers also have cross-functional roles, for example a manager of learning to encourage learning across all the building society's activities.

Organisational changes within BMW are bringing together functions that were once widely separated. Thus at the BMW Research and Engineering Centre one can find 'scientists, engineers, skilled and semi-skilled employees from different divisions' working together in project groups. Functions have been brought together into single units and reporting and decision-making structures and processes are being shortened. A significant increase in flexibility and speed at a lower cost is being sought.

Network re-engineering

When a process extends across supply chain partners they may need to be involved if significant improvements are to be achieved.[5] This area of 'network re-engineering' is one in which there are often the greatest opportunities to achieve radical transformation.

Virtual shopping now occurs on the Internet. Virtual reality allows people to 'experience' houses or cars they are thinking of buying without actually 'being there'. A small company such as Rodenstock can transform the market for spectacles by almost eliminating the need for stock as a result of modelling alternative frames on a VDU.

Network re-engineering is particularly relevant to SMEs. Collectively, the virtual network of SMEs supported by appropriate electronic 'front ends' can appear to an actual or a potential customer as largely indistinguishable from the major multinational. Associated Independent Stores is a network of smaller stores who are cooperating to achieve many of the economies of scale of their larger competitors.

Applications of EDI can also make it easier for selected SMEs to maintain relationships with larger customers. The advantages of networking may even encourage rivals to work together. At times both factors come together. Thus 'white goods' suppliers such as Braun, Moulinex, Philips and Tefal have cooperated via the Electrical Appliance Service Agents System to form a network that links up the many SMEs and small traders who effect repairs to goods returned within guarantee periods.

In the case of some sectors, such as pharmaceuticals, there are also the activities of regulatory authorities to take into account. These can constrain the speed of new product commercialisation. In Leicester, linking up the police with the courts is speeding up the justice system, while within the Oxfordshire region linking general practitioners to hospitals is enabling patients to receive the results of tests much more quickly than before.

The transition to a network organisation and the network's supporting technology can facilitate both process flexibility and the creation of a global process.[4] Thus within Ford the global network links the factory in Spain with the engineer in Brussels and the designer in Detroit.

Implications of the network organisation for re-engineering

Paradoxically, the move away from a bureaucratic form of organisation and the replacement of repetitive routines with the fluid adhocracy of the network organisation is making it increasingly difficult to apply the first generation of approaches to process re-engineering. In some contexts, they have been found to be redundant even before people have had an opportunity to become familiar with them.

Developments in technology from video conferencing to groupware are making it easier for groups and teams to come together to solve particular problems as required. Repetitive processes do not exist long enough to be documented, while there is little point undertaking a fundamental first principles review of a particular pattern of communication which may never be used again.

The network organisation is constantly evolving as roles and responsibilities move around the network according to changing circumstances and customer needs. Processes exist only for the time required for tasks to be completed and may take the form of ever changing patterns of communication. The use of second and third generation re-engineering tools copes with this fluidity to the extent that certain paths and flows tend to be used more than others as problem-solvers return to certain connections and patterns that have worked well in the past.

What has been achieved?

The fundamental re-engineering of management and business processes is a key element of the corporate transformation programmes of a growing number of companies. For example, Rank Xerox (UK) is restructuring around its key business processes. A wide ranging programme is replacing traditional functional departments, and has led to a board composed of business unit leaders and horizontal process owners rather than heads of vertical specialist groups. In Rank Xerox and other 'customer-focused' companies the benefits are apparent:

- 3M, in its approach to service excellence, examines its processes from the perspective of the customer. In the industrial and consumer sector of the company's business, the ordering, packaging, shipping and billing systems are tailored to the individual requirements of customers.

● Process improvement is a significant element of ABB's 'Customer Focus Program'. Reducing cycle times and raising quality and service levels are seen as the main means of delivering better value to the customer and achieving operational excellence.

Within Rank Xerox, a certain category of re-engineering project is referred to as a '10× project' as performance typically improves by a factor of ten. Similar levels of performance improvements have been achieved in other companies, particularly in respect of projects designed to 'speed things up':

● At Ford, following a process improvement study, the time taken to settle accounts relating to construction projects was reduced from 220 to 22 days.

● The time taken to process certain transactions in Mutual Benefit Life has fallen from 24 days to 24 hours.

● The Dutch PTT has reduced the time it takes to provide a customer with a new telephone number, a contract and connection time from two weeks to two days as a result of linking together relevant internal databases. 'Front office' terminals now allow sales staff to obtain a comprehensive overview of the PTT's relationship with individual customers. Further improvements are sought, and the goal is instantaneous connection.

● Within ABB there have been some very significant reduction in cycle times. A 70 per cent reduction in process times has been achieved in transformer operations in Finland, Germany and the US. Delivery times for low-voltage apparatus in Sweden have been cut from 33 to three days, while in Switzerland the quotation time for gas-insulated switchgear has fallen from 30 to three days.

However, these outcomes could be atypical. A word of caution is needed as most re-engineering projects do not chalk up such impressive gains. According to two authorities, 'most companies that begin re-engineering ... end their efforts precisely where they began, making no significant changes, achieving no major performance improvement.'[13]

Some cautions

In many cases there is disappointment because the BPR concept is being misapplied. Improvement approaches, overly prescriptive methodologies and modest goals are not likely to result in radical performance improvements. Rarely do significant changes of attitude, perspective or behaviour appear to occur.

Currently, and to be expected given the depth of the bureaucratic heritage, the focus in the first wave of re-engineering is very much upon internal applications. As people and organisations become more confident, more exercises are likely to encompass supply chains and alternative patterns of market operation. New markets and new forms of market could grow out of vision-led exercises.

Problems may also be moved rather than solved. Hiving off, 'market testing', 'outsourcing' and subcontracting can all be undertaken for a variety of reasons, and on some occasions deliver the hoped for benefits. Within the network organisation, from time to time responsibilities are likely to be shuffled among partners. However, a distinction needs to be made between relocating activities and redesigning them. Doing one without the other can rule out substantial payoffs.

Redesign and re-engineering can sometimes lead to disaster. For example:

- The very term 're-engineering' suggests a mechanical approach to changing a living organism. Most organisations were not designed in the first place, they evolved, grew and have adapted and aged in a variety of ways. Hacking off limbs, or moving about organs, can create shocks from which the organism may not recover.[4] Living organisms that recover from surgery are often a shadow of their former selves.
- Re-engineering can be a distraction from more pressing matters. One well positioned company lost an opportunity to gain significant market share as it was thought that the introduction of an innovatory product would 'hold up' a BPR exercise. Needless to say, some time later the opportunity went to a competitor that launched an alternative and, as a consequence, has secured a commanding lead in the marketplace.

Once a BPR exercise is complete there is a tendency to 'relax' and fundamental rethinking is put to one side as the 'blueprint' of the new model organisation is implemented. This is a dangerous practice, as conditions and circumstances, challenges and opportunities, etc, can rapidly change. Within ICL a review of organisation structure and people's roles and responsibilities is undertaken on a quarterly basis to ensure that each is appropriate to the current context.

Learning from experience of BPR

Where are we going wrong? Let us look in more detail at the European experience of BPR. Mention has already been made of the 'improvement' nature of most BPR projects. In the main, improvement delivers benefits in terms of cost and time savings. Practical methodologies and consultancy skills are available. However, with re-engineering exercises aimed at more radical change the results are disappointing:[1,3]

- There is a considerable gap between the rhetoric of BPR and its practical achievements. In general, attitudes and behaviour are proving resistant to the approaches being adopted.
- Overall goals and strategy are generally not clear or shared, while very often the resources and capability required for implementation have not been assembled. Often the goals are not sufficiently demanding to encourage radical change.
- The focus is invariably on the needs of the organisation and its internal processes rather than on 'what represents value for the customer' and the wider supply chain.
- Many approaches to BPR are procedural rather than creative. They are often 'light' on the people aspects because these are perceived as 'difficult' or 'intangible', and generally questions relating to new ways of working and learning are not asked.
- There is a tendency to reduce discretion in the search for standard processes. This can deskill and may be less flexible than trusting people to devise a process to handle a particular project.
- The use of many BPR methodologies is almost guaranteed to produce incremental rather than radical improvements. Given most consultants' methodologies, one should certainly not expect innovation in the areas of working and learning.
- Initiatives are often doomed from the start as other 'complementary' change elements are not in place, in many cases the experience and 'credentials' of those applying the methodologies almost guaranteeing these will remain absent.
- Excessive amounts of time are devoted to documenting and understanding 'what is' rather than thinking about what ought to be. The timescale to implement BPR is often longer than the change requirement.
- People become bogged down in either the trivial or time-consuming exercises that take an age to demonstrate any benefits. Colleagues simply get bored. In some cases, the 'day of action' is postponed indefinitely while complex process models are developed that resemble plates of spaghetti.
- Pioneers are finding that process owners can squabble and have 'boundary' problems just like heads of functions.
- BPR is 'done to people', ie they are not actively involved, motivated or empowered. This causes resentment as BPR is perceived as being about job cuts or 'turning up the speed of the treadmill'.
- Little effort is being devoted to improving the quality of either learning or working life through the introduction of new ways of working

or learning. Those organisations that are innovating in the areas of working and learning are often achieving very significant performance improvements.

● Many companies are not as open as they could be about the real motivation behind BPR. Often it is 'all about' downsizing and headcount reduction in order to reduce the cost base rather than value to customers.

In general, the emphasis is negative rather than positive, ie upon short-term savings in cost rather than the building of longer-term capability. The approaches adopted are mechanical and incomplete. For example, people are changing structures and processes without agreeing and building the roles, competencies and behaviours that would breathe life into them. Organisations are viewed as machines rather than as living and learning organisms.[4]

Most re-engineering programmes of the 'blue skies' variety begin with a pilot programme. This allows the risks to be contained, and enables the organisation to gain experience and build confidence. To get the benefits of prudence and caution it is important that whatever lessons are learned are widely shared. This is not always the case.

Helping professionals to learn

The most valuable professionals are those who continually question and learn, critiquing both activities and processes and the tools and techniques that are applied to them and used within them. Key processes within any organisation are those that encourage learning (Figure 10.7).[4]

General models or summary diagrams of organisations can appear simplistic. However, diagrammatic representations along the lines of the Rank Xerox Business Excellence Model, IBM (UK)'s Customer Satisfaction Management System, or DEC's Service Excellence Model can be of value in helping to 'close loops' and ensure that learning and feedback occurs.

Technique of itself is rarely sufficient when appropriate attitudes are lacking. The Belgian company Solvay distinguishes three aspects of continuous improvement, namely 'listening to all clients', the 'personal effectiveness' of Solvay's people 'in all areas of activity' and 'command of the techniques and methods' of the 'improvement process itself'. Continuous improvements in all three aspects are sought 'day by day'.

Step or 'frame-breaking' change requires that people discard what is comfortable, avoid groupthink and break free from constraining corporate prejudices and assumptions. Having got all their people facing in the same direction, corporations are now encouraging them to look around. One CEO lamented: 'We've spent a small fortune spreading ... or I should say sharing ... our agreed corporate view around the organisation and getting it understood, I'm now inviting people to tear holes in it.'

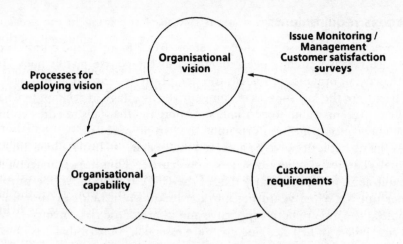

Figure 10.7 Organisational learning

Source: Colin Coulson-Thomas, *Transforming the Company*, Kogan Page, 1992.

The use of elaborate tools or packaged solutions by consultants or quality specialists can inhibit questioning and learning 'in the line'. People should be encouraged themselves to create and make use of simple tools. Martin Bartholomew, as Director of Mercury Mobile Services, involved his people in the use of simple lifecycle and constituency diagrams, responsibility matrices and added value and benchmarking tools to encourage learning and sharing.

Information overload

A commitment to the learning organisation can result in so much information being collected as to cause a degree of paralysis. When the results of customer satisfaction surveys, customer interviews, feedback sessions, research reports and other 'inputs' are collected together, many management teams find it very difficult to make sense of it all.

There is a tendency to devote much more effort to collecting information than to its analysis. The approaches and tools that can enable people to make use of what has been collected are frequently overlooked.

Effective marketing strategies do not just 'jump out' of the data. Requirements may interrelate. What is important, the drivers and root causes, may not be obvious. Sources of differentiation and trade-offs may require discussion.

When a management team finds it difficult to extract meaning and relevant understanding from the data it has collected, a loss of momentum can occur. Staff who have enthusiastically collected information find that 'nothing has happened', and after a time may become disillusioned.

Success requirements

So how can we increase the success rate of BPR? Many of the critical success factors have already been identified in the course of this book. In particular, an organisation needs to establish the essence of its distinctive contribution, the key sources of competitive advantage in relation to what really represents value to customers. A company that fails to address this issue may concentrate its efforts upon the 'wrong processes'.

At the outset it needs to be accepted that seeking to bring about fundamental change is generally a risky enterprise. Thus top management commitment, and particularly that of the CEO, is crucial. As one practitioner put it: 'When venturing into the unknown, it helps to know that people at the top are both supportive and aware of the risks involved.'

Clear vision and challenging goals are essential. A board that sets objectives that are undemanding can constrain and stunt the development of an enterprise. A willingness to act is also important, as there will be those who withhold their commitment until some 'results' are apparent. Action depends very much upon selecting the right 'champion' and assembling the right core team. We will consider the latter issue in the next section.

The 'analysis-paralysis' syndrome and excessive complexity also need to be avoided. Many elegant solutions are in essence quite simple. Very often the best guarantee of progress is to ask bold and penetrating questions.

Some companies seem destined to be forever documenting existing processes or devising elaborate models of new ones that are unlikely ever to see the light of day. One director complained: 'We all knew where we had to start, but we kept identifying and documenting ever more obscure sub-processes until it was almost too late.' Xerox has refined its 'top level' process model into seven core processes, while other companies claim fewer.

Finally, before going operational with radical changes it is usually advisable to 'test run' or prototype. An existing system or process should not be junked until its intended replacement has proved its worth. The demonstration of positive results can also be very conducive of more widespread adoption.

Assembling the BPR team

Clear accountability for the achievement of BPR outcomes needs to be established. Each BPR project should be the responsibility of an appropriately led and qualified project team or steering group with a wide-ranging and demanding brief.[6] Multidisciplinary groups and teams are a must. While the right consultants can push and challenge, visible internal 'ownership' and leadership should normally be maintained throughout a BPR project.

Competent staff should be included within the BPR team and engaged on key BPR tasks.[6] All those likely to be affected should be involved. In many cases, they may need to be equipped and motivated to participate, and not everyone will respond or be able to make the necessary transition. Some people may 'vote with their feet', while others may have to be asked to leave.

Someone involved in an exercise should have an understanding of the overall process and of techniques that can be used. Otherwise there is the risk of not knowing where to start, false starts and general confusion. Undertaking a first principles review of value, technology, working and learning options can make it easier to achieve substantial improvements.

Given the total process scope of most reviews, the demanding goals which ought to be set and the fundamental nature of the issues and choices which may emerge, sustained and intense involvement of appropriate members of the senior management team is usually needed.

To ensure 'buy in', commitment and effective implementation, the review process has to be seen to be authoritative and comprehensive. The various divisions and operations functions affected must be involved. Facilitated sessions can ensure their active participation at each phase. Workshops should be arranged to introduce staff to the necessary corporate transformation or process review, improvement, re-engineering and learning tools and approaches.

A support team should be at a high level and include those with direct line experience of similar exercises. Professional project management of parallel activities is essential, and an experienced project manager could be included in the support team. The cost of any external support that is required will depend upon the extent to which the staff of areas under review are available to undertake particular work tasks and their calibre and potential.

Empowerment and BPR

For significant improvements to occur people must often be given and accept a greater level of involvement and personal responsibility. Also if change is to be initiated at the grass roots in many organisations a greater degree of empowerment is needed. As we saw in the last chapter, involvement and participation of themselves tend not to extend the total time required for BPR and they can greatly ease the acceptance of changes.

The consequences of empowerment for how an organisation operates and the role of the manager can be profound. In the longer term HYPO-BANK expects that its bottom-up 'Better Still' programme will ' lead to a change of culture as employees are provided with the ability to solve their tasks and problems within the group to a large extent on their own responsibility.'

Rolf Börjesson, President and CEO of PLM Plastics, is seeking 'a decentralised organisation in order to create a company which operates efficiently and functions in a rational manner, with short decision paths. This presupposes that PLM's objectives, strategies and values are well known and that overall policies are implemented in each unit according to local conditions. This is the responsibility of each manager.'

For Börjesson: 'Individual responsibility means that all PLM employees must be willing to contribute and take on responsibility. Individual potential is developed by practical and theoretical training.' In too many companies, people are not being properly equipped to handle the extra responsibilities that are being placed upon them. Within Rank Xerox (UK) the combination and sequence of processes illustrated in Figure 10.6 have been used to help ensure that people are empowered and equipped to undertake what they are expected to do.

Radical change

On the whole, evidence suggests that, when presented with a choice, boards feel threatened by, and avoid, the more radical options. Many more examples of frustrated innovations are found than those which have been encouraged. People may understand how the rules of a market game might be changed while at the same time doubting their ability to play well under an alternative regime.

Where radical and innovatory changes are encountered, these are invariably not the result of BPR. Often people come into an area without prior experience and simply ask basic and fundamental questions.

The innovators do not seem to 'grow up' to become as inhibited, embittered and cynical as most senior managers. In comparison, they often appear to exhibit the simplicity of the innocent. They retain enthusiasms and they still expect, seek and manage to find some mystery and magic in life. For them, the 'best is yet to come' is a belief, not a slogan. Above all, they are open-minded and willing to learn. They leap out of bed each morning as eager as ever to explore and discover.

Checklist

Has your organisation identified its learning processes and the key management, business and support processes that identify and deliver what represents value to customers and achieve business objectives?

Are these processes understood and documented? Who is responsible for them?

To what extent are the processes cross-functional and inter-organisational?

Are they tailored to the unique and distinct needs of their purpose and those involved?

Have cost, time, quality, flexibility and learning objectives been established?

Are these processes supported and their activities facilitated by appropriate technology?

Is the level of process capability measured? Are the key processes periodically reviewed and improved or re-engineered?

What do customers, suppliers and business partners think of them? To what extent are these groups involved in process improvement and re-engineering?

Are investments in training and information technology applied to the activities and processes that identify and deliver value to customers?

How effectively are information and knowledge accessed, shared, deployed and used?

Have the people of your organisation been equipped and empowered to simplify and re-engineer management, business, support and learning processes?

Do their approaches and methodologies represent best practice? Are 'helps and hinders' and obstacles and barriers to the effective operation of processes identified, understood and addressed?

References

1. Colin Coulson-Thomas (ed), *Business Process Re-engineering: Myth and Reality*, London, Kogan Page, 1994.
2. J M Juran, *Breakthrough Management*, London, Macmillan, 1964.
3. Colin Coulson-Thomas, (executive ed), *The Responsive Organisation: Re-engineering New Patterns of Work*, London, Policy Publications, 1995.
4. Colin Coulson-Thomas, *Transforming the Company: Bridging the Gap Between Management Myth and Corporate Reality*, London, Kogan Page, 1992.
5. Peter Bartram, *The Competitive Network*, London, Policy Publications, 1996.
6. Colin Coulson-Thomas, 'Competencies for Business Process Re-engineering', *Competency*, Vol 2, No 1, Autumn 1994, pp 35–9.
7. H James Harrington, *Business Process Improvement: The Breakthrough Strategy for Total Quality, Productivity, and Competitiveness*, New York, McGraw-Hill, 1991.
8. Lester Thurow, Foreword, p vi, in Michael Scott Morton (ed), *The Corporation of the 1990s: Information Technology and Organizational Transformation*, New York, Oxford University Press, 1991.
9. Colin Coulson-Thomas, *Transforming the Company: Bridging the Gap Between Management Myth and Corporate Reality*, London, Kogan Page, 1992, p 249.
10. Roger Woolfe, *The Role of Information Technology in Transforming the Business*, London, Butler Cox Foundation, 1991.
11. Peter Bartram, *Re-inventing the Company, The Use of IT to Re-engineer Corporate Processes*, Wimbledon, London, Business Intelligence, 1992.
12. Peter Bartram, *IT and Corporate Transformation*, Wimbledon, London, Business Intelligence, 1995.
13. Michael Hammer and James Champy, *Re-engineering The Corporation: A Manifesto for Business Revolution*, London, Nicholas Brealey, 1993.

11

Approaches, tools and techniques: future prospects

You don't need it anymore than a toad needs side pockets.

In many companies, people have not been properly equipped to do what is expected of them. Senior management teams have a tendency to restructure or introduce new goals without thinking through the implications in terms of the roles, competencies, tools or behaviours that may be required.

A typical comment is: 'People get results of sorts, but are held back because they don't focus, involve colleagues or use the right tools.' A common complaint is that people are struggling rather than thinking: 'People do not have time to think.' This may be another way of saying they are disinterested, resigned or have given up. For one reason or another they are going automatic.

Many management techniques do more harm than good when mechanically or unthinkingly applied. Approaches, tools and techniques can work in some contexts better than in others. For example, preliminary results of a Cambridge study suggest that many UK companies which adopt Japanese approaches such as total quality management are less profitable than those which do not.[1] Adoption and application needs to reflect the local situation.

Approaches, tools and techniques

We saw in the last chapter that mechanical and prescriptive approaches to business process re-engineering can actually reduce the prospects of radical change. Approaches, tools and techniques need to be appropriate to the context, task and people involved. While the right ones can liberate and delight, the wrong ones can inhibit and frustrate.

There is little value in tools for their own sake. One director of an international company explained: 'The approach adopted must depend upon the situation and culture. A high degree of flexibility and tolerance of diversity may be needed when there is considerable variety in the circumstances of different customers.' Relevance is the key to the effective use of approaches, tools and techniques.

One needs to avoid an unhealthy obsession with tools. While they can be an aid to thinking, they should not be allowed to become a substitute for it. The encouragement of lateral thinking, bringing in different people or mixing backgrounds and levels may be more important than the introduction of additional tools.

On many occasions more thought appears to be devoted to the choice of tool than to the selection of the problem to address. Management tools and techniques were not responsible for any of the original ideas behind the innovations examined in the course of preparing this book. Their roots generally lay outside the world of work, when seeing a link or connection with 'something different' caused someone to ask a simple, yet fundamental, question.

The problems companies don't think or know they have are often the issue, for example the hidden delays that occur at the interfaces or handover points between departments.[2] This invisible dimension generally consists of areas that fall between departmental responsibilities. It can represent enormous potential for performance improvement when brought into the open.

Motivations for use

Too many of the existing management approaches and tools are concerned with working people harder or with the depressing task of downsizing or reducing the organisation to its 'core'. The lifeblood of many organisations, their people and the spirit of those that remain, is draining away. They are becoming weaker rather than stronger relative to their more positive competitors.

Some reductionist strategies resemble cutting your wrists, lying in a bath and bleeding to death, rather than stepping outside and energetically and creatively looking for opportunities. By the time the body corporate has been thoroughly pummelled and steamed by the full range of tools, only dry and lifeless bones are likely to remain.

What is often missing is the willingness to ask fundamental questions about the opportunities and capabilities that could sustain a positive spiral of growth and development. Weight watching by itself can be negative. At one extreme is anorexia. As suggested in Chapter 1, adopting a healthier lifestyle, for example taking regular exercise, is generally a more positive approach. What is needed is will, vision and purpose rather than the latest dietary fad.

Attitudes and behaviours

Attitudes and behaviours can be more important than approaches and techniques. There are companies that perceive and define themselves as sick. Many of these corporate malingerers avoid confronting the reality that their problems are actually 'in the mind'. The 'quick fix', the needle, the sticking plaster, the bandage and all sorts of potions and spells are of little value if the patient has lost the will and desire to live.

Attitudes of mind are more positive in some contexts than others. ASK Europe plc has a conscious policy of operating on a human scale through business units of 'family size' based at aesthetically pleasing locations that are conducive of reflection and creativity. Group Chief Executive Robert Terry puts the highest priority upon safeguarding the 'learning' ethos of the company.

Rather than become small in vision and mind, some larger companies seek to emulate what are perceived as desirable qualities associated with smallness such as flexibility and entrepreneurial attitudes. These can then be coupled with the scale and reach needed to operate effectively in confronting targeted areas of opportunity. This is the route taken by such US companies as Alcoa, Corning and Xerox.

Large companies can also form close relationships with specialist suppliers that have attitudes and behaviours, or tools and techniques, which they lack. Those in possession of distinctive competences can find themselves in great demand as a potential 'member' of virtual corporations and other forms of network organisation.

Companies at risk are reactive users of tools, companies that grasp at fashionable methodologies in order to cope with challenges and threats they do not fully understand. Those they select may do little more than give them some temporary peace of mind and a 'stay of execution'. In struggling to 'make it work' there is often a fine line between perseverance which can be a noble quality and stubbornness which is generally plain stupid.

Changing the architecture of the corporation may have little impact upon its feelings, its heart and its soul. The future belongs to proactive creators and users of tools, the companies that initiate trends, fashions and opportunities. They have vision and purpose, and adopt pragmatic criteria for developing and selecting tools that will help them get to where they want to be. If the situation and circumstances change, they have the flexibility and maturity to try something else.

Attitudes can be influenced positively or negatively by the successful or unsuccessful use of tools. This cumulative experience is reflected in an organisation's approach to its activities and operations. Satisfaction and confidence results in a more pragmatic selection of tools, those employed reflecting current issues and priorities.

US manufacturer Federal-Mogul Corporation has been committed to 'continuous improvement' for 'several years'. By building upon its experience and pragmatically experimenting with new ways of adding value, the company has made 'sweeping process changes' at all its locations to reach its 'goal of becoming world class'. As a consequence, Federal-Mogul has the flexibility to resupply its demanding customers on a daily basis.

Matching tools to objectives and priorities

Approaches, tools and techniques are often neutral instruments, an organisation's objectives and priorities determining how they are used and for what purpose. In the financial services sector it is possible to see the same expert system used in one bank to reduce lending risks, in another primarily as a training tool, while elsewhere it is used as the basis for delivering additional services to customers.

A management approach should reflect corporate goals and priorities, and support whatever is thought necessary to safeguard and secure the future of a company. Quality *per se* may or may not be explicit in a short-list of 'critical success factors'. For example, consider the factors considered by BASF to be important:

> We want to remain successful in worldwide competition and to consolidate our position in the markets. The requirements for this are attractive products and services based on successful R&D, our long-term capital expenditure policy, our high standard in environmental protection and safety, and the skills, imaginativeness, qualifications and commitment of our employees.[3]

Such a list of corporate priorities suggests an implicit requirement for quality products and services, a quality research and development process, quality investment decisions, an environmental quality policy and quality attitudes and skills. In each of these areas the approaches, tools and techniques required could be quite different.

In another context, a similar approach could be applicable to different situations. Sweden's SCA group is Europe's largest private owner of forest land, and the second largest recycled fibre company. Throughout the company in recent years there have been drives to restructure and reduce the cost base. In order to be more flexible in response to the requirements of individual customers the priority in research and development is incorporating customer requirements while at the same time speeding up the delivery of products to the marketplace. A process improvement approach could have applicability in each of these areas.

The achievement of corporate objectives should drive the use of tools and techniques. Internationalisation is a key priority of Statoil. President and CEO, Harald Norvik, believes internationalisation will give the Norwegian company 'a sharper edge and create the basis for improved profitability and increased strength'. Helps and hinders analysis could be employed within such a company to identify the enablers and inhibitors of successful internationalisation.

For other companies, multiskilling is the priority – equipping people with the capability and flexibility to undertake a range of tasks. One director greeting visitors with the question: 'How many people are you?' claimed to have a team of 'eighty or thereabout' as a result of multi-skilling, even though the establishment strength was only seven. In such a context general problem-solving rather than narrow specialist skills may be sought.

Selection criteria

Approaches, tools and techniques should be selected with care. A corporate toolkit could be assembled or a diversity of different tools maintained by a central team that is able to advise on their use. Some companies establish centres of excellence similar to a learning resources centre at a university. Others resort to learning partners or a network of approved consultancy suppliers.

People may need help in identifying the techniques, tools and approaches that are most relevant to their particular situation and context. Wherever possible, they should be encouraged to create their own tools, for example identifying the key factors and expressing these in matrix form. If chimpanzees in forests can develop tools to tackle their problems, highly paid managers in the corporate jungle ought to be able to do likewise.

There are no 'right' or 'wrong' tools. It is horses for courses. For example, the selection could depend upon the degree of change that is required, or how much time is available. Figure 11.1 illustrates an approach that could be used. One similar to this has been utilised within Rank Xerox.

Whether or not a simple quality tool or some form of BPR is employed will depend upon the 'width' of the problem. For example, does it relate to one activity or a sequence of activities along a process? There are other factors to consider (Figure 11.1):

● At the quality end of the 'difficulty' spectrum the barriers to use are relatively low. For example, large numbers of people, perhaps everyone, could be empowered to use a problem-solving process and 'left to get on with it'.

● In contrast, BPR methodologies are more complex. Their use needs to be more sparing and controlled. Expert or consultancy support may be required. Information and communications technologies are more likely to be involved, as are senior management where applications are strategically significant.

The most useful tools are those that can be used in the line by managers themselves. For example, a process might be improved by simply asking: 'Would I do this if it were my business?' or 'Would the customer pay for this?' Rough rules of thumb can sometimes quickly yield as much as 90 per cent of the benefits which would arise from the much more protracted use of a detailed methodology.

Assembling toolkits

Tool and approach selection should reflect timescale. Thus a management team that feels 'pressured' to demonstrate results might opt for the simplification of a process within three or four months, rather than undertake a more fundamental re-engineering exercise which might require a year or more to complete.

The impact of benchmarking is largely due to the decision of pioneers such as AT&T, Du Pont, Milliken and Xerox to devise approaches for the

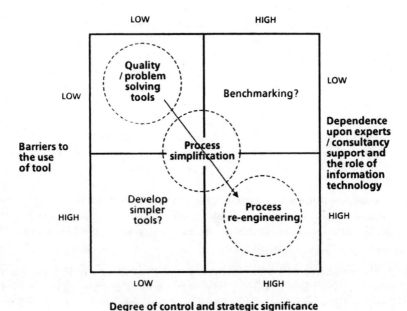

Figure 11.1   Tool selection

use of people in general, rather than just the experts. In the field of re-engineering the opposite is occurring in many companies, even though certain approaches are designed to be used by non-specialists in a wide range of circumstances.[4] Elaborate methodologies are adopted that require experts or consultants to implement.

Benchmarking could be used to investigate the sorts of tools being used to address similar problems in other organisations. It could also help identify improvements and refinements which could be introduced. An evolving capability is preferable to 'dipping into a toolbox' and 'returning' a technique after use to be forgotten until required again.

A general core 'toolkit' could be supplemented by specialist techniques that are developed or imported for particular purposes. To provide customers with freedom of choice, SCA has 'to produce and deliver in a highly flexible manner'. Across many areas of the business the emphasis is upon the twin objectives of cost reduction and 'increasing the dependability of just-in-time deliveries'. To achieve improvements, specific materials handling tools and expertise may be required in addition to a 'quality' technique such as benchmarking.

Sophistication for its own sake should be avoided. People may find it difficult to quickly 'buy in' or 'take ownership' of complex tools and techniques. It may be advisable to start with relatively simple tools in order to encourage their early adoption. Then when people are comfortable with them, and their use has delivered some tangible benefits, more sophisticated techniques can be introduced. According to one quality director: 'Charge straight into complexity and you hit a brick wall.'

Not all applications of tools and techniques will be successful. John Melo was responsible for assembling the combination of approaches in use within the Thomas Cook Group worldwide on a wide range of quality and re-engineering projects. He stresses the importance of learning from disappointments: 'Expect to make mistakes and to continue making them, but ensure that the organisation learns and shares these experiences.'

Network quality

Within the network organisation, not all members need be equally expert in all areas of competence and capability. Some division of responsibility for tool development and use may be advisable, with each member agreeing to maintain a centre of competence in a certain area. Such centres could be outsourced or encouraged to seek business opportunities outside of an organisation or network.

Non-core activities are being contracted out or shared as network relationships are being forged with customers and suppliers. Nothing should be taken for granted. While many organisations consider research and development a core activity to be undertaken 'in house', others such as

US natural resources company Freeport-McMoRan take a different view. Freeport-McMoRan has undertaken a continuing programme of restructuring. The Chairman and CEO explains: 'We have outsourced our research and engineering, environmental, and safety functions to an independent consulting firm staffed by retired Freeport-McMoRan experts who had long tenure with the company.'

Ex-employees may have some empathy with, and sympathy for, a company's approach and philosophy, but new partners and people without any previous contacts or experience of working together may not. Many companies in growth markets are now making a conscious choice to remain small in order to retain flexibility. According to one director: 'Success is transient. Markets are here today and gone tomorrow. You can't afford to get locked in.'

The Japanese game company Nintendo operates in a market that has mushroomed. Yet overheads are kept to a minimum, with much of the manufacturing and other activities subcontracted. With employee levels still in three figures, Nintendo operates through a network of contract relationships. The role of the core 'head office' team is largely to coordinate and manage relationships with business partners rather than the activities of subordinate employees.

Management approaches need to cope with the virtual enterprise or *ad hoc* company. People may join shared learning groups, 'quality clubs' or other consortia of organisations that agree to adopt compatible approaches and from among whose members future business partners might be drawn. A shared set of approaches, tools and techniques can help to hold a network organisation together. Where steps are taken to refine and develop them they can become one of the benefits of network membership.

The learning culture

The most valuable tools are those that encourage continuing learning and development. The corporate environment should be supportive and conducive of learning. Learning role models should be encouraged. People should be enabled to explore, to be open-minded and to share insights across functional, business unit, geographic and cultural barriers.

A learning culture does not automatically occur. A company should consider the appointment of a director of learning or thinking:

● While Managing Director at the National & Provincial Building Society, David O'Brien put a high priority upon the encouragement of learning throughout the organisation. A Manager of Learning was appointed and learning was built into all management processes.
● Much of the recent performance improvement achieved by the Rover

Group has been due to the creation of a learning culture. A dedicated team has been established to encourage and support learning.

● Xerox has recognised that learning is such an important activity as to constitute a 'business within a business'. A 'learning institute' has been developed to deliver internal and external learning solutions.

Kirster Ahlstrom, President of the Finnish company Ahlstrom, encourages people to challenge what they collectively believe they know and to search for new ways of increasing their collective capacity and capability to implement a shared vision. As a consequence of this collective restlessness the company has grown rapidly in a decade from being a local supplier to a global player.

If innovation, experimentation and risk-taking are to be encouraged, people should not be unfairly penalised for mistakes. If failure is not tolerated, staff are likely to be inhibited from 'having a go'. Risk and return are related. It is often difficult for the overly safe organisation to generate returns that are significantly above average. The probability of success can be increased through the use of appropriate tools and supporting systems.

Within the network organisation an open and free market in ideas should be encouraged, if ideas are to be translated into action. Individuals who are good at initiating proposals should be motivated and enabled to form alliances with others who may have a greater ability at putting them into effect. The technology of the network could be used to raise issues, canvas support and seek help with development and implementation.

Values and learning

MashreqBank, the first winner of the Dubai Quality Award, has adopted a comprehensive approach to quality. Abdul Aziz Abdulla Al Ghurair, the Chief Executive Officer, puts particular stress upon the importance of such fundamental quality values as trust and honesty of purpose. At MashreqBank these are not just words but key elements of 'a culture based upon fundamental values'. Senior executives express their career aspirations in terms of moral purpose and younger staff are attracted to the bank by the values embedded in its culture.

The Birmingham Midshires Building Society also has a 'first choice' strategy and aims to exceed customer expectations by being Friendly, Informed, Responsive, Service oriented and Trustworthy. Again the emphasis is moving from tools and techniques to attitudes and values.

Corporate values should stimulate thinking rather than impose a sanitised or bland view of the world. A too heavy handed approach can stifle and inhibit. Within a federal network, a top-down approach needs to tolerate a degree of diversity and recognise the variety of situations and circumstances that can be found at the local level.

The most fruitful collaborations are those between individuals with particular and distinctive, but complementary, qualities and talents. This may require a greater tolerance of those who may have obvious deficiencies, but at the same time possess compensating strengths. So long as weaknesses are identified and understood they can be balanced by the attributes and qualities of other members of the team.

There are many dimensions to the building of diversity. For example:

- At Xerox PARC a conscious effort was made to increase the diversity of experience within groups and teams to the extent of adding the occasional sociologist or musician to join teams of electronic engineers.
- People brought in from other functions as non-executive managers can introduce the questioning and challenging independence and objectivity which the good non-executive director brings to the boardroom.
- Learning partnerships can be forged with other organisations that have distinctive and complementary learning approaches and competences. Thus ASK Europe plc has strategic learning partnerships with selected international organisations based upon a shared commitment to collaborative learning.

If values are to shape attitudes and behaviour they need to be more than mere 'words on paper'. A commitment to learning should be clearly demonstrated through corporate practice. Thus:

- Mouchel, the international firm of consulting engineers, links progression through a sequence of more demanding roles to the acquisition and demonstration of appropriate competencies.
- The University of Luton, the first university to gain the UK's 'Investor in People' award, allows significant time to all staff, both academic and support, for personal development and such activities are an important feature of promotion discussions.

Reward and remuneration strategy will often reflect corporate values. Thus because most organisations value delivery of short-term priorities rather than the building of longer-term capability they do not reward learning or the enhancement of competence.

Flexible learning

Some companies recognise the central importance of learning. William Saurin, a company within the French Group Saint Louis, established a series of working parties to examine how internal communications might be improved and decision-making speeded up. Training is 'central to the management philosophy' of the Group Saint Louis, and the development activities of the various subsidiaries are 'tailored to the particular circumstances of their different industries'.

The growing emphasis upon tailoring is associated with recognition of 'training' as a core activity. The most effective learning occurs when working and learning are integrated. This matches the preferences of major companies across Europe for learning that is both tailored and flexible. Table 11.1 summarises the relevance attached by survey respondents to various modes of study according to 'very relevant' responses.[5]

The challenge is to support and facilitate the learning of individuals, groups and organisations by means of an appropriate and tailored combination of content, process and delivery mechanisms that matches the situation, circumstances and context and both enables people to harness more of their potential and allows them to learn at the time and place, and in a mode, that best suits their preferences and natural aptitudes for learning.

In order to implement a flexible learning strategy, learning opportunities and environments need to be created, people as individuals and groups need to be allowed to discover their learning potential and preferred learning styles, and appropriate learning processes and supporting learning technologies should be put in place.

Table 11.1 *Corporate training requirements: relevance of various modes of study in order of 'very relevant' replies*

Tailored company-specific programmes	52%
Project component	36%
In-company delivery	30%
Open programmes	24%
Modular programme	23%
Self-managed	21%
Issue based	21%
Part-time day release	20%
Evening	19%
Distance learning	18%
Portability of credits/qualifications within UK	14%
Mutual recognition of qualifications within EC	14%
Joint programme/joint validation	13%
Residential element	13%
Period of study in another EC country	13%
Full time	13%
Study visit abroad	11%
Discipline centred	11%
Industry-specific programmes	11%
Block release	3%

Source: *Human Resource Development for International Operation*, 1990.[5]

Quality and thinking

Does quality broaden or narrow thinking? The pursuit of any drive to extreme, for example a succession of new and prescriptive models all embracing 'continuous improvements' that cause confusion and leaves the palate jaded, can be counter-productive.

Quality thinking about tomorrow may be more important than thinking quality today. Companies need to question what represents intellectual leadership in areas of opportunity. How dependent is the organisation upon its past and how prepared is it for the future? What is relevant will depend in large part upon the nature of windows of opportunity created by 'frame-breaking' change.

The quality of thought can be a particular problem for the task and output focused network organisation that lives in a world of contracting and outsourcing. Rather than allowing time for thinking, or investing in training or the building of capability, it buys in specific skills and knowledge as and when required. People are used and then discarded. Individuals making up the contractual fringe, the independent contractors many of whom may lack the resources to invest in their own development or renewal, may need shared learning support.

The common toolkit and diversity

Common techniques and tools can encourage and facilitate communication and sharing, but this benefit should not be achieved at the cost of encouraging a standard approach to all problems and opportunities. Innovation is often the result of an unconventional approach and the perception of links and relationships between different elements that hitherto have not been connected. To foster creativity a variety and diversity of approaches should be encouraged.

The additional workloads that many managers are experiencing as a result of delayering and the allocation of the work of those that leave to those that remain can drive out any time to explore alternative ways of tackling problems. The long hours of work that many people are having to put in is reducing thinking time. As a consequence, too many people are surviving rather than challenging. 3M is a corporation that has developed a reputation for encouraging its people to think, challenge and take risks.

The desire to learn, a penchant for benchmarking and the search for patterns, links and relationships should not be pursued to the extent of over-generalisation, excessive simplification or a selective vision that screens out what is special and different about a particular situation. Origin, an international supplier of software services, recognises that 'over-specialization can lead to fixed views and preconceived ideas.' The company approaches every project with an open mind, as 'our experience has shown that it is not, of course, the sameness from project to project which presents the challenge, but the differences.'

The human factor

There is a tendency when applying tools to focus upon the more visible and tangible 'hardware', 'structural' or 'formal' factors. Thus processes are documented and re-routed, and organisation charts are changed to reflect the latest restructuring. The more tricky 'software', 'behavioural' or 'informal' side, the question of attitudes, feelings and values, is avoided.[6] The essence of the corporate organism is described and redesigned in terms of its skeleton and bones rather than its senses and nerves.

Simplicity is sought, not superficiality. Complexity is often an indication of lack of rigour and limited understanding. The impact of the simple solution can be profound. It is usually easier to communicate and share, and thus can represent a threat to those whose specialist positions depend upon the relative ignorance or lack of awareness of others. Complex tools are more likely to require expert support.

Rigour must be complemented by sensitivity and relevance. According to one CEO: 'Too many of my people, especially the ex-consultants, seem anaemic – devoid of humanity. Our customers are human beings.' Recognising that people have feelings is realistic and not naive.

Tools in themselves may not have an impact unless attention is also given to the 'human factors' and the ambiance, context and framework within which they are employed. Bernard Fournier, Managing Director of Rank Xerox, believes: 'Productivity should be achieved by doing things differently and by simplifying our processes, using additional tools and further empowering our people.'

In many companies survival as an employee depends upon a willingness to 'act tough', to fire or protect the 'corporate interest'. What value should a corporation put upon personal anguish or risk to human life? Should a company spend whatever is necessary to remove all reasonable risk of damage or injury? A growing number of corporate 'toolkits' contain approaches to handling human dilemmas and ethical issues.

The rationality that can accompany the use of quantitative tools should never be allowed to crowd out the sensitivity that comes from a concern for humanity and human values. Ford decided not to pay an additional cost of $11 per car to reduce the risk of the fuel tanks in its Pinto car exploding when they were struck from the rear when cost-benefit analysis showed that the probability of this occurring was minimal. In the event, accidents and deaths occurred.

The cultural dimension and diversity

Management approaches travel better in some cultures than in others. Their focus, true cost and potential benefits likewise depend upon the context. Thus while the American manager might seek inspiration from 'gurus' or suppliers of quality tools and techniques, an Italian colleague could prefer to learn from the experiences of business role models.

The culture of Walt Disney puts great stress upon the consistent quality of customer experience. Yet it appears to capture some of the magic associated with its early products and the youthful optimism of many of its customers, and exudes a sense of enterprise.

Some companies recognise that cultural and other forms of diversity should be built upon rather than suppressed. For example:

- Hutchinson Whampoa, one of the 'hongs' of Hong Kong, treasures 'its ability to blend successfully the best business techniques of East and West.'
- While chairman of BP, Robert Horton reported that 'managing a complex organisation like BP demands a variety of skills which are supplied by different groups and individuals.'
- Paul Allaire, as Chairman of Xerox Corporation, has launched a corporation-wide initiative to not only recognise and understand cultural diversity, but also to encourage it.

To better reap economies of scale, the internal sharing of ideas, resources and best practice should be encouraged. At the same time, those aspects which distinguish a particular case must be recognised.

Care needs to be taken to ensure that the use of standard approaches does not result in an organisation losing the benefits of diversity and variety. Enterprising though it is, perhaps Walt Disney should have devoted more effort to tailoring its Euro-Disney theme park to the distinct nature of local cultures.

Companies vary greatly in the extent to which they appreciate the value of diversity. The corporate logo of the Malaysian Berjaya Group Berhad 'taken in totality ... signifies Strength In Diversity.' Vincent Tan Chee Yioun, the Group CEO of Berjaya has devoted much effort to encouraging 'companies within the Group to exploit the Group's strength in diversity ... management has responded through numerous cross-selling of ideas and promotions.'

Basic quality tools

While surveys considered earlier in this book (eg in Chapters 1 and 2) have revealed much criticism in certain contexts of quality assurance approaches, tools and techniques, there are companies that find them of value and innovation continues to occur. For example:

- The VIAG subsidiary VAW aluminium has introduced a computer-aided quality management system. This covers the full production process from incoming inspections to final testing, and detects and immediately remedies production-related deviations from agreed standards. VAW aluminium's customers were closely involved in the design of the system to ensure that it meets their requirements.
- Open-minded and imaginative use of simple quality tools can result in more radical outcomes than the uninspired and plodding application of so-called 're-engineering' approaches whose ostensible purpose is to help bring about radical change.

Many quality tools are unfairly criticised by those who fail to use them properly. Basic quality tools like cause and effect diagrams, Pareto charts, histograms, etc, can be used as aids to learning by enabling us to structure data or spot trends, while quality management and planning tools such as inter-relationship diagrams can assist us in making connections.[7] Other techniques such as gap or attribute analysis, perspective shifting, association or substitute search can be specifically used to stimulate creative thinking.

Problem-solving

Let us look at the tools mentioned in Figure 11.1. Most companies, irrespective of their approach to quality, would benefit from more effective problem-solving. Many do not specifically address the problem-solving skills of their people or, when action is taken, they adopt the 'easy route' of equipping people with a simple and general approach which may offer little practical help in addressing contextual issues.

A basic problem-solving process is illustrated in Figure 11.2. There are many such approaches. What matters is not the number of stages or what they are called, but how the process is approached. Thus:

- Asking the right questions can prevent good work being done on the wrong problem.
- When analysing the situation it is important to get at the root causes.
- The quality and significance of solutions can depend greatly upon the nature of the objectives set.
- A minimum number of options of varying degrees of risk or step change could, and perhaps should, be demanded.
- Strategic as well as tactical factors may need to be taken into account when selecting a preferred option.
- Planning and implementation should be followed by a review stage, and any significant lessons learned should be widely shared.

The management and 'peer review' of a portfolio of projects becomes

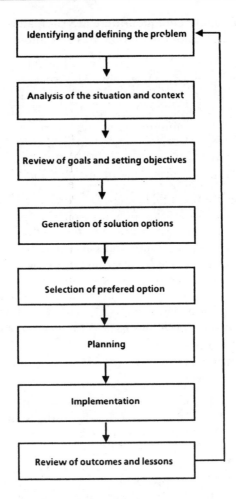

Figure 11.2   The problem-solving process

easier when a common framework or process is adopted. The progress of each can be charted upon an appropriate matrix.

Some companies that record analyses, objectives, options and outcomes practise 'open problem-solving', inviting all members of an organisational unit to browse through, and where appropriate comment upon, each other's projects. Very often people can add value to the projects of colleagues without delaying the progress of their own.

Benchmarking

The mission or philosophy of a company might suggest the use of certain tools. For example, in the case of Hero Supermarket: 'The Company's philosophy is clear: the best quality and the best service for the customer who is king.' It would be difficult for this Indonesian company to determine whether or not it is the 'best' without the use of benchmarking.

Benchmarking can be particularly valuable for organisations that feel they need to catch up. Volvo, the Swedish car company, sensed it had fallen behind. Chief Executive Soren Gyll has initiated an extensive benchmarking programme.

The principle of benchmarking is not new. According to Israel Sieff, who together with Simon Marks led Marks & Spencer during the period 1916 to 1964, quality is very much a question of 'doing what other people are doing but doing it better.' More recently companies such as AT&T, Eastman Kodak, Elida Gibbs, Du Pont, Ford Motor, Milliken and Xerox have derived significant benefits from the systematic use of benchmarking.

Xerox defines benchmarking as: 'A continuous, systematic process of evaluating companies recognised as industry leaders, to determine business and work processes that represent "Best Practices" and establish rational performance goals.' Figure 11.3 illustrates a simple approach to benchmarking based upon the problem-solving process of Figure 11.2. In many companies too much emphasis is placed upon measuring gaps and too little attention and effort is devoted to closing them.

A survey of benchmarking in the UK has found that, while there is general satisfaction with its use, the 'many different definitions of benchmarking suggest considerable confusion as to the meaning of the term.'[8] In addition, 'comparison with direct competitors is the most widespread form of benchmarking; relatively few yet benchmark against best in class.' By focusing on direct competitors, these companies are missing opportunities to identify means of breaking away from the pack. Winners overtake as well as catch up.

As with other tools, much depends upon creative and imaginative use. A drawback of 'inter-firm comparisons' is that companies in self-contained sectors tend to gravitate to similar levels of performance. Xerox initially benchmarked itself against outfitter L L Bean rather than other office equipment suppliers in view of Bean's impressive response times.[9] Activities to benchmark are those which are most critical to the achievement of organisational goals.

Benchmarking can be a strong incentive to act. Thus the management teams at both Xerox and Ford were galvanised when they became aware of the levels of performance their Japanese competitors were achieving. As Vern Zelmer, when Managing Director of Rank Xerox (UK), put it: 'Like hanging it concentrates the mind.'

As with any form of analysis, the key to success is understanding how the findings relate to one's own situation. Many are ruthlessly objective at examining others while harbouring all sorts of delusions regarding themselves.

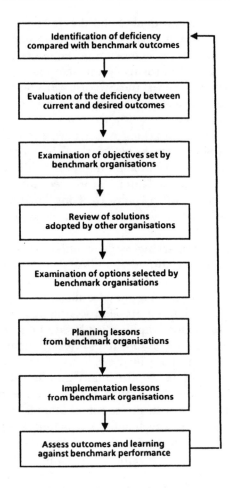

Figure 11.3   Benchmarking and the problem-solving process

The Xerox internal booklet on competitive benchmarking begins with the Sun Tzu quote: 'Know your enemy and know yourself; in a hundred battles you will never be in peril.' Underestimate one and exaggerate the other, and you are in trouble.

Process tools

A wide range of process improvement tools are now available.[4] Their relative merits vary, and which is the most suitable will depend upon the situation and circumstances. A number of mutual help and experience sharing networks are in operation that can help organisations to share experiences and benchmark.

Almost every major consultancy appears to have its own approach, some being recycled older methodologies, while others are differentiated sufficiently to conceal from whom they have been 'creatively swiped'. Consulting an accessible overview (eg *Business Re-engineering*[10]) and examining a more holistic methodology with case studies and notes on relevant tools and techniques (eg *The Responsive Organisation*[4]) can result in the perspective to make more sensible and relevant choices.

The complete spectrum of tools of Figure 11.1 could be applied to process improvement:

● For example, the problem-solving process of Figure 11.2 could be used, and rather like Chinese boxes, different tools can be used at each stage of other tools. Thus Figure 11.4 illustrates how certain other quality tools could be used at particular stages of a problem-solving process.
● Simplification methodologies (Figure 11.5) are at the low-risk end of the spectrum, while the more challenging and risky re-engineering methodologies are at the other end (Figure 11.6). A distinction between these two approaches was made in the last chapter.

Figures 11.5 and 11.6 are both based upon the methodology resulting from the European Commission's COBRA project, and notes on 101 tools and techniques to support these approaches are given in the published results of the project:[4]

● At the simplification end (Figure 11.5) greater attention is paid to examining the current situation as a point of departure. The focus is upon obtaining more from an existing capability by such means as empowerment and changing departmental boundaries.
● Re-engineering (Figure 11.6) begins with what could be, or ought to be, in order to encourage people to 'think outside the square' and not be overly concerned with what is. The role of emerging technologies and new ways of working and learning ought to be more important.

It may be possible to make visible progress with simplification by starting with the internal organisation. With re-engineering, it is generally advisable to begin with the external business environment and a first principles review of current and future customer requirements.

The re-engineering process (Figure 11.6) is vision led. People look beyond their own context for inspiration and ideas concerning new ways in which people, information and emerging technologies can be brought together. Once design principles are established it may be worth examining whether certain elements of an existing situation could be reused. Because the new alternative is likely to be fundamentally different, a pilot test should be run ahead of full implementation.

Most process improvement methodologies appear to be of a simplification rather than 're-engineering' variety, and unless challenging goals are

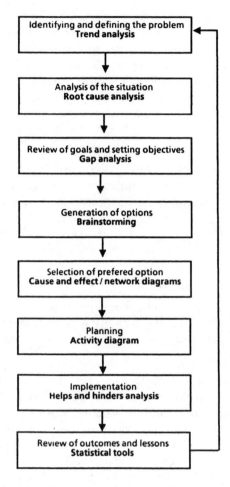

Figure 11.4 'Quality and quality management tools' and the problem-solving process

set there is a tendency to regress towards the achievement of incremental rather than radical change. Paul O'Neill, Chairman of Alcoa, has sought to set the tone and raise expectations by collectively referring to the company's change initiatives as its 'Quantum Leap' programme.

Using process tools

Purpose and motivation are crucial as significant payoffs from using many of the tools on offer are likely to go to the courageous and creative rather than to the timid and the blinkered. The aim should be to encourage challenging first principles reviews that lead to imaginative but practical

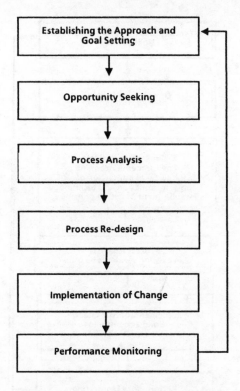

Figure 11.5   Process simplification

Source: Colin Coulson-Thomas, *The Responsive Organisation*, Policy Publications, 1995.

solutions, and substantially enhance learning and performance improvement capability. The more ambitious an exercise, the greater is the need for insight, imagination and innovation, and top management courage and sustained commitment.

The goal of an ambitious re-engineering project could be a world-class capability that delivers value and benchmark levels of satisfaction to customers, employees and business partners, differentiates in the marketplace, and supports ambitious commercial, business and core competence development objectives. The review process, and subsequent implementation and operation, should invigorate the people and teams concerned and provide them with enhanced personal development and shared learning opportunities.

The Rank Xerox re-engineering process will typically pass through modelling, analysis, design and implementation planning phases and be tailored to the client situation and context. It involves the assessment of internal and external requirements; the use of benchmarking, environmental scanning, modelling, visioning, design and planning tools; and

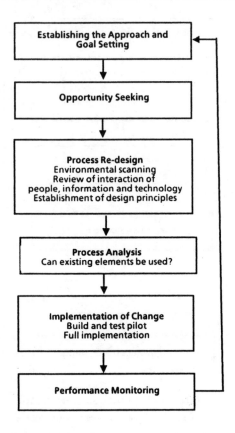

Figure 11.6   Process re-engineering

Source: Colin Coulson-Thomas, *The Responsive Organisation*, Policy Publications, 1995.

the analysis of the interaction of people, work processes, information and technology. In view of the attitudinal and behavioural changes that are likely to be required, particular attention is paid to internal communication, involvement and other people issues.

Organisations should be wary of IT suppliers that 'jump on the re-engineering' bandwagon by suggesting packaged methodologies which lead inexorably to further opportunities for them to sell their products. According to two pioneers of re-engineering: 'There is no package, either of methodologies or software products, that will help companies re-engineer.'[11]

More companies should focus upon their supply chains and make full use of the potential offered by such emerging technologies as electronic commerce.[12] Applications of IT can be trivial or profound. When used appropriately, groupware can fundamentally change the pattern of communications within an organisation, and by subverting positions of power based upon possession of information it can facilitate the transition to a new model of organisation.[13]

The extent to which the use of groupware is relevant to the achievement of corporate change will depend upon the significance and nature of the tasks and objectives concerned. Table 11.2 identifies a number of the factors that may be associated with the isolated or pervasive use of groupware according to whether changes sought are limited and incremental or significant and fundamental.

World-class project management

An often overlooked process is that which is used to manage projects. Major projects constitute a significant proportion of the income of companies in sectors as varied as shipbuilding and software development. More companies are becoming organised by project. They are the vehicle for delivering value to customers. Differentiation can result from better project management.

Table 11.2 *The degree of change and its impacts*

Factor	Limited/incremental	Significant/ fundamental
Senior management involvement	Symbolic	Substantial
Timescale	Short	Long
Purpose	Limited/Modest	Profound
Objectives	Simple	Complex/multiple
Effect upon business	Normal activity	Disruptive
Responsibilities	Usual	Special project
Focus	Individual tasks	Management and business processes
Communication	Within departments	Cross-functional
Importance of information technology	Limited or incidental	Fundamental
Use of groupware	Isolated	Pervasive
Motivation	Weak	Strong
Risk	Low	High
Visibility	Low	High
Activities	Continuous	Discontinuous
Impact	Comparatively small	Relatively large

There are many ways to improve the status of project management. Project managers could be regarded as the heroes of an organisation, listed on organisation charts, and encouraged with appropriate incentives and rewards. Often the most relevant skills are not allocated to project teams, as there are disincentives to using people outside of an immediate business unit.

The project management process itself could be re-engineered or supported by management and systems processes that 'add value' rather than simply check:

- Managers could undertake peer reviews of each other's projects and should be encouraged to look for patterns, trends, links, common features, etc, across projects.
- The emphasis in reporting and reviews should be upon the early identification of project risks, ie of not meeting customer requirements or corporate objectives.
- To encourage the open and early reporting and anticipation of problem areas, 'brownie points' could be given for the energetic identification and tackling of root causes, obstacles and barriers.

Project managers and their teams may need to be provided with relevant analysis, planning and problem-solving tools, and counselling and support regarding their selection and use. Perhaps estimating and budgeting could be more realistic. Maybe more time could be allowed for testing, assessing and learning.

In many companies, greater learning from experience is needed, especially of how problems encountered on projects were overcome. Continual learning, sharing and improvement should be built into a project management process, particularly by means of peer reviews at each stage and debrief reports.

People should be encouraged to assume personal responsibility. for learning. No longer should reports just be sent on to someone else 'who is paid to think'. Great stress has been placed upon employee involvement and personal responsibility at both Xerox and Ford. At Xerox people are consciously equipped with learning skills, while at one Ford location the hourly paid persuaded those on salaries to stay away for a week while they demonstrated what they themselves were capable of achieving.

'Re-engineering' management

Management approaches such as quality should themselves be challenged. Re-engineering is concerned with outcomes. Too often, quality professionals behave as though the quality process is an end in itself. As one quality director put it: 'Output quality is the acid test, quality from the perspective of the customer.'

Rolf Börjesson, President and CEO of PLM Plastics, believes: 'Quality cannot be compromised and therefore it is of utmost importance for PLM. It means that we must match customer expectations at all times.' While a company may question and continuously refine the means employed to achieve it, the goal of output quality needs to be sustained in order to remain a player in a growing number of markets.

Some companies continue with 'care and maintenance' quality, with some risk to their competitive positioning and quality registration and in the knowledge that the quality of output as delivered to customers is below what is possible. Others view their current approach to quality as but a stage on an ongoing journey and undertake regular and collective reviews.

The more ambitious move beyond 'maintenance', for example updating what is in order to retain a recognised quality registration, while introducing initiatives to improve the quality of the product delivered to customers. Various considerations can emerge while undertaking such an approach.

A first step is to understand current expectations. The priorities might be to maintain a quality registration at minimum financial and time cost, or to reduce project 'risk'. They could be more positive, such as to encourage rather than replace thinking and learning, or to maximise contribution to 'delivered' quality.

Customers like to feel that they and their requirements are both understood and driving a supplier's activities. A company might view customer satisfaction in terms of technical quality, while 'value' from a customer perspective might be defined in terms of meeting business requirements rather than technical excellence *per se*. Product quality may be assumed, with empathy and quality of relationships with the customer being the key differentiator.

It is often difficult to change quality priorities and a quality perspective without a combination of measures that will collectively modify attitudes and behaviours. Consideration could be given to the extent to which the 'cost of quality' (eg cost of rework, lost clients, deficient processes, etc) could be used to build project management or account management competencies.

As well as improving performance on individual customer projects, the approach adopted should increase the general capability of an organisation to deliver satisfaction and value. The aim should be to break out of declining spirals towards commodity work, and into ascending spirals towards broader partnership relationships with customers and higher margin activity.

Focus on risk to delivered quality

The demanding customer has little interest in the cosmetics or rituals of quality, and is likely to be resistant to initiatives that are not thought through, or which are not seen to be clearly beneficial. A broader approach to quality in a project-based organisation could focus upon reducing risks to the quality of output or quality 'delivered' to the customer.

A 'delivered' quality approach can yield benefits to a range of stakeholders. For example:

- value and flexibility to customers;
- satisfaction to employees and project teams;
- reduced rework costs and fewer 'surprises' for corporate management;
- enhanced and 'safer' returns to shareholders;
- the company itself could make progress towards becoming a learning organisation.

All stakeholders could have a common interest in reducing risks on projects. However, being a 'safe' organisation may not be compatible with the generation of high returns. Given that risk and return are related, a company that adopts a narrow technical view of its role and takes every step to deny responsibility or protect its contractual position could limit itself to commodity work. Higher returns and broader partnership business relationships, as we saw in Chapter 7, could require greater openness, flexibility and sharing of risk with the customer.

At the same time, a significant proportion of 'bottom line' returns can be swallowed up by a small proportion of projects that 'go wrong'. It is imperative that organisations take every step to ensure that potential risks to project delivery are identified as early as possible and energetically tackled.

Developing an integrated approach

The route to greater 'delivered' quality in project-based organisations often lies in the integration of quality and commercial concerns and the management of technical and legal risks into an integrated management process that focuses upon:

- greater involvement of customers in the initial agreement of quality criteria;
- supportive peer reviews during the course of projects to enable the customer to benefit from a broader pool of experience;
- open and honest reporting to achieve an earlier identification of risks to project performance;

- the continual use of relevant and practical tools such as root cause and barrier analysis to identify likely obstacles and barriers;
- access to, and application of, lessons and experience from other projects;
- dialogue with customers in terms of their expectations concerning deliverable quality;
- a post-delivery relationship, shared learning and ongoing responsibility for customer satisfaction;
- holistic reviews at each stage of a project, to ask questions such as: What went wrong? What could have been done better? What lessons could be learned?

The optimum review points will depend upon the project. Start-up reviews to clarify objectives and requirements are particularly important for ensuring a project sets off in the right direction. Technical peer reviews can be of value at a design stage. While work is in progress, it may be worth asking periodically: 'Is the project doing what it should be doing?' and 'Is the project on track in terms of delivery time and cost?'

The emphasis at each stage should be upon the customer rather than the quality system and its requirements. The focus should be upon identifying and tackling problem areas rather than just producing reports to management which may or may not get read.

Such an integrated process framework might need to be applicable to 'products', 'one-offs', consultancy, large and small projects, etc. Its use should help, over time, to build more competent project managers.

Implications of an integrated approach

Many professionals are ambivalent about integrating their role into business and management processes. For example, a quality specialist might feel quality assurance and the maintenance of a quality registration demands independence and objectivity, or may fear conflict between 'quality' and 'commercial' drivers.

Views may differ as to the timing and priority of different 'dimensions'. Thus the 'quality' aspect might be needed early on, while a technology review may be required some way into a project. Some might consider such a division artificial.

Among project managers, there is often interest, indeed a degree of enthusiasm, for the use of supportive screening processes through which projects can be passed in order to determine the nature and extent of any further analysis that might be required. The intelligent monitoring of projects via a series of screens could involve:

- 'thinking' rather than 'automatic' or procedural reviews;
- the use by a multiskilled team of 'trigger' checklists to detect symptoms of possible problems;

- root cause analysis, and an examination of the implications for different stakeholders prior to determining next steps;
- 'getting to grips' with issues, rather than just reporting them, for example learning from others or instituting a programmes of corrective actions;
- line management participation in the decision of whether to probe further.

Learning can occur as review screens and checklists are refined and, through their use, people become more alert and sensitive to possible problem areas. The focus upon identifying and overcoming obstacles and barriers to performance helps to ensure people are actively working towards 'delivered' quality.

Project managers ought to perceive themselves as customers of holistic reviews which should be supportive, learning experiences rather than 'checking up' exercises. Peer review reports should go initially, or exclusively, to the project manager and team. Reporting elsewhere could undermine their receptiveness and responsibility. Ideally, reviews should be positively sought by project teams.

Organisational learning could be fostered by the use of debrief reports or records of how problems are overcome. A knowledge-based system could be developed concerning how project managers overcome common problems. The results of project reviews could be used to raise issues, modify expectations or generally build customer relationships.

Advantages of an integrated approach

There are many advantages of more integrated approaches. Holistic central, business unit and peer reviews help people to develop an overview of projects and can encourage a more customer-focused approach to account management. Reviews with project teams can bring issues and root causes to the surface.

Reviews that 'add value' represent a learning opportunity for those involved. Review team assignments could be used to encourage sensitivity to problem areas and to select, train and develop project managers with a more holistic approach to project management. People should 'do' quality rather than talk about it. Over time, holistic and peer reviews can result in the development of a cadre of people who are better able to manage large and complex projects.

There may be opportunities to involve customers in the review process and thus develop a broader and shared view of what represents quality. Peer reviews could be 'sold' as an additional customer benefit. They might also lead to incremental earnings opportunities. The consequences of direct and open customer participation might need to be thought through in certain contexts.

For the fully stretched who do not want an increase in their workloads, peer reviews represent 'swings and roundabouts' – people help others and in turn are helped themselves, in both cases building their competence. Reviewing other people's problems sometimes allows one's own to be viewed in a different light. A peer review culture can reduce the need for incremental resources.

When a broader approach to 'delivered' quality is adopted, some thought may need to be given to roles and responsibilities. For example, who determines overall quality policy, goals and objectives? Should subsidiaries or business units develop their own 'business excellence' or transformation programmes?

A balance may need to be struck between central and local reviews. Central reviews could be undertaken of projects that impact upon overall corporate objectives and ratios, and local reviews of other projects. Centres of competence for certain approaches could be established centrally or locally according to need.

Widening ownership of quality

In some organisations quality is perceived as largely the concern of quality professionals in a quality assurance department. Widening involvement in, and ownership of, quality and extending it to cover output or 'delivered' quality can be encouraged by moving from an audit or checking culture to a support culture. Line accountability for 'delivered' quality may need to be made more explicit. Introducing a peer review system can also help encourage shared ownership.

Some potential for possible conflict could exist between the competing claims of registration and centralisation on the one hand versus involvement and devolution on the other. Quality professionals might fear that delegation of responsibility to operating units could lead to:

- a loss of focus, objectivity and independence in relation to the quality assurance role;
- less breadth and perspective in quality reviews;
- reduced learning across departmental, business unit and other organisational boundaries.

A 'lowering of standards' should not necessarily occur, and there may be some who would welcome less emphasis upon quality documentation as a result of cost and time pressure. The relevance of quality from a customer perspective could be enhanced by locating it closer to the customer.

Where it is thought a central quality unit should be maintained, line managers could be passed through it by means of an assignment system.

'Widening ownership' becomes more of an issue if an organisation opts to adopt a broader approach to delivering higher output quality. To bring about the changes of attitude and culture required, 'everyone' may need to be involved.

Related initiatives within a holistic approach

Quality will, of itself, not necessarily cause the improvements in output or 'delivered' quality many would like to see. Organisations often adopt a family of related initiatives as a 'customer focus' or project performance drive. A corporate transformation programme can help to distinguish a broader, more holistic approach from past quality assurance activity designed to maintain a quality registration. While aspects of such an approach may be relatively easy to introduce at the subsidiary or business unit level, and comparatively difficult at the group level, the payback is often relatively greater if complementary changes can be introduced at the level of the organisation as a whole.

The following initiatives have featured in one corporate transformation programme:

- A policy development and deployment cycle to ensure corporate vision and mission, and goals, values and objectives, are understood and shared.
- The ongoing measurement and tracking of customer satisfaction, leading to appropriate analyses and 'vital few' programmes.
- Benchmarking or business excellence reviews at subsidiary or business unit level, leading to the development of local action plans.
- Encouragement of more holistic and perceptive line reviews of local activities and projects, for example through the use of a peer review system.
- Creation and encouragement of a more open, learning and sharing culture.
- Adoption of new ways of working and learning that are more responsive to the distinct tasks and preferences of particular individuals and groups.
- The definition, agreement, development and practice of roles, competencies and appropriate role model behaviour.
- Reviews of management, support and learning processes as well as business processes, for example the account management or project management process.
- Learning support resources, 'learning labs' and learning partnerships.
- More focus during recruitment upon values, diversity and people skills.
- A reward system that encourages breadth, people, presentational and sharing skills, and learning from experience.
- Redefinition of the role of the line manager in terms of coaching, counselling, advising and mentoring, rather than the checking associated with 'command and control'.

A combination of change elements are normally required to bring about transformational change.[2] The mix of elements will need to reflect the evolving nature of the context, situation and circumstances at each stage of the change process. In the final two chapters we will examine how to go about setting priorities and objectives in a particular setting and how to ensure all the pieces of the jigsaw puzzle needed to turn aspiration into reality are in place.

Checklist

Have the people of your organisation been equipped with the approaches, tools and techniques to implement its quality, learning, re-engineering or transformation programmes and satisfy customers?

Are the tools practical and relatively easy to use? Do they require the support of experts and specialists?

How effective is the use of quality and re-engineering tools within your organisation? Are they used routinely and appropriately to tackle problems and build individual competence and group capacity?

How demanding is your organisation's approach to benchmarking? Does the organisation benchmark other quality, learning, re-engineering or transformation programmes in order to ensure its own toolkit is up to date?

Is there a comprehensive toolkit? How pervasive is its use? What are the main gaps? What action is being taken to remedy any deficiencies?

Is the toolkit common to different functions and business units? Does its content and selection reflect the local situation? Are the tools used appropriate and according to the context?

Who is responsible for ensuring that the toolkit is comprehensive, appropriate and up to date?

What is done to learn from the use of tools and to develop and refine them?

Are there accessible centres of competence in the use of certain tools? Are they effectively used by those 'in the field'?

References

1. Nick Oliver and Gillian Hunter, *The Financial Impact of Japanese Production Methods in UK Companies*, Cambridge, Judge Institute of Management Studies, 1995.
2. Colin Coulson-Thomas, *Transforming the Company: Bridging the Gap Between Management Myth and Corporate Reality*, London, Kogan Page, 1992.
3. 'Management Analysis', *BASF Annual Report 1992*, Ludwigshafen am Rhein, BASF, 1993, p 11.

4. Colin Coulson-Thomas (executive ed), *The Responsive Organisation: Re-engineering New Patterns of Work*, London, Policy Publications, 1995.
5. Colin Coulson-Thomas, *Human Resource Development for International Operation*, survey report for Surrey European Management School, London, Adaptation Ltd, 1990.
6. Colin Coulson-Thomas (ed), *Business Process Re-engineering: Myth and Reality*, London, Kogan Page, 1994.
7. Michael Brassard, *The Memory Jogger Plus+*, Methuen, MA, GOAL/QPC, 1989.
8. *Survey of Benchmarking in the UK*, executive summary of a survey undertaken by Gallup, Coopers & Lybrand and CBI National Manufacturing Council, London, Gallup/Coopers & Lybrand/CBI, 1993.
9. Robert C Camp, *Benchmarking: The Search for Industry Best Practices that Lead to Superior Performance*, Milwaukee, Wisconsin, Quality Press, 1989.
10. Peter Bartram, *Business Re-Engineering: The Use of Process Redesign and IT to Transform Corporate Performance*, Wimbledon, Business Intelligence, 1992.
11. James Champy and Michael Hammer, *Re-engineering the Corporation: A Manifesto for Business Revolution*, London, Nicholas Brealey, 1993.
12. Peter Bartram, *The Competitive Network*, London, Policy Publications, 1996.
13. Colin Coulson-Thomas, *Harnessing the Potential of Groups*, a survey sponsored by Lotus Development, London, Adaptation Ltd, 1993.

Priorities and performance, objectives and outcomes

Quietness is the best noise.

For an elderly craftsman making serpentine objects at the Lizard in Cornwall the most perfect lighthouse he had ever made remained in his shop. For years no one wanted it, because of its size and weight. When eventually a potential customer appeared the old man was unable to bring himself to let it go. It was a perpetual reminder of what could be achieved. For him it was a pinnacle of achievement.

Only among the self-employed is there the freedom to pursue excellence to the extent of our serpentine maker. The board of a company has to be mindful of the interests of the key stakeholders in the enterprise. From time to time these may be in conflict, and accordingly, as one CEO explains: 'Management and Quality are about balance, an equilibrium of interests. A situation in which too much of the benefits accrue exclusively to one party cannot be sustained.'

Should we 'thump the tub' about quality or transformation and further raise their profile with stakeholders, or quietly incorporate quality and related considerations into a new generation of corporate priorities and objectives?

Stakeholders

Who are the groups with a legal, financial, social or economic stake in a company? Some managements adopt a broad view of who the stakeholders are:

- Japanese companies such as Canon and Matsushita articulate their purpose in terms of serving the interests of mankind.

- ASK Europe has a mission of helping people around the world to harness more of their potential.

In the UK, the 'Tomorrow's Company' initiative of the Royal Society for the encouragement of Arts, Manufacturers and Commerce has been seeking to encourage a more balanced approach to identifying and reconciling stakeholder interests.

The key stakeholders for most boards are shareholders, customers, employees and business partners. In the case of the virtual corporation, or network organisation, most 'employees' could be contractors and most suppliers and business partners could be members of the network. A balance has to be maintained, and the core requirements of all groups must be satisfied if a company is to survive. Where an equilibrium has been achieved, any new management initiatives should not be allowed to further the interests of one group to the extent that those of another are neglected.

Treat stakeholders well and they are more likely to stand by you, whether shareholders during a takeover battle or employees approached by a poacher. British Airways found that few of its customers changed airlines following the considerable publicity surrounding revelations of its 'dirty tricks' activities. Its focus upon the customer has established strong bonds of loyalty.

Pehr Gyllenhammar, Executive Chairman of Volvo, recognises the 'tricky trinity' and points out that his company's 'continuing development efforts are concentrating on meeting customer needs, creating confidence in the future on the part of employees, and providing an attractive return for our shareholders.' A different form of relationship is required for each group, but the relative significance a board attaches to each of them can be very revealing.

Stakeholder priorities

Stakeholder priorities reflect many factors, their relative power, the business climate and culture, and directorial drives. Given their role in the establishment of priorities, the pressures upon boards are particularly influential. As one US CEO put it: 'I've read all the stakeholder stuff, but at the end of the day my future here and my prospects of another job somewhere else depend upon the financials.'

The priority many boards attach to the financial imperative is sometimes an indication of the economic health of their business sector rather than evidence they are not customer oriented. For example, producers of white goods entered the 1990s facing a significant fall in demand in their key markets. For Anders Scharp and Leif Johansson, Chairman and

CEO, and President, respectively of Electrolux: 'Top priority has been assigned to improving profitability through internal programmes.'

The amendment of the Baldrige award criteria to include business results reflected the view that even among its enthusiasts 'doing quality is not enough'. Quality needs to be functional rather than an absolute abstraction pursued for its own sake. Management concepts and philosophies must be shown to contribute to business performance. The challenge is very often to ensure that short-term improvements are not secured at the expense of longer-term performance.

Thinking longer term about the customer

The impact of corporate activity upon the customer may be no less certain for being indirect and longer term. For example, customers can benefit from improved learning and understanding:

- ASK Europe puts the priority upon creating a learning culture for its people and the review of learning processes, believing this is the best guarantee of remaining at the leading edge and thus being able to act as a strategic learning partner of large 'blue chip' organisations.
- Thames Water actively searches for new technologies that might offer solutions to the waste water disposal problems of its customers. Similarly with quality, a company could begin with customer problems and issues, and then evaluate various approaches and tools that might make a useful contribution to addressing them, rather than automatically apply a standard toolkit.

Thames Water also helps its customers to assemble networks of organisations that share certain interests and concerns and have the potential to learn from or help each other. A customer-focused approach to quality and learning would lead a supplier to investigate which of its various customers might have all or part of the answer to the problems of others.

Longer-term exercises to change corporate structures or management processes can also be customer driven. For Continental, the 'ultimate goal of the quality concept' is 'to enhance customer satisfaction'. At the beginning of 1992 the company restructured its executive board, replacing functional with business responsibilities, reflecting its transition to a decentralised and divisional form of organisation in order to achieve closer contact with customers.

BPR and stakeholders

The focus upon an external or end customer is a key feature of the rhetoric of BPR. With some approaches to quality much more emphasis is given to 'internal customers', some of whom may be engaged in activities of little significance to final consumers. Bureaucratic processes often serve 'internal customers' and in many organisations these consume an excessive amount of time and resource. In general, the focus and a greater proportion of corporate capability needs to be switched to activities that generate value for external customers and sustain beneficial customer, supply chain and shared learning relationships.

While priorities for re-engineering were being set at Apple's Cork manufacturing plant, Joe Gantly, customer operations manager, encouraged colleagues to consider whether the customer would notice the difference. A number of suggestions for action failed this simple test.

Not all change initiatives or improvement models are driven exclusively, or directly, by the immediate interests of customers. Many applications of BPR are not really about the customer. They are driven primarily by the organisation's own requirements to cut costs, or to reduce headcount levels as a means of achieving the same objective.[1]

Even fewer BPR exercises put much priority upon the interests of another group of stakeholders, the people of the organisation. Those responsible, the early packagers of BPR, are now acknowledging the lack of attention given to the 'people' factors.[2,3] Improving the quality of working life or thinking do not feature highly among BPR goals.

Ideal outcomes are those that represent success from the perspectives of the long-term interests of all stakeholders. Such outcomes are conducive of lasting partnership relationships. Where one party does not regard outcomes as beneficial there are likely to be pressures to end a relationship. In mature relationships all parties are able to be open about the benefits they each derive.

Corporate drivers

For most companies the key drivers of restructuring or downsizing are financial such as 'reducing the cost base', 'boosting profitability' or 'strengthening cash flow'. Many exercises fail to achieve their primary purpose and contribute little to secondary objectives such as 'improving flexibility and responsiveness'. Behind many of the numbers that are 'achieved' is the world of disappointment, anguish and pain of those whose hopes and dreams are dashed.

Scratch the rhetoric about quality, and the imperative of reducing the cost base quickly becomes apparent. Quality multiple award winner Xerox is quite open about the need to reduce the cost of its operations and this is an underlying priority driver of productivity, process improvement and empowerment.

It is noticeable that survey participants increasingly refer to the need to confront reality. As one put it: 'Too many initiatives give the corporate smoothies a fresh opportunity to "keep in", "play the game" or demonstrate they are "role models".' Complacency still reigns in those quarters where people are able to avoid reality.

Confronting the right realities is important. In 'macho-management' cultures ruthlessness at cutting current costs is the virility test that offers entry to the inner sanctum. Yet ultimate survival depends upon the continuing willingness of customers to buy future generations of products and services. Cost could be just one factor in the purchase decision.

A preoccupation with internal costs should not detract from the strategic importance of the customer. According to one director: 'Cutting costs seems tangible ... you can take discrete decisions and feel you have done something ... The more strategic developments that will have a longer-term impact upon the customer relationship are more difficult ... They tend to get put off.'

One reason why traditionally bureaucratic companies such as IBM are being split into 'autonomous business units' and ICI 'demerged' into two separate corporate groups is to bring more of their people into closer contact with the realities of the marketplace. Given the tendency for a disturbed system to return to a previous equilibrium or trend, a succession of shocks may be needed to keep people on their toes.

Ends or means?

Certain companies consider quality an end, an aspiration or goal, while others regard it as a means, a combination of approaches, tools and techniques that may be employed to help achieve business objectives. Thus BP Oil is aiming to become 'The Quality Oil Brand', while Telefonica de España's 'total quality management system' is 'aimed at achieving the ambitious targets established in the company's strategic plans and at providing the support for the necessary change in corporate culture.' As a result of liberalisation, Telefonica has had to restructure its organisation, 'transform a monopolistic corporate culture', and create a new operating framework which 'is far more focused on meeting customers needs within a competitive environment'.

Collectively quality and other corporate objectives should cover the full range of elements that need to be in place to ensure a company satisfies its various stakeholders, and carries on satisfying them in the future. To achieve the latter may require actively learning and working with customers to create the future.

During an economic recession, companies in a wide range of sectors from construction and furnishings to motor cars and steel, and the many suppliers of goods and services that support them, are confronted with the harsh reality that bottom line profit can no longer be assumed to automatically rise as the volume of production inexorably increases. Emphasis switches to productivity as a source of profit improvement. Quality in many companies has to become a contributor rather than a beneficiary.

Ends and means

Some companies view quality as both an end and a means. Pacific Rim companies put especial emphasis upon the need for a company's business philosophy and corporate culture to match its goals. For example, consider the case of the Indonesian company PT Semen Cibinong:

> Our corporate mission is the development of competitive advantage in cement and concrete products through a customer oriented, cost conscious, quality focused, and shareholder value oriented management ... We are also committed to being a socially responsible citizen to the environment and the community.

> The Company has reinforced the need for a strong corporate philosophy and culture which are consistent with its corporate goals. The principal elements are a belief in, and respect for, the individual and the creativity of its employees, the creation of a competitive advantage in cement and concrete products, the achievement and enhancement of higher value for self development, our customers, our shareholders and for the nation.[4]

Concepts such as quality, unless qualified or explained, can mean so many different things. Companies often pull out and stress certain features in order to focus attention on those aspects thought to be particularly important. For example, BICC is 'dedicated to total quality, technical excellence and customer satisfaction' rather than simply to 'total quality'. BICC's objective is 'to be the most efficient and customer-friendly cables business in the world. Each company within the Group pursues total quality programmes aimed at a thorough understanding of customer needs and meeting those needs without error, on time, every time, at minimum cost.'

Setting corporate objectives

Fumio Sato, President and CEO of Toshiba Corporation, can claim: 'We have a huge potential to contribute to the progress of world society. The way I see it, that contribution is Toshiba's mission.' Other CEOs would not be taken seriously if they made such a claim. In the case of a US company both the analysts and non-executive directors would be worried. Quality and other objectives have to be related to the situation and context.

Those adopting 'balanced scorecards' of multiple objectives still tend to plump for 'hard' or quantifiable objectives such as response times or meeting a project deadline. Less tangible factors are sidelined. Peter Smith of Coopers & Lybrand acknowledges that 'at first sight' even client or customer satisfaction 'can seem vague and intangible. Certainly it is broad ranging and aspects of it are "soft" in that it is partly about impressions –

"are they helpful?", "do they value my business?"' It is upon such perceptions and impressions that many decisions concerning whether or not to continue a business relationship are based.

Objectives also need to reflect local and sectoral requirements. For example, for Eastman Chemical Company 'a capable process is a stable process' and 'process capability improvement is the continual reduction of variation'. In other contexts, for example a network of consultants, processes may be *ad hoc* and established to match the requirements of particular assignments and combinations of expertise in different locations.

The cultural context can have a significant impact upon the ease and speed with which corporate objectives can be implemented. Switzerland's Ciba has found that different cultures vary greatly in their response to empowerment. US companies like Xerox are currently reviewing how approaches to quality can be better tailored to the local context, business excellence exercises having considerable potential in this respect.

Figure 12.1 sets out a process which could be used to review corporate performance and identify what needs to be changed.[5] Before getting into

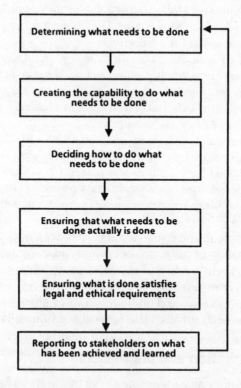

Figure 12.1 The strategy review process

Source: Colin Coulson-Thomas, *Transforming the Company*, Kogan Page, 1992.

the question of 'deciding how to do what needs to be done', the normal focus of quality, and then measuring achievement, there are two earlier stages. Both could involve quality considerations. Thus quality of life or experience considerations could help determine 'what needs to be done', while without elements of capability of the right quality, for example people or technology, there may be little point proceeding.

Organisations miss the various stages of Figure 12.1 at their peril. Thus, some companies seek to improve the quality of activities that do not relate to 'what needs to be done'. Others launch a great many management initiatives that make incompatible or impossible claims upon resources. They have not first identified and created 'the capability to do what needs to be done'.

Timescale

Creating new markets and industries can take a long time. Some twenty years elapsed between Chester Carlson's production of the first xerographic image in 1938 and the first office copier to use ordinary paper. The Japanese company JVC persisted for even longer in perfecting the video cassette recorder. Xerox and JVC have had a profound impact upon working and social life respectively.

During times of economic recession, many quality professionals hold the view that long-term quality objectives are being sacrificed for short-term considerations. Similar concerns are likely to be expressed by colleagues responsible for other activities such as research and development or the introduction of new technology.

Rover adopted total quality in the late 1980s. Its 'Rover Tomorrow' programme addressed the culture of the organisation, its people and its processes and particular emphasis was placed upon flexibility. By 1992 its Discovery vehicle emerged as a world-class product. However, at the end of a couple of years into the programme there was activity but little in the way of tangible results to show.

Thought and action are interrelated. Whereas it can take some time for 'thinking quality' to influence behaviour, adaptive people often find it easier to adjust their views and attitudes to accommodate the results of actions. Where time horizons are necessarily short, priority should be given to relevant action and initiatives rather than grandiose plans to change people's views through the advocacy of unfamiliar concepts.

Balancing aspiration and pragmatism

The realist planning any corporate programme ensures that the balance between activity and outcome, and the point at which tangible benefits are likely to arise, matches prevailing time horizons. People get bored and lose interest. It is naive to expect that in turbulent and uncertain market conditions corporate leaders will be prepared to wait indefinitely for returns that in any event might be questionable. More than faith is required when other people's money and careers are at stake.

In many companies in straightened circumstances, quality and re-engineering are being judged in relation to their contribution to current business objectives. As one CEO put it: 'For me there will be no long term unless we tackle some immediate and pressing issues ... To avoid them would be negligent, to suggest otherwise would be to live in "cloud cuckoo land"'.

Some motivations inhibit flexibility. In litigious societies, companies are under pressure to play it safe and avoid risks that could lead to liabilities. Not having a quality assurance system could come to represent prima facie evidence that one has not taken all reasonable steps.

While some companies view 'downsizing' as a necessary if unpleasant interference with their longer-term drives, others view it in a more positive light. For example, Euroc 'aims to be a lean enterprise that meets customer needs faster, using less resources, and with higher quality than competitors.'

A compact, tight and focused organisation can prove more flexible and responsive. As one manager put it: 'We have always talked about the need for a more responsive organisation, economic adversity has speeded things up. We are now doing what we needed to do in any case.' Companies like Virgin and ASK Europe set up new business units to preserve the entrepreneurial benefits of 'human scale' enterprise rather than just drive for economies of scale.

Large corporations find it difficult to preserve the flexibility and sense of mutual support found in family or 'human scale' enterprises. The competitive nature of the business environment can lead to defensive behaviour and a hardening of attitudes. Many corporate organisations become arenas of conflict rather than friendly and supportive working and learning environments.

To guarantee or not to guarantee 'deliverables'?

A key issue for many organisations is what if any aspects of 'output' can be guaranteed to the customer. Practice varies by business sector. Software suppliers have traditionally been reluctant to give quality guarantees. According to one manager: 'It's a minefield. We avoid any hint of guaranteeing anything. There is so much that can go wrong, and whether a system meets a spec can be very subjective. You can't just weigh it or take its temperature. With guarantees, almost all our projects would end in legal disputes.'

There seems to be a trend towards guarantees, and the 'Citizen's Charter' in the UK is an example of this. Guarantees can be a differentiator for early users or innovators, but they can also be matched or exceeded by competitors:

- In the office products field, Rank Xerox took out full-page advertisements to announce its innovatory 'customer satisfaction guarantee' by which any customer not satisfied with a copier could demand a replacement.
- British Airports Authority offers with the convenience of its touch screen shopping terminals at airports an absolute return guarantee, which it hopes will assuage the concerns of first-time users of the technology.

In some areas, guaranteed quality is assumed. Government funding can depend upon it. For years many component and other suppliers have had to meet and guarantee strict standards of output quality. Marks & Spencer insists upon the achievement of stipulated levels of quality.

In a wide range of process industries output has to meet exacting standards. These standards may themselves be dynamic, changing as requirements change and customers become ever more demanding. Ciments Français' success depends upon 'the group's commitment to anticipating demand for constantly improved products and providing customer service that spans both product use and quality guarantees.'

Demanding and aware customers are allies of innovators. Production technology increasingly allows variety and tailoring to be reconciled with economies of scale. Both customers and individuals need to be encouraged to articulate their requirements in order that they can be satisfied.

Speed as an objective

According to one international executive: 'In the US everyone tries to speed you up. In Ireland, they try to slow you down.' Who is right? It all depends upon what you are trying to achieve. Firing people to cut costs can be done the same day as a decision is made to reduce headcount. Learning can take longer.

Companies such as Apple, Deere & Company, Ford and Xerox have been focusing upon speed and responsiveness for some years. They are 'competing against the clock', encouraging a 'throughput orientation', undertaking activities in parallel and 'compressing' activity times in order to beat competitors to the market with new products.

In Chapter 10 we examined the results of some re-engineering exercises that have been particularly successful. Dramatic reductions in the total time taken to produce a product to meet the needs of an individual customer are possible. For example:

- An AT&T plant reduced the time taken to design and deliver a tailored power supply to a producer of PCs from 53 to five days.

- The Japanese bicycle manufacturer National combines flexibility and sensitivity to the needs of the individual customer with speed of response. The company requires only two weeks to produce a made-to-order machine.

In the karaoke bar we can all be instant stars. Children demand toys while the television commercials are still running. Bosses put on the pressure for quick results. Subordinates strive for immediate impact. We live in an impatient society.

The pressure is on to be fast and first. As one manager put it: 'The spirit of the western gunfighter is about the place – come second and you are dead.' Time driven companies can achieve competitive advantage and when non-value added activities are intelligently eliminated it may be possible to both improve quality without a corresponding increase in cost, and ensure faster delivery without impairing quality.[6]

An obvious aspect of performance to measure is response times. Legal & General has established response, delivery or throughput times for 38 processes. In some corporate cultures measurement may be a necessary precondition of improvement. In others, the establishment of throughput times could inhibit developments through fear that, while reviews and changes may well promise substantial gains in the future, their introduction could compromise the achievement of today's targets.

Speed as an obsession

Speed may or may not be important to customers, but it appears to be an obsession of a growing number of companies. Processes are being re-engineered in some organisations, while corners are cut in others. In both cases, caution may need to be exercised. The 'wasted time' may turn out to have been used for reflection or 'second thoughts'.

Time may be saved today at the cost of storing up trouble for the future. Consider the following comments:

There used to be time to think. Now everything is wanted yesterday. I just pass things onto the next person in the chain. I don't really add value anymore.

You would think we were all trying to catch a bus ... [that's] disappearing around a corner. People put their heads down and go automatic.

I do sometimes think ... things occur to me. I'm tempted to speak up, but I'm afraid I'll interrupt. Questions delay things. People here like to get on with it.

Around here the brownie points are earned by quick tongues rather than considered thoughts.

Within Ford, an important aspect of the Education Training Quality Improvement Plan is to encourage thinking. People, including professionals such as engineers, are invited to challenge established ways of doing things and fundamental assumptions. Without radical thinking, the company believes it will become increasingly difficult for it to differentiate its products.

Negative consequences of a focus on speed, such as the 'lure of the simple' and the avoidance of longer-term issues, can be reduced through greater tolerance for uncertainty and diversity, and providing some security with a framework of long-term partnership relationships. Disposable cultures that use people and move on are often seen to hover around fashionable trends without actually causing any of them. Insecurity can cause people to focus on immediate issues.

Speed in perspective

Speed cannot be dismissed. Of itself it can represent value to a customer. Opportunistic suppliers take advantage of transient, fleeting, impulse and urgent needs. One CEO explained: 'Few of our customers ask for things more slowly.' However, for some customers other considerations may be more important than time of delivery.

The urge to squeeze out time may be strengthened by a preoccupation with short-term financial results. Delaying delivery, and spending more time to tailor or test a product, may result in a more satisfied customer at the end of the day. In some fields it could also lead to lower litigation, maintenance or lifecycle costs.

There may be considerable potential for time saving. Improvement teams at Rolls Royce have found that 40 per cent of time in certain areas does not add value from a customer perspective.

However, time may need to be spent to save time. Within the Post Office teams have spent 18 months mapping various processes to determine how they interrelate before feeling able to introduce any time-saving changes. Inappropriate approaches to re-engineering can be the cause of frustration and delay.

Roughly right

Ideally we should be economical in the use of time, simplify things and take the heat off people. For a start, many people waste time by doing too much. At the margin, the incremental benefits of the extra work or learning may be minimal or even negative. Getting things roughly right may enable progress to be made, even though many quality professionals find this concept difficult to accept.

How much needs to be done depends upon the requirements and circumstances. The insurance team of one well known MNC were asked by the chairman: 'How much insurance cover have we got?' Rather than explore the reasoning behind the question, the group panicked.

Nowhere could they find a master list of all the company's insurance cover. It was a Friday.

The insurance team worked through the weekend, burning the midnight oil, living on 'fast food' and accumulating vast quantities of data. The final report, several inches thick, was deposited on the chairman's desk during the course of Monday morning. Its arrival was greeted by: 'I only wanted to know if we're covered when, after dropping me off, the chauffeur takes my car down to the village to fill it up with petrol.'

Circumstances are important, because the real value may be added early or late. With some tasks, the obvious issues hit you up front. Thus, when simplifying business processes, most of the potential time savings may come from relatively straightforward changes such as giving more discretion or altering organisational boundaries. In other cases, the real benefits come right at the end, and it may be well worth 'going the extra mile'.

Returning to a process simplification example, perhaps massive investments in retraining and information technology could yield further improvements. But at what cost, and will the situation or requirement change before they are achieved? Presenting the project in the aggregate may deny the decision-maker or client the opportunity to say: 'Let's get it roughly right, and go for 80 per cent of the benefit at 20 per cent of the cost.'

Reporting formats

Many managers spend too much time drafting and presenting, and too little time thinking about what is really important. Xerox and other companies have tired of 'slogan management' and introduced drives to encourage 'management by fact'. Opinion, unsupported by analysis and reason, and feeding off prejudice, can be destructive, but speculative musings can sometimes lead to creative and innovative ideas that could well be subsequently supported by fact. Insight and intuition do not always travel with the evidence to support them, but when pursued they can sometimes have a revolutionary impact.

The use of common reporting formats can make it easier for people to identify key points, although in many organisations there will be those opponents of this approach who stress the differences between various departments and business units. Notwithstanding such arguments and concerns, a requirement that reports show trends and identify root causes and corrective actions can assist understanding, reduce concealment and help ensure that remedial action is taken.

The greater use of common formats can also make it easier for management and reporting processes to be supported by appropriate information technology, break down internal organisational barriers, and facilitate shared learning and the movement of people between roles. It can also help to prevent the production of information that does little to contribute to organisational learning or individual understanding. However, such benefits should not be achieved at the cost of denying people the opportunity to work, learn and communicate in ways that best enable them to harness their potential.

Longer-term issues such as environmental quality

Not every company is obsessed with saving time or the desire for an almost instant response. The focus of Lyonnaise des Eaux-Dumez is upon: 'Enhancing quality of life for this generation without sacrificing the needs of generations to come ... By the nature of its activities – designing, building and operating facilities and services – group companies give precedence to the long-term future, and to the sustainable use of nature's resources.'

According to one cynical and jaundiced manager: 'You risk mugging, or being run over or poisoned with fumes, to struggle to work each day to find out whether or not you are fired.' A few moments of personal ease at the end of many hours of anxiety, if not misery, might seem a poor 'trade-off'. A priority could be to make companies and the environment within which they operate more friendly.[7]

For the Swiss pharmaceutical company Sandoz the quality of the environment ranks alongside research and development as a corporate priority. Chairman and CEO Marc Moret explains that:

> For Sandoz this is not simply a matter of feeling obligated to follow the fashion or of jumping on the bandwagon, but of facing up to everyday reality ... We believe that in future companies will increasingly be judged not merely on their commercial record but equally on how they handle their responsibility to the community. This means that, in addition to traditional managerial skills, those responsible for directing their affairs will have to show genuine concern for people's well-being and quality of life.

Sandoz has a 'commitment to a responsible approach to man and the environment.' The company's quality priorities are designed to help bring about 'a lower environmental impact'. The German tyre company Continental has established a joint quality and environmental affairs function which reflects the integration of its environmental protection efforts into its quality philosophy.

A network organisation or an entrepreneurial company like Body Shop can deploy corporate values such as concern with lifestyle and environmental quality as a differentiator. People tend to network with others who share their values. The values made explicit by Body Shop founder Anita Roddick are used to attract customers, employees and ethical investors.

The working environment

A corporate drive to focus externally on the customer or the environment should not allow the quality of working life and environment within the company to be overlooked. The managing directors within one group of companies concluded at the end of an exercise to determine development needs that the greatest priority was 'improving lifestyle'. A course was subsequently run to help them to 'slow down' and lead lives with more of a balance between work and leisure.

The broader and more deeply rooted a management approach is, the greater the likelihood that it will impact upon both the internal and external dimensions. One of the major challenges facing managers along-side handling ambiguity, paradox, conflicts of interests, etc, is achieving a balance between the internal and external dimensions. We saw in Chapter 8 some examples of enlightened action.

There is little point developing externally focused corporate visions if, internally, an organisation lacks the means of achieving them.[8] Too many boards craft strategies without putting in place the capabilities to implement them.[9] Figure 12.2 extends the review process of Figure 12.1 to

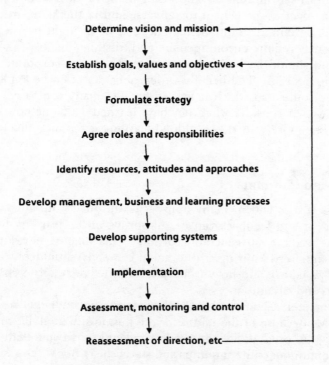

Figure 12.2 The board review process

Source: Colin Coulson-Thomas, *Developing Directors*, McGraw-Hill, 1993.

embrace the roles, resources, attitudes, approaches, processes and systems needed for effective implementation.

Learning objectives

In a growing number of 'knowledge' industries learning is a critical core competence for both development and implementation. Its importance was highlighted in the last chapter. In many sectors the basis of competition, whether or not it is perceived as such, is willingness and ability to learn. The quality of learning can be a critical determinant of an organisation's future.

Learning should be a top priority. People should leave home in the mornings, or log on saying 'I am going to learn', not 'I am going to work'. Rover Group is an example of a company for whom 'corporate learning' is a key business process. 'An organisation which can learn' is a fundamental principle of Rover's quality strategy, and like BOC or London Electricity it engages in shared learning.

A focus upon learning and creativity can be hard-nosed. Learning can lead to intellectual property and high price-earnings ratios. It also requires practical approaches and recognition of such realities as that people may need to be helped to converse and to think. In order to be challenged, certain assumptions may need to be brought to the surface. Again this may require encouragement and trust.

Learning should be built into processes to review corporate performance (Figure 12.3). The benefits of learning can often be applied outside of the context in which it has arisen. Yet many companies do not even consciously consider what they have learned, let alone how it might be used. The more valued and utilised learning is the more likely it is to occur.

Quality and learning

The stress that is laid in many approaches to quality upon continuous improvement and feedback can be supportive of the learning organisation. Whereas the bureaucratic corporate machine requires periodic overhaul and restructuring, the organic company should continuously evolve in its nature and how it operates in order to adapt to changes in conditions and circumstances.[5]

Lou Gerstner, Chairman of IBM, acknowledges: 'We will never stop fixing IBM. Because of the nature of the business, we will be constantly renewing this organisation and our challenge is to get that renewal process continuous without bumps and starts.'

A distinction needs to be drawn between knowledge and learning. Knowledge is a stock while learning is an ongoing activity. Knowledge can

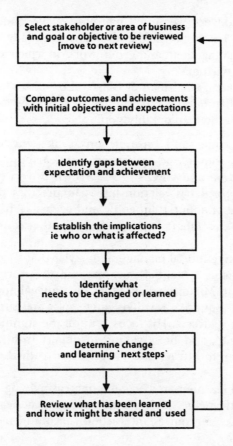

Figure 12.3 Reviewing corporate performance

exist in abundance, but as General Motors, IBM and Sears Roebuck have discovered, that accumulated yesterday may not be relevant to today's issues. Commodity knowledge may be without value unless used creatively. Its value lies in its application to activities that themselves add value. In this sense, what is needed is a capable and competent, rather than a clever and knowledgeable, organisation.

Encouraging learning

Learning should not be taken for granted. Many companies would be embarrassed by the responses to such questions as: what has been learned from a particular joint venture, subsidiary companies, foreign subsidiaries, subordinates or junior staff? Not everyone jumps out of bed each morning wondering what new things they will learn. Collaborative learning may need to be encouraged:

- Daniel Goeudevert, Deputy Chairman of Volkswagen, encourages employees to be 'responsible and creative'. He advocates a 'cooperative style of management and group work' in which 'every employee is involved as a partner'.
- Sir Paul Girolami, Chairman of Glaxo, also stresses 'trust and partnership, rather than bureaucratic control' as providing a sounder basis for learning throughout an organisation.

Subsidiary companies and business units, like employees, customers and suppliers, should be regarded as learning partners. Percy Barnevik, President and CEO of Asea Brown Boveri dislikes the traditional 'parent–subsidiary relationship'. He presides in Zurich over a small head office of about 100 people and regards ABB operating companies as 'sisters', members of the ABB family that count and have their say.

Today's unconventional management styles that succeed in attracting talent and releasing potential may become the norm for knowledge industries. Tetsuo Mizuno believes that his unusual approach to people management at Square, a video game software supplier, is largely responsible for its success. His focus is upon the stimulation of imagination and creativity, and he is willing to depart from normal Japanese practice in order to attract and retain those with the attributes he is seeking.

Thinking and learning are becoming increasingly significant as sources of competitive advantage. Like change management, learning tends to be a 'contact sport'. It requires interaction, encouragement and commitment.

More companies should select learning partners and appoint 'learning catalysts', teams and directors with specific responsibilities for assessing and improving the quality of individual, group and organisational learning. For example:

- Within the National & Provincial Building Society there is a group that actively monitors learning best practice.
- Philips audits the 'thinking styles' of its scientists and engineers in order to build learning capability and creativity, and identify and tackle barriers to learning and thinking.

A theme of this book is the desirability of 'positive' rather than 'negative' approaches to business, management, quality and transformation. Thus when an analysis such as that in Figure 12.3 reveals a gap between aspiration and achievement[5] one should aim to raise achievement rather than reduce aspiration (Figure 12.4). Investment in the conscious improvement of learning could represent a key means of building the 'capability to deliver'.

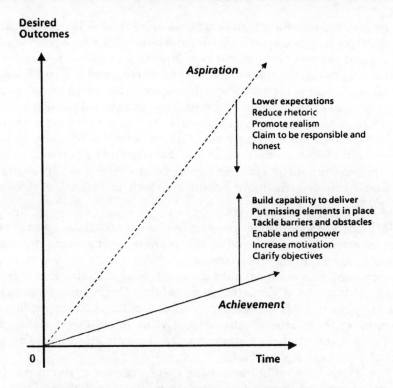

Desired
Outcomes

Aspiration

Lower expectations
Reduce rhetoric
Promote realism
Claim to be responsible and
honest

Build capability to deliver
Put missing elements in place
Tackle barriers and obstacles
Enable and empower
Increase motivation
Clarify objectives

Achievement

0   Time

Figure 12.4 Bridging the aspiration/achievement gap
Source: Colin Coulson-Thomas, *Transforming the Company*, Kogan Page, 1992.

Redefining specialist roles

One positive approach is to use potential 'headcount reduction targets' as
catalysts, developers and learners. Reskilling and redeployment, redefin-
ing and relocating roles can be a creative alternative to redundancy. For
example, once everyone is involved in quality, certain specialists or 'centres of competence' could assume learning roles. Members of a central or
core team could be used to:

● facilitate subsidiary and business unit benchmarking or business excellence reviews and, where required, provide support to peer reviews;
● support shared learning, quality, improvement and re-engineering
  teams;
● identify and overcome common obstacles and barriers to learning;
● encourage the use of relevant approaches, tools and techniques;
● help define, understand and build roles, competencies and behaviours;
● spur development of more holistic and people-centred approaches;

- undertake, or support, international and external benchmarking to match or improve upon the 'best', and internal benchmarking to identify and share key lessons and 'best practice';
- facilitate horizontal and supply chain networking and shared learning;
- identify areas of capability or competence which could be outsourced or bought in, or for which there could be an external market;
- advise, counsel, mentor, facilitate and encourage new ways of working and learning and the better use of information that has been collected to build understanding, and ensure that learning takes place;
- communicate the purpose and contribution of both quality assurance and a broader and more holistic approach to output or 'delivered' quality.

Sometimes when a broader approach is adopted not all the members of a current management team will be able to make the transition. An organisation needs players not passengers.

Increasingly, operational units are questioning the value that staff specialists and 'overhead' departments are adding. Quality professionals who are sensitive to such criticisms concentrate upon applying quality and learning to those activities that deliver value to customers rather than 'things that are nice to do'. Many companies cannot afford the blind pursuit of improvements in all areas.

In part, the interest in outsourcing that has grown in recent years has been the result of some frustration with in-house specialists. Many have become too technical, obsessed with their techniques, and remote from the practical concerns and priorities of customers and colleagues.

Use of non-chargeable time or 'downtime'

Let's look at other learning opportunities. Many organisations could make much better use of 'downtime', the spare capacity people may have between projects. Such intervals can represent rich opportunities for learning and the building of longer-term capabilities. People should:

- visit customers to learn about their current priorities and concerns;
- share their experiences, including by means of verbal debriefs where there are general lessons to be learned;
- develop, or learn the use of, new tools and approaches to handle new situations, eg activity based costing could be evaluated where it is not used;
- update corporate credentials and sales and marketing materials;
- apply problem-solving tools and root cause, 'helps' and 'hinders' and other analyses to corporate issues and activities;
- participate in study visits, workshops and other learning and sharing activities;

- analyse collected information such as project debrief reports for trends, links and patterns;
- undertake *ad hoc* issue monitoring and benchmarking assignments;
- carry out peer reviews of other projects that are still in progress;
- form quality improvement or process review and improvement teams.

Time between assignments represents a development opportunity and a key means of encouraging a more open learning and sharing culture. It should be used positively and creatively. Saving time could reduce learning opportunities.

Professionalism

Many companies are suffering the disadvantages of professionalism rather than reaping what ought to be the benefits. Instead of seeing business issues 'in the round', people address them from the perspective of a particular profession. This can distort their approach and considerations. Certain aspects may be exaggerated or viewed out of context, while others are overlooked or ignored.

Problems are problems. It is various groups of professionals who categorise them as financial, marketing, production or quality issues and seek to advise on particular aspects of what is perceived. What may be needed is a holistic review that reflects an organisation's vision, goals, values and objectives and the requirements of customers rather than narrow professional concerns.

Traditional professionals distinguish themselves and their contributions by stressing their ethics and values. The professional probes and questions, and offers independent and objective advice. Yet the modern company demands that its people share corporate objectives and values and become team players. In many cases, individuals feel under tremendous pressure to conform.

In some companies independent spirits tend to be seen as 'rocking the boat'. To be regarded as 'role models' people feel they must be politically correct. As one director put it: 'Around here you wouldn't expect me to say anything like that would you? Its all "saluting the flag" and "praise the lord". I'm one of the team. Outsiders are soon out of a job.'

Rich learning environments are those that not only tolerate a variety of approaches but actively encourage them. While UK Secretary of State John Patten identified 'diversity' as one of the keys to the success of higher education: 'The enormous expansion we have seen in higher education does not mean mass production of students in a factory-like environment.'

At the same time senior executives are questioning the value of absolute advice that exists outside of a particular situation, within a certain corporate context at one moment in time. Because people are being asked to tailor advice and make it relevant to circumstances and requirements, it does not follow that impartiality, caution and critical questioning should be put to one side. Many corporate programmes suffer because first principles questions are not asked.

A company with a commitment to ethics may need to discourage certain forms of learning. For example, when does benchmarking become 'creative swiping', intellectual piracy or even industrial espionage? The 'full range of techniques' are used by some corporations. Inhibitions are sometimes reduced when 'targets' are foreign organisations.

Intellectual capital

Companies also need to remember, particularly those that are 'world class', that the greater their achievements the more they themselves become 'targets' of the 'learning' of others. Management teams face the corporate equivalent of the 'dilemma of democracy', or how to protect it without destroying it. A degree of freedom and openness encourages enquiry and creativity, and care needs to be taken to ensure that measures introduced to protect intellectual property do not stifle their development.

The 'open corporation', with its multiple relationships and electronic links with network partners that cooperate in some areas and compete in others, is particularly at risk of being intellectually asset stripped. One director complained: 'We are well on the way to becoming a virtual company in that what hasn't been subcontracted has been stolen. I've no idea where we go from here.'

A key role of boards is to preserve the assets of an organisation. While paying considerable attention to physical and financial assets, many boards are naive in the extreme when it comes to intellectual capital. For example:

- Some large companies are hollow shells, their intellectual capital having 'walked out of the door' as their 'brightest and best' left to establish their own businesses. Only the time servers, the consumers rather than producers of intellectual capital, remain.
- Parasitic adventurers join virtual and network organisations with a view to sucking them dry of intellectual capital. Within seconds all of value that is stored electronically can be downloaded on any number of linked terminals.

Companies that merely consume rather than produce intellectual capital need to be parasitic in order to survive. Mature boards take account of the implications of decisions for 'know-how' and learning capability. However, many others are not so enlightened. Their standards and proceedures increase the number of people drawing from the corporate well. Ever more creative uses of a finite resource need to be balanced by the breakthroughs that create new sources of supply.

Many companies approach downsizing and outsourcing in a way that loses them the intellectual resources and capacity to operate in tomorrow's markets. Cutting out capabilities that are not directly related to immediate priorities or putting people under so much pressure that they no longer have time to think are widespread phenomena.

A prime challenge of directors of learning and thinking is to replenish the well of inspiration and creativity, the life force that represents the intellectual capital and capacity of their organisations. Many companies drain the well dry, and wake up one day to find there is not much in the way of intellectual energy left. They become an IBM, the large estate that thought it had so much land and water that it did not need to bore new holes and was forced to seek supplies from surrounding small farms.

Reference has already been made to the drive within Xerox to reduce the cost base. At the same time the need for corporate learning is not forgotten. 'Small, slim and smart' could be the motto of the Rank Xerox drive to boost creativity in identifying new sources of value opportunity and continual learning in generating extra value for existing customers. In some areas of its activity Rank Xerox does not mind sharing what it has learned, as it is confident that its commitment to learning will keep it one step ahead of competitors.

Corporate objectives and assessing relative contributions

Learning and other objectives need to be related to the situation, circumstances and context, and each of these may be in a state of flux. Aiming at a rigid and quantified target can result in aiming too high or too low, resulting in cost penalties or losing the business respectively. What is needed is an empathy with the customer that creates a sense of what represents, and contributes to, value and quality in the context of a particular customer relationship.

In deciding where to focus effort it is helpful to identify the extent to which different factors impact upon business results or customer satisfaction. Thus many companies carry out some form of sensitivity or risk analysis. For example:

- The Skandia Group, an insurance company, has quantified the extent to which changes in inflation, wages, interest rates and claims frequency impact upon financial performance. This allows areas of potential vulnerability to be assessed.
- US MNCs such as Xerox Corporation carry out international issue monitoring and management exercises to identify developments in the

business environment that are likely to affect the business, assess their impact and suggest corporate responses at local, regional and international levels.

Helps and hinders analysis could also be used (Figure 12.5) to identify the factors that are contributing to, or detracting from, the achievement of corporate objectives. Such an exercise can enable the potential contributions of learning, quality, etc, to be assessed in the context of what else needs to be done.

The successful performance of some companies, for example Nissan Motors (UK), is due not only to quality but to various factors other than quality. Where quality does have a beneficial impact, we have seen that this is usually because it is used in combination with other elements.

Assessing and measuring the contributions of learning or quality, rather than just assuming they are a 'good thing' assists their selective, focused and relevant use. Quality attitudes could help review exercises to focus upon customer-related issues, quality tools could be used at appropriate points in the analysis and to determine what needs to be done, while quality processes could facilitate the delivery of a response. It was emphasised in the last chapter that learning and quality should be

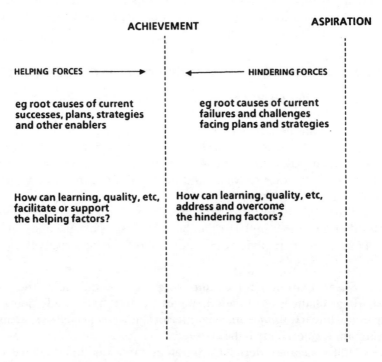

Figure 12.5 'Helps and hinders' analysis

regarded as integral elements of the management process, rather than as self-contained initiatives.

Management measures

Since its origins, quality has been inseparable from quantified targets and measures. People find it difficult to proceed without targets, objectives or goals. However, what is important is a satisfied customer, not the achievement of a quantified target that represents a manager's assessment of one aspect of what was important to 'the customer' at the time the target was established.

There is a tendency to relate quality measures to 'what is', for example today's products, rather than 'what ought to be' in terms of, say, the quality of customer experience. When Bill Gates and Paul Allen established Microsoft in 1975 their vision was not simply of lower costs but of a world in which technology was more accessible and convenient from a user perspective. They set out to put 'a personal computer on every desk and in every home'. This focus upon quality of working experience has made Bill Gates the richest person in the US.

Percy Barnevik, President and CEO of ABB, reports that as part of the company's 'Customer Focus Program': 'New systematic measurements of quality and of delivery service have also been introduced. Companies which used to operate at 70-80 per cent on-time delivery level are now up to 95–98 per cent.'

By their measures you will know them. While those at the top of a US company have traditionally pored over the 'financials', their equivalents in the Japanese competitor have been similarly preoccupied, only this time with physical performance. Whether the information is reported vertically or shared horizontally, in neither case will it necessarily result in sufficient of a focus upon the customer.

Holistic approaches to measurement

Performance assessment should be holistic. Thus measurement of quality achievement should encompass all those activities that are necessary to deliver value to customers. While 'customer satisfaction' is highly desirable, employing it as a sole measure can be counter-productive. For example, driving the people of an organisation too hard in order to achieve higher levels of customer satisfaction may frustrate further improvements if, in future, they 'burn out'.

There are many areas in which a 'balanced scorecard' company might wish to track progress, for example: the extent to which communications are horizontal, learning is occurring or feedback loops are short; how close to the customer decisions are taken; or how far a unifying and shared vision extends.

Corporate goals and objectives should embrace all the elements needed to bring about a future desired state. Thus for Rank Xerox, while customer satisfaction is the number one objective, the second is employee satisfaction. As Vern Zelmer put it while Managing Director of Rank Xerox (UK): 'We couldn't figure out a way to get 100 per cent of our customers satisfied while only 50 per cent of our employees were satisfied.'

Wherever possible measures of performance improvements in intangible areas such as attitudes and perceptions should be independent and objective. Companies such as IBM and Xerox commission external surveys of customer satisfaction and employee attitudes.

The value of customer satisfaction as a goal or objective will also depend upon what is measured. The key questions sometimes don't get asked. Requirements can change, and there may be subtle variations between contexts. Reporting systems may require order, and high levels of formality and predictability, so that those who operate them can prevent adaptation. Measurements should be a lodestar not a shrine, they should enable and guide rather than constrain or block.

Professionals frequently complain about excessive management fixation with financial performance, which is in any event heavily dependent upon whatever accounting convention or practice is followed. They are more reluctant to acknowledge that many of their own measures are arbitrary, governed by practice and what is measurable rather than importance to the customer.

One company allowed each major subsidiary to develop and test its own measures of quality. In the main, questionnaire surveys were used. The results were misleading:

- The operating companies with the highest apparent levels of quality were those that posed questions, and hence received replies, relating to their strengths.
- Those with the lower levels of customer satisfaction were often found to have included questions that related to less successful aspects of corporate performance.

In the case just mentioned, some people were measuring what they were good at, while others measured their weaknesses. The problem areas turned out to be those with the higher levels of measured customer satisfaction. These were often the operating units that were least aware of their deficiencies, and who focused upon their view of what was important, which was not always what represented value to the customer. Some of the subsidiaries with the lowest levels of measured customer satisfaction had both identified areas of weakness and put action programmes in place to deal with them.

Measurement of customer satisfaction

Some thought needs to be given to the question of how best to measure customer satisfaction. In some sectors those sending out a questionnaire might be thanked by the recipients for showing an interest in their companies, while in others letters would be received from company secretaries pointing out that in view of the great and growing number of questionnaires received, and the time taken to complete them, it was now company policy not to respond.

Dissatisfaction can be understated when customers 'vote with their feet'. They are simply not around to record their displeasure. It is important to understand why such customers do not come back. Did something go wrong? Are they simply disinterested, or are they actively telling others of their disappointment? Quality is decided by the customer, and their assessments need to be understood.

It is important that what is measured are root causes rather than symptoms (Figure 12.5). Too many quality teams are focused upon consequences rather than key drivers. The use of quality has been likened by some interviewees to a placebo or anesthetic: 'You deceive yourself into thinking you are tackling real issues by going through the motions, while the real root causes of poor financial performance are not tackled.'

Measures are not ends in themselves. Some organisations meticulously assess but do little with the results. A key question is: what happens to measures? Also, is remuneration linked to improvements in customer satisfaction? It is in companies like Rank Xerox. At the London Business School pay and promotion now reflects student feedback.

The 'S' curve of quality improvement and learning

Levels of customer satisfaction rarely rise at a steady rate (Figure 12.6). Initially, improvements in levels of satisfaction may appear slow in coming. As one manager put it: 'Success, where it occurs, is seen as a flash in the pan.' It may take some time before customers accept that improvements are 'for real'.

During the 'early phase', and before 'take-off' occurs, those new to quality or a learning initiative may experience some anxiety. Senior management may become impatient and wonder where the tangible benefits are.

After some sustained effort, levels of satisfaction or achievement often pick up and for a period may rise at a steadily increasing rate. The reason for this is often that expectations are changing. Once initial barriers to customer satisfaction are tackled, suppliers may find that incremental improvements in satisfaction become easier to achieve. Customers may no longer expect their previous sources of frustration to periodically recur. Learners become more confident.

At this 'take-off' stage, people may become accustomed to steadily

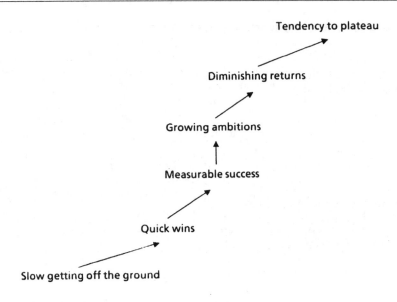

Figure 12.6   The 'S' curve of quality and learning

improving levels of achievement. Ambitious customer satisfaction targets may be set, or negotiated, for future years. However, it should not be assumed that such a trend will continue as over time customers may take higher levels of performance and service for granted. Learners may experience 'diminishing returns'.

In many sectors 100 per cent 'quality' is the aspiration. For the network services division of Televerket, 'quality is the point of departure for all strategic planning' and is 'measured as both availability and performance'. In 1991 Televerket achieved average performance levels of 98.9 per cent in terms of successful and 'good quality' long-distance calls during office hours. Once accustomed to such performance, customers notice the 1 per cent of calls that may not be to their satisfaction.

There is often a tendency to plateau. Paradoxically, the closer one gets to 100 per cent, the more success is assumed and failure is noticed. A supplier may need to work disproportionately harder in order to achieve incremental improvements at higher levels of customer satisfaction as customer expectations rise. In business, as in sport, the final effort at the limit is often the differentiator.

Financial performance and quality within the 'balanced scorecard'

A 'balanced scorecard' must both balance and have a fulcrum. Ultimately quality, satisfaction, competence, learning, relevance, innovation, etc, will have a collective impact upon the 'financials'. A 'guiding principle' of Hoechst is that: 'Hoechst needs profits. Profit is the yardstick of success in business and also its reward. Good profits are a sign of a healthy company with a sound future. Hoechst aims to give its shareholders an appropriate return on their capital.'

While an exclusive obsession with 'the financials' can be self-defeating, no one should·be ashamed of a focus upon profitability and the generation of shareholder value. As a key stakeholder, the owners of an enterprise are a crucial 'customer' for quality. The aim of providing shareholders with a 'long-term growth in assets per share and dividends which exceed the rate of inflation' could be regarded as a specification of the quality of earnings to be provided.

Business priorities can change, and recent economic circumstances have caused a degree of convergence across national cultures. For example, previously many German and Japanese companies have stressed turnover growth rather than profits *per se*. More recently, greater emphasis has been placed upon cost-base reduction, productivity and profitability. Relative costs are important for such decisions as whether to produce at home or offshore.

Quality as implemented is not always free. 'Learning' can also be very costly. Hence the cost-impact of proposals for new initiatives should be assessed (Figure 12.7). The investment required could be of scarce resources other than the financial, for example time. High cost investments that have high impacts from a customer perspective can sometimes be the basis for collaborative activity, turning a supplier relationship into one of joint-venture or 'partnership'.

According to one director of quality: 'We have seen from the PIMS [PIMS Associates] database that there is a link between relative quality and financial performance. However, good performance is usually the result of a number of factors that come together. The combination makes it happen ... it is the right combination for us that we are seeking.'

The right combination at one moment may be inappropriate the next.[5] One CEO used the analogy of a pack of cards:

> The game just goes on ... you don't want it to end because that means you are out of it. You need to know what cards to hold in the hand, and what combinations of cards to play at each stage of the game. Financial performance ebbs and flows ... the winning streak is difficult to sustain, when others can copy your moves ... when others are always trying to outguess you.

Charles Handy has pointed out that a sense of personal frustration, emptiness and growing alienation can exist alongside corporate success in terms of the various economic indicators of performance.[10] We need to move on from the 'hard' quality of product and of process, through supply chain quality, the 'softer' quality of relationships and learning, to the quality of life.

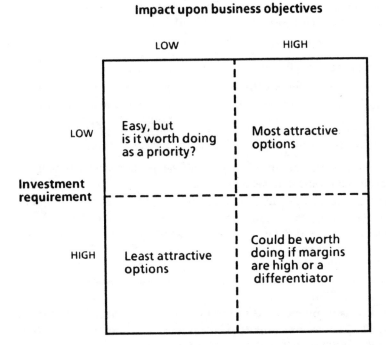

Impact upon business objectives

Figure 12.7   Cost-impact analysis

All may not be lost. A latent desire for loyalty, given a shared purpose, appears widespread and is worth encouraging.[11] Priorities and objectives can be broadened and made more compelling. It is possible to establish or create 'human scale' enterprises, with whom people can identify. Larger companies such as Unipart can exhibit the 'family feel' of successful family owned businesses such as JCB. In the final two chapters we consider the next steps in the adoption of a more holistic and people-centred approach to management.

Checklist

How are the interests of key stakeholders in your organisation ranked in priority by the board?

Where do learning and the pursuit of quality rank alongside other priorities such as financial, market share and employee satisfaction measures?

In terms of what really drives the organisation, is there sufficient focus upon positive objectives such as building core competencies and longer-term capability?

To what extent does learning, quality or re-engineering contribute to the achievement of each key business objective?

Does your organisation measure the achievement of its objectives?

How would each be affected if different elements of your company's approach to learning, quality or transformation were withdrawn?

Is there a feedback loop from measurement through analysis to action?

Has learning, quality or re-engineering had a significant impact upon 'bottom line' performance? Are learning outcomes assessed?

How 'balanced' are both the objectives and the outcomes in terms of their impacts upon various stakeholders?

Are the 'root causes' of a failure to achieve objectives and targets identified and tackled?

What are the 'vital few' tasks, initiatives or 'next steps' that would contribute most to the achievement of desired objectives and outcomes?

References

1. Colin Coulson-Thomas (executive ed), *The Responsive Organisation: Re-engineering New Patterns of Work*, London, Policy Publications, 1995.
2. James Champy, *Re-engineering Management: The Mandate for New Leadership*, London, HarperCollins, 1994.
3. Michael Hammer and Steven A Stanton, *The Re-engineering Revolution: The Handbook*, London, HarperCollins, 1995.
4. Suyono Sosrodarsono and Hashim Djojohadikusumo, PT Semen Cibinong, 'Report of the President Commissioner and President Director', *1991 Annual Report*, Jakarta, June 1992, p 5–6.
5. Colin Coulson-Thomas, *Transforming the Company: Bridging the Gap Between Management Myth and Corporate Reality*, London, Kogan Page, 1992.
6. George Stalk and Thomas Hout, *Competing Against Time*, New York, Free Press, 1990.
7. Francis Tibbalds, *Making People Friendly Towns: Improving the Public Environment in Towns and Cities*, Harlow, Longman, 1992.
8. Colin Coulson-Thomas, *Creating Excellence in the Boardroom*, London, McGraw-Hill, 1993.
9. Colin Coulson-Thomas, *Developing Directors: Building an Effective Boardroom Team*, London, McGraw-Hill, 1993.
10. Charles Handy, *The Empty Raincoat: Making Sense of the Future*, London, Hutchinson, 1994.
11. Charles Heckscher, *White Collar Blues: Management Loyalties in an Age of Corporate Restructuring*, London, Basic Books/HarperCollins, 1995.

Next steps: identifying the missing elements

Seagulls face the wind.

Quality, re-engineering and related approaches to management are American in origin. Imported into Europe and elsewhere, they work best when they impact upon attitudes in certain ways, and yet their implementation generally has had either little or a counter-productive influence. They also assume behaviours such as teamwork which in certain contexts may be difficult to achieve.

Overall, quality is too general and non-focused, and has a tendency to become formalised and rigid, while re-engineering tends to ignore people factors and motivational aspects. Neither is by itself sufficient. Something is missing. More holistic approaches are required. To develop them we need to reassess the basic purpose of an enterprise. Natural forces such as the capabilities of people should be used to aid flight rather than ruffle feathers.

The need for next steps

David Kearns introduced quality to Xerox while CEO. He understood: 'Quality is a race without a finish line. A focus on quality has made Xerox a stronger company, but we know we'll never be as good as we can be, because we'll always try to be better. We are on a mission of continuous quality improvement.'

In David Kearn's terms quality could be developed to match the changing contexts in which people are struggling to apply it. There is insecurity and discontent. There is striving, a restlessness, a hungering for new ways of coping with a combination of challenges that threaten to overwhelm. Now is the time to review next steps and move ahead.

Is quality 'a dog whose day is done'? The network or relationship organisation and the 'virtual corporation', composed as they are of self-managed and empowered groups and continually learning and adapting within a turbulent, even chaotic environment, represent very complex social systems. They present dilemmas to those who manage them. If we are to learn we may need to identify links and patterns. However, if too much order, procedure and predictability is imposed upon a system it cannot effectively change and may die.

The harsh reality of the contemporary business environment represents a profound challenge for movements whose origins are rooted in predictability and the reduction of variation. It is conceivable that quality, as practiced hitherto, will be unable to cope. It may only survive by mutation, as its advocates adopt and place under the quality banner whatever enables organisations to cope. While we should not discard elements of value when thoughtfully applied, much of what has previously been associated with quality may pass into history.

President Bill Clinton said in his inaugural address: 'To renew America we must be bold. We must do what no generation has had to do before. We must invest more in our own people and in our own future ...' Clinton represents a new generation of US political leaders. Among major corporations during the late 1990s a new generation of corporate leaders is likely to emerge whose formative influences are more likely to be the free-thinking 1960s rather than the austerity of war or the paranoiac conformism of the 1950s.

Raymond Levy, President of the European Foundation for Quality Management, acknowledges: 'We are living through the third industrial revolution which does not imply so much technological change as a change in management philosophy which is geared to satisfying the customer.'

Change can involve refinement as well as invention. A Canadian CEO points out: 'Quality moves – it's dynamic. It's a balance between changing expectations, competitor claims and your own intentions and capability to deliver. You need to look ahead at what will drive the industry up a notch.' Maintaining a balance requires judgement – enough has to be done to differentiate, but not so much so soon as to put a company at a competitive disadvantage.

Corporate transformation

In the turbulent and demanding business environment we examined in Chapter 3, companies are having to undergo fundamental transformations in order to survive. In the ruthlessly competitive personal computer marketplace prices have tumbled and suppliers are having to simultaneously downsize and transform. The restructuring of IBM has resulted in job losses at the rate of 40,000 per annum. This is 'rightsizing' on a scale that is fitting for a bureaucratic corporation.

James Treybig, President and CEO of Tandem Computers, summarises the scale of the challenge: 'To become a low-price provider requires that we adopt a new business model if we are going to achieve our profitability goals. This requires more than just cutting costs; it requires re-engineering the business, changing our culture, and continuously reducing our cost structure.'

Although there are many approaches to corporate transformation, in some quarters it has almost become synonymous with process re-engineering. While the wary and cautious may see this as a new and more sophisticated attempt to sell IT, others who accept a latent need to achieve more fundamental change are encouraged by an apparent willingness to envisage radical alternatives rather than incremental or 'small step' evolution.

Most transformation programmes consist of a wide variety of elements and a multiplicity of different approaches are being used. For example:

- Schindler has introduced a range of initiatives to 'reduce costs' and 'further accelerate internal throughput times'. A modular elevator line is enabling the company 'to introduce at the same time more cost-effective order processing, assembly, and servicing methods.'
- First principles reviews of organisations can lead to fundamental restructuring. In the case of Control Data Corporation it led to the division of the company into Control Data Systems, a computer systems integrator, and Ceridian Corporation, an information services company. The headquarters product marketing and development resources have been reorganised into Competency Centres that bring together all the skills needed to focus on specific technological issues.
- A combination of change elements at Berkshire County Council that includes transition to a network model of organisation, the building of a team and learning culture and the externalisation of services amounts almost to a reinvention of the local authority.

During the process of organisational transformation additional opportunities may be created for fraud and deception. Audit and control arrangements need to keep pace with changing opportunities for the unscrupulous to take advantage. However, a sense of balance needs to be maintained as in traditional organisations opportunities to 'take advantage' can often occur at the boundaries between functions. A re-engineered process with appropriate controls can represent a more secure environment.

Corporate and environmental realities

The core corporate team needs to possess and share a holistic and realistic understanding of the essence and dynamics of the business they are in.

No attempt should be made to embrace quality, re-engineering, transformation or anything else that is not absolutely relevant to the central purpose and core goals, values and priorities of an enterprise. Time and resource for distractions cannot be afforded.

Sadly, success appears to be becoming ever more difficult to sustain. Many management teams do not find it easy to put their fingers upon those 'vital few' factors that will lead inevitably to a continuing harvest. This complicates a review of the ongoing relevance of management approaches such as re-engineering.

Organisations are created for particular purposes. They are all to some extent unique, even though it sometimes appears that just about everyone is seeking to categorise them as this or that type. General concepts such as 'empowerment' can seem as remote as the moon to many of the practical people who run organisations. A typical comment might be: 'This is all very well for consultancies, the media and the professions, but what does it mean for me?'

Pragmatism suggests that when assessing alternative business philosophies and approaches during a period of uncertainty, the simple, quick and cheap have the advantage of limiting risk and keeping options open. How else does one prepare for success in markets that have not yet been created? We may not yet know what skills, attitudes, tools and techniques will be at a premium.

For a company interested in grabbing a share of future opportunities, building a community of people who are open minded and free thinking may be a more sensible strategy than the adoption of a complete framework such as quality that may end up acting as a protective cocoon. No more than spells and charms will many approaches to management keep adversity at bay.

Danger areas

Once everything is explained, people tend to go to sleep. Fads, obsessions and 'single solutions' should not be allowed to become the opium of the manager. When we have an answer for everything the sparks of innovation may no longer light up corners of the mind and the spirit of creativity may fly away.

For too many companies quality is viewed as 'something to take on board' or as a 'system' or 'approach' to adopt. A package is acquired and implemented. Quality numbs rather than feeds the mind. To achieve a fundamental impact a quality programme needs to be subtle, sensitive and adaptive. To live it needs to be in the hands of creative, thinking and sensitive people.

John Symes, a member of the Executive Committee of BSO/Beheer, has the job title: 'Group Vice-President, Quality Innovation'. Terms such as, 'creative quality', 'quality and thinking' or 'quality and learning' are likely to become more widely used at the expense of 'quality assurance' and 'quality control'. Traditional quality is too rational, too statistical and too engineering oriented in the 'softer', sensitive, thinking, feeling world of values and relationships.

Taking any approach to an extreme has its dangers. Thus an excessive and exclusive focus upon today's core capability might lead to the loss or sale of many viable and embryonic businesses, some of which could represent a key to the future. It can also result in an introverted company that fails to pick up and run with ideas generated elsewhere.

A crisis can be a catalyst and energizer. Action can be motivated by actual and latent threats, opportunities or expected outcomes. A threat could be external such as a social trend or internal, for example short-termism. Will there be radical competitor initiatives? Are there obvious problem areas? Could some of the company's most talented people be attracted elsewhere for lifestyle reasons? Are there potential economic 'payoffs' or new business opportunities? One company calculated that reducing project overruns by half could result in a doubling of 'bottom line' profit.

Need for imagination

Ultimately some groups have a drive and will to move on and look for new opportunities while others don't. There is always room for creativity and imagination, even on death row. Mitchell Rupe, an inmate in the US, increased his weight in prison to such an extent as to claim he could not be hanged as this would result in decapitation which was unconstitutional.

To build the capability and competencies to cope with unknown futures requires communities of people who can sense and feel. It requires the freshness, perhaps the innocence, to look at things in new ways. How does one preserve the wonder and curiosity of the child? Many innovators throughout the ages would not have got anywhere if they had been equipped with a standard toolkit that caused them to look at the world and its problems in the same way as everyone else.

Innovative, adaptive and creative cultures do not spontaneously come into existence when constraints are removed and empowerments are put in place. They can be sensitive plants that require much nurturing and support, and are vulnerable to the cold winds of retrenchment and the frost of central control. Order and formal structure can produce sterile conditions. Those which are more promising are identified by fluidity, tolerance, legitimacy and debate.

The pitch for next steps has been thoroughly spoiled in many companies. Cynicism, negativism, reluctance to change or face reality, a 'flavour of the month mentality', an obsession with short-term 'financials', lack of awareness, skills and process, the 'not invented here' reaction, a lack of management commitment and vision – one could go on – do not represent ideal conditions in which new approaches are likely to succeed.

Companies that are now embracing quality towards the end of what may come to be known as the 'age of quality' are probably too late. Smart companies, whether or not they have been through it, are looking elsewhere for inspiration and help. The survivors are likely to be from among those who have the courage to say no to comprehensive frameworks such as quality and rely instead upon attracting whatever capability and competences are relevant to the opportunities they define and the markets their imaginations create.

The board and management approaches

Enthusiasts of particular management approaches expect members of the board and senior management to act as role models. This usually means they are expected to be enthusiastic. But what if they have concerns? Legitimate reservations can lead to accusations of lack of commitment.

A board needs a balanced perspective, and what other people may claim should be taken with a pinch of salt. For example, alleged success may be nothing to do with 'quality' as it has been packaged by internal or external consultants. On occasion quality can be a placebo – it just happens to be there. Elsewhere, quality may be associated with success without being a decisive root cause.

Success usually comes from the assembly of a relevant combination of factors that work in one context at one moment in time.[1] While not the result of quality *per se*, success in the marketplace can provide the resources to fund quality. In this sense the corporate quality programme could be regarded as a form of conspicuous consumption.

Corporate performance can be assessed in terms of relating the outcomes of corporate programmes to corporate vision, values and goals. While the execution of programmes might be in the hands of management, their performance will reflect the framework and context established by the board, and the extent to which the people of the organisation are equipped, empowered and motivated to act and achieve.[2]

The chairman chairs meetings of the board and should ensure it concentrates upon the determination and monitoring of strategic direction. The chief executive should ensure the management team implements the agreed strategy within the policy and enabling framework established by the board. There needs to be a high degree of mutual trust and respect if the two are to observe and support each other's roles and responsibilities.

The board should recognise its own responsibility for turning aspiration and intention into achievement and reality.[2] The effectiveness of a board could in part be assessed in relation to the value it adds to major corporate programmes through its understanding, encouragement, guidance and support, and its policies, specific actions and general conduct.

Commitment

Top management commitment has been identified as a key requirement for the successful implementation of a corporate programme or philosophy such as total quality.[1,3,4] In many companies the lack of it is mentioned as a constraint more often than its existence is referred to as an enabler.

Success rarely walks alone. Just about every employee and endless consultants and advisers claim their share of credit when things go well. However, when quality initiatives and corporate transformation run out of steam the blame is usually attached to a lack of 'top management commitment'. How justified is the criticism?

The extent to which the board needs to be committed, and the nature of this commitment, will depend upon the degree of transformation challenge (Figure 13.1). If a minimum level or threshold of commitment is not achieved there may be little point in launching an initiative that is likely to fail. The role and performance of the board in confronting the major barriers, whether attitudinal or technical, that are impeding the quest for total quality can be decisive.

Much will depend upon a board's assessment of an initiative's likely contribution in areas of particular concern. Surveys suggest that quality is perceived as relevant to key concerns of the board relating to satisfying customers.[3,5] According to one chairman: 'The lure is not quality *per se*, but the prospect of using the goal or spur of quality to achieve key corporate objectives.'

Creating a quality or customer-focused organisation generally requires sustained commitment on the part of the board.[6,7] The extent to which the board itself uses quality tools and approaches, and whether its members behave as quality role models, could represent evidence of such commitment.

It is particularly important that the board keeps an organisation's feet on the ground. Directors should think through the likely impacts of what is advocated upon stakeholders, and particularly the customer. For example, will new ways of working, involvement, empowerment, etc, prolong decision-making? How many people need to be involved when a relatively simple response is required? How valuable are customer satisfaction figures when only delighted customers repeat buy? Are the customers taken into account when investment decisions are taken?

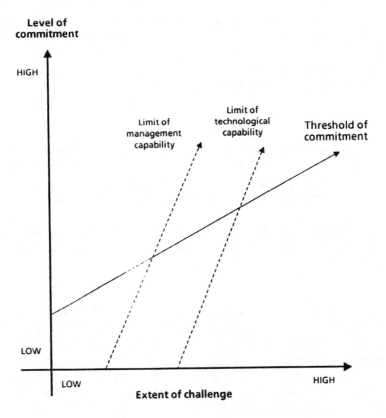

Figure 13.1 Commitment and challenge

Vision and the boardroom

In some quarters there has been a reaction against 'the vision thing'. Too many visions are bland and instantly forgettable. Motherhood statements are no substitute for rigorous thinking.

Imagine someone arriving from Mars with a brief to create a form of organisation which guarantees that most people plateau, work on tasks unrelated to business objectives, play organisational games, are denied their individuality and are deterred from creativity during their working hours. They need look no further than the bureaucratic form of organisation with its job descriptions, hierarchy and procedures.

The truly machiavellian, intent on causing frustration, would make people live in one place and work a commuting journey away, establish professions and specialisms that inhibit holistic views of problems and create approaches to learning that ensure the desire of most people to learn is destroyed. They could even throw in standard tools appropriate for identikit clones, or tie people up with the bureaucracy of quality certification. Such a scenario could be viewed as a bad dream, or a cynic's portrayal of corporations that need to be transformed.

Lou Gerstner faced one of the world's greatest transformation challenges. Soon after assuming the Chairmanship of IBM he expressed the view: 'The last thing IBM needs right now is a vision.' In Gerstner's opinion: 'What IBM needs right now is a series of very tough-minded, market driven, highly effective strategies that deliver performance in the marketplace and shareholder value.'

A vision for quality?

So what vision should the board have for quality? A number of conclusions concerning the status of traditional approaches to quality which emerge from the *Quality: The Next Steps* survey[8] and interviews undertaken for two related surveys[9,10] appear still very relevant:

- Quality has been thought to be a critical success factor and a source of competitive advantage. However confining a 'quality focus' to the product may limit a company to the role of a commodity supplier. Higher margin business may require more of an emphasis upon the quality of relationships and the quality of learning.

- Broader and more comprehensive approaches to quality have been pioneered, but they could be more widely used. Some boards appear determined not to learn from the experiences of other companies. For example, Xerox, a pioneer of both quality and process management, has concluded that if they 'are separate you have a problem', yet companies with quality programmes are still launching self-contained process initiatives.

- Few companies can deliver the whole of the value sought by customers without working closely with other organisations in the supply chain. There is a natural progression from quality product to quality organisation and then on to quality network or supply chain. The perspective of the board should lead this 'natural evolution'.

- Tapping greater added value opportunities may require a more holistic directorial view, and closer relationships with both suppliers and customers. For many companies the key to continuing quality improvement and differentiation from competitors lies in their relationships with customers, suppliers and business partners. Implementation of quality within 'quality networks' is a joint responsibility and depends upon the agreement of 'equal' partners, rather than the 'traditional' approach of 'cascading down from above'.

- As technical quality is increasingly assumed, the competitive focus has shifted to quality of process, attitude, understanding, behaviour, relationships and management. These areas can be addressed with beneficial results, but few boards have provided the necessary drive and commitment to adopt holistic approaches.

- Where management and business processes have been systematically re-engineered the results have been dramatic. However, many boards composed of directors who are engrossed in their 'departmental' responsibilities are still blind to 'cross-functional' opportunities. Exercises that focus upon learning processes are extremely rare.

An organisation should periodically reassess its management approaches. Interview discussions suggest that quality may have outgrown some of its 'gurus' and many of its pioneers. It is more complex and subtle than many have suspected. General solutions can be dangerous. Each organisation and board needs to formulate, and refine in the light of experience and changes of circumstance, its own approach to quality.

The contribution of a management approach such as quality

So what might the contribution of quality be? Much will depend upon the context. For example, is a supply chain involved? There are so many potential issues that could arise in a particular situation. Thus improving the quality of learning could involve selection of a learning partner, the encouragement of reflection and the introduction of a peer review system.

In general, we need to be less prescriptive. Quality systems and management approaches need to be enablers, not bureaucratic constraints. A practical and comprehensive quality toolkit is valuable, but no substitute for a holistic and comprehensive approach to output or 'delivered' quality.

While the mechanical use of checklists can discourage initiative, there are basic questions concerning the contribution of a management approach which could be addressed. For example:

- Is there a common understanding of the situation and context, and the purpose of the organisation?
- How much agreement is there on the fundamentals and principles of an approach? Are there agreed definitions or shared values?
- How clear, appropriate and achievable are the goals and objectives?
- Is the programme integrated into other corporate initiatives?
- How should it be managed? Who should 'own' it and 'lead' it?
- What should it be called? What are the 'pros' and 'cons' of using or dropping a name such as quality or re-engineering? Should a universal name be used?
- When should we start or introduce a fundamental change? Should an initiative be phased in everywhere, or commence at different times according to location, business unit or function?
- How much opportunity for local variation and flexibility should there be?

- What needs to be done in advance of a 'start date'?
- How long will implementation take, or how realistic is whatever timescale has been established?
- What are our expectations and those of stakeholders?
- Has adequate support been arranged or planned? Is shared learning, or a learning or transformation partner, involved?
- How appropriate is measurement and monitoring? Are supply chain involvement and feedback, review, learning and refinement 'built in'?

Creating the required corporate environment may demand a combination of attitudes, competencies, processes, tools and other enablers. A project-based company, whose priority is to maximise the contribution of its people to 'delivered' quality, might need to redefine roles, encourage quality values, review project management, relationship and learning processes, and introduce problem-solving, process review, learning and other tools.

Many corporate perceptions of quality are heavily influenced by where they are in relation to the 'quality hump'¹ of Figure 13.2. Many of the more optimistic assessments are from those recently starting the quality

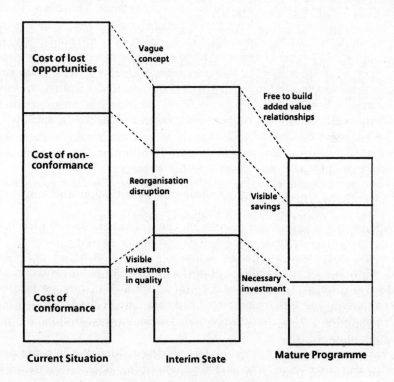

Figure 13.2 The quality hump

Source: Colin Coulson-Thomas, *Transforming the Company*, Kogan Page, 1992.

journey. For those who have travelled through the valley of the shadow, the promised land can sometimes turn out to be unsettling. Having 'done quality' they face the question: 'What now?'

From quality through business excellence to corporate transformation

Companies are finding that the maintenance of a basic quality registration is not sufficient to differentiate them from competitors in demanding and competitive marketplaces, or ensure that desired levels of quality are delivered to their customers. To become a world-class player in all key aspects of its operations a company needs to move 'beyond quality' and aspire to excellence and 'best in class' performance within its field.

The European Foundation for Quality Management (EFQM) adopts a broad view of quality which embraces the future and stakeholders other than the customer. EFQM describes its approach as 'The European Model for Business Excellence'. According to Secretary General, Geert de Raad: 'Ultimately every CEO is concerned with achieving the positive continuity of the business and the added value required to meet the expectations of all stakeholders.'

The number of issues raised by interviewees suggests that for many companies a broad, holistic 'business excellence' approach is required, and that 'all the people' may need to be involved in tackling them. Rank Xerox adopts this approach. To develop an action programme for moving ahead, a company should identify:

- requirements, opportunities, needs, values and preferences;
- goals, objectives and priorities;
- obstacles and barriers, and 'helps and hinders';
- core competencies and potential differentiators;
- relevant capabilities, values, tools, approaches, allies and partners;
- any missing change elements;
- roles and responsibilities and related competencies;
- vital few actions.

The output from such an analysis should consist of an action programme to achieve the agreed quality, business excellence or transformation goals, values and objectives. The areas to focus upon could vary according to the situation and circumstances of the company. The elements listed in the appendix to this chapter received particular attention in one major transformation exercise.

For many companies, total quality represents the chosen route to corporate transformation.[1] We have throughout this book encountered various barriers to quality that are being experienced. The lessons that can be learned from 'benchmark' companies such as Rank Xerox which have journeyed from crisis, through quality and on via business excellence towards transformation suggest that strategic visions should not be allowed to become a strategic con which can itself represent an obstacle to change.[11] For a vision to live and influence, flexibility is required in both planning and execution.

Corporate planning, or learning and steering?

Members of a board are trustees of the interests of stakeholders. Their time horizon may be for the duration of a specific venture or much longer. In the UK during the late 1980s and early 1990s a 'business expansion scheme' company might plan for a life of five or six years. In contrast, Abdulaziz Al-Zamil, Chairman of the Board of the Saudi Basic Industries Corporation, refers to SABIC's contribution to the Kingdom's industrial growth and environmental health 'today and for generations to come'.

In a dynamic business environment a high degree of flexibility may be required in the implementation of strategy. Many of those launching assured tenancy BES schemes did not anticipate a static property market, while not all of SABIC's executives would have foreseen the 'Gulf War' and its consequences.

Perstorp defines its business as 'Creative Chemistry', and considers the 'commitment and creativity' of its employees to be 'decisive factors in the implementation' of its customer-focused strategy. According to the Perstorp President Gösta Wiking the company's 'corporate culture is based on creativity and entrepreneurship'. The company's training programmes positively seek to develop flexible, creative and entrepreneurial people.

The boards of many companies should be learning and steering rather than planning and implementing. They ought to be more involved in anticipating, supporting and enabling. Reliance on numbers can lead to a focus upon the consequences of past actions rather than future opportunities. Learning ensures that growth and evolution as well as change occurs. Steering increases the opportunity of the board to influence and add value.

Figure 13.3 overviews a planning model that illustrates the impact of selective and biased perceptions of events, developments, activities and situations.[12] Many companies screen out evidence, including that from their own customer surveys, that does not coincide with their own view of the world. Their own perceptions of what is important in relationships with customers and suppliers may be very different from those of the external parties concerned. A process lacking in awareness, perception, learning and judgement can be dangerous.

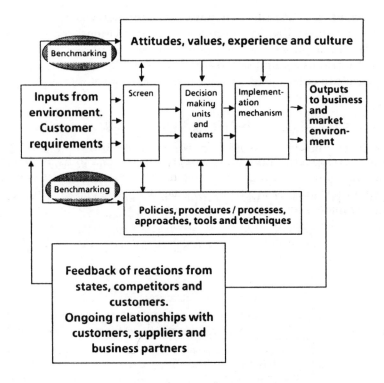

Figure 13.3 Planning models

Source: Colin Coulson-Thomas, *Creating the Global Company*, McGraw-Hill, 1992.

At the same time, a corporate initiative that is focused and sustained, and which has board, top management and budgetary commitment, is more likely to have a company-wide impact than one which is not and does not.

Assessment of the role of quality

Certain companies have concentrated upon corporate change programmes that have yielded measurable results while not being considered to be an exclusively, or wholly, quality initiative. For example, ABB's 'Customer Focus Program' is resulting in measurable and significant improvements. For the 30,000 employees in Sweden the intention is to reduce throughput times in all areas by 50 per cent. More dramatic results have been achieved in many areas.

Quality is but one element of ABB's 'Customer Focus Program', yet other companies have quality programmes within which customer focus is a significant element. The 'corporate philosophies' of the Lucky-

Goldstar Group are 'Creating Value for the Customer and Management that Respects Human Dignity'. Even with such an approach the company had to declare a 'Month of the Customer' in order to demonstrate around the world its commitment to the customer.

It is possible to enter into a semantic debate about what is or is not quality, irrespective of what it is called. What many would associate with elements of quality appears to be a significant component of a wide range of transformation programmes that operate under various other names. The use of a name other than quality may be an indication that a company is seeking to develop and distinguish a programme related to its own situation and circumstances, and which contains features and aspects beyond those found previously, or in a typical or imagined quality programme.

Many companies avoid the use of terms such as 're-engineeering' or 'total quality' because of their associations.[13] Figure 13.4 illustrates a process that could be used to review a corporate programme or an organisation's approach to quality. The more frequently an approach is reviewed the less likely it is to become typecast. A dynamic is created as new elements or refinements may be introduced and others discarded as a result of each iteration of the review process.

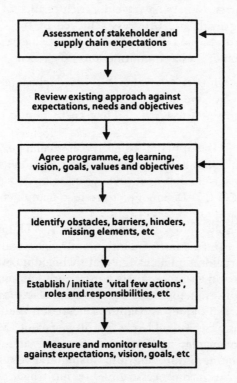

Figure 13.4 Reviewing a corporate programme

Avoiding throwing out the baby with the bathwater

When planning next steps, it is important to retain a sense of balance. While quality is being questioned and reassessment is healthy, it needs to be remembered that certain companies consider elements of quality to be a key cause of their success. For example:

- In 1990 and 1991 Saab Automobile AB introduced a number of measures to 'improve productivity and quality'. During a two-year period a reduction in the average manufacturing time per car of 50 per cent was achieved, and continuing improvements are being sought.
- 3M believes the three keys to the achievement of its business goals are 'a strong flow of new products, continued quality and productivity improvement, and increased penetration of international markets'. L D DeSimone, Chairman and CEO of 3M, has reported that one five-year improvement programme 'reduced by 35 per cent the amount of labour needed to produce our products.'
- Saleh Kurnia, Presiden Direktur of the rapidly expanding Indonesian company Hero Supermarket believes: 'Quality, service and an integrated management approach that have created a strong company image with our customers have yielded rich results for us, reflected in the excellent growth and progress achieved by the Company in the short span of three years.' In particular, quality has resulted in a focus upon the customer and a commitment to excellence.

Very often those who feel they have 'done quality' have experienced indifferent results. As one quality director put it: 'Those who have done well tend to acquire a taste for it ... They keep coming back and asking for more.'

Success can whet the appetite for a greater challenge. In the five-year period, ending in 1990, 3M's manufacturing cycle time was reduced by 21 per cent and over the next five years 3M strove, according to Chairman and CEO L D DeSimone, 'to reduce manufacturing cycle time by more than an additional 35 per cent.'

Rather than simply embrace or trash quality, the Thomas Cook Group went through an assessment, consultation and review process to assemble an approach to organisational change that matched its own mission, situation and context and also those of its partner organisations. The result is a holistic framework that embraces a philosophy of management, current and future tools, techniques and approaches, and attitudes and behaviours. The company has assembled 'a comprehensive set of consistent and complementary principles and practices for analysing, understanding, supporting, facilitating, improving, simplifying and re-engineering' both management and business processes.

In the last three chapters, considerable stress has been placed upon the importance of learning and learning processes. The most effective form of strategic and quality planning is a process of continual and organic learning and adaptation. Sensitivity to feedback is particularly important (Figure 13.3). A board should put the highest priority upon organisational learning processes (see Figure 10.7 in Chapter 10) that ensure organisational vision and corporate capability both evolve to match changing customer requirements.[1] In turbulent environments and uncertain conditions, the quality of learning can be a crucial differentiator.

Organising for quality, learning and transformation

If there is to be a new role for quality within the context of learning, renewal, business excellence or transformation, who within the corporate organisation should be responsible for its contribution? A favourite and frequent response to this question is 'everyone'. When everyone is, in theory, responsible for quality it may be found in practice that no one regards themselves as responsible.

In some companies quality has its own department. In others it may be linked with information technology, organisational change or personnel. There is no general right answer to the question of how best to organise for quality, or for learning. Like so many things, it all depends upon the situation and circumstances of the individual case.

Considerations to bear in mind could include the reasons for quality, how it relates to other corporate initiatives, and the position reached in terms of quality implementation. While the goal may well be 'ownership of quality by the line' and 'making quality the way we work around here', a series of intermediate steps may be required. At the same time, early approaches that are adopted can inhibit or further next steps, and should be selected with an end point in view.

More broadly, companies need to put more effort into learning from each other. Networks along the lines of Japan's Union of Scientists and Engineers are enabling companies and universities to work together to share understanding and practice, and research and develop new tools and approaches. Even the largest of corporations can struggle to keep up with developments in 'world-class' technique and practice, and a greater degree of cooperation seems both desirable and likely. In time there may be a wider choice of quality and learning networks to which one can belong according to interests and priorities.

The human dimension

Organisations are communities of people. Too many corporate plans consist of numbers on paper. There is little trace of implementation requirements and scant evidence that anyone outside of the boardroom, as individually thinking and feeling people, are involved. Those at the top of organisations may assume or believe they understand their cultures, but many appear out of touch with 'the realities' at the levels that impact more directly upon the customer.[14]

Managers need to focus more upon the hidden dimensions, the contents of the cards played close to chests and the 'inner persons' within those chests.

> Similarly, much consultancy effort is devoted to the application of tried and tested tools and techniques to existing approaches and activities, rather than to identifying missing elements, and devising and adopting new approaches that may have greater relevance. Expertise, training and technology are devoted to what is, rather than to bringing about what ought to be.[15]

Plans need to be communicated and shared. The top-down approaches adopted by many companies do not recognise the importance of horizontal communication. Within the total quality drive of the Belgian Solvay Group: 'Particular emphasis is given to operational and communications networks to break down barriers and encourage common involvement.'

Legalism, or a reliance upon small print, can represent an abdication of responsibility, while nitpicking can result in the avoidance of fundamental questions. The detail of plans, their rigidity and uniformity can inhibit diversity and creativity. Rather than plan activity, more companies are considering what support groups exploring new ventures and initiatives might require. They define a framework of goals and values and create a context within which legitimised change can occur. All the small print and detail in the world cannot defend a corporation against a breach of accepted morals or values.

There is no law which states that organisations have to be cold and unfeeling. Quality of life can be more than a slogan. Companies such as ASK Europe put great importance upon human values and sensitivity to individual requirements. It is possible to demonstrate both care and a responsiveness to the needs of particular customers. For example, British Gas operates Gascare, a computer-based register which records those of its customers, such as the elderly, who have special needs.

Another arena in which it is possible to care is in helping people to achieve a better balance between family and work. BMW operates a Family Break Programme allowing people to spend up to ten years with their family before returning to work. During this period 'employees are given an opportunity to keep their knowledge and skills up-to-date through upgrading and holiday replacements.' In addition, the BMW Children's Office provides help, advice and contacts on a range of issues to do with children and parenting.

Practical considerations

When planning quality, re-engineering or transformation initiatives, it needs to be recognised that different groups within a company may vary greatly in terms of the time it takes for them to react and implement. For example, the experience of the 'Courtelle' business within Courtaulds was that: 'The time horizons of different sections of the workforce vary from one week to several months.' In this case, a lesson which emerges is that once objectives are agreed 'appropriate resources' need to be 'made available within the time horizon of the specific group.'

A key issue to address is the extent to which a change programme needs to create new forms of the 'three Cs', capacity, capability and competence, and establish from scratch the commitment and motivation to apply them, or the degree to which each of these is already latent (Figure 13.5). The challenge is the greatest where both are new, but it is sometimes difficult to identify and assess latent potential. As one CEO put it: 'How do you know?'

In some cases, where the potential does exist, results may be the product of greater awareness, application and visibility of existing 'change

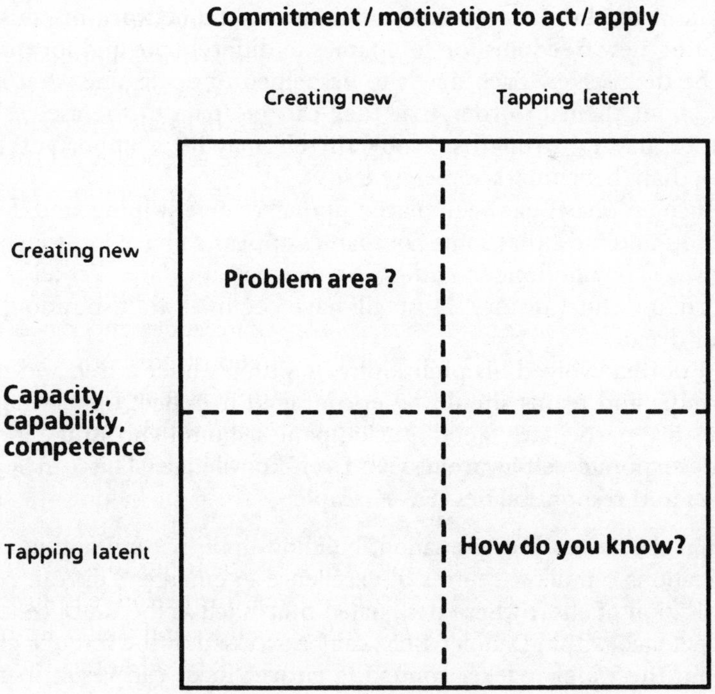

Figure 13.5 Assessing the challenge

elements' rather than the development of new ones. On occasion, the motivation to act is born out of frustration and what is needed is a trigger or catalyst.

Future approaches need to acknowledge the changing patterns of behaviour of both corporations and individuals, especially those that are 'above average'. Just as ambitious corporations are breaking free of the constraints of government and particular national frameworks as they become global players, so 'buy-out' teams and the more capable individuals are seeking independence from the shackles of an over-tight corporate embrace.

At the level of global competition, rival networks are engaged in a ruthless struggle for survival. People today require both competitive instincts and the qualities to build partnership relations based upon trust. They have to simultaneously play zero-sum and positive-sum games. Internally, they need to ensure a challenging environment within which competing ideas can seek support while at the same time ensuring an environment conducive of individual and collective fulfilment.

Self-knowledge and awareness

The privatisation and deregulation programmes of governments and the transition of the bureaucratic corporation into the network organisation are creating new freedoms for companies to differentiate and for individuals to be themselves. Each needs to be helped to determine what is distinctive about them in order that they can be 'true to themselves' and build upon natural strengths. 'Know thyself' may be as important, if not more so, than 'benchmark someone else'.

So much emphasis has been placed upon 'creative swiping' and 'following fashion and fads' that some companies appear to have lost touch with themselves. They no longer know 'who or what' they are. Yet all are the product of a distinct history. Most will have begun as an inspiration, aspiration or dream.

The Buddha evolved his philosophy by sitting under a tree and thinking. Groups and teams should be encouraged to reflect upon what it is that they are particularly good at. Companies should encourage individual and corporate self-awareness and self-knowledge. This can lead to new roles and responsibilities. For example:

- Within the network organisation, building upon natural aptitudes and inclinations can allow centres of excellence to emerge. This can reduce duplication of effort where designated units such as the R&D 'centres of competence' within Daimler-Benz can be accessed by the rest of a group.
- Within the wider market context, a clearer focus can result in membership of further networks. As one manager put it: 'People now know what we are about. Before we were all things to all people.'

Lewis Galoob Toys of the US subcontracts all but a small core of corporate functions, such as network coordination, to various organisations each of which aims to be outstanding within its chosen field of focus. Activities such as design, manufacturing, distribution and account collection are all undertaken by network partners.

Fritz Gerber, Chairman and CEO of the Swiss company Roche, cautions: 'We should at all times keep a watchful eye on events and be prepared to adapt ourselves proactively to the needs of our customers, however rapidly these needs may change.' Gerber concludes: 'Only by responding flexibly will we stay on top.'

Big companies can benefit from relationships with small partners. Yamaha has people on the ground associating with its individual customers. By working with musicians the company hopes not only to spot emerging developments but also to be a pioneering participant in opportunities and trends.

Network quality

The quality professional with the backing of a CEO has an easy ride compared with the challenge of achieving joint, supply chain or network quality. Within alliances between equal partners, and when network members are significant organisations in their own right, progress is by negotiation and agreement.

So far as roles within the network or supply chain relationship are concerned, those who have looked outwards are likely to have an advantage over those who have hitherto adopted a largely internal and product-focused approach. A degree of openness and trust is also required, given the greater opportunities for partner organisations to learn from each other.

Many organisations have no particular reason for continuing to exist. They just happen to be there. Within the network organisation a more ephemeral venture culture can be evolved. People can be encouraged to come to the centre with proposals for ventures or projects. The core team exists to provide counselling and advice. Where opportunities are fleeting, there may not be sufficient time to change attitudes and behaviours.

Within the bureaucracy there are pressures to fit in with the prevailing 'way of doing things'. Identikit clones can be the result. By contrast, within the context of a network composed of venture teams and project-based units there is a greater opportunity for people to be themselves. Thus some could focus upon innovating while others concentrate upon maintaining relationships.

Overall, the network community may need to maintain a pool of approaches, modules of processes, learning technologies, creative environments, tools and techniques which could be drawn upon and used as and when required to support groups and teams in whatever it is they are wishing to do. Variety, tailoring and the tolerance of very different approaches is the key to individual fulfilment. Network members need to be allowed to be themselves.

Not everyone is attracted to the notion of an ephemeral society of nomads and transients. There will be those who desire to operate at a slower pace, return to the same source, or hang onto their goods for longer between replacements. New balances between the supply and demand for different patterns and modes of work and lifestyles will emerge. Entrepreneurs will create opportunities for people to add value in their terms, according to their lifestyle preferences.

To create a particular lifestyle environment could involve the conscious removal of certain approaches that put people under greater pressure than they are comfortable with. The expertise of the new professional could lie in identifying which aspects of what we take for granted today cause the most aggravation, and which when removed might release or liberate enthusiasm and talent.

Network values

Increasingly, vision and values will differentiate one network from another. People will decide whether or not to join a particular network according to what it stands for and what it is seeking to do. These considerations are particularly important for knowledge workers.

Shared values can encourage the loyalty of both customers and employees that is an important requirement for longer-term success.[16] Hence publisher HarperCollins has its Vision and Values programme, MashreqBank stresses its values and matches them to the aspirations of its people, and the learning company ASK Europe actively seeks to network with those who share its values.

Generalised concepts such as quality or excellence are of little value. As articulated within many organisations they are meaningless and can be dangerous when used as a substitute for thought. Many people have an inherent and deeply rooted need to believe in something, and some grasp the all-embracing as a form of secular religion.

Concepts need to be given meaning and made relevant in the context of individual roles and particular situations. The role of the manager, and especially of senior management, is to encourage people to think and find relevance, meaning and purpose. These should not be assumed, or regarded as inherent in something that, once deployed, becomes self-explanatory.

If direction comes to be all about leading the search for meaning and purpose, then organisational leaders must be honest when and where these are found not to exist. This could result in some of the accumulated baggage of quality and re-engineering being discarded.

Network organisations are likely to be choosy about who joins them. The admissions process will resemble that for becoming the member of a club or the fellow of a college. Problems, issues and questions, challenges and opportunities will be fed into the network community for comment.

Rather than pass along a linear or standard review and evaluation process, proposals will be tossed around like a hailstone in a cloud according to the degree and sources of interest it stimulates and the support it attracts. When it has accumulated sufficient weight of backing to justify implementation, like the hailstone it will break out and come down to earth.

The extent of people's commitment to the network will reflect how much they get out of it. Some individuals might hold multiple memberships of, for example, a shared learning collective, a learning technologies club, a problem-solving community, a new concept development group and a project management team.

Assembling the pieces of the jigsaw puzzle

The failure of many companies to turn intention into outcomes often results from missing elements in the corporate transformation strategy that is adopted by the board.[1] Companies whose management teams have already recognised the existence of a gap between plans and results are at an advantage, especially when such awareness coexists with a determination to reassess previous, standard or traditional approaches (Figure 13.6).

Next steps are likely to be built upon foundations of sand, unless the combination of elements that will bridge the gap between aspirations and achievement in the particular situation, circumstances and context are identified.[1] So what 'building blocks' or 'pieces of the jigsaw puzzle' might be needed to effect a successful transformation?

From the issues raised during the course of this book, it is suggested there are elements that most organisations will need, for example a distinctive and compelling vision, clear and measurable objectives and demonstrable top management commitment. In addition, an individual company may need to focus upon such areas as improving the quality of both management and learning, role model behaviour, a more open and sharing culture, and processes that identify and deliver customer value or employee involvement.

There is widespread agreement on many of the elements needed for competitive success. Thus a joint Department of Trade and Industry and CBI study of 100 of the best UK companies has identified such familiar ingredients as visionary and enthusiastic leaders who champion change, empowered and customer-focused people, a learning culture, innovation and commitment to quality, continuous improvement and winning.[17] Few

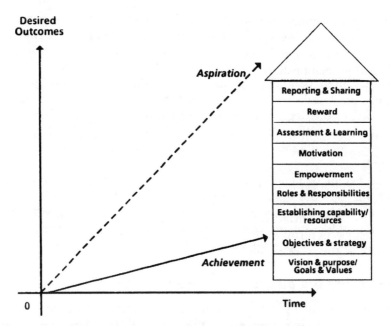

Figure 13.6 Assembling the building blocks

Source: Colin Coulson-Thomas, *Transforming the Company*, Kogan Page, 1992.

would argue these are not 'nice to have', the challenge is to give such terms meaning in the context of a particular situation and set of circumstances.

Many companies adopt a 'pick-n-mix' approach, either by thinking through what elements are particularly appropriate or useful, or on the basis of such factors as what is 'doable', 'interesting' or practical. In so far as individual tasks are concerned a degree of 'pick' can be especially important, while the overall mix of elements can be a significant determinant of whether or not transformation occurs. A list of questions along the lines of the following could be used to identify the broad location of areas of deficiency:

- The vision:
  – Is there a shared and compelling vision? Is the vision rooted in the customer?
  – Does the organisation care? Does it have 'heart'?
  – What is special or distinctive about it? What is its rationale and purpose?
  – Is there sustained 'top management' commitment? Do directors and senior executives exude role model behaviour?
- The customer:
  – Is priority given to the customer? Is the board motivated and the company 'run' according to customer related objectives?

- Is performance measured in terms of its impact upon the customer? Are corporate processes and procedures focused on the customer?
- Is sufficient importance attached to establishing and sustaining partnership relationships?
- Does the organisation learn from and with its customers?
- The people:
  - Are employees involved, committed and enabled to learn? Is empowerment for real, eg is work undertaken by self-managed work groups?
  - Is reward strategy consistent with corporate goals and objectives? Are people actually remunerated to generate value for customers and to learn?
  - How appropriate are roles, competencies, attitudes, values and perspectives in terms of the achievement of the vision?
  - Does the working and learning environment enable people to give of their best?
- The processes and the tools:
  - Are people equipped to cope? Are relevant tools and approaches used?
  - Is there active learning at individual, group and corporate levels? Is there learning from and with others, eg benchmarking and shared learning?
  - Have the key cross-functional management and business processes that determine and deliver value for customers been identified?
  - Are they, and learning and support processes, re-engineered, as appropriate, in order to focus more clearly upon customer requirements? Who is responsible for them within the boardroom?
  - Is the company competing on response, delivery or learning time, and are learning and working integrated?

These are just a selection of the areas in which pieces of the jigsaw might be found to be lacking. Mention has already been made of the appendix to this chapter which lists a wider range of 'change elements'.

One common missing element is the space and time for reflection. The children of the 1960s who spent hours considering a patch of sky or the colour of the water have become executives who are expected to decide between restructuring options on the basis of a few slides at a hurried meeting. Outside, the customers are coming to expect responses in the fractions of a second it takes to call up information from their CD-Rom discs. Yet paradoxically, because so much can be programmed and quickly disseminated, the return upon original thinking has never been higher.

Once areas of deficiency have been identified, appropriate director, staff and partner development responses can be determined. For example, perhaps the board would benefit from an 'away day' specifically on corporate transformation and the role of the board in relation to its achievement.[2]

The key to success generally lies in the criteria which are employed to select the elements which are used and the extent to which the interrelationships between them are understood. Factors such as ease of use, familiarity and timescale need to be taken into account, but in the main the mix of elements used should be based upon what is most relevant to the situation and context.

Some professionals and consultants are attracted to the use of elements they feel represent the 'cutting edge' or which will add value to their CVs. Thus the high profile re-engineering exercise may have more appeal than less risky and quicker simplification exercises. The latter may have a more tangible and immediate impact upon business results.

Managing the elements

Once the combination of change elements needed by a particular company have been identified, they will need to be managed, both individually and collectively. In some companies, for example Rank Xerox, each of the elements is the subject of both benchmarking and SWOT analysis. These review activities should also lead to the establishment of performance measures and the formulation of vital few programmes to bring about any improvements that are required.

A company should avoid concentrating upon the individual elements at the expense of overlooking how they interreact. By analogy, a director is not competent in any absolute sense, the contribution made by a particular individual depends upon the interplay of people and personalities within the context of a particular boardroom, while the situations and circumstances of different companies can greatly vary.[2] So it is with change elements. How they complement and reinforce each other within the dynamics of a particular change environment may be much more important than individual levels of attainment.

Some corporate transformation programmes have become derailed because certain change elements have been developed to an excessive degree in relation to others. A sense of balance and proportion between the elements may be necessary. To manage a portfolio of change elements one must retain a holistic perspective.

Figure 13.7 illustrates the need for a balance to be struck between complexity and commitment in the course of implementation. One could aim to gradually build confidence, and with it ownership, involvement and commitment, by tackling the less complex areas first (strategy (a)). Another approach, often adopted by revolutionaries (strategy (b)), is to storm the areas of difficulty using a cadre of the committed and

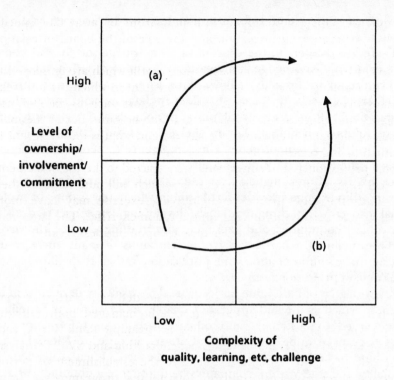

Figure 13.7   Routes to implementation

involved. A common dilemma is the need to sustain commitment for long enough to have an impact, while in the meantime requirements are changing.

The sequence of steps adopted can be critical if each is to build upon and complement previous initiatives and achievements. Charles Baden-Fuller and John Stopford suggest a four-stage process of galvanising the top team in order to secure their commitment to change, simplification of the context and what needs to be done, building the multiple capabilities needed to effect changes, and leveraging achievements by maintaining momentum and extending competitive advantages.[18]

The knowledge society

Many pundits have heralded the passing of industrial society and the emergence of the knowledge society. The rapid increase in the numbers of knowledge workers relative to other groups in society is seen as a consequence. The dramatic growth of Microsoft and decline of IBM are cited as evidence of this trend. Information and knowledge are seen as the key resource areas.

There are dangers in the concept of a knowledge society and knowledge company. Knowledge is increasingly a commodity. It is all around us, like the air we breathe. It flows along wires and cables and through the ether as waves and signals. It resides in databases and spreads like a fungus via CD-Rom discs, proliferating periodicals and a growing number of volumes on bulging library shelves. It is duplicated, shared and can spread like a mutant gene. The competence to beneficially use and apply it can be more difficult to acquire.

An excess of information can cause confusion and inaction. The growth of knowledge provides fertile soil in which new groups of professionals can grow, attaching new labels, developing new concepts, drawing new subject boundaries, and packaging and freezing areas of knowledge as the domain of a particular group. The aims of many such groups appear to be differentiation and justification rather than illumination. The curse of professionalism lives on.

Knowledge is of little value for its own sake – its utility derives from the extent to which its use and application enables more value and benefits to be delivered to customers and other stakeholders. Information and knowledge need to be harnessed and utilised in order to add value and contribute to both business and human objectives. What is needed is a capability society. Within companies and other communities what is required is the capability to act and to do.

Information, understanding and expertise is only of relevance if it relates to the shared vision, purpose and objectives of the enterprise or network. Many of those who claim to 'have knowledge' that may be equally accessible to anyone via the terminals on their desks should be greeted with 'so what?' or 'good for you'. Knowledge that has taken years to acquire may not be accompanied by human understanding or sensitivity, and it may also be rendered irrelevant overnight by innovation or the flow of events. Knowledge workers are expensive and should be recruited and used with care.

Human endeavour will continue to need collective and cooperative organisations of some form. The essentials, the essence of humanity, feelings and values rather than the transient and trendy, should form the soil from which our people-centred communities and networks will evolve to provide various combinations of physical environment and electronic space that offer their members more than can be communicated or shared via the Internet or by e-mail alone.

Checklist

How satisfied is your organisation with its approach to learning, and to quality, re-engineering or transformation?

Are people contributing to the building of tomorrow's competencies and capability?

Are the expectations of customers, employees and other stakeholders understood?

Is there a gap between aspiration and achievement?

Have obstacles and barriers and 'helps and hinders' been identified?

Is effective learning occurring at individual, group, corporate and supply chain levels?

Has your organisation's approach to learning, quality, re-engineering or transformation been recently reviewed and reassessed?

How objective, comprehensive and fundamental has the review been?

Do the vision, values, goals and objectives need to be changed?

Can they be implemented? Have missing elements been identified? Is action being taken to put them in place?

Are roles and responsibilities relating to these actions and the required competencies and behaviours clear and understood?

Is there sufficient will, commitment and imagination to effect the transition?

Have the implications of achieving the transition been thought through?

References

1. Colin Coulson-Thomas, *Transforming the Company: Bridging the Gap Between Management Myth and Corporate Reality*, London, Kogan Page, 1992.
2. Colin Coulson-Thomas, *Creating Excellence in the Boardroom*, London, McGraw-Hill, 1993.
3. Colin Coulson-Thomas and Richard Brown, *Beyond Quality: Managing the Relationship with the Customer*, Corby, British Institute of Management (BIM), 1990.
4. George Binney, *Making Quality Work: Lessons from Europe's Leading Companies*, Special Report No P655, London, Economist Intelligence Unit, 1992.
5. Colin Coulson-Thomas, *Professional Development of and for the Board*, a survey undertaken by Adaptation for the Institute of Directors (IOD). A summary has been published: London, Institute of Directors (IOD), February 1990.
6. Kees van Ham and Roger Williams, 'The Quest for Quality at Philips', in Bernard Taylor (ed), *Strategic Planning: The Chief Executive and the Board*, Oxford, Pergamon Press, 1988 pp 93–8.

7. Richard C Whiteley, *The Customer-Driven Company: Moving from Talk to Action*, London, Business Books, 1991.
8. Colin and Susan Coulson-Thomas, *Quality: The Next Steps*, an Adaptation Ltd survey for ODI , London, Adaptation, 1991; executive summary available from ODI Europe, Wimbledon, ODI Europe, 1991.
9. Colin Coulson-Thomas and Trudy Coe, *The Flat Organisation: Philosophy and Practice*, Corby, British Institute of Management (BIM), 1991.
10. Colin and Susan Coulson-Thomas, *Communicating for Change*, an Adaptation Ltd survey for Granada Business Services, London, Adaptation Ltd, 1991.
11. Colin Coulson-Thomas, 'Strategic Vision or Strategic Con?: Rhetoric or Reality?', *Long Range Planning*, Vol 25, No 1, 1992, pp 81–9.
12. Colin Coulson-Thomas, *Creating the Global Company: Successful Internationalisation*, London, McGraw-Hill, 1992.
13. Colin Coulson-Thomas, *The Responsive Organisation: Re-engineering New Patterns of Work*, London, Policy Publications, 1995
14. G Hofstede, *Cultures and Organisations: Software of the Mind*, London, McGraw-Hill, 1991.
15. Colin Coulson-Thomas, *Transforming the Company: Bridging the Gap Between Management Myth and Corporate Reality*, London, Kogan Page, 1992, p 242.
16. Frederick F Reichheld, *The Loyalty Effect: The Hidden Force Behind Growth, Profits and Lasting Value*, Boston, Mass, Harvard Business School Press, 1996.
17. Department of Trade and Industry and Confederation of British Industry, *Competitiveness – How the Best UK Companies Are Winning*, London, DTI/CBI, 1994.
18. Charles Baden-Fuller and John Stopford, *Rejuvenating the Mature Business: The Competitive Challenge*, London, Routledge, 1993.

Appendix: Corporate transformation elements

- Establish vision, purpose, values, goals and objectives
  - Understanding of stakeholder requirements
  - Clarity and distinct nature of the vision
  - Agreed purpose, philosophy, values and policies
  - Degree of top management leadership and commitment
  - Issue and opportunity monitoring and management
  - Rigour of corporate planning / learning process
  - Focus on the customer
  - Willingness to challenge assumptions / confront reality
  - Clear goals and measurable objectives
  - Shared time horizon and agreed timescales
  - Board and director development

- Involve, motivate and empower people
  - Sharing of vision, mission, goals and values
  - Deployment of policies and objectives
  - Two-way communication
  - Extent of involvement
  - Reality of empowerment
  - Selection and promotion process and criteria

- Equal treatment and tolerance of diversity
- Learning and self-development
- Relevance of reward and recognition
- Quality of working and learning environments
- Access to learning technologies
- Positive redeployment

● Develop quality attitudes, processes and tools
- Definition and practice of role model conduct
- Openness, sensitivity and trust
- Management by fact
- Use of information
- Learning and sharing
- Prioritisation, integration and focus
- Customer responsibility and empathy
- Handling of problems and crises
- Management, support and learning process review
- Business process review
- Process improvement, simplification and re-engineering
- Maintenance of quality registration
- Quality, learning, benchmarking and other tools
- Innovation and creativity
- Management development

● Build relationships with customers, suppliers and business partners
- Customer/supplier/partner/supply chain relationships
- Focus on customer requirements/satisfaction
- Customer information
- Learning from the customer
- Learning and transformation partnerships/knowledge transfer
- Customer communications/involvement
- Segmentation and tailoring
- Prioritisation
- Differentiation
- Exploitation of value added opportunity
- Trade-off of time, cost and quality
- Account and relationship management
- Commitment to the customer
- Customer gains and losses
- Quality networks/supply chain quality
- Partner development

● Initiate and support activities that identify and deliver value
- Clear and measurable task/account objectives
- Clear roles and responsibilities
- Redefinition of roles

- Shared understanding of what needs to be done
- Assessment and development of competencies
- Access to relevant resources, skills and capability
- Application of resources, skills and capability to value generating activity
- Extent of management counselling, mentoring and support
- Cross-functional and inter-organisational cooperation
- Integration of working and learning
- Participation in shared learning groups and networks
- Focus upon 'hinders', obstacles and barriers

● Measure/monitor customer satisfaction and achievement of goals/objectives
  - Market/opportunity/supply chain positioning measures
  - Measurement of customer satisfaction
  - People measures
  - Financial and added value measures
  - Measures of learning and of competence and capability development
  - Innovation and intellectual property measures
  - Priority given to customer-related measures within 'measure portfolio'
  - Gap analysis
  - Reality and openness of reporting
  - Reporting of performance to stakeholders

Holistic and people-focused management

Do the work and leave your boasting.

Where we have been

Our journey has taken us from various desires and intentions that were expressed at the start of the 1990s, through the very mixed experience of subsequent years of struggle with delivery and implementation, to what now needs to be done to prepare our organisations for the twenty-first century.

Much of the initial assessment of what is needed in terms of flexibility and responsiveness to cope with economic, social, market and other changes is still valid. The rationale and purpose of organisations remains to access, develop, harness and apply the collective capabilities and potential of people in pursuit of such goals as profitably identifying and delivering whatever represents value to customers and clients.

The range of viable options and practical choices for overcoming functional, organisational, geographic, scale and other barriers to communication, working and learning has greatly increased. The utility and cost-effectiveness of a growing universe of technologies, from learning technologies to those of electronic commerce, have eroded barriers to involvement, innovation and market entry, and are democratising entrepreneurship and expertise.

Contemporary concerns

Investigation of our collective efforts to turn aspirations into corporate realities reveals that, while many organisations have manged to survive in the face of formidable challenges, there is widespread disappointment and frustration that more positive outcomes have not been achieved in relation to the effort that has been expended and the human and financial costs involved. Our visions remain as intangible as holograms.

Many managers experience a sense of schizophrenia when, following 'hard-nosed' behaviour in the office, occasional and quieter moments of reflection on the consequences of their actions lead to doubts if not feelings of remorse. While management initiatives and programmes are often as numerous as the dragonflies in a Chinese garden our transformation goals continue to elude us.

Many organisations, as they slim down through headcount reduction and sink deeper into the mire, have become more dependent upon external consultants, some of whom appear intent on securing control of the corporate organism in order to divert cash flow into further IT or re-engineering projects. Certain consultants have become powerful and self-interested inside stakeholders.

Other consultants are less satisfied. To retain control, organisations have pursued divide and rule strategies, using different consultants for a range of self-contained projects. As a consequence, there is much jockeying for power at court and an excess of uncoordinated initiatives, some of which may be in conflict. When 'work packages' are defined internally and put out to tender, successful consultants have little opportunity to influence the critical scoping stages when approaches are determined and goals are selected, while slim margins resulting from the competitive process may encourage them to limit themselves to delivering the contracted brief.

A time for reflection and reassessment

Innovations are occurring in many areas that collectively have the potential to radically transform the nature of our lives. However, many social institutions, corporate mind-sets and certain social values are inhibiting rather than enabling beneficial change. We are lagging ever further behind where we need to be if we are to fully embrace the opportunities open to us and secure the advantages they promise. We are defensive where we should be bold.

The time has come to forsake the executive support systems of the executive suite in favour of the hermit's hut or park bench. We need to stop boasting about the cost-cutting and efficiency savings that have enabled survival and concentrate instead upon the work of renewal and transformation that will allow us to live richer and more balanced lives. We must pause and think about how to escape from the traps we have set for ourselves and the treadmills that burn us out.

Interviewees have displayed a healthy scepticism towards management fashions and fads. We require sensitive, balanced, thinking and responsible approaches rather than slavish reliance upon the hyped and packaged. Reflection and rigorous thinking 'up front' can ease subsequent implementation.

We need the courage to formulate our own philosophies of business and develop our own tools and approaches. Inspiration should be sought from what is simple yet fundamental, and from within rather than from what is trendy.

Where we need to be

We are surrounded by opportunities to re-engineer supply chains, create learning environments and liberate potential, establish new markets and introduce new services. As information, communications and learning technologies come to be taken for granted and integrated into the physical and social fabric, greater priority should be given to our social needs.

We should stress the fun of shared learning and future discovery rather than dwell on the pain of past restructuring. People should be encouraged to work and learn in whatever ways suit their circumstances and preferences, match their aptitudes and otherwise allow them to give of their best. Social creatures thrive on trust, and the interaction and interdependence that allow individuals to create and negotiate roles that enable them to contribute while being true to themselves.

Pioneers of new ways of working, organising, managing and learning should be valued as highly as inventors of new technologies and creators of new services. The impact of their innovations can be equally profound. However, those developing new models of organisation should remember that we are people and not peripherals or input–output devices. We breathe and sweat.

Management must focus primarily upon people, whether customers, suppliers, employees or partners, and upon their anxieties and dreams as well as their needs and requirements. The emphasis should be upon values and relationships; roles, competencies and behaviours rather than procedures and structures; flexibility and intuition rather than prescriptive and mechanical approaches; the fostering of diversity and creativity rather than the enforcement of standards; learning rather than control.

Management also needs to be holistic if we are to understand interrelationships and trade-offs and assemble the combination of elements to deliver multiple objectives and longer-term goals such as renewal and transformation, and if people are to become beneficiaries of change and not its victims.

Different transformation roles have their own distinct competency requirements, and these can change during the transformation journey.

Organisations should explore a broader range of options for establishing relationships with various providers of required skills and experience.

Learning and transformation partners that share our visions, goals and values can help us to develop and adapt. Legal, remuneration and other arrangements should be such that 'positive sum' rather than 'zero sum' games result, collective learning rather than intellectual asset stripping. Longer-term relationships support continuity of strategic programme direction and management.

Organisations will still be needed

Organisations have no divine right of existence. Some do little to enrich our lives. The true cost of others exceed the value they add. Their passing releases resources and energies for more positive activities and thoughts.

However, there are more people who wish to be employees, or members, than have the desire, drive or capability to be instigators, innovators and pioneers of new enterprises or founders of new networks. Most of us depend for our current livelihoods and our future pensions upon the renewal, transformation and continuance of sufficient current organisations, institutions and relationships to prevent a melt-down into collective confusion, insecurity and chaos.

A society of empowered and enabled citizens still requires institutions and organisations. When participation and interaction are as limited as browsing on, and communicating via, the Internet, awareness and tolerence of others and some shared principles of conduct can benefit all users. Frameworks of common and shared values will enable us to reap greater benefits from cooperative activities. Agreement to observe certain codes and rules may be a necessary precondition of network membership and more effective operation.

The challenge

Choices have to be made. There are new visions, values and priorities to agree. We must focus upon what is important, such as end customers in supply chains. Self-awareness is demanded, and honesty with ourselves and with others. Focusing upon what we are particularly good at rather than striving to 'improve everything' makes it easier for us to work cooperatively with others who have complementary capabilities.

Ultimately, we are citizens as well as consumers. Networks, consortia and learning clubs will supplement, and should complement and balance rather than replace, families, communities and societies. We only have one life on this earth. More attention should be given to improving its quality.

The options, examples and opportunities we have examined suggest that, given a shared sense of purpose, supportive learning and transformation partners, and an appropriate mix of change elements, renewal and transformation can be achieved. The potential payoffs, for both ourselves and for others, more than justify the incremental effort. Go for it.

Index

References in italic indicate figures or tables